THE WAY OF THE WHITE CLOUDS

THE WAY OF

THE WAY OF THE WHITE CLOUDS

LAMA ANAGARIKA GOVINDA

WITH AN INTRODUCTION BY ROBERT A.F. THURMAN

THE OVERLOOK PRESS
WOODSTOCK & NEW YORK

First published in the United States in 2005 by
The Overlook Press, Peter Mayer Publishers, Inc.
Woodstock & New York

WOODSTOCK:
One Overlook Drive
Woodstock, NY 12498
www.overlookpress.com
[for individual orders, bulk and special sales, contact our Woodstock office]

NEW YORK:
141 Wooster Street
New York, NY 10012

∞ The paper used in this book meets the requirements for paper permanence as described in the ANSI Z39.48-1992 standard.

Cataloging-in-Publication Data Library of Congress

Book design and type formatting by Bernard Schleifer
Manufactured in the United States of America
ISBN 1-58567-465-6 (hc)
ISBN 1-58567-785-X (pb)
1 3 5 7 9 8 6 4 2

TO

LI GOTAMI

(Śākya Dölma)

MY COMPANION

IN THE LAND OF THE THOUSAND BUDDHAS

CONTENTS

CONTENTS

Illustrations

Introduction

LAMA ANAGARIKA GOVINDA was undoubtedly one of the West's greatest minds of the twentieth century, and should be considered among the group that includes Einstein, Heisenberg, Wittgenstein, Solzhenitsyn, Gandhi, and the Dalai Lama. He is not as well known as the others except in Buddhist circles. In spite of the fact that many scholars, including historian, Arnold Toynbee, claim that the West's most important event of the twentieth century was its encounter with the Buddhist Dharma, most cultured people still have no idea of what that really means. Even academic scholars of Buddhism, either its ancient forms in Asia or its current manifestations in the West, accepting a definition of themselves as marginal investigators laboring in a field of marginalia, think of Lama Govinda, invariably without having read his writings, as a rather quaint figure. They consider him a German romantic who fled the disaster of the "world war century" into a romanticized myth of "The East," living and promoting the fantasy of Shangri-la about the backward and benighted culture and superstitious, primitive, or feudal, at the very least "pre-modern" or "underdeveloped," society of Tibet.

However, as we begin the twenty-first common era century in hopes of not repeating the violence of the world wars and genocides of the previous ones—it is crucial that we face up to some important lessons that Lama Govinda tirelessly taught. Western culture, based on the religious forms of Christianity and Islam, which, in Lama's words, "lost themselves . . . by overpowering the human mind through the dictatorship of a partially world-creating and at the same time world-negating spirit," is still relatively uncivilized, focused on the external conquest of other civilizations, violence, war, imperialism, and a rampant need for material possession and self-aggrandizement. Contrary to its inflated self-image, it is not the most advanced culture the world has yet seen. Its very developed material technology is, in fact, put to the childish uses of violent destruction and thoughtless consumption. Its worst problem is its foundational confusion, which leads those of us under its thrall to feel disconnected from nature. Hence we tend to be not responsible for the consequences of our actions, and distract ourselves from the extreme danger of destroying everything in our path by the irrational promise of either a blissful salvation by an absolutely disconnected omnipotent "God" or else a blissful oblivion.

Hence our barbarous culture—I do not call it a "civilization"—poses the ultimate threat to planetary life, to all the human beings of other more ancient and better balanced cultures, all other life forms, and the eco-system itself. We are deploying the five horsemen of our imminent man-made apocalypse; population explosion, epidemic disease, unlivable pollution, resource depletion, and wars of mass destruction. The urgent need, therefore, is for we bearers of this imbalanced, disconnection culture to rediscover our interconnection with the rest of life, our infinite responsibility to ourselves and all other living beings, the extreme negative danger of our continuing on the path of destruction and consumption, and the positive potential for us to find a reliable happiness within our own souls, to conquer our own inner negative habits, and to cultivate our infinite capacity for love and joy.

The Buddhist world movement is not accurately thought of simply as a "world religion," understood as a set system of beliefs and institutions that parallel those of religions. It can be viewed that way with some validity—indeed both proponents and opponents do so—but it is only one- third a religion at most. It is more fundamentally a way of living and a pattern of ethics, a basis for numerous civilizations that emphasized individualism, wisdom, gentleness, altruism, and universal equality. And it is a way of understanding the world, a tradition of sciences based on the possibility of human beings developing a complete and accurate understanding of the realities of life and death. Its fundamental teaching intends to help beings understand their causal interconnection with all life, find the causes of all their sufferings, intervene to prevent those causes from giving their effects, and achieve the evolutionary goal of enduring and shareable happiness. It is therefore just what the victim/bearers of a confusion, violence-, and greed-based culture need to cure their self-imprisoning malaise and world-endangering malfunction.

So in the history of the process of the West discovering the new frontier it requires, namely the inner continent of the human heart, the last possibility for a hopeful future for humankind and its hard-pressed planet, Lama Anagarika Govinda (Indo-Tibetan Buddhist name Anangavajra Khamsum Wangchuk), emerges as one of the great heroes of the century, a pioneer and prophetic leader of an outwardly triumphant and inwardly desperate Western culture. He himself broke free from the collective hypnosis about the superiority of the West and found traces of the civilization that met his standards in Asia, in Lanka, Burma, India, and ultimately Tibet. While he never proclaimed himself fully enlightened, he attained his personal visionary goals and turned back to his home culture to open up for the thoughtful the vista of a new possibility for human life. The first book I read on Tibet was his elegant and epochal *Foundations of Tibetan Mysticism*, which I read in France when I was eighteen, and I am still grateful every day for the path on which it very much helped to set me.

His preface below begins with the words, written already in the sixties, "Why is it that the fate of Tibet has found such a deep echo in the world? . . . What is happening in Tibet is symbolical for the fate of humanity. As on a gigantically raised stage we witness the struggle between two worlds, which may be interpreted, according to the standpoint of the spectator, either [if you are still so persuaded] as a struggle between the past and the future, between backwardness and progress, belief and science, superstition and knowledge—or [much better] as the struggle between spiritual freedom and material power, between the wisdom of the heart and the knowledge of the brain, between the dignity of the individual and the herd-instinct of the mass, between the faith in the higher destiny of man through inner development and the belief in material prosperity through an ever-increasing production of goods."

This is prophetic utterance, profoundly wise, courageous, and well ahead of its time. I believe it is accurate to say that Lama Govinda was the first Western scholar-explorer-experimenter-practitioner to experience and articulate the radical individualism at the heart of the Buddhist tradition. To this day, I use his wonderful simile for the difference between Buddhist enlightenment and the mystical experience of oneness that Vedantic Hinduism and many other mysticisms anticipate. He said that those mysticisms perceive the ultimate goal as being the moment when the little individual drop of water—which has fallen from the rain cloud to the mountain top, melted down from glacial snows, flowed with myriad others into streams and waterfalls and broad rivers—finally merges itself indivisibly in the vast and shining sea. But Buddhist enlightenment is rather when the individual drop itself becomes the repository of the whole vast ocean, when the shining sea slips into the individual drop! I cannot get over my admiration for this insight; it teaches enlightenment as the inconceivable reconciliation of the seemingly absolute dichotomy between individual and universal. It reveals it to be the complex, ecstatic, yet responsible state of supreme awareness that it is, rather than some sort of escapist extinction of the individual into some oblivious collective security.

The time has long since come to take a deeper look at the Venerable Lama, and when would it be more appropriate than on the occasion of this new edition of his classic autobiographical work, *The Way of the White Clouds*. Lama was much too humble to have written a detailed autobiography, greatly to our loss, it must be said, but he gives us considerable insight into his inner life, important insights and spiritual experiences in this work, and in bits and pieces of personal accounts scattered throughout his other works. He was born in 1896, the Year of the Fire Monkey, in Waldheim, Germany, as Ernst Hoffmann. His father was German, his mother Bolivian. During his early childhood he was ill with consumption, pneumonia or pleurisy, and had to go to a sanatorium in Switzerland, in the Swiss Tessin area (Ticino, where Hermann Hesse also retreated after the First World War). His later adolescence was spent in Capri, Italy, as his parents were part of a small circle of international, wealthy, artistic expatriates who were disaffected and in self-imposed exile from the imperialistic, industrial, and militaristic European-American culture of the time, the culture described so well by Barbara Tuchman in her classic, *The Proud Tower*. Reportedly, he began to meditate using Buddhist methods in 1914, during the year of the outbreak of the First World War, while completing his first book, *The Fundamental Ideas of Buddhism and Their Relation to the Concept of God*. He also studied Pali at the University of Naples. Around this time, in 1917 (I have to guess from clues dropped here and there in his writings), he had an extraordinary experience of one of his previous incarnations, that of a German writer (he doesn't give the name) of about a century previous who had embarked upon a massive project of writing, in Lama's words, a "morphology of human thought and culture, resulting in a magic vision of the universe," the same project that Lama, as the young Ernst Hoffmann, found himself absorbed in from adolescence. The unnamed German writer had suffered from the same lung disease young Hoffmann had, and had died young, leaving behind an unfinished metaphysical novel, which, when Hoffmann read it, contained not only the same general ideas as his novel, but even whole sentences and paragraphs of nearly identical prose! A scholar he met in Capri who was researching the earlier writer was amazed at the young Hoffmann's resemblance to the unnamed German writer. There were many details of this experience that provide convincing evidence of a genuine former life remembrance, and the young Hoffmann must have thereby adopted the determination to deepen his investigation of the teachings of Buddhism.

Around this time, he must have visited North Africa from Capri, since he mentions an anecdote that occurred when he was "spending some time" among the Aissaouas tribes of Muslim Sufis. He also mentions a journey in the Bolivian highlands, visiting his maternal grandmother, and learning about his great-grandfather, who had been a comrade in arms of Bolivar, the George Washington of South America, given the title of Field Marshal de Montenegro. His mother's fortune seems to have come from ownership of silver mines in Bolivia, and at one time he thought of becoming a mining engineer.

Eventually he went to Sri Lanka, eight years after his first book was published, say in 1922 or 1923. He was eventually ordained as a novice by the Venerable Bhikkhu Nyanatiloka Mahathera (also of German descent) at the Island Hermitage of Dodanduwa, and he spent the next twenty years as a virtual bhikkhu—monk, celibate, enrobed and ascetical. He never took the full bhikkhu ordination, as he objected to the "innumerable rules" of the formal Sangha. During this time, as a monk pilgrim, he visited Burma and perhaps even Hunan in Southwest China, which we gather from another anecdote he recites. He expected to stay for life in Lanka, and built himself a hermitage between Kandy and Nuwara-Eliya. He also worked on his first major work of Buddhist scholarship, *The Psychological Attitude of Early Buddhist Philosophy*, a learned and comprehensive study of the Pali Abhidhamma psychology.

He mentions that he was not originally attracted to Tibet, and was prey to the usual misconception of those times (and in some quarters, sadly, still today) that it was a degenerate form of Buddhism polluted by demon-worship, shamanism, and other weird elements from the rough cultures of the Himalayas. He was therefore astonished, when invited to Darjeeling to a conference to present on Theravāda Buddhism and its literature, to feel strangely drawn to the world of "Lamaism." He spent some time in a monastery high above the town, and began his immersion in the world of Tibet. It's hard to tell exactly, but this must have been in the late '20s. The monastery was called Yi-gah Cho-ling (Lama's phonetic spelling), and was the retreat residence of Tomo Géshé Rimpoché. After spending months there in Tibetan studies with other teachers, while the Rimpoché was on a long retreat, Lama met the Rimpoché, was accepted by him as a disciple, and formally became a Tibetan Buddhist. During these same times, he spent time at Tagore's University in Bengal, Shantiniketan, and lectured at other Indian universities. In the early 1930s he began trips to Tibet, going up through Sikkim into the Chumbi valley, and then in 1933 visiting Ladakh and the Chang-Thang or northern plain, coming from the west. In 1936 Tomo Géshé Rimpoché passed away, soon taking reincarnation in Sikkim. In 1937 Lama himself went to Sikkim and visited the lama of the famous French scholar-adventurer, Alexandra David-Neel, the Gomchen of Lachen, up on the Tibetan border. During his years in India, he had become friendly with Tagore, Nehru, and other Indian independence leaders, and so during the war years, the British held him in an internment camp for five years, despite the fact that he held a British passport at this time. After his release, he met the beautiful artist and scholar Li Gotami, born in the Fire Horse Year, 1906, to a Parsee family in Bombay, who had been studying for years at Shantiniketan. He renounced his monastic novice vows to marry her, and she became his inseparable companion until his death.

With Indian independence in 1947, he became an Indian citizen, and he and Li were finally able to make the extensive pilgrimage and study travels in Tibet that took him to Mount Kailash and Lake Manasarovar, and beyond to the ruins of the great temples and monasteries of Tsaparang, which he describes so eloquently in this book. After the Chinese invasion of Tibet in 1950 they moved to the small and beautiful Kasar Devi hermitage at Almora, in the Kumaon hills of Uttar Pradesh, given to him and Li by the great translator W. H. Y Evans-Wentz, where he lived and wrote his major works over the next thirty years, with occasional trips to Europe and America in the late '70s and early '80s.

It was in Almora, a little town in the Kumaon Hills of Utter Pradesh, India, that I first met Lama and Li in 1971, while on a year-long fellowship for dissertation research. My wife Nena had already met them six years earlier on her own pilgrimage to India, and Lama and Li were obviously very fond of her, in a parental sort of way. When she introduced me to the gentle but reclusive scholar, he looked me over as a fastidious father might inspect a son-in-law. Whatever my own shortcomings, he and Li were immediately enchanted with our three-year-old boy, Ganden, and our smiling baby girl, Uma. On the scholarly level, Lama was a bit concerned that my approach to Buddhism might be too one-sidedly intellectual, as I was translating a work of Centrist Madhyamaka philosophy, and, though he knew I had been a monk myself for some years, he was afraid I might become enmired in scholasticism and not get deeply enough into the meditative side of the practice. He brought out his old study notebooks—I particularly remember his translation of Aryadeva's *Four Hundred*, a work of the same Centrist school, and I was impressed with the high level of his critical scholarship. He was intent that I acknowledge the key role of the great hermit yogins of Tibet, and of the *Chakrasamvara Tantra* in particular, the favorite spiritual technology of the Great Adepts he was so fond of.

We had wonderful times at his ashram, celebrating his birthday, taking Li down to the bazaar for shopping in our Volkswagen, hearing spellbinding tales of their visit to Kailash. They were wonderful in conversation, as they would correct each other meticulously as to the fine details of particular adventures, to make sure the facts were clear. On the other hand, when Lama was engaged in his writing, Li was like a guardian angel and would not allow visitors or anything to disturb him. This became more and more of a problem during the '70s, as Lama's books were beginning to attract a wider readership in Europe and America, and visitors were more and more frequent. To reach the ashram retreat was quite a hike up the mountain onto "Crank's Ridge," as the place was affectionately called, due to the presence of Lama and other Indian intellectuals and old-guard expatriate yogins, artists, and writers. So when Lama reached his eightieth year, in 1976, it seemed more and more difficult to live there. He began to stay longer in the West, finally settling down in California, with the help of the San Francisco Zen Center and a growing circle of friends.

I remember meeting him out there during his last years, after he had already suffered a few strokes. His reaction to old age and approaching death was truly amazing. He assured me that the strokes were the greatest of blessings, not a hardship at all. He said that he had previously thought he had achieved some understanding of emptiness, *shunyata*, the great void of blissful freedom at the core of Buddhist reality, only to realize *with each stroke*, how much more profound, how much more miraculous it was! He expressed his extreme gratitude that he was getting the chance to disentagle from his embodiment so gradually, so able to observe the process, unravelling the web of attachments strand by strand. The few visits we had in those last days were a great privilege and an encouragement about dealing with all aspects of life that I am only beginning to appreciate in my own later years.

I am grateful to Peter Mayer and Overlook Press that they are now reprinting Lama's amazing memoir. I have tried to extract the details of his life from the little nuggets he drops here and there in his text and from what he told to Peter Matthiessen. I can't believe I was so busy and preoccupied when I had the chance that I didn't sit him down and get him to provide me a clear and detailed chronology, but Lama was not an easy person to sit down and put to a task not of his own choosing. Out of humility he chose not to author a full autobiography, as in the Tibetan tradition only the most enlightened saint is thought worthy of biography—the very term for which literally translates as "Liberation." He gave us instead his many works of teaching, and the marvelous account of his pilgrimages and discoveries in Tibet that you now have before you. Enjoy it, and may it help you open your heart and mind to the white-cloud-like quality of your own existence, floating freely through the clear blue sky!

—ROBERT A. F. THURMAN
Ganden Dekyiling, Woodstock, New York
January 1, 2005, Year of the Wood Monkey

Foreword

WHY IS IT that the fate of Tibet has found such a deep echo in the world? There can only be one answer: Tibet has become the symbol of all that present-day humanity is longing for, either because it has been lost or not yet been realised or because it is in danger of disappearing from human sight: the stability of a tradition, which has its roots not only in a historical or cultural past, but within the innermost being of man, in whose depth this past is enshrined as an ever-present source of inspiration.

But more than that: what is happening in Tibet is symbolical for the fate of humanity. As on a gigantically raised stage we witness the struggle between two worlds, which may be interpreted, according to the standpoint of the spectator, either as the struggle between the past and the future, between backwardness and progress, belief and science, superstition and knowledge—or as the struggle between spiritual freedom and material power, between the wisdom of the heart and the knowledge of the brain, between the dignity of the human individual and the herd-instinct of the mass, between the faith in the higher destiny of man through inner development and the belief in material prosperity through an ever-increasing production of goods.

We witness the tragedy of a peaceful people without political ambitions and with the sole desire to be left alone, being deprived of its freedom and trampled underfoot by a powerful neighbour in the name of 'progress', which as ever must serve as a cover for all the brutalities of the human race. The living present is sacrificed to the moloch of the future, the organic connection with a fruitful past is destroyed for the chimera of a machine-made prosperity.

Thus cut off from their past, men lose their roots and can find security only in the herd, and happiness only in the satisfaction of their ephemeral needs and desires. For, from the standpoint of 'progress' the past is a negligible, if not negative, value, bearing the stigma of imperfection and being synonymous with backwardness and 'reaction'.

What, however, is it that distinguishes man from the animal, if not the consciousness of the past, a consciousness which stretches beyond his short life-span, beyond his own little ego, in short, beyond the limitations of his momentary time-conditioned individuality? It is this wider and richer consciousness, this oneness with the creative seeds hidden in the womb of an ever-young past, which makes the difference, not only between the human and the animal consciousness, but between a cultured and an uncultured mind.

The same is true for nations and peoples. Only such nations are truly civilised, or better, truly cultured, which are rich in tradition and conscious of their past. It is in this sense that we speak of Tibet as a deeply cultured nation, in spite of the primitive conditions of life and the wildness of nature prevailing over the greater part of the country. In fact, it is the very harshness of life, and the unrelenting struggle against the powers of nature, that has steeled the spirit of its inhabitants and built their character. Herein lies the unconquerable strength of the Tibetan, which in the end will prevail over all external powers and calamities. This strength has shown itself throughout Tibet's history. Tibet has been overrun more than once by hostile powers and has gone through worse calamities than the present one—as in the times of King Langdarma, who usurped the throne of Lhasa and persecuted Buddhism with fire and sword. But the Tibetans never bowed to any conqueror or to any tyrant. When the hordes of Genghis Khan drowned half the world in blood and Mongols overran the mighty Chinese empire and threatened to conquer Tibet, it was the spiritual superiority of Tibet that saved its independence, by converting Kublai Khan and his people to Buddhism and transforming this warlike race into a peaceful nation. Nobody has yet entered Tibet without falling under its spell, and who knows whether the Chinese themselves, instead of converting the Tibetans to Communism, may not be subtly transformed in their ideas like the Mongolian hordes of yore.

One thing is sure, and that is, that while the Chinese are trying their utmost to crush Tibet by brutal force, the spirit of Tibet is gaining an ever-increasing influence upon the world—just as the persecution of the early Christians by the might of the Roman empire carried the new faith into the remotest corners of the then-known world, converted a small religious sect into a world-religion and finally triumphed over the very empire that had tried to crush it.

We know that Tibet will never be the same again, even if it regains its independence, but this is not what really matters. What matters is that the continuity of Tibet's spiritual culture, which is based on a *living* tradition and a conscious connection with its origins, should not be lost. Buddhism is not opposed to change—in fact, it is recognising it as the nature of all life—it is, therefore, not opposed to new forms of life and thought or to new discoveries in the fields of science and technique.

On the contrary, the challenge of modern life, the widening horizon of scientific knowledge, will be an incentive to explore the very depths of the human mind and to rediscover the true meaning of the teachings and symbols of the past, which had been hidden under the accumulated dross of centuries. Much that had been merely accepted as an article of faith, or that had become a matter of mere routine, will again have to be consciously acquired and resuscitated.

In the meantime, however, it is our task to keep alive the remembrance of the beauty and greatness of the spirit that informed the history and the religious life of Tibet, so that future generations may feel encouraged and inspired to build a new life on the foundations of a noble past.

The Way of the White Clouds as an eye-witness account and the description of a pilgrimage in Tibet during the last decenniums of its independence and unbroken cultural tradition, is the attempt to do justice to the above-mentioned task, as far as this is possible within the frame of personal experiences and impressions. It is not a travelogue, but the description of a *pilgrimage* in the truest sense of the word, because a pilgrimage distinguishes itself from an ordinary journey by the fact that it does not follow a laid-out plan or itinerary, that it does not pursue a fixed aim or a limited purpose, but that it carries its meaning in itself, by relying on an inner urge which operates on two planes: on the physical as well as on the spiritual plane. It is a movement not only in the outer, but equally in the inner space, a movement whose spontaneity is that of the nature of all life, i.e. of all that grows continually beyond its momentary form, a movement that always starts from an invisible inner core.

It is for this reason that we begin our description with a prologue in one of the temples of Tsaparang, a poetic vision corresponding to that inner reality (or core) which contains the germs of all outer events that later on unfold themselves before our eyes in temporal succession.

In the great solitude and stillness of the abandoned city of Tsaparang and in the mysterious semi-darkness of its temple-halls, in which the spiritual experiences and achievements of countless generations seemed to be projected into the magic forms of images—an insight into hidden connections dawned upon me, which gave a new perspective to my life and revealed apparently accidental events and human relationships as being parts of a meaningful interplay of psychic forces. The coincidence of certain happenings and experiences, which are not causally connected and therefore not time-conditioned, seem to have their origin in a time-free dimension, which can be experienced only on a higher level of consciousness.

Indeed, the temples of Tsaparang seemed to be lifted out of the stream of time; preserving in them the concentrated atmosphere of a whole epoch of Tibetan culture. And this atmosphere grew in intensity the longer one dwelled in it, until the images took on a life of their own and an almost supernatural reality. Their very presence filled the temples with the voices of an undying past. What, therefore, may appear to the reader as merely poetical imagination, contains a deeper reality than any matter-of-fact description of outer events and situations could ever have conveyed, because these events and facts become meaningful only if seen against the background of inner experience.

Thus the pilgrimage in the outer space is actually the mirrored reflection of an inner movement or development, directed towards a yet unknown, distant aim which, however, is intrinsically and seed-like contained in the very direction of that movement. Herefrom springs the readiness to cross the horizons of the known and the familiar, the readiness to accept people and new environments as parts of our destiny, and the confidence in the ultimate significance of all that happens and is in harmony with the depth of our being and the universality of a greater life.

Just as a white summer-cloud, in harmony with heaven and earth, freely floats in the blue sky from horizon to horizon, following the breath of the atmosphere—in the same way the pilgrim abandons himself to the breath of the greater life that wells up from the depth of his being and leads him beyond the farthest horizons to an aim which is already present within him, though yet hidden from his sight.

In Tibetan Buddhism the symbol of the cloud is of such far-reaching importance, that a glance upon Tibetan Thankas (scrolls) or temple-frescoes would suffice to convince the beholder. The figures of Buddhas, Bodhisattvas (enlightened beings), saints, gods and genii manifest themselves from cloud-formations which surround their haloes. The cloud represents the creative power of the mind, which can assume any imaginable form. The white cloud especially (or even a cloud shining in delicate rainbow-colours) is regarded as the ideal medium of creation for the enlightened or enraptured mind, which manifests itself on the plane of meditative vision as *sambhogakāya,* the mind-created 'body of delight'.

Even the earlier Sanskrit-Buddhism speaks of the 'Cloud of Truth' or the 'Cloud of the Universal Law' *(dharma-megha),* from which descends the rain of bliss and liberating knowledge upon a world burning with passions.

Thus the 'White Cloud' becomes the symbol of the Guru's wisdom and compassion, and therefore 'the Way of the White Clouds' hints at the same time at the way of spiritual unfoldment, the way of a pilgrimage that leads to the realisation of final completeness.

The relationship to the Guru, the highest teacher, is beautifully expressed in the Tibetan *Song of the Eastern Snow Mountain:*

'On the peak of the white snow mountain in the East
A white cloud seems to be rising towards the sky.
At the instance of beholding it, I remember my teacher
And, pondering over his kindness, faith stirs in me.'[1]

1. Quoted in Tibetan and translated by Johan van. Manen. Asiatic Society, Calcutta 1919.

PART ONE

Three Visions

I

The Poet's Vision

Prologue in the Red Temple of Tsaparang

Clothed in facts
truth feels oppressed;
in the garb of poetry
it moves easy and free.
—Rabindranath Tagore

It was a stormy night over the rocks and ruins of Tsaparang, the abandoned capital of the once powerful kingdom of Western Tibet. Clouds were drifting across the sky, alternately hiding and revealing the full moon, throwing its ghostly spotlights upon the gigantic stage on which history played one of its immortal dramas. Immortal? Yes: because it was the same old theme of the impermanency of all things, the wondrous play of power and beauty, spiritual achievement and worldly splendour.

The power vanished, while beauty still hovered over the ruins and in the works of art, which had been created patiently and humbly under the shadow of power. The splendour crumbled while the spirit of culture and devotion retired into far-off hermitages and survived in the words and deeds of saints and scholars, poets and artists—illustrating the words of Lao-tse, that what is yielding and tender belongs to the realm of life, and what is hard and strong belongs to the realm of death.

The fate of Tsaparang is sealed. The work of man and the work of nature have become almost indistinguishable. The ruins have taken the form of rocks, and rocks stand out like Cyclopean buildings. The whole huge mountain looks like one huge block of marble, out of which a fairy city has been carved, with lofty castles, towers, and turrets which seem to touch the clouds, with mighty walls and battlements on perpendicular rocks, which on their part are honeycombed with hundreds and hundreds of caves.

The changing light of the moon made all this still more unreal, like a vision that flared up and disappeared as unexpectedly as it came into existence.

The great Red Temple of Buddha Śākyamuni was filled with darkness and silence. Only from the golden face of the giant image of Buddha Śākyamuni a soft light seemed to radiate and to be reflected faintly on the golden images of the Dhyāni-Buddhas, seated on both sides below his throne.

Suddenly a tremor, accompanied by the rumbling sounds of falling masonry, shook the walls of the temple. The wooden shutters above the head of Buddha Śākyamuni sprang open, and the Buddha's face was lit up brightly by the rays of the full moon flooding the whole temple with a pale light.

At the same time the air was filled with the moaning and groaning of innumerable voices. It was as if the whole building were groaning under the weight of the many centuries of its existence. A huge crack appeared by the side of the White Tārā, almost touching one of the flowers flanking her beautiful throne.

The spirit who inhabited this flower rushed out in fear, and with clasped hands prayed to Tārā: 'Oh, Thou Saviouress of all who are in danger, save us, save this sacred place from destruction!'

Tārā looked with merciful eyes in the direction from where the voice came and asked: 'Who art thou, little spirit?'

'I am the Spirit of Beauty, living in this flower by your side.'

Tārā smiled her motherly smile and, pointing towards the other side of the temple, replied:

'Among the priceless treasures of wisdom which are collected in those ancient half-destroyed manuscripts, heaped up in the corner, there is one called Prajñāpāramitā. In it these words of the Tathāgata are recorded:

'"Thus shall ye think of all this fleeting world:
A star at dawn, a bubble in a stream,
A flash of lightning in a summer cloud,
A flickering lamp, a phantom, and a dream.'"

The Spirit of Beauty had tears in his eyes: 'Oh, how true are these words, how true! And where there is beauty, even for a flashing moment, there some immortal chord is touched in us. Yes, we are all in a great dream, and we hope to awaken from it, as our Lord the Tathāgata, who in his mercy appears before us in his dream-form in order to guide us towards enlightenment.'

The Spirit of Beauty, while speaking thus, bowed down towards the gigantic statue of Buddha Śākyamuni, which had come to life like all the other images in this magic hour.

'It is not for myself,' the Spirit continued, 'that I pray for help. I know that all the forms which we inhabit have to perish—as even the priceless words of the Tathāgata, stored up in those dust-covered manuscripts. But what I pray for is: let them not perish before they have fulfilled the purpose for which they were created; let them not perish before we have delivered the great message which is embodied in them.

'I, therefore, pray to thee, O mother of all suffering beings, and to all the Buddhas here present, to have mercy upon those among humans whose eyes are covered with only a little dust, and who would see and understand if only we would linger a little in these our dream-forms until our message has reached them or has been handed on to those who are able to spread it for the benefit of all living beings.

'Our Lord Śākyamuni himself was deterred thus by the gods from entering Parinirvāṇa after the attainment of Perfect Enlightenment. May I appeal to him again with the same motive and take my refuge in him and all his innumerable forms of appearance.'

Again he bowed with clasped hands before his forehead towards the mighty, radiating figure of Śākyamuni and to all the assembled Buddhas and Bodhisattvas.

Tārā raised her hands in a tender attitude of blessing and wish-granting, and Śākyamuni's radiant features smiled in approval.

'The Spirit of Beauty has spoken the truth and his heart is sincere. And how could it be otherwise? Is not beauty the greatest messenger and servant of truth? Beauty is the revelation of harmony through forms, whether visible or audible, material or immaterial. However transient the forms may be, the harmony they express and embody belongs to the eternal realm of the spirit, the innermost law of truth, which we call Dharma.

'Had I not expressed this eternal Dharma through perfect harmony of word and thought, had I not appealed to humanity through the spirit of beauty, my teaching would never have moved the hearts of men, it would never have survived even one generation.

'This temple is doomed to destruction like those precious manuscripts, in which ardent disciples have recorded my words with infinite pain and devotion. But others have copied them and carried on my teachings both in word and deed. In a similar way the work of those devoted artists and saints who created this sanctuary may be saved for future generations.

'Thy wish shall be granted, Spirit of Beauty! Thy form, as well as that of the others inhabiting this temple, shall not perish until their message has been delivered to the world, their sacred purpose fulfilled.'

A stir went through the rows of Dhyāni-Buddhas inhabiting the temple.

Akṣobhya, whose nature is as vast and immutable as space, said: 'I will give stability to this sanctuary until it has fulfilled its purpose.'

Ratnasambhava, whose nature is gift-bestowing, said: 'I will bestow the gift of the Dharma on those who are ready to receive it. I will inspire the generosity of those who are able to contribute to the preservation of the Dharma.'

Amitābha, whose nature is infinite light, said: 'Those who have eyes to see, I shall make them see the beauty of the Dharma. And those who have minds to understand, I shall make them discern the profound truth of the Dharma.'

Amoghasiddhi, whose nature is to accomplish the works of the Dharma by the magic power of compassion, penetrating the four quarters, the ten directions, of the universe, said: 'Those who are fit to do the work of the Dharma, I will inspire them with energy and compassion.'

Vairocana, who is the embodiment of the all-comprising reality of the Dharma, said: 'I will combine all your efforts and direct them towards the individuals ready for this task.' And with his heavenly eye penetrating the four directions of the universe he said: 'Even in this age of strife and spiritual decay there are some saintly men, and among them in this very country of Tibet there lives a great hermit, whose abode is in the Southern Wheat Valley. His name is Lama Ngawang Kalzang. I shall request him to go forth from his retreat into the world and kindle the flame of the Dharma in the hearts of men.

'I shall call him through the mouth of the Great Oracle to the sacred spot, where heaven and earth meet, and where Padmasambhava, the great apostle of the Buddha-Dharma, left the traces of his magic power in the miraculous spring of Chorten Nyima. In the utter solitude and purity of this place I shall allow the radiance of our transcendent forms to appear before him. Having acquired during long years of meditation the power to communicate his visions to others, he will open their eyes to the eternal beauty of Buddha-hood and guide those who 'will be able to save these our perishing forms from oblivion, so that all who understand the language of beauty will be inspired and uplifted and be put upon the path of deliverance.'

2

The Guru's Vision

A lonely hermitage on a mountain peak,
Towering above a thousand others—
One half is occupied by an old monk,
The other by a cloud!

Last night it was stormy
And the cloud was blown away;
After all a cloud is not equal
To the old man's quiet way.

—Ryokwan

The Lama Ngawang Kalzang had been meditating for twelve years in various caves and retreats in the wilderness of the mountains of Southern Tibet. Nobody knew him, nobody had heard of him. He was one of the many thousands of unknown monks who had received his higher education in one of the great monastic universities in the vicinity of Lhasa, and though he had acquired the title of Géshé (i.e. Doctor of Divinity), he had come to the conclusion that realisation can only be found in the stillness and solitude of nature, as far away from the noisy crowds of market-places as from the monkish routine of big monasteries and the intellectual atmosphere of famous colleges.

The world had forgotten him, and he had forgotten the world. This was not the outcome of indifference on his part but, on the contrary, because he had ceased to make a distinction between himself and the world. What actually he had forgotten was not the world but his own self, because the 'world' is something that exists only in contrast to one's own ego.

Wild animals visited him in his caves and made friends with him, and his spirit went out in sympathy to all living beings. Thus he never felt lonely in his solitude, and enjoyed the bliss of emancipation, born out of the exalted visions of Dhyāna.

One day a herdsman in search of new grazing grounds had lost his way in the inaccessible wilderness of rocks high above the valley when he heard the rhythmic beats of a *damaru* (a small hour-glass-like hand-drum, used by Lamas and wandering ascetics during their invocations) mingled with the silvery sound of a ritual bell. At first he did not believe his ears, because he could not imagine that any human being could exist in this forbidding place. But when the sound came again and again fear filled him, because if these sounds had no human origin then they could only have some supernatural cause.

Torn between fear and curiosity, he followed the sound, as if drawn by the irresistible force of a magnet, and soon he saw the figure of a hermit, seated before a cave, deeply absorbed in his devotional practice. The hermit's body was lean but not emaciated, and his face serene, lit up with the fire of inspiration and devotion. The herdsman immediately lost all fear, and after the hermit had finished his invocations he confidently approached the Lama and asked for his blessing.

When the hermit's hand touched the crown of his head he felt a stream of bliss flowing through his body, and he was filled with such unspeakable peace and happiness that he forgot all the questions he had wanted to ask, and hurried down into the valley to bring the happy news of his discovery to the people there.

These people at first could hardly believe the news, and when the herdsman led some of them to the hermit's cave they were wonder-struck. How could any human being live in this almost inaccessible mountain fastness? From where did he get his food, since nobody knew of his existence? How could he endure the hardships of winter, when the mountains were covered with snow and ice and even the smallest footpaths were obliterated, so that neither fuel nor food could be obtained? Certainly only a hermit endowed with superhuman yogic powers could survive under such conditions.

The people threw themselves at the feet of the Hermit-Lama, and when he blessed them they felt as if their whole being was transformed into a vessel of peace and happiness. It gave them a foretaste of what every human being can attain to when he realises the dormant powers of light, which are buried like seeds deep within his soul.

The Hermit-Lama merely made them participate in the bliss of his own achievement, so that they might be encouraged to follow the same path towards liberation.

The rumour of the wondrous hermit spread in the valleys like wildfire. But, alas, only those who were strong enough could venture to climb up to the hermit's cave, and since there were many who were thirsting for spiritual guidance, the people of the valley implored the Lama to settle among them for the benefit of all who needed his help. The hermit knew that the hour had come for him to return to the world of men, and true to his Bodhisattva-vow he renounced the bliss of solitude for the welfare of the many.

There was a very small and poor monastery in the valley from which the people had come, called the Monastery of the White Conch (Dungkar Gompa). It was situated on a steep hill with a rocky crest in the middle of a fertile wheat-growing valley called Tomo ('To' = wheat). This place was given to the Hermit-Lama, who from now on was known as 'Tomo Géshé, Rimpoché', 'The Learned Jewel of the Wheat Valley'.

Soon monks and laymen came from far and wide to learn at the feet of Tomo Géshé and in a very short time the Monastery of the White Conch grew into an important place of study and worship, with beautiful temples and spacious living-quarters. In the great hall of the main temple Tomo Géshé erected a gigantic golden statue of Buddha Maitreya, the Coming One, as a symbol of the spiritual future and rebirth of the Eternal Truth of the Dharma, which is reincarnated in every Enlightened One and is to be rediscovered in every human heart.

Tomo Géshé, however, did not content himself with the success of his work at Dungkar. He erected statues of Maitreya in many other places and made the followers of the Buddha-Dharma conscious of the fact that it was not sufficient to bask in the glories of the past, but that one must take active part in the shaping of the future, and thus make it possible for the coming Buddha to appear in this world by preparing our minds for his reception.

In the midst of all these activities an event took place which was as startling as the Hermit-Lama's discovery and return to the world.

It came about through the intervention of the State Oracle of Lhasa (Nächung), which directed Tomo Géshé to make a pilgrimage to Chorten Nyima, a place sacred to Padmasambhava, who was the first to establish Buddhism in Tibet and who, therefore, is held in the highest esteem, especially by the older schools of Tibetan tradition.

This is of particular significance because it throws light upon the interesting fact that one of the most important events in Tomo Géshé's life was thus connected with the earliest period of Tibetan Buddhism, in which Western Tibet—and especially Tsaparang—played an important part.

Chorten Nyima is situated in one of the highest parts of the Tibetan plateau near the northern border of Sikkim. The place is wide and open, with snow-peaks here and there piercing the deep blue sky characteristic of these altitudes. It is a place where heaven and earth meet on equal terms, where the landscape has the vastness and rhythm of the open sea, and the sky the depth of universal space. It is a place where you feel near to the celestial bodies, where sun and moon are your neighbours and the stars your friends.

And here it happened that those very Buddhas and Bodhisattvas, who inspired the artists of Tsaparang and took visible shape through their hands, appeared again in visible form before the eyes of Tomo Géshé Rimpoché. They appeared against the dark blue sky, as if woven of light, dazzling in all the colours of the rainbow, while slowly moving from the eastern to the western horizon.

The vision was first seen by the Rimpoché alone, but just as a great artist is able to make his visions visible to others by re-creating them in various materials, the Guru, by the creative power of his mind, made this wonderful vision visible to all who were present. Not all of them were able to see the full extent of it, or to see it as completely as the Guru. It varied according to the capacity or receptivity of the individual mind.

It is not possible for anybody who was not present, and perhaps even for those who were, to put into adequate words the sublime beauty and the profound effect of this vision upon the beholders. However, in the Śūraṅgama Sūtra we find the description of a similar event (said to have taken place in the presence of Buddha Śākyamuni), of which a paraphrase may serve as the nearest approach to the vision of Chorten Nyima.

'The Blessed Lord, sitting upon the throne in the midst of Buddhas and Bodhisattvas from all the ten quarters of the universe, manifested his transcendental glory, surpassing them all. From his hands and feet and body radiated supernal beams of light that rested upon the crown of each Buddha and Bodhisattva assembled here.

'And equally from the hands and feet and bodies of all those Buddhas and Bodhisattvas of the ten quarters of the universe went forth rays of glorious brightness that converged upon the crown of the Lord Buddha, and upon the crowns of all the Buddhas and Bodhisattvas and Saints present.

'At the same time, the waters and waves of brooks and streams were singing the music of the Dharma, and all the intersecting rays of brightness were like a net of splendour, set with jewels and over-arching them all.

'Such a marvellous sight had never been imagined and held all who were present in silence and awe. Unwittingly they passed into the blissful state of Samādhi. And upon them all an unspeakable peace and happiness descended like a gentle rain of soft petals of many different-coloured lotus-blossoms, all blending together and being reflected into the open space of heaven in all the tints of the spectrum.

'Moreover, all the differentiations of mountains and waters and rocks and plants, and all that makes up our common world, blended into one another and faded away, leaving only the indescribable experience of primordial unity—not dull and inert, but vibrant with rhythmic life and light, with celestial sounds of songs and harmonies, melodiously rising and falling and merging and then fading away into silence.'

After the party had returned to Dungkar Gompa each of the eyewitnesses described what he had seen, and from the combined records, with the final sanction of the Guru (who reluctantly gave in to the wishes of his disciples to have the scene recorded in the form of a fresco), the painting was conscientiously executed.

One of the last witnesses of this memorable incident is the present abbot of Dungkar Gompa. He not only gave his permission to take photographs of this interesting fresco in one of Tomo Géshé's private apartments, but explained every detail of the painting, while relating his own experiences of this pilgrimage. He pointed out what he had seen with his own eyes, and also what he had not been able to see, but what apparently had been visible to others. He also mentioned the strange fact that the vision had remained visible for hours, so that all who saw it could observe and point out to each other the minutest details.

This vision had far-reaching effects upon Tomo Géshé as well as upon his disciples. It invested him with that superior authority which in Tibet is ascribed only to Tulkus, i.e. those in whom the Bodhisattva-spirit, or the ideal of Buddhahood, has taken firm root, so that they have become its living embodiment. They have the power to direct their future rebirths according to the needs of their fellow-men.

And from now on Tomo Géshé conceived the idea to bring the teachings of the Enlightened Ones not only to the people of his own country but to the world at large, irrespective of race, caste, colour, or creed.

And so he stepped out of his quiet valley and travelled all over the countries of the Himalayas and to the sacred places of Buddhism in India. And wherever he went he planted hope and inspiration in the hearts of men; he healed the sick, taught those who were ready to receive the truth of the Dharma, and left in his wake many a disciple to carry on the work which the Buddhas had ordained him to do.

3

The Monastery of Yi-Gah Chö-Ling

In order to understand the significance of events in our lives, in fact, in order to perceive the strange patterns of our destiny (which according to Buddhist conviction are the outcome of our own Karma, our own former deeds), which condition our present thoughts and actions, we have to look back from time to time and trace the origin and the course of the main threads of the complicated fabric which we call life.

Sometimes a glance, a few casual words, fragments of a melody floating through the quiet air of a summer evening, a book that accidentally comes into our hands, a poem or a memory-laden fragrance, may bring about the impulse which changes and determines our whole life.

While writing this, the delicate resinous scent of Tibetan incense is wafted through the shrine-room of my little hermitage and immediately calls up the memory of the place where for the first time I became acquainted with this particular variety. I see myself seated in the dimly lit hall of a Tibetan temple, surrounded by a pantheon of fantastic figures, some of them peaceful and benevolent, some wild and frightening, and others enigmatic and mysterious; but all full of life and colour, though emanating from the depth of dark shadows.

I had taken refuge in this temple during a terrible blizzard which for days on end covered the roads with snow and ice. The suddenness and violence of the storm were something which even the local people had not experienced in their lifetime, and for me, who had come straight from Ceylon clad only in the yellow robes of a Theravāda monk and a light woollen shawl, the contrast was such that I seemed to live in a weird dream. The monastery itself, situated on a mountain-spur jutting out high above the deep valleys which surround the Darjeeling range, seemed to be tossed about in a cauldron of boiling clouds, rising up from invisible dark valleys, lit up only by continual lightning, while other clouds seemed to be sweeping down from the icy ranges of the Central Himalayas from which they were rebounding, thus adding to the confusion of the elements. The uninterrupted rumble of thunder, the deafening noise of hail on the roof, and the howling of the storm filled the air.

The abbot kindly invited me to stay with him in his own room, supplied me with blankets and food, and made me as comfortable as possible under the circumstances. His little room, however, was so overheated, and filled with the smoke of incense and deodar-needles which he sprinkled upon the charcoal fire as offerings during his devotions and long recitations, that I felt almost suffocated and was unable to sleep. The next day he therefore allowed me to settle down in a corner of the big temple as soon as it was possible to cross the courtyard which separated it from the main building of the monastery.

How did I get from the placid life of Ceylon's tropical paradise into this pandemonium of an Himalayan blizzard and the strange surroundings of a Tibetan monastery? Tibet had never figured in my plans or stirred my imagination. To me Ceylon had seemed the fulfilment of all my dreams; and in the certainty of living there to the end of my days I had built myself a hermitage in the heart of the island, midway between Kandy and Nuwara-Eliya in a country of eternal spring, which was neither touched by the heat of the summer nor by the cold of the winter, and where trees and flowers blossomed all through the year.

But one day I received an invitation to take part in an international Buddhist Conference at Darjeeling as a delegate from Ceylon and to preside over the literary section of this conference. After some initial hesitation I suddenly made up my mind, encouraged by the idea that here was an opportunity to uphold the purity of the Buddha's teaching, as preserved in Ceylon, and to spread its message in a country where the Buddha-Dharma had degenerated into a system of demon-worship and weird beliefs.

And here I was in the middle of this weird world of Lamaism, neither knowing the language of the country nor the meaning of those countless images and symbols which surrounded me in the frescoes and statues of this temple, except when they represented the universally known figures of Buddhas and Bodhisattvas.

And yet when the day came on which the skies and the roads were open again and nothing stood in the way of my returning to the comforts of Darjeeling and the soft loveliness of Ceylon I was no more interested in making use of these opportunities. Some inexplicable force seemed to keep me back, and the longer I stayed on in this magic world into which I had dropped by a strange concatenation of circumstances, the more I felt that a hitherto unknown form of reality was revealed to me and that I was on the threshold of a new life.

I never realised it as strongly as on this occasion that the absence of the spoken word, the silent communion with things and people, which was forced upon me due to the lack of a common language, can bring about a deeper awareness and a directness of experience which generally is drowned by the incessant chatter under which human beings hide their fear of meeting each other in the nakedness of their natural being. (I say 'generally' because in the East a form of silent communion is still known under the concept of *darshan,* which denotes the meeting and contemplating a person in silence, merely partaking of the person's presence, without the necessity of making conversation. Thus, religious leaders or other spiritually advanced people are expected to 'give *darshan*' to their devotees or disciples. To 'have *darshan*' of a saint is the equivalent of receiving his blessings.)

As I said before, I had been given the privilege of being allowed to live in a corner of the temple: a big square hall, presided over by the gigantic statue of Buddha Maitreya, whose head would have lost itself in the darkness of the temple's upper regions had it not received the daylight coming through an opening of the raised central part of the roof, which was supported by tall red-lacquered pillars with richly carved and gilded brackets. During the night Maitreya's golden face reflected the mellow light of the Eternal Lamp, which stood in the centre of the hall before a marble table with offerings, consisting of rows of water-bowls, small butter-lamps, bowls with rice, and conical ritual cakes *(torma).*

The floor to the right and to the left of this altar-like offering-table was occupied by long rows of low, carpeted seats and equally low and narrow, box-like tables *(chogtse),* stretching from the open space near the entrance towards the back wall of the temple, against which the giant figure of Maitreya was seated (in European fashion), flanked by other Buddhas and Bodhisattvas and the statues of the founder of the temple and of the thirteenth Dalai Lama. The remainder of the back wall, as well as a substantial part of the two side walls, were covered with a collection of sacred books *(Kanjur* and *Tanjur),* each volume wrapped in red and yellow cloth, resting in wooden pigeon-holes, surmounted by beautifully carved and painted panels.

The walls, as far as their surface was visible to the eye—even above the tall wooden bookstands and behind the statues—were covered with frescoes, alive with the denizens of all the realms of existence: human, superhuman and non-human, divine and demonic, awe-inspiring and reassuring, fierce and compassionate ones. There were many-armed monsters embracing each other in sexual union, surrounded by flames and smoke, and close to them enhaloed saints, serenely resting on lotus-flowers, with devotees at their feet. There were fairies of tender beauty and fierce goddesses in ecstatic dance, adorned with skulls and garlands of human heads, while ascetics were absorbed in meditation and scholars in teaching their disciples. In between appeared wooded hills and snow-clad mountains, trees and waterfalls, clouds and deep blue space and celestial bodies, while manifold birds and beasts and flowering trees animated the landscapes. At the bottom of all, the waters of the ocean with their treasures of pearls, jewels, and corals, as well as the serpent-spirits, the guardians of these treasures, became visible.

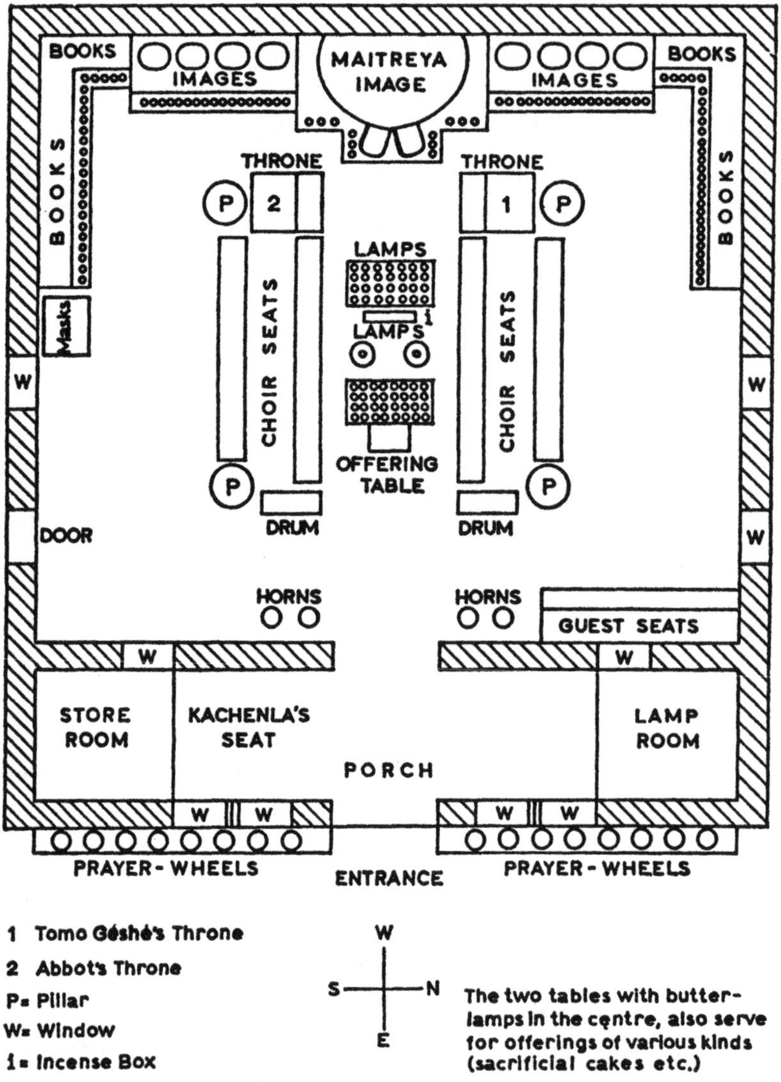

GROUND-PLAN OF THE TEMPLE OF YI-GAH CHÖ-LING

The whole universe seemed to be assembled in this temple, whose walls opened, as it were, into the depths of unheard-of dimensions. And in the midst of this thousand-eyed, form-filled universe, overbrimming with life and possibilities of conscious experience, I lived in a state of wonder, contemplating and absorbing an infinite variety of impressions without trying to define or reason out their meaning—accepting them, as one accepts the landscapes of a foreign country through which one travels.

Had I had somebody to explain to me the details of these my surroundings, my attention would probably have been diverted towards iconographical and historical facts, and this intellectual preoccupation would have robbed me of the direct impact and the spontaneous reaction which these mysterious images exerted upon me. Here I was not confronted only with the outgrowths of individual human imagination but with the accumulated visions of untold generations, visions based on inner experience and on a spiritual reality over which my intellect had neither power nor judgement.

And slowly this reality took possession of me, penetrating and superimposing itself upon my conception and evaluation of the material world and bringing about a subtle transformation in my conscious attitude towards it. I realised that religious truths and spiritual life are more a matter of transcending our habitual consciousness than of changing our opinions or building our convictions on the strength of intellectual arguments and syllogisms, of the laws of reason, which will never lead us beyond the circle of what is already known in the form of ready-made concepts: the cut-and-dried bricks with which we have constructed the present world of 'material reality' and common sense. These have always been the greatest obstacles of creative vision and of the exploration of further dimensions of consciousness and deeper realms of reality. Spiritual life is based on inner awareness and experience, which no amount of thinking could create, thinking and reasoning merely being a process of digestion or mental assimilation which follows but does not precede the above-mentioned faculties.

4

KACHENLA, THE FATHERLY FRIEND AND MENTOR

WHENEVER I HAPPENED TO WAKE UP during the night I beheld the benign features of Buddha Maitreya's golden face, which seemed to float high above the shadowy forms that filled the temple in the dim light of the Eternal Lamp. And in the golden, softly radiating face the large deep blue eyes seemed to be filled with supernatural life, and I felt their glance resting upon me with infinite tenderness.

Sometimes in the middle of the night a strange shuffling sound awoke me, accompanied by what appeared to be the sound of heavy breathing. As the nights were very cold and I was well wrapped up, it took me some time before I could make up my mind to raise myself up and to look around. But the knowledge that the temple was closed at night, and that there was no living soul in it except myself, aroused my curiosity.

And then I saw the slowly moving dark figure of an old man in the open space before the altar, raising his joined hands above his head, going down upon his knees and hands, and then stretching himself out upon the floor in his full length, after which he would again get up and repeat the same exercise over and over again, until his breath was heavy with exertion. After that he moved silently along the walls, bowing before each of the images and touching the lower rows of the sacred books and the feet of Maitreya reverently with his forehead. He moved in a clockwise direction, and when coming back along the right wall towards my corner, I recognised him as the venerable old monk who lived in a small room flanking the porch that formed the entrance of the temple.

It was easy to recognise him because of his slightly bent figure and his long beard, which is comparatively rare among Tibetans. He was the oldest monk in the monastery and hailed from Shigatse. In his younger days he had been one of the personal attendants of the Tashi Lama (or Panchen Rimpoché, as he is known in Tibet), from whom he still received a small pension which, as I found out later, he mainly used for the improvement and beautification of the temple, while he himself lived like the poorest and humblest of monks at the temple door with no other personal possessions than his sitting-mat and his monastic robes. He was bent not so much from age, perhaps, as from sitting for years and years in the posture of meditation, and, in fact, his whole life seemed to be a continuous *sādhanā* (religious practice).

But this did not preclude him from playing occasionally with the children who ran about in the courtyard of the monastery and sometimes invaded the temple in order to tease old Kachenla, who good-naturedly would pretend to chase them among the low benches and the little tea-tables of the temple hall. His friendly little eyes would twinkle in such a way that even his most threatening gestures could not frighten the smallest of the little urchins, who would pull his flapping robes and scream with pleasure when die old man made an attempt to catch him.

In spite of his old age I never saw Kachenla unoccupied: whether he would glide about the temple on two square pieces of felt, in order to keep the floor polished, or whether he would attend to the hundreds of butter-lamps, water-bowls, and other altar-vessels, which had to be kept clean and shining and filled with their various ingredients—ever was he busy in the service of the temple or in the performance of his spiritual duties: reading the sacred texts, reciting prayers for the welfare of all living beings, and performing the daily rituals for their protection and well-being. On special occasions he would be making small clay images of great beauty, and I was fascinated to see how every phase of the work, from the mixing and kneading of the clay, the modelling or pressing into forms, to the drying or baking in the charcoal fire and the subsequent gilding or painting (or both) of the delicate details, every process was accompanied by *mantras* and prayers, invoking the blessings of the Enlightened Ones and the beneficent forces of the universe, present in earth and air, water and fire, i.e. in all the elements which support our life and serve win the accomplishment of our work. Thus even a manual occupation was turned into a ritual of profound meaning and an act of devotion and meditation, whose forces would saturate even the material objects created in this way.

What Kachenla taught me in his humble way was more than I shall ever be able to convey in words. His devotion and his utter humility prepared my mind for the meeting with my Guru—in fact, he was part and parcel of the Guru who was ever present in his mind and so inseparably united with him that the gratitude and veneration which I feel towards my Guru includes Kachenla.

He looked after my welfare as if I was his own son. He taught me the first words of Tibetan by pointing at things and pronouncing their names. In the morning he would bring me warm water—a luxury in which he himself would not indulge and which none of the other monks could afford—and while doing so he would say *chu tsawo.* He would share with me his beloved *sö-cha* (Tibetan butter-tea), which was simmering the whole day long on his little charcoal stove behind which he had his seat. That I relished this strange concoction of Chinese tea, slightly 'matured' butter, soda, and salt—which few non-Tibetans seem to be able to stomach—must have been due to Kachenla's overwhelming kindness. And how important it was to get accustomed to this indispensible and nourishing drink I realised in my later wanderings on the frozen highlands of Tibet.

Before enjoying his morning tea Kachenla would take a pinchful of black seeds, arrange them on the palm of his left hand in the form of a scorpion, and while reciting the *mantra* for protection from all evils, he would drop them into the charcoal fire. On other occasions he would sprinkle some incense upon the charcoal and describe with various beautiful gestures *(mudrā)* of his hands a variety of symbolical gifts which he offered to the Buddhas, at the same time pronouncing a formula of dedication for each of them. This was done in such perfect and naturally flowing movements that I could almost see the various objects appearing before my eyes and that I had no doubt of the sincerity with which they were given. There was nothing theatrical or pompous or artificial in these little rituals. They seemed to be the natural expression of the man's inner life, as natural as the breathing of his lungs or the beating of his heart. He moved among the multitude of enlightened beings, as well as among gods and demons, as naturally as among humans and animals, giving to each of them the recognition or attention due to them.

In the evenings Kachenla would generally come into my quiet corner in the temple with a lit butter-lamp, sit down before me on the floor, and motion me to take out paper and pencil; and with infinite patience he would recite and dictate one prayer after another and make me repeat it until I caught the right pronunciation and intonation. It never bothered him that I could not understand a single word in the beginning, though he pointed out the image of the Buddhas and Bodhisattvas concerned, so that I was not left entirely without guidance and could connect the words with a definite mental picture.

He seemed to be confident that he transmitted to me something that was of infinite value, whether I knew it or not; and to say the truth I experienced a similar satisfaction, because I was convinced that a gift given with such infinite love and devotion was valuable through this very fact, and, indeed, I felt that something was streaming over from the old man to me that filled me with happiness, though I could find no reasonable explanation for it. It was the first time that—without knowing it—I experienced the power of *mantra,* of sacred speech, in which the transcendental sound of the spirit that dwells in the human heart is perceived. And because it is the sound of the heart it cannot be heard by the ear or understood by the brain. But this I did not know yet, though I began to experience it.

Later on I was able to understand the contents and the meaning of those prayers, but this knowledge did not surpass the initial benefit I had derived from them, and now I know that more important than the intellectual meaning of the words were the circumstances under which they were transmitted and the spiritual purity and conviction of the transmitter.

5

Religious Practice and Ritual Symbolism

Under Kachenla's kindly guidance I soon learned to become conscious of many of the small things to which formerly I would not have given any importance or attention, and which yet proved to be very useful as means of keeping the mind tuned to a higher level and in consonance with one's aspirations, by making one's movements and behaviour part of one's *sādhanā* (religious practice) and meditation.

I learned how to unwrap and handle a sacred book—treating it with the respect due to the embodiment of wisdom—how to turn the pages of the loose sheets of which the books consisted, without upsetting their order—and how to look upon each letter of the alphabet as a *mantric* symbol, so that even a discarded or damaged piece of writing was not to be thrown away carelessly, lest it might be trampled underfoot. To dispose of such things there was a special little structure outside the temple which looked like a wayside shrine but was meant for depositing unwanted pieces of writing or any ritual objects that had served their purpose.

I learned how to move about within the precincts of the monastery: always in the direction in which the planets move around the sun—signifying that one should always feel oneself in the presence of the Buddha, the Enlightened One, who used to be honoured by circumambulation in this direction, as being the spiritual sun, the illuminator of mankind.

Thus, even if I merely wanted to cross over the courtyard to the buildings on my left side (when leaving the temple), I had to turn to the right and circumambulate the whole temple in order to reach my destination. And while doing this I had to pass rows of copper cylinders on which the Great Mantra of Six Syllables, OṀ MAṆI PADME HŪṀ, was embossed and which contained thousands of repetitions of the same *mantra,* written on long rolls of thin but extremely durable Tibetan paper.

As in the preparation of clay images and seal *(ts'ha-ts'ha),* these rolls had been prepared with special rites and as an act of devotion, with the intention to bestow blessings to all those whose minds are susceptible to good thoughts and the effects of spiritual influences.

While passing, I would give each of these 'prayer-wheels' a quick jerk and at the same time repeat the *mantra* in my heart, as Kachenla had taught me, because no Tibetan who has any deeper knowledge of his religion is so crude as to believe that a mere mechanical action can benefit him, or that with every turn of the drum as many thousands of prayers as are written on the paper roll rise up to heaven. This silly nonsense is mainly the invention of Westerners, who feel themselves superior by ridiculing the religious customs of other peoples, without understanding their psychological approach or the origin of those customs.

The Tibetan is not out to 'cheat the gods' by placating them with sham prayers, or to escape the trouble of exerting himself and escaping the responsibility for his own deeds and conduct *(karma).* Prayers in the Buddhist sense are not requests to a power outside ourselves and for personal advantages but the calling up of the forces that dwell within ourselves and that can only be effective if we are free from selfish desires. In other words, Buddhists do not put their faith in the power of gods, residing in some heavens beyond, but they believe in the power of motive and the purity of faith (or purity of intention).

If a simple peasant installs a *maṇi-chö-khor* (which is a more appropriate name than prayer-wheel) in the brook or channel that brings water to his village and his fields, with the motive of blessing the water and all those who partake of it—whether man or animals, down to the smallest creatures and plants—then this act of sincere faith is as good and valid as that of the Christian priest who by his blessings converts ordinary water into 'holy water'. And, apart from this, the sound of the little bell, which the prayer-wheel emits with each revolution, is a reminder for all who hear it to repeat the sacred *mantra* in their own mind.

But what is the origin of the revolving wheel? The 'turning of the Wheel of the Dharma' *(chö-ki khor-lo khor-ba)* is a metaphor known to every Buddhist, meaning 'the setting in motion of the forces of the Universal and Moral Law', and in turning the prayer-wheel he becomes conscious of the supreme law which the Buddha proclaimed when he set the Wheel of the Dharma rolling 2,500 years ago. For the Buddhist it is not sufficient that this act has been performed once by the Enlightened One—every single human being that strives for Enlightenment must repeat this creative act by realising it in his own mind.

The profundity and the cosmic parallelism of this symbol will easily be understood if we realise that the life of the whole universe is dependent on rotation: be it the rotation of stars and planets around their own axis or the rotation of planets around a central sun, or the similar movements of atoms. If the mere rotation of a dynamo can produce the power of electricity (an altogether inexplicable phenomenon), and if the turning of the human mind around a particular subject of his consciousness can produce a state of concentration that can lead to world-shaking discoveries or to the realization of higher dimensions or Perfect Enlightenment, is it under such circumstances to be wondered if there is a belief among the Tibetans that the beneficent forces which were concentrated in the ritual act of preparing the contents of the prayer-wheel are somehow retained even in its material form and are transmitted or activated when they are set in motion? If matter can be impregnated with psychic energies—as has been demonstrated by experiments in psychometry, which has been defined as the 'faculty of divining from physical contact or proximity the qualities of an object or of persons, etc. [i.e. forces, events, or conditions], that have been in contact with it'—then we must admit that the Tibetan belief is not quite so absurd as it might have appeared in the first instance. But even though a thing might be psychometrically effective, and even beneficent in a certain way, I am convinced that without our conscious co-operation no spiritual profit can be gained through any mechanical or material device. But whatever helps us to concentrate our mind or to achieve that 'inner turning about' in the deepest seat of our consciousness, of which the Laṅkāvatāra Sūtra speaks—in fact, whatever puts us into a creative or intuitively receptive frame of mind—is worthy of our attention, whether it be a 'prayer-wheel', a rosary, or any other device. Those who think that prayers can be delivered by anything else but the human heart do not know what prayers are—and still less the meaning of a *mantra,* in which no powers outside ourselves are implored or placated. So there is no question of gaining favours or 'cheating the gods'. On the contrary, the *maṅi-khor-eo* is an expression of supreme faith in the infinite power of goodwill and love that may act through an infinite number of means: through the thoughts of the wise, the single-hearted devotion of simple minds, nay, even through a child's toy.

All these thoughts came flooding through me during my frequent circumambulations around the temple and in the grounds of the monastery which—though hardly a mile from the little Tibetan settlement of Ghoom—seemed to belong to an altogether different world, separated as it was from the village by a steep terraced hill, crowned by whitewashed Chortens (*stūpa*-like religious monuments), and surrounded by a grove of tall white prayer-flags. Each of the flagpoles was about twenty-five feet in height and surmounted by the symbols of sun, moon and fire, or a flaming sword or trident. The white flag-cloth, upon which prayers and auspicious symbols were printed, was about two feet wide and ran along the length of the pole, starting from about four or five feet above the ground. Each of these prayer-flags was an offering of a devotee (or a family) as a blessing and a reminder of the Dharma to all who approached it or lived within its sight.

During the greater part of the day the whole hill was generally hidden in a huge cloud, so that lamps had to be lit at noon inside the buildings, while the outside was wrapped in thick white fog. One felt as if the whole place was floating on a cloud and driven by the ghostlike white sails of innumerable prayer-flags standing guard over the monastery and the many small sanctuaries scattered over the hillside. But, far from being depressing, the fog rather heightened the mysterious atmosphere of the place and gave one a feeling of protection, seclusion, and security, a feeling of being far away from the vicissitudes and hustle of ordinary human life.

When wandering about on this magic hill it appeared to me that the buildings materialised out of nowhere, having no more substance than my own mind, while I myself moved about invisible to others like a discarnate spirit. Everything took on an air of supernatural animation, and the general silence seemed to heighten the effect of the strange sounds that pervaded the air in swelling and ebbing cadences. I had never heard such sounds before; they were produced by the peculiar vibrating movement of the long, narrow prayer-flags in the constant breeze that came up from the Indian plains, some seven and a half thousand feet below (and incidentally produced the eternal cloud by condensing the warm moist air when it suddenly came in contact with the cold prevailing in higher altitudes). Mingled with these strange sounds was the silvery tinkle of the great prayer-wheel, which was housed in a small building next to the temple and was kept in motion by a blind old man, who accompanied the rhythm of the bell with the hum of his incessant recitation of the sacred *mantra*.

A little farther up the hillside the deep sound of a ritual drum emerged during certain hours of the day from a small temple. I was drawn to this little building by this sound and its rhythm, which was sometimes interrupted by the crash of cymbals. When coming nearer, I heard the sonorous voice of a monk, reciting to the rhythm of the drum, and as I did not dare to disturb him, it took me some days until I found an opportunity of approaching him and asking his permission to enter the sanctuary that was otherwise not open to the public.

I soon began to understand the reason. It was dedicated to the terrible and awe-inspiring deities, the forces of dissolution and transformation, which appear destructive and frightening to those who cling to the things of this world and to their own limited existence, but which prove to be the forces of liberation to those who accept them and make use of them in the right spirit, by realising their true nature. They are the removers of obstacles, the liberators from bondage, the symbols of the ultimate mystery of self-transcendence in the ecstasy of breaking through the darkness of ignorance.

They are the embodiment of the highest knowledge, which like a blinding flash would destroy those who are not yet prepared for it, like the youth who lifted the veil in the Temple of Sais. It is for this reason that many of the images of this temple are veiled and only initiates are allowed to enter it alone. To them these forces or aspects of reality are as much symbols of Enlightenment as the compassionate embodiments of Buddhas and Bodhisattvas. Indeed, they are *one* in their ultimate nature. The universal law is beneficent to those who accept it, terrible to those who try to oppose it. Therefore the forces of light (the forces that urge us towards Enlightenment) appear in fearful forms to the enemies of light and truth, for which reason those forms are called Protectors of the Law *(chö-kyong gon-po)* and are invoked as tutelary deities by those who have received initiation and realised their meaning.

But there was one more mystery to be solved for me in this monastery, which seemed to be connected with a third sanctuary, bigger than the Gönkhang, but small compared with the other buildings. It was perfectly square, with a yellow-coloured, curved Chinese temple-roof and a closed glass veranda in front. Due to the sloping ground the veranda rested on stilts, so that one could not look into the interior of the building, and the only door, that led to the veranda from the back, was permanently closed.

What intrigued me especially was that this building was connected with the main temple below by a garland of silvery-white seed-pods. When asking Kachenla about it, he told me with awed voice that the 'Great Lama', who was one with the Buddhas, was engaged there in meditation. He spoke in whispers, as if in the presence of the great Lama, and though I could not make out the details of his explanation, nor who this Lama was, I began to wonder whether the powerful atmosphere of this place, and the spiritual transformation which I began to experience, had something to do with him. The fact that Kachenla, whose goodness and sincerity had made a deep impression upon me, spoke with such veneration of this Lama, aroused in me the desire to become his pupil, and when I mentioned this to Kachenla he approved of it immediately and promised to talk to the abbot, who might be able to convey my wish in due time.

6

The Guru Appears

One or two weeks passed by and I did not know whether the abbot had succeeded in passing on my request, when one day, after returning from my meditation cave at the back of the hill, below the *chortens,* I found on my place in the temple a huge mango of the most costly and rare variety, growing only in the plains and not yet in season at that time of the year. I could hardly believe my eyes, nor could I understand how it got there, until Kachenla came, beaming with pleasure and pointing up in the direction of the meditation-cubicle *(ts'hang-khang),* and told me it was a gift from the Great Lama. I have never received a more precious gift, because it told me that my wish had been granted, that I had been accepted as a disciple.

Kachenla shared with me my happiness, and no matter how long I would have to wait I knew it was worth waiting even for a lifetime to find a real Guru, i.e. one who not only imparted intellectual knowledge but who could awaken the inner forces of one's own mind by the power of his spiritual achievements and realisation.

The term *'guru'* is generally translated as 'teacher', but actually it has no equivalent in any Western language, because a Guru is far more than a teacher in the ordinary sense of the word. A teacher gives knowledge, but a Guru gives himself. The real teachings of a Guru are not his words but what remains unspoken, because it goes beyond the power of human speech. The Guru is an *inspirer* in the truest sense of this word, i.e. one who infuses us with his own living spirit.

And consequently the term *'chela'* means more than an ordinary pupil, who goes through a course of instructions, but a disciple who has established a profound spiritual relationship with the Guru, a relationship that is founded on the act of initiation, during which a direct 'transference of power' takes place and is embodied in the sacred formula *(mantra)* through which this power can be called up by the Chela at any time and through which a permanent contact with the Guru is maintained.

The 'power' of which I speak here is not a force that overwhelms one's mind, but the power that makes one participate in an experience belonging to a higher state of consciousness and realisation, which gives one a foretaste or glimpse of the aim towards which we strive, so that it is no more a vague ideal but an *experienced* reality. Such power can only be created through a life of meditation and becomes intensified with each period of complete seclusion, like the cumulative force of the waters of a dammed-up river.

This became apparent to me on the day when the Great Lama—whose name did not yet mean anything to me at that time, but who was none other than the famous Tomo Géshé Rimpoché—emerged from the Ts'hang-khang after his many weeks of silent meditation.

From the early morning I noticed an uncommon stir in the monastery, whose population suddenly seemed to have doubled or tripled. I did not know from where all those monks, whom I did not remember to have seen before, suddenly had come, but apparently they belonged to the monastery, though they did not live within its premises. Even those whom I knew seemed to look different, not only because all of them wore their best robes but also because they all looked exceptionally washed and clean.

The long rows of seats in the temple hall were filled to the last place, and some new rows had been added. The huge cauldrons in the adjacent kitchen building were filled with boiling tea and soup, to be served in the intervals during the service in the temple. The temple hall was lit up by more than a thousand butter-lamps, and bundles of incense-sticks wafted clouds of fragrant smoke into the air and wove bluish veils around the golden images high above the congregation.

Suddenly the deep, thundering sound of alp-horn-like tubas, punctuated by the slow rhythm of bass-drums and accompanied by the vibrating voices of oboes, was heard from outside, the doors of the temple swung wide open, and Tomo Géshé Rimpoché, flanked by two Lamas in full ornate and high ceremonial hats, entered the temple. A large orange-coloured silken shawl (representing the upper garment or *civaram* of an orthodox Buddhist monk) was draped around him and a prayer-carpet was spread before his feet. He raised his hands with joined palms above his head in salutation of the Buddhas, knelt down on the carpet, and prostrated himself with his forehead on the ground. This he repeated three times, while the choir of the assembled monks chanted the formulas of refuge in deep melodious voices which formed a rhythmically moving background to the continued blasts of the *radongs* (the twelve-foot-long bass-horns) outside the temple.

After the Rimpoché had finished his devotions the tall pointed yellow cap, the symbol of his high office, was put upon his head, and then he slowly moved through the middle of the hall and ascended the high throne, opposite that of the Umdzé, the leader of the choir and the head of the monastery in his absence. While he moved through the hall a deep silence fell upon the congregation and all sat motionless as if spellbound by the magic presence of this one man, who seemed to fill the whole temple with the accumulated power gained through a long period of concentration and complete absorption. I now began to understand what Kachenla meant when he said that the Great Lama had become one with the Buddhas.

As soon as he was seated the Umdzé began to chant the liturgy in a voice so deep as to make one wonder whether it came from a human throat or from the very depths of the earth. After a few bars of solo chant the choir of monks and novices joined in, the higher voices of the younger harmoniously blending with the deeper ones of the older monks and the bass of the leader of the choir. Sometimes the chant would end abruptly and only the voice of the Umdzé would be heard, and then again the entire congregation would fall in and continue until another climax had been reached with a clash of cymbals and an acceleration of drum-beats.

7

Tibetan Sacred Music

The soul-stirring quality of Tibetan ritual music which accompanies and often precedes the liturgy is not based on melody but on rhythm and pure sound-values: the latter in the sense that the different instruments do not try to imitate the variations and movements of a human song or its emotions, but each of them represents the tonal value of a fundamental quality of nature, in which the human voice is merely one of the many vibrations that make up the symphony of the universe. This symphony does not follow the laws of Western musical harmony, and yet it achieves an effect that is far from disharmonious, because each sound has its fixed place and corresponds to the others in a way that establishes an unmistakable parallelism on different levels.

I am not a musician, so as to be able to describe or to analyse Tibetan music in technical terms. But I am deeply moved by music, and therefore I can only describe my own reaction. Moreover, the few references I have read about Tibetan sacred music are so scanty and inadequate that I have come to the conclusion that either Western terminology is unsuitable to express the nature of Tibetan music or that those who have attempted to give an idea of it were not able to enter into its spirit.

To do this one has to experience the religious as well as the natural background from which this music grew, and this is only possible if one has lived in those surroundings and has taken part in the spiritual and emotional life of which this music is the most immediate expression. Tibetan Buddhism regards man not as a solitary figure but always in connection with and against a universal background. In the same way Tibetan ritual music is not concerned with the emotions of temporal individuality, but with the ever-present, timeless qualities of universal life, in which our personal joys and sorrows do not exist, so that we feel in communion with the very sources of reality in the deepest core of our being. To bring us in touch with this realm is the very purpose of meditation as well as of Tibetan ritual music, which is built upon the deepest vibrations that an instrument or a human voice can produce: sounds that seem to come from the womb of the earth or from the depth of space like rolling thunder, the *mantric* sound of nature, which symbolise the creative vibrations of the universe, the origin of all things. They form the foundation as well as the background from which the modulations of the higher voices and the plaintive notes of the reed instruments rise like the forms of sentient life from the elementary forces of nature—which are nowhere more apparent than in the gigantic mountain ranges and in the vast, lonely highlands of Tibet.

Just as the bass-voice of the precentor forms the basis of the choir, from which the liturgy starts and to which it sinks back in a peculiarly sliding way at the end of each part of the recitation, in the same way the huge twelve-foot *radongs* form the basis and the starting-point of the orchestral music. They are always in pairs and are alternately blown in such a way that the sounds of the one merge into the other without breaking its continuity and at the same time producing the effect of gradually swelling and ebbing tides of an ocean of sound. And on the surface of this ocean the breeze of individual life creates and plays with a multitude of waves and wavelets which, like the high-pitched tremolo of the oboes, add vivacity and melody to the vastness of the ocean, whose sound seems to be that of the all-embracing OM, the prototype of all *mantric* sounds.

It is in imitation of this sound that *mantras* are recited in that peculiar, deep bass-voice with which the Umdzé begins and conducts the liturgy. The liturgy, after all, is mainly mantric in character, especially the opening and closing passages of each section. Certain important *mantras* are accompanied by hand-bells and *damarus* (small, hour-glass-shaped hand-drums, which can be played with one hand).

In contrast to the more or less static sound of the *radongs,* the bass-drums and the big cymbals introduce a dynamic element into the orchestra. Not only does the rhythm change according to the metre of the recitation, but—what is more important from the musical and emotional point of view, as it creates a feeling of liberation and a release from a slowly mounting tension—towards the end of each section the rhythm is accelerated until it merges into one great finale, in which the big cymbals by a peculiar rotating movement produce triumphantly upsurging sound, rising above the thundering rumble of the bass-drums, and ending in a mighty clash. After this a new slow rhythm marks the beginning of another section of the liturgy.

If the *radong* or the human bass-voice represent the primeval cosmic sound, in which we experience the infinity of space, the drum represents the infinity of life and movement, governed by the supreme law of its inherent rhythm, in which we experience the alternating cycles of creation and dissolution, culminating in manifestation and liberation.

While melody plays only the ephemeral part of the passing moods of individual life, the rhythm (of the bass-drum in particular) gives the real significance and structure to the music. With the drum, therefore, the Tibetan (and perhaps the East in general) associates quite different emotions than the West, where it is not regarded as a basic or independent musical instrument. The importance of the drum from the very beginnings of Indian civilisation may be seen from one of the most significant similes of the Buddha, in which he compared the eternal law of the universe *(dharma)* with the rhythm of the drum, when in his first utterance after the attainment of enlightenment he spoke of 'the drum of immortality' *(amata-dundubhin)* which he wanted to make heard throughout the world.

Since I could not follow yet the details of the liturgy and the particular service which was conducted that morning in the presence and under the guidance of Tomo Géshé Rimpoché, my whole attention was given to the effects of the music and the meaning it conveyed to me. The inspiring atmosphere, which prevailed all through the service, put me into a state of greater receptiveness than ever before. I had attended during the last weeks many liturgic services and ceremonies in the temple, but never had I witnessed them in such perfection and complete harmony. All who took part in it seemed to be moved by the same spirit—united, as I felt, in the bigger consciousness of the great Guru, so that they acted and chanted in perfect unison, as if merged into *one* body.

All this moved me all the more as during the last years in Ceylon I had been starved of all musical inspiration, which is entirely absent in Southern Buddhism *(Theravāda)* on account of the mistaken view that music is merely a form of sense-pleasure. In consequence of this the religious life had taken on a dry, intellectual form of expression, in which together with the lower also the higher emotions were suppressed and all negative virtues were fostered to the extent that no great personality could arise—i.e. rise above the level of the accepted norm. Book-knowledge had become more important than experience, the letter more important than the spirit.

No wonder, therefore, that it was believed that no *Arahans* (realised saints) could arise after the first millennium of the Buddhist era, in other words, that for the last 1,500 years the Buddhadharma in Ceylon had existed only in theory, or at the best as a belief, since (according to the Sinhalese themselves) Ceylon had not produced a single saint during this long period and it was no more possible to enter into the higher states of *dhyāna* or direct spiritual insight. It was, therefore, impossible even to discuss deeper experiences of meditation, as it was regarded preposterous to assume that anybody could actually realise any of the states of higher consciousness of which the sacred texts speak so often. Thus Buddhism had become a matter of the past, a creed or a distant ideal towards which one could strive by leading a moral life and committing to heart as many sacred texts as possible.

8

MEETING WITH THE GURU

HOW GREAT, THEREFORE, WAS MY JOY to find before my very eyes the living embodiment of those far-off ideals: a man who impressed all those who came in touch with him not merely by his learning but by his mere presence, and thus gave proof that what the sacred texts teach can be realised here and now, as in the days of the Buddha.

What greater opportunity could fate offer me than meeting such a man and coming into living contact with the spirit that had moved the Buddhas and saints of the past and would inspire those of the future!

Soon my first meeting with the Guru came about. It took place in one of the little shrine-rooms on the upper floor of the Lhabrang (the main residential building of the monastery) which served as his private apartments whenever he stayed at Yi-Gah Chö-Ling, and which even during his absence were regarded as the monastery's innermost sanctuary. Like in the temple, the Great Abbot's seat is a place of special sanctity, as it is here that he performs his daily devotions and spends many hours in meditation, even during the night, which he spends in a cross-legged position in the confined space of his seat, which allows him neither to lie down nor to stretch out. The high back of this box-like, slightly raised meditation seat bore the emblem of the Lama's high office, the Wheel of the Law, and was surmounted by the traditional canopy with a seven-coloured volant, representing the aura of the Buddha.

The whole room breathed an atmosphere of peace and beauty, the natural outflow of a mind to whom harmony is not merely an aesthetic pleasure but the adequate expression of a life devoted to the realm of the spirit. Exquisite religious paintings, minutely executed and mounted on old Chinese brocades, harmonised with the mellow colours of hand-woven Tibetan rugs which covered the low seats behind lacquer-topped, delicately carved and painted *Chogtses.* On the opposite side golden images of the finest workmanship rested in glazed shrines, flanked by dragons and crowned by multi-coloured, carved cornices, and on the narrow ledge before the images stood silver bowls filled with clear water and butter-lamps of chased silver. There was not a single object in the room that was not connected with the symbols and functions of religious life and practice, and nothing that could have been regarded as the Guru's personal possession.[1] In fact, long after he had left the body of his present incarnation, when, according to the Guru's special instructions, I had the unique privilege to dwell in this hallowed room, I found everything in it as it had been in the Guru's presence—even the silver-mounted jade teacup and the ritual vessels, beside vajra-sceptre and bell, on the *Chogtse* before his seat.

But all these details fused into one general impression of supreme peace and harmony on that first day, when I bowed down before the Guru and his hands lay on my head: hands whose lightest touch sent a stream of bliss through one's whole body, nay, one's whole being, so that all that one had intended to say or to ask, vanished from one's mind like smoke into blue

---

1. When moving from one monastery to the other he would take with him only the bare necessities for the journey. To him a cave was as good as a palace, and a palace as good as a cave. As little as he cared for riches and comforts, as little was he afraid of making use of them. He was neither attached to comfort nor to asceticism. He knew that the vanity of asceticism can be as great a hindrance as the vanity of possession. Whatever gifts he received from devotees were either distributed among those who were in need or utilised for the maintainance of temples, monasteries, libraries, or similar purposes.

air. Merely to be in this man's presence seemed to be enough to dissolve all problems, to make them non-existent, like darkness in the presence of light.

As he sat on his meditation-seat under the canopy, clad in the simple maroon-coloured robes of a Tibetan monk, I found it difficult to determine his age, though he must have been already about sixty-five years old at that time. His short-cropped hair was still dark and his body looked sturdy and erect. His clean-shaven face showed the features of a strong character, but his friendly eyes and his mouth that was slightly turned up at the corners, as if ready to smile, gave me an immediate feeling of reassurance.

It is a strange fact that nobody ever succeeded in taking a photograph of Tomo Géshé Rimpoché, though many people tried to do so surreptitiously, because they knew that he never allowed anybody to take a picture of him. Those who tried found out that their films had turned into blanks or were blurred beyond recognition or that something else happened to the films. Whatever happened, the Guru's face was never visible. He detested any kind of hero-worship and did not want his person made into an object of veneration.

On the day on which he formally accepted me as his Chela, he said:

'If you wish me to be your Guru, do not look upon my person as the Guru, because every human personality has its shortcomings, and so long as we are engaged in observing the imperfections of others we deprive ourselves of the opportunities of learning from them. Remember that every being carries within itself the spark of Buddhahood *(bodhicitta),* but as long as we concentrate on other people's faults we deprive ourselves of the light that in various degrees shines out from our fellow-beings.

'When searching for a teacher, we surely should search for one who is worthy of our trust, but once we have found him, we should accept whatever he has to teach us as a gift of the Buddhas, and we should look upon the Guru not as one who speaks with his own voice but as the mouthpiece of the Buddha, to whom alone all honour is due. Therefore, if you bow down before the Guru, it is not the mortal personality of the teacher that you worship, but the Buddha, who is the eternal Guru and who reveals his teaching through the mouth of your human teacher who forms a living link in the chain of initiated teachers and pupils who have transmitted the Dharma in an unbroken line from the times of Sākyamuni. Those who transmit to us the teachings of the Buddha are the vessels of the Dharma, and as far as they master the Dharma and have realised the Dharma within themselves, they are the embodiment of the Dharma.

'It is not the robes, nor the body, nor the words that make the Guru, but that which lives in him of truth and knowledge and light *(bodhi)*. The more he possesses of this, and the more his outer conduct and appearance is in harmony with it, the easier it is for the Chela to see the Buddha in his Guru. Therefore he should be as careful in his choice as the Guru in his acceptance of a Chela.

'However, one should never forget that in every living being *bodhicitta* is present as a potentiality (I, therefore, rather prefer to call it a "spark" of enlightenment-consciousness than a "thought" of enlightenment, which only arises when this latent spark becomes fully conscious) and that only our own blindness prevents us from recognising this. The greater our imperfections, the more we are inclined to see the faults of others, while those who have gained deeper insight can see through these faults into their essential nature. Therefore the greatest among men were those who recognised the divine qualities in their fellow-beings and were always ready to respect even the lowliest among them.

'As long as we regard ourselves superior to others or look down upon the world, we cannot make any real progress. As soon, however, as we understand that we live in exactly that world which we deserve, we shall recognise the faults of others as our own—though they may appear in different form. It is our own *karma* that we live in this "imperfect" world, which in the ultimate sense is our own creation. This is the only attitude which can help us to overcome our difficulties, because it replaces fruitless negation by an impulse towards self-perfection, which not only makes us worthy of a better world but partners in its creation.'

The Guru then went on to explain some of the preconditions and preliminary exercises of meditation for bringing about this positive and creative attitude: Unselfish love and compassion towards all living beings was, according to him, the first prerequisite of meditation, as it removed all self-created emotional and intellectual limitations; and in order to gain this attitude one should look upon all beings like upon one's own mother or one's own children, since there was not a single being in the universe that in the infinity of time had not been closely related to us in one way or another. In order to be conscious of the preciousness of time one should realise that any moment might be the last of this life and that the opportunity which it offers might not come again easily. Finally he pointed out that what we learned from books about meditation was not comparable to the direct transmission of experience and the spiritual impetus that a living Guru could give us, if we open ourselves to him in all sincerity.

To this purpose one should imagine the Buddha in the form of one's Guru, and having done so to a degree that one feels his very presence, one should visualise him seated in the posture of meditation above one's head and finally merging into one's own person, to take his seat on the lotus-throne of our heart. For, as long as the Buddha is still imagined outside ourselves, we cannot realise him in our own life. The moment, however, we become conscious of him as the light in our innermost being, the Mantra OṀ MAṆI PADME HŪṀ begins to reveal its meaning, because now the 'lotus' *(padma)* is our own heart, in which the 'jewel' *(maṇi)*, namely the Buddha, is present. The OṀ and the HŪṀ, however, represent the universe in its highest and deepest aspects, in all its forms of appearance and experience, which we should embrace with unlimited love and compassion like the Buddha. Do not think of your own salvation, but make yourself an instrument for the liberation of all living beings. Once the Buddha has become awakened within you, you are no more able to act other than in accordance with his Law. Therefore it is said in the *Bodhicaryāvatāra*: 'As soon as the thought of Enlightenment takes root in him, the miserable one who is fettered by passions to the prison of existence, becomes immediately a son of the Buddhas, he becomes worthy of veneration for men and gods. As soon as this thought has taken possession of this unclean body, it becomes transformed into the precious jewel of a Buddha's body. Therefore take hold of this elixir which causes such a wonderful transformation and which is called the thought of Enlightenment.'

9

INITIATION

IT WAS MY GREAT GOOD LUCK that I had not only been well prepared by Kachenla's patient teachings but that I had found a friend in a learned Mongolian Lama, who knew English and helped me with my Tibetan studies in exchange for Pāli and practice in English. He had studied for about twenty years in one of the great monastic universities near Lhasa, where he acquired the degree of 'Géshé', and he had subsequently worked with the well-known scholar von Staël-Holstein in Peking. His name was Thubden Sherab, though he was generally referred to as 'Géshéla'.

With him as interpreter I was able to converse with the Guru, though—as I was to find out soon—the Guru was in no need of an interpreter, as he was able to read my thoughts like an open book. As he knew that I had devoted the greater part of my adult life to the study of Buddhism, he did not waste time in explaining doctrinal points, but went straight to the practice of meditation, which he regarded as more important than all theoretical knowledge. It was, indeed, also the most important thing to me.

So far I had practised meditation following my own intuition as well as certain instructions which I had found in the sacred texts—especially in the *Satipaṭṭhāna-Sutta* (which in those days had not yet been popularised in the modern, rather one-sided fashion of the Rangoon School). All the more I felt eager to see the further steps and to be introduced into the traditional methods which could guide one step by step into the deeper realms of meditative experience.

On the day on which Tomo Géshé Rimpoché formally accepted me as his Chela in a special ritual of initiation, in which I received my first *mantra,* I realised one of the most important things that hitherto had been lacking in my religious life: the impetus of a spiritual force that required no philosophical argument or intellectual justification, because it was not based on theoretical knowledge, but on fact and direct experience, and thus gave one the certainty that what one was striving after was not merely an abstract idea, a mere shadow of a thought, but an attainable state of mind, the only 'tangible' reality of which we can speak.

And yet the experience through which this 'tangible' reality is transmitted is so intangible that to describe the details of an initiation and the essential experiences connected with it would be as inadequate as describing in words the contents or the impact of music. Indeed, any description of factual details would destroy the very basis of the emotional appeal and significance, because 'emotion', in the word's truest meaning, is that which *moves* our mind, intensifies and awakens it to a higher life and a wider awareness, which finally turn into Enlightenment, a state of pure Light—which at the same time is pure, unhindered, infinite movement and highest tranquillity. Movement is the nature of the mind as much as it is the nature of light. All that tries to arrest, to hinder, or to confine the free, infinite movement of the mind, is ignorance—whether it be caused by conceptual thought, desires, or attachments. Tranquillity is not standstill, it does not consist in stopping the mind, but in not obstructing its movement by artificial concepts (or by breaking its flow by dissecting its movement into momentary phases in the futile attempt to analyse its nature). This does not mean that we should give up thinking or conceptual thought—which would be impossible—but that we should not get caught up in it.

Just as a single note in a melody has no meaning in itself but only in relationship to preceding and following notes—i.e. as a moment in a meaningful or organic movement, which cannot be held on to without destroying the melody—in the same way we cannot stop thinking or hold on to a particular concept without destroying its value. The moment we try to analyse, to conceptualise, or to rationalise the details and experiences of initiation, we are dealing only with dead fragments, but not with the living flow of force, which is expressed in the Tibetan word *'dam-ts'hig'*, the inner relationship between Guru and Chela and the spontaneous movement, emotion, and realisation on which this relationship is based.

There is nothing secret in the process of initiation, but everybody has to experience it for himself. By trying to explain what goes beyond words we only succeed in dragging the sacred down to the level of the profane, thus losing our own *dam-ts'hig* without benefiting others. By glibly talking about the mystery, we destroy the purity and spontaneity of our inner attitude and the deep reverence which is the key to the temple of revelations. Just as the mystery of love can only unfold when it is withdrawn from the eyes of the crowd, and as a lover will not discuss the beloved with outsiders, in the same way the mystery of inner transformation can only take place if the secret force of its symbols is hidden from the profane eyes and the idle talk of the world.

What is communicable are only those experiences that belong to the plane of our mundane consciousness, and beyond this we may be able to speak about the results and conclusions to which our experiences have led us, or about the teachings in which the experiences of former generations and of our Gurus were summarised. I have tried to do this in a previous book of mine, and I will, therefore, confine myself in the present volume as far as possible to my personal impressions and the most memorable events and personalities that had a lasting influence on my inner life.

Among those personalities Tomo Géshé Rimpoché was undoubtedly the greatest. The inner bond which was created on the day on which I received the *abhiśeka,* my first and therefore most important initiation, became a constant source of strength and inspiration. How much the Guru would be able to help me by his presence, even beyond his death, this I guessed as little in those days as I was conscious of the fact that he was one of the most highly revered religious teachers of Tibet and that for millions of people his name was equated with the highest attainments on the Buddha's spiritual path.

My ignorance of his position, however, had the advantage that it enabled me to observe impartially and uninfluenced by others some of the extraordinary faculties of the Guru, which convinced me that he really possessed the yogic powers *(siddhi)* which traditionally were ascribed to the saints of the past. In fact, it all came about quite by chance, when one day my Mongolian friend and I were discussing with the Guru certain aspects of meditation, as we often used to do. Our questions were mostly concerned with problems arising out of practical experience. In the course of this it happened that my friend had some personal questions to ask, and since I could not follow the trend of the discussion, I allowed myself to let my thoughts wander in other directions. In the course of this it came to my mind that the day might not be far when the Guru would have to leave in order to return to his main monastery beyond the border, and that years might pass before I had another opportunity to sit at his feet. And in a sudden impulse I formulated in my mind the following request: 'Please give me a visible sign of the inner bond that unites me with you, my Guru, something that beyond all words reminds me daily of your kindness and of the ultimate aim: be it a small image of the Buddha blessed by your hands or whatever you might think fit . . .' Hardly had I pronounced these words in my mind when the Guru, suddenly interrupting his talk, turned to me and said: 'Before I leave I shall give you a small Buddha-image as remembrance.'

I was thundersrtuck and hardly able to stutter a few words of thanks—partly from joy and partly from being taken aback at the effect of my thought. At the same time I could not help feeling a little ashamed that I had dared to put the Guru to the test in such a direct way; because as little as I would have dared to interrupt the Guru's talk with audible words, would I have dared to do this even in thoughts, if I had really believed that he could hear them as clearly as if I had uttered them aloud.

That the Guru reacted as he did, even while his attention was absorbed by other things, proved to me that he was able to perceive other people's thoughts not only when his mind was directed towards them or as the result of a conscious effort, but that he possessed the faculty which in the Buddhist Scriptures is described as the 'divine ear' or the faculty of clairaudience, which enabled him to hear and to respond to thoughts that were directed to him, as other people would hear spoken words. And, what was more, I had not addressed him in Tibetan but in my own language, which shows that what was audible to the Guru were not the words but their meaning or the impulse that prompted them.

When finally the day of leave-taking came I found myself in a state of great tension. Weeks had passed since that memorable talk, but on no other occasion had the Guru mentioned this subject again, and I naturally had not dared to remind him, knowing full well that he was as conscious of his promise as I myself. Since he knew how much it meant to me, I could only think that perhaps he wanted to test my patience and my faith in him, and that made me all the more determined to remain silent.

But when during the last days of his stay at Yi-Gah Chö-ling all his time was taken up by people who came to receive his blessings before he would leave, I felt afraid that the Guru might be too occupied to remember my request or that other circumstances had prevented him from carrying out his intention.

How great was therefore my surprise and my joy when during our last meeting—even before I could say a word about this matter—he handed me a small but exquisitely finished terracotta statue of Buddha Śākyamuni and told me that he had kept this image in his hands during his daily meditations.

Now I realised the greatness of his gift and the reason for its delay, and while receiving it from his hands, it was only with the greatest effort that I controlled my tears. I bowed down, unable to speak, and then I felt his hands resting on my head with great tenderness; and again a wave of bliss streamed through my whole being and gave me the certainty that I would never be separated from the Guru, though a thousand miles might lie between us.

The little image has since been my constant companion: it has accompanied me over countless snow-clad passes in and beyond the Himalayas, it has roamed with me the deserted highlands of the Chang-Thang and the fertile valleys of South and Central Tibet. It has saved me in difficult situations in Western Tibet, when the Guru's seal, with which it had been consecrated, gave evidence of the fact that I was not a Chinese agent, but a personal pupil of Tomo Géshé Rimpoché; and in 1948, it pacified the armed tribesmen who surrounded our camp with hostile intentions and left with the Guru's blessings, only to come back with gifts and asking that also their women and children and their flocks might be blessed.

But there is something more to this little image, something that is as important to me as the Guru's seal and benediction: namely the fact that it was not created by some unknown artisan, but by the hands of my Guru's humblest and most devoted disciple Kachenla, whose remembrance is for me inseparable from that of Tomo Géshé Rimpoché. During the years that elapsed before the Guru's return to Yi-Gah Chö-Ling, Kachenla remained my faithful friend and Gurubhai (i.e. one who has become a brother by having been initiated by the same Guru), and whenever I came back to Yi-Gah Chö-Ling—either to stay in or near the monastery—it was Kachenla who would receive me and look after me, especially when later on a younger caretaker was appointed for the main temple, while Kachenla took charge of the Guru's private apartments and their shrines. Thus, when according to the Guru's wishes I made use of the privilege to stay in those hallowed rooms, it was again Kachenla who surrounded me with his love and care and made me feel more than ever that the Guru was with us, as in the days of our first meeting.

10

On the Way of the White Clouds

Before settling down at Ghoom—where later on I had taken a solitary little country house, in order to live undisturbed in the vicinity of the monastery—the urge to follow the Guru beyond the snow-covered passes into the forbidden land beyond the horizon was such that soon I found myself on the caravan road across the mountains to have my first glimpse of Tibet.

Though it was late in the season and I knew that I could not proceed far, as otherwise the passes might get blocked by snow and prevent my return within the time that was at my disposal (and within the restrictions of a limited travelling permit), I shall never forget the first impression of the 'promised land'—for that was what Tibet had become to me since the Guru had left.

The journey had a dream-like quality: rain, fog, and clouds transformed the virgin forest, the rocks and mountains, gorges and precipices into a world of uncannily changing, fantastic forms, which appeared and dissolved with such suddenness that one began to doubt their reality as well as one's own. Mighty waterfalls hurled from invisible heights into an equally invisible bottomless depth. Clouds above and clouds below the narrow path, surging up and sinking again, revealing views of breathtaking grandeur for one moment and blotting them out in the next.

Trees appeared like many-armed giants with long grey beards of moss, entangled in creepers and festooned with delicate light green garlands that swung from tree to tree. In the lower altitudes blossoming orchids and ferns sprouted from tree-trunks and branches, while an impenetrable undergrowth hid the ground from view. Clouds, rocks, trees, and waterfalls created a fairyland worthy of the imagination of a romantic Chinese landscape painter, and the small caravan of men and horses moved through it like miniature figures in a vast landscape scroll.

Up and up the caravan went, through one cloud-layer after another. What was yesterday our sky, lay today at our feet like a vast turbulent ocean, at the bottom of which the human world was hidden. It was like a journey through different world-planes into the Far Beyond. The ascent seemed to have no end—indeed, even the sky was no more the limit!—and each stage revealed a new type of landscape, climate, and vegetation.

The exuberant, moist-warm, leech-infested, and fever-laden tropical virgin forest, in which ferns grew to the size of trees and bamboos exploded like green fireworks into gracefully curved bunches of feathery-leaved tall stalks, gave way to the more sober forests of subtropical and temperate zones, where trees regained their individuality and flowers were able to compete with the lighter undergrowth until they formed carpets of bright yellow, orange, and purple colours under the sombre needle-trees of weatherbeaten alpine forests.

Soon even these were left behind, and we entered the near-arctic zone, in which only stunted fir and dwarf rhododendron, besides heather, mosses, and lichen, could survive in a world of titanic rocks, snow-covered peaks, and deep green lakes, among which low-hanging clouds and sudden bursts of sunshine created a constantly changing play of light and shadow. The landscape was in a continual state of transformation, as if it was being created from moment to moment. What was here a minute ago had disappeared in the next, and a new feature of the landscape revealed itself before our eyes.

And then came the great miracle—a miracle that repeated itself and thrilled me each time I crossed over to Tibet: on the highest point of the pass the clouds that in huge masses surged angrily and threateningly dark against the mountain walls, dissolved into thin air as if by magic, the gates of heaven were opened, and a world of luminous colours under a deep blue sky stretched before one's eyes and a fierce sun lit up the snow-covered slopes on the other side of the pass so that one was almost blinded by their brilliance.

After the cloud- and fog-veiled landscapes of Sikkim it almost went beyond one's capacity to take in so much colour and light. Even the deep colours of the shadows seemed to radiate, and the isolated white summer-clouds which blissfully floated in the velvety dark blue sky and between the far-off purple-coloured mountain ranges only enhanced and intensified the feeling of the immensity and depth of space and the luminosity of colours.

It was in this moment, when for the first time I set eyes upon the sacred land of Tibet, that I knew that from now on I would follow the *Way of the White Clouds* into this enchanted land of my Guru, to learn more of its wisdom and to find inspiration in the immense peace and beauty of its nature. I knew that from now on I would ever be drawn back into this luminous world and that my life would be dedicated to its exploration.

Like many a pilgrim before me, I solemnly circumambulated the cairn that marked the highest point of the pass, and, repeating the Guru's *mantra,* I gratefully added a stone to the monument as a token of gratitude for having been safely guided up to here, as a pledge for the future pursuance of the path I had chosen, and as a blessing to all the pilgrims and travellers who would pass this way after me. And then the words of a Chinese stanza, ascribed to Maitreya, the future Buddha, when he roamed the world as a wandering monk, came to my mind: *'Alone I wander a thousand miles . . . and I ask my way from the white clouds.'*

All the way down into the Chumbi Valley I was filled with happiness. Soon the snow gave way to carpets of flowers and the storm-beaten crippled fir trees to magnificent forests of needle-trees with birds and butterflies flitting about in the sunny, clear atmosphere. The air felt so unearthly light and exhilarating that I could hardly contain my joy, though I was conscious that soon I would have to turn back into the sombre shadow-world on the other side of the pass and to descend again into the steamy tropical jungles. But I felt confident that sooner or later I would be able to follow the way of the white clouds beyond my present horizon, on which the white pyramid of the sacred mountain Chomolhari, the throne of the goddess Dorjé Phagmo, seemed to beckon me.

And, indeed, through circumstances of the most unexpected kind —which, when looking back, I can only conceive as the effect of a directing force, both within me as in those who were instrumental in removing all existing difficulties—I soon found myself again on the caravan path into the unknown regions beyond the Himalayas.

This time, however, my aim was the north-western part of Tibet, and in the spring of 1933 I joined for the first part of my journey a caravan in the Yarkand Sarai at Srinagar, travelling through Kashmir, Baltistan, and Little Tibet (Ladak), which latter was formerly part of the kingdom of Gugé. Leaving the caravan at Kargil and my travel-companion, the well-known Indian scholar Rahula Sankrityayana (who at that time was still a Buddhist monk), at Leh, I travelled on alone, accompanied by only two Tibetans, whose horses carried my scanty luggage and food-supplies.

During the previous weeks I had hardened myself to the climatic conditions, sleeping in the open without a tent, protected against snow and rain only by a more or less waterproof *namda* (a large felt rug) which I spread over my camp-cot. Rahula was inclined to regard the latter as a luxury, until when crossing our first pass over the main Himalayan range we got into a thunderstorm, accompanied by rain and sleet, which finally turned into a heavy snowfall during the night. The next morning, when peeping out from under my heavy, snow-covered and solidly frozen *namda,* I could not discover my companion—until he emerged shivering and rather crestfallen from what had appeared to me as a snowdrift.

Fortunately on the whole the weather was dry and sunny, in fact the sun proved to be fiercer than in India, though on account of the cold air one did not realise it until one's skin came off in flakes from face and hands in spite of the use of protective ointments.

However, now I was on my way to the Chang-Thang, the vast northern highlands of Tibet, the country of blue lakes, gold- and copper-coloured hills and wide valleys with green grazing-grounds, where the nomads of the north live with their flocks and their black yak-hair tents. I felt fresh and rested, after having spent some time in the hospitable monasteries of Ladak, and now I looked forward to the uncharted solitudes of the land beyond the snow-covered mountain ranges that stretched between the upper reaches of the Indus and the Karakorum.

A pass of more than 18,000 feet lay ahead of us, and we followed a wide, slowly rising valley. The sun, which for weeks without end had mercilessly beaten down upon the arid country, had been hidden behind dark clouds since the early hours of the morning, and a cold drizzling thin rain lashed with a thousand fine needles against our faces. Everything had suddenly taken on a sinister, threatening aspect, and the valley, leading up into the darkness of clouds and flanked by the rocky teeth of mountains whose peaks were lost in the gloomy vapours, appeared like the open mouth of a gigantic monster.

The two men who accompanied me seemed gripped by the same mood. Nobody spoke a word. Everybody was absorbed in his own thoughts, and even the horses were walking on mechanically in a dream-like state. I felt rather uneasy when thinking of the coming night and the prospect of being caught in a blizzard while crossing the dreaded pass, one of the highest on our present journey.

11

The Rock Monastery

Late in the afternoon we reached the entrance of a gorge from which the final ascent of the pass was to start. At the foot of a group of ragged rocks, piled one upon the other on the flank of a steep mountain, there appeared to be a few stone hovels, whose cubic forms were hardly distinguishable from the tumbled rocks. A strange contrast, however, was provided by innumerable whitewashed *chorten,* religious monuments which have their origin in the ancient *stūpas* of India, consisting of a cubic base, a hemispherical or vase-shaped middle piece, and a long conical spire of brick-red disks, crowned with the symbols of sun and moon.

Millions of such monuments are scattered all over Tibet. They are found wherever human beings live or have lived, and even on dangerous passes, at the entrances of precariously constructed suspension bridges, or on strange rock formations near the caravan routes. The great number of *chortens* which appeared here, as if the rocks had been transformed into these shapes by magic, indicated the vicinity of a temple or a monastery. As I had heard of a very ancient rock monastery, situated in one of the gorges of these mountains, I followed the narrow path leading through the *chortens,* and soon I found myself in a maze of huge boulders and towering rock-walls.

The path became steeper, and finally the horses refused to go on and had to be left behind. But now masonry appeared, and out of the rocks there developed a group of high cubic buildings with balconies protruding here and there from their sloping walls. It was difficult to say where the rocks ended and the architecture began, since they were fitted into each other as if the one had grown out of the other.

Hoping to find some shelter for the night, I climbed on through a labyrinth of rocks and buildings, but the farther I proceeded the more I lost hope. No living being was to be seen anywhere, not even one of those dreadful watchdogs which generally rush at any stranger who approaches a Tibetan dwelling, be it a house, a monastery, or a nomad's tent. I did not dare to enter any of these apparently uninhabited buildings.

Near each entrance I observed a small stone pyramid, and each of them was crowned with a flat, plate-like stone slab, upon which a small round stone had been placed. I was just about to ask the one of my two men, who had accompanied me, while the other had remained behind with the horses, whether these structures were a kind of miniature *chorten,* when he picked up one of the small round stones and let it fall upon the slab, from which he had taken it. The slab emitted a clear, glassy sound. So this was the house-bell! I could not help admiring the ingenuity of these simple people.

We sounded several of these resonant slabs, but no response came. So we climbed on until we reached a little courtyard, which on one side was bordered by a veranda-like covered passage. The other side consisted of a temple façade, built into the rock, which projected like a roof over it, while the side opposite the entrance was formed by a two-storeyed building (with open verandas) behind which strangely eroded rock formations rose into the sky. In the middle of the courtyard stood a tall white prayer-flag. It was the courtyard of a monastery. But even here not a living soul!

Nevertheless I felt that finally we were somewhere where one could spend a peaceful night and find shelter from rain and cold. Suddenly I heard the barking of a dog behind me, and instinctively I looked for an exit. But there was nothing of the kind. We were nicely trapped!

Fortunately the dog was not one of those ferocious creatures as I had feared, and I felt even more reassured when it was followed by an old friendly looking Lama, who welcomed me with great politeness. I told him that I was a pilgrim from a far-off country, and, seeing my monastic robes, he opened without hesitation the heavy door at the base of the rock temple and beckoned me to follow him.

He led me through a steep, dark staircase into a big cave. The smooth walls were covered with apparently very ancient frescoes. In the mellow light of an altar-lamp I could see the statue of the great Buddhist Apostle Padmasambhava, the founder of the Old Sect (Nying-ma-pa), to which this monastery belonged. The image was flanked by two statues of Bodhisattvas and Padmasambhava's two chief disciples, the Indian princess Mandāravā and the Tibetan incarnate *Khadoma* (fairy) Yeshé Tshogyal (who are persistently and wrongly represented as Padmasambhava's two wives!).

After having finished my *pūjā,* the ritual of devotion, I was conducted into a second Lhakhang in the upper storey of the adjoining building. Judging from the frescoes, this temple seemed to have been renovated not long ago. The central place of the shrine was occupied by the historical Buddha Śākyamuni, attended by his two chief disciples Maudgalyāyana and Śāriputra, and flanked by the Buddhas of the past and the future.

Returning to the courtyard, we found several other Lamas waiting there, and after answering the usual questions I was conducted into a spacious, rather rough but clean-looking room which, as I was told, had never been inhabited yet. A steep open staircase led up to it and a window opened towards the valley. The wall opposite the window was partly formed by a natural rock protruding into the room and giving it a rustic atmosphere. It reminded me of the close co-operation of man and nature, through which this strange Gompa had come into existence.

While I was still talking to the Lamas, my man carried my luggage into the room, and when I started unfolding my camp-cot and screwing together my primus stove the Lamas settled down around me in a semicircle to enjoy this rare spectacle. Even the open door was filled with spectators, who tried to peep in from outside, since there was no more space in the room. The unfolding of the camp-bed had already been followed with exclamations of surprise and various explanatory comments.

However, when I started to fill the circular contrivance of the primus stove with a mysterious water-like liquid the tension of the onlookers reached its climax. An awe-inspired silence fell upon the spectators and, conscious of the dramatic character of the moment, I struck a match and lit the spirit. The spectators clicked their tongues with surprise when the ghostly flame shot up from what seemed to them plain water.

They shook their heads, as if doubting the reality of what they saw. Certainly this foreign Lama was a master magician! In order to convince them of the reality of the fire I asked those who were next to the stove to hold their hands over the flame, and it caused great hilarity when each of them quickly withdrew his hand and testified that the fire was real.

However, the miracle had not yet reached its end. When the flame suddenly receded after the liquid had been consumed, and in its place there appeared around the silencer rows of blue-green fire-beads with a light hissing sound, there was no limit to their wonderment.

If I had flown away through the air with crossed legs this would have been an adequate end to the performance and would not have surprised the people around me at all. But when they saw me nonchalantly putting an ordinary cooking-pot upon the magic flame their tension collapsed like a pricked balloon and gave place to a laugh of understanding. We had reached the human plane again.

During the preparation of my food, as well as during my meal, all eyes rested upon me, and all ingredients were closely scrutinised and discussed. When they saw me eat with chopsticks (as was and still is my habit) they concluded that I must be a Chinese monk. But even when my meal was over they made no move to leave me. So I finally stretched out on my camp-bed, turned towards the wall, and feigned sleep.

Opening my eyes a few minutes later, I found myself alone.

12

The Chela's Vision

THE SUN HAD NOT YET SET, so that it was too early to go to bed, and actually I did not feel sleepy. It was agreeable to stretch one's legs after a long day's ride, and so I remained at rest. As my eyes fell on the freshly plastered wall opposite me, I observed the irregular surface, and it seemed to me as if it had a strange life of its own.

At the same time I became conscious that this room, in spite of its emptiness, had something that appealed to me in an extraordinary way, though I was unable to discover any reason for it. The gloomy weather and the poor prospects for the following day were in no way conducive to an elated state of mind. But since I had entered this room my depression had vanished and had given place to a feeling of great inner peace and serenity.

Was it the general atmosphere of this ancient sanctuary, which from the cave of a pious hermit had grown in the course of centuries into a monastery in which uncounted generations of monks had lived a life of devotion and contemplation? Or was it owing to the special atmosphere of this room that the change had taken place in me? I did not know.

I only felt that there was something about the surface of this wall that held my attention, as if it were a fascinating landscape. But no, it was far from suggesting a landscape. These apparently accidental forms were related to each other in some mysterious way; they grew more and more plastic and coherent. Their outlines became clearly defined and raised from the flat background. It was like a process of crystallisation, or like an organic growth; and the transformation which took place on the surface of the wall was as natural and convincing as if I had watched an invisible sculptor in the creation of a life-size relief. The only difference was that the invisible sculptor worked from *within* his material and in all places at the same time.

Before I knew how it all happened, a majestic human figure took shape before my eyes. It was seated upon a throne, with both feet on the ground, the head crowned with a diadem, the hands raised in a gesture, as if explaining the points of an intricate problem: it was the figure of Buddha Maitreya, the Coming One, who already now is on his way to Buddhahood, and who, like the sun before it rises over the horizon, sends his rays of love into this world of darkness, through which he has been wandering in innumerable forms, through innumerable births and deaths.

I felt a wave of joy passing through me, as I had felt in the presence of my Guru, who had initiated me into the mystic circle *(maṇḍala)* of Maitreya and had caused his images to be erected all over Tibet.

I closed my eyes and opened them again: the figure in the wall had not changed. There it stood like a graven image, and yet full of life!

I looked around me to assure myself that I was not dreaming, but everything was as before: there was the projecting rock in the wall to the right, my cooking utensils on the ground, my luggage in the corner.

Again my glance fell upon the opposite wall. The figure was there—or was I mistaken? What I saw was no more the figure of a compassionately preaching Buddha but rather that of a terrifying demon. His body was thick-set and bulky, his feet wide apart, as if ready to jump: his raised, flame-like hair was adorned with human skulls, his right arm stretched out in a threatening gesture, wielding a diamond sceptre *(vajra)* in his hand, while the other hand held a ritual bell before his chest.

If all this had not appeared before me like a skilfully modelled relief, as if created by the hand of a great artist, my blood would have frozen with terror. But as it was I rather felt the strange beauty in the powerful expression of this terrifying form of Vajrapāni, the defender of truth against the powers of darkness and ignorance, the Master of Unfathomed Mysteries.

While I was still under the spell of this awe-inspiring figure, the diamond sceptre transformed itself into a flaming sword, and in place of the bell the long stem of a lotus-flower grew out of the left hand. It grew up to the height of the left shoulder, unfolded its leaves and petals, and upon them appeared the book of wisdom. The body of the figure had in the meantime become that of a well-formed youth, sitting cross-legged on a lotus-throne. His face took on a benign expression, lit up with the youthful vigour and charm of an Enlightened One. Instead of the flaming hair and the human skulls, his head was adorned with the Bodhisattva-crown of the Five Wisdoms. It was the figure of Mañjuśrī, the embodiment of active wisdom, who cuts through the knots of doubt with the flaming sword of knowledge.

After some time a new change took place, and a female figure formed itself before my eyes. She had the same youthful grace as Mañjuśrī, and even the lotus, which grew from her left hand, seemed to be the same. But instead of wielding the flaming sword her opened right hand was resting on the knee of her right leg, which was extended, as if she were about to descend from her lotus-throne in answer to some prayer of supplication. The wish-granting gesture, the loving expression of her face, which seemed to be inclined towards some invisible suppliant, were the liveliest embodiment of Buddha Śākyamuni's words:

'Like a mother, who protects her child, her only child, with her own life, thus one should cultivate a heart of unlimited love and compassion towards all living beings.'

I felt deeply moved, and trying to concentrate my whole attention upon the lovely expression of her divine face, it seemed to me as if an almost imperceptible, sorrowful smile was hovering about her mouth, as though she wanted to say: 'Indeed, my love is unlimited; but the number of suffering beings is unlimited too. How can I, who have only one head and two eyes, soothe the unspeakable sufferings of numberless beings?'

Were these not the words of Avalokiteśvara which reverberated in my mind? Indeed, I recognised in Tārā's face the features of the Great Compassionate One, out of whose tears Tārā is said to have sprung.

And, as if overpowered by grief, the head burst and grew into a thousand heads, and the arms split into a thousand arms, whose helping hands were stretched out in all directions of the universe like the rays of the sun. And now everything was dissolving into light, for in each of those innumerable hands there was a radiating eye, as loving and compassionate as that in the face of Avalokiteśvara; and as I closed my eyes, bewildered and blinded by so much radiance, it struck me that I had met this face before: and now I knew—it was that of the Coming One, the Buddha Maitreya!

When I looked up again everything .had disappeared; but the wall was lit up by a warm light, and when I turned round I saw that the last rays of the evening sun had broken through the clouds. I jumped up with joy and looked out of the window. All the gloom and darkness had disappeared. The landscape was bathed in the soft colours of the parting day. Above the green pastures of the valley there rose the brown- and ochre-coloured slopes of rocky mountains, and behind them appeared sunlit snow-fields against the remnants of dark purple clouds, now and then lit up by lightning. A distant rumbling from beyond the mountains showed that Vajrapāni was still wielding his diamond sceptre in the struggle with the powers of darkness.

Deep below me in the valley I saw my horses grazing, small as toys, and not far from them rose the smoke of a camp-fire, where the men were preparing their evening meal. From the cave temple came the deep, vibrating sound of a big bass-drum. It came like a voice out of the bowels of the earth, like a call from the depths to the light above: the light that conquers all darkness and fear of the eternal abyss.

And out of the gladness of my heart words formed themselves spontaneously like a prayer and a pledge:

'Who art Thou, Mighty One,
Thou, who art knocking
at the portals of my heart?
Art Thou a ray of wisdom and of love,
emerging from the dazzling aura
of a silent Muni,
illuminating those
whose minds are ready
to receive the noble message
of deliverance?

Art Thou the Coming One,
the Saviour of all beings,
who wanders through the world
in thousand unknown forms?

Art Thou the messenger
of one who reached the shore
and left the raft for us
to cross the raging stream?

Whoever Thou may be,
Mighty Enlightened One:
wide open are the petals
of my heart,
prepared the lotus-throne
for Thy reception.

Do I not meet Thee
ever where I go?—
I find Thee dwelling
in my brothers' eyes;
I hear Thee speaking

in the Guru's voice;
I feel Thee
in the mother's loving care.

Was it not Thou,
who turned the stone to life,
who made Thy Form
appear before my eyes,
whose presence sanctified
the rite of initiation,
who shone into my dreams
and filled my life with light?

Thou Sun of Thousand Helping Arms,
All-comprehending and compassionate,
O Thousand-Eyed One, Thou,
whose all-perceiving glance,
while penetrating all,
hurts none, nor judges, nor condemns,
but warms and helps to ripen,
like fertile summer rain.

Thou Light!
Whose rays transform and sanctify
compassionately
our weakness even;
Turning death's poison thus
into the wine of life—

Wherever in the sea
of hate and gloom
A ray of wisdom
and compassion shines:
There I know Thee,
O Mighty One!
Whose radiant light

leads us to harmony,
Whose peaceful power
overcomes all worldly strife.

O Loving One!
Take this my earthly life
and let me be reborn
in Thee!'

13

An Awakening and a Glimpse into the Future

The next morning I was awakened by brilliant sunshine. My things had been packed in the evening, so that we could start without delay. Everything around me seemed to be transformed by the morning sun.

I would have liked to take leave of the friendly Lamas and to thank them for their hospitality. But no living soul was to be seen or heard anywhere. I decided to wait a little, and in order to pass the time I made a sketch of the courtyard. But even after I had finished no sign of life emerged. It was as if the monastery was under a magic spell, due to which time had stopped a thousand years ago and life had gone to sleep, while nature around went on in its own way and rocks were growing into strange shapes, assuming an unusual vitality, ever encroaching on the works of man.

Was it perhaps one of those haunted places, where a long-buried past comes to life again and again, and where the lonely traveller sees and hears all sorts of strange things, which after some time disappear like a *fata morgana*? 'Well,' I thought to myself, 'the monastery at any rate is still here, and if it should disappear, I have at least my sketch!'

Slowly I descended through the narrow lanes between rocks and walls, lost in thought about all that had happened during my short stay here. My syce, who had come for the luggage, saw my pensive mood and said: 'Was Kushog Rimpoché not satisfied with this place?'

'Indeed,' I said, 'I never liked any place better than this.'

'No wonder,' he replied, 'if one sleeps in a consecrated room.'

'What do you mean?' I enquired with surprise.

'Don't you remember, Kushog-la, that the old Lama, who led you into the room, mentioned that never had anybody dwelt in it before?'

'Yes. I remember.'

'Then I will tell you the reason. While you were in the cave temple the monks consulted each other whether they should give you that room for the night, because it had been dedicated to Chamba, the Buddha Maitreya.'

Suddenly a strange idea struck me.

What gave them the idea to build a Lhakhang to Buddha Maitreya?' I asked.

'Oh,' said my man, 'don't you know that all over Tibet sanctuaries are being built to Chamba, the Great Coming One, through the power of a great Lama from the southern part of Tibet?'

'Do you know his name?' I asked, almost quivering with excitement.

'I don't know his name, but I was told that people call him Tomo Géshé.'

'He is my own Guru!' I exclaimed. 'Did I not tell you?' I then remembered that he had asked me about my 'Tsawai-Lama' and that, very casually, I had replied: 'My Guru's place is more than a thousand miles away, you wouldn't know him anyway.'

Now my experience of the previous evening took on a new significance, and suddenly it dawned upon me: *This was my second initiation!*

Whether it was due to the Guru's direct influence (as in the events of Chorten Nyima and other, similar cases, of which I came to know later on), or due to the ripening of the seeds which he had sown into my mind, one thing was sure, namely that it was no mere coincidence.

For the first time I now realised what the Guru had meant when he spoke to me of the '*kerim*', the creative state of meditation. 'One day you will be able to see the transcendental bodies [Tibetan: *long-ku;* Sanskrit: *sambhoga-kāya]* of Buddhas and Bodhisattvas, which are the powers of light within you, but which now only exist as faint ideas in your mind. When they have become to you as real as what you now believe to be the material world around you, then you will understand that the reality of the inner and the outer world are interchangeable, and that it depends on *you* in which of the two you want to live: whether you want to be a slave of the one or the inheritor and master of the other.'

More than ever I felt the nearness of the Guru, and I was so elated that I did not even feel the exertion while climbing that formidable pass, which I had dreaded so much the previous day. My thoughts went on in a steady flow, as if an inner voice was speaking to me and revealing bit by bit the solutions of many problems which had troubled my mind for a long time.

I now realised what I had dimly felt during my first stay at Yi-Gah Chö-Ling, namely that the images and frescoes around me were not merely beautiful decorations of aesthetic value but representations of a higher reality, born from visions and inner experience. They were put into as precise a language of forms as is contained in a geographical map or a scientific formula, while being as natural in expression and as direct in appeal as a flower or a sunset.

Was it not this language of forms which opened the gates to the mystery of the human soul and its hidden forces, a language that would be understood by all who were honestly knocking at this innermost gate, if only a little guidance was given?

Since my Guru had opened my eyes to this mystery, was it not my duty to pass on to others what I had received?

Indeed, I now saw clearly the message which he had communicated to me through this vision; and out of the wish to convey to others what I had seen and experienced the idea was born in me to follow the way of the Lama-artists of yore and faithfully to reproduce in line and colour the traditions of a great past, which had been treasured in the temples and mountain fastnesses of Tibet.

It was from this very journey that I brought back my first simple tracings of the stone engravings of the 'Eighty-Four Siddhas', or medieval Buddhist Mystics, which later on were housed in a special hall, dedicated to my work in the Municipal Museum of Allahabad.

And as if some invisible hand had guided me and had made come to pass everything necessary for the fulfilment of this desire, on my way I hit upon one of the ancient temples, founded by Lotsava Rinchen Zangpo, in which for the first time I saw some of the magnificent frescoes and statues of the early eleventh century A.D.

I was so deeply impressed by this unique art that I lost no time in collecting whatever information I could get concerning the history of Western Tibet. Thus I learned that Rinchen Zangpo was one of the greatest torch-bearers of Buddhism in Tibet, equally great as scholar, builder, artist, and saint. A substantial part of the sacred scriptures of Tibet (*Kanjur* and *Tanjur*) was translated by him from Sanskrit in collaboration with Indian scholars, a work which earned him the highly prized title *Lotsava* (the Translator). While spreading the Buddha's teachings in word and script, he built monasteries, temples, and shrines wherever he went. His main activities were in and around Tholing and Tsaparang (see the Historical Appendix). Tholing was the most important monastery and seat of learning in Western Tibet and remained so until the recent Chinese invasion, while Tsaparang was abandoned centuries ago.

The last-mentioned fact aroused my interest, because in a climate like that of Tibet I had good reason to believe that a considerable part of the earliest works of art could still be found among the ruins, and that the very remoteness and solitude of the place would make it possible to investigate and explore undisturbed whatever had survived the ravages of man and time. All the information that I could gather convinced me that this was the very place where I could study in peace, and retrieve some of the glories of the past. Thus the idea of an expedition to Tsaparang was born, though many years had still to pass before my dream could become reality.

PART TWO

Pilgrim Life

I

The Nature of the Highlands

WE HAD CROSSED THE FEARED 18,000-foot pass in perfect ease and under a cloudless sky. The sun was so hot during the ascent that I had discarded my warm things, but hardly had we entered the shadows on the other side of the pass when we were plunged into icy cold, that made me regret not having kept my warm clothing at hand. Tibet is a country where one is ever up against the unexpected and where all accepted rules of nature seem to be changed. The contrast between sunshine and shade is such that if for any length of time one part of one's body would be exposed to the sun, while the other remained in the shade, one could develop simultaneously blisters, due to severe sunburn, and chilblains due to the icy air in the shade. The air is too rarefied to absorb the sun's heat and thus to create a medium shadow temperature, nor is it able to protect one from the fierceness of the sun and its ultra-violet rays.

The difference in temperature between sun and shade can be as much as 100° Fahrenheit, according to some observers, and I can well believe it, for when riding I often found my feet getting numb with cold, while the backs of my hands, which were exposed to the sun while holding the reins, got blistered as if I had poured boiling water over them, and the skin of my face came off in flakes, before I got sufficiently acclimatised. In spite of applying various ointments, my lips cracked open, so that eating and drinking became difficult and painful, but fortunately after three or four weeks my skin grew sufficiently sun-resistant to make me immune against these troubles for the rest of my journey. Even Tibetans, except those who live permanently in the open air, like herdsmen, farmers, or muleteers, often wear face-masks when travelling to protect themselves from the fierce sun and the still fiercer winds, which at certain seasons sweep over the highlands, carrying with them clouds of fine stinging sand that penetrate even the heaviest clothing. To meet a caravan or a group of masked and armed men somewhere in the wilderness, far away from the haunts of men, was a rather frightening experience, as one never could be sure whether the masks were worn merely for protection against the inclemencies of the climate or for hiding the faces of robbers who, especially in times of unrest, infested the more remote regions of Tibet.

However, I was not unduly worried about these things at that time (though I knew that fighting was going on in neighbouring Chinese Turkestan), because after leaving the last check-post on the Ladakh side at Tankse I branched off from the caravan route into the no-man's-land which stretched from the region of the great lakes, Pangong and Nyak-Tso, towards the Aksai-Chin plateau. In those days there were no frontiers between Ladakh and Tibet in this region. It was one of the few spots in the world where man and nature had been left to themselves without interference of man-made 'authorities' and governments. Here the inner law of man and the physical law of nature were the only authorities, and I felt thrilled at the thought of being for once entirely on my own, alone in the immensity of nature, facing the earth and the universe as they were before the creation of man, accompanied only by my two faithful Ladakhis and their horses. The horses more or less determined the choice of our camping-places, as we could stop only where there was sufficient grazing ground for them as well as water.

In spite of the feeling of smallness in the vastness and grandeur of the mountain landscape, in spite of the knowledge of human limitations and dependence on the whims of wind and weather, water and grazing-grounds, food and fuel and other material circumstances, I had never felt a sense of greater freedom and independence. I realised more than ever how narrow and circumscribed our so-called civilised life is, how much we pay for the security of a sheltered life by way of freedom and real independence of thought and action.

When every detail of our life is planned and regulated, and every fraction of time determined beforehand, then the last trace of our boundless and timeless being, in which the freedom of our soul exists, will be suffocated. This freedom does not consist in being able 'to do what we want', it is neither arbitrariness nor waywardness, nor the thirst for adventures, but the capacity to accept the unexpected, the unthought-of situations of life, good as well as bad, with an open mind; it is the capacity to adapt oneself to the infinite variety of conditions without losing confidence in the deeper connections between the inner and the outer world. It is the spontaneous certainty of being neither bound by space nor by time, the ability to experience the fulness of both without clinging to any of their aspects, without trying to take possession of them by way of arbitrary fragmentation.

The machine-made time of modern man has not made him the master but the slave of time; the more he tries to 'save' time, the less he possesses it. It is like trying to catch a river in a bucket. It is the flow, the continuity of its movement, that makes the river; and it is the same with time. Only he who accepts it in its fulness, in its eternal and life-giving rhythm, in which its continuity consists, can master it and make it his own. By accepting time in this way, by not-resisting its flow, it loses its power over us and we are carried by it like on the crest of a wave, without being submerged and without losing sight of our essential timelessness.

Nowhere have I experienced this deeper than under the open skies of Tibet, in the vastness of its solitudes, the clarity of its atmosphere, the luminosity of its colours and the plastic, almost abstract, purity of its mountain forms. Organic life is reduced to a minimum and does not play any role in the formation and appearance of the landscape or interfere with its plastic purity, but the landscape itself appears like the organic expression of primeval forces. Bare mountains expose in far-swinging lines the fundamental laws of gravitation, modified only by the continuous action of wind and weather, revealing their geological structure and the nature of their material, which shines forth in pure and vivid colours.

The roles of heaven and earth are reversed. While normally the sky appears lighter than the landscape, the sky here is dark and deep, while the landscape stands out against it in radiating colours, as if it were the source of light. Red and yellow rocks rise like flames against the dark blue velvet curtain of the sky.

But at night the curtain is drawn back and allows a view into the depth of the universe. The stars are seen as bright and near as if they were part of the landscape. One can see them come right down to the horizon and suddenly vanish with a flicker, as if a man with a lantern had disappeared round the next corner. The universe here is no more a mere concept or a pale abstraction but a matter of direct experience; and nobody thinks of time other than in terms of sun, moon, and stars. The celestial bodies govern the rhythm of life, and thus even time loses its negative aspect and becomes the almost tangible experience of the ever-present, ever-recurring, self-renewing *movement* that is the essence of all existence. As the sky is hardly ever hidden by clouds, man never loses contact with the celestial bodies. The nights are never completely dark. Even when there is no moon a strange diffused light pervades the landscape, a truly 'astral' light, that reveals the bare outlines of forms without shadows or substance and without colour, yet clearly discernible.

Even the waters of rivers and brooks rise and fall in accordance with this celestial rhythm, because during the twelve hours of daytime the snow on the mountains melts due to the intensity of the sun's rays (in spite of the low temperature of the air), while at night it freezes again, so that the supply of water is stopped. But as it takes the water twelve hours on the average to come down from the mountains, the high tide of the rivers begins in the evening and ebbs off in the morning. Often the smaller water-courses dry out completely during the daytime and appear only at night, so that one who unknowingly pitches his tent in the dry bed of such rivulet may suddenly be washed away at night by the rushing waters. (It happened to me, but fortunately I managed to save myself and my equipment.)

The great rhythm of nature pervades everything, and man is woven into it with mind and body. Even his imagination does not belong so much to the realm of the individual as to the soul of the landscape, in which the rhythm of the universe is condensed into a melody of irresistible charm. Imagination here becomes an adequate expression of reality on the plane of human consciousness, and this consciousness seems to communicate itself from individual to individual till it forms a spiritual atmosphere that envelops the whole of Tibet.

Thus a strange transformation takes place under the influence of this country, in which the valleys are as high as the highest peaks of Europe and where mountains soar into space beyond the reach of humans. It is as if a weight were lifted from one's mind, or as if certain hindrances were removed. Thoughts flow easily and spontaneously without losing their direction and coherence, a high degree of concentration and clarity is attained almost without effort and a feeling of elevated joy keeps one's mind in a creative mood. Consciousness seems to be raised to a higher level, where the obstacles and disturbances of our ordinary life do not exist, except as a faint memory of things which have lost all their importance and attraction. At the same time one becomes more sensitive and open to new forms of reality; the intuitive qualities of our mind are awakened and stimulated—in short, there are all the conditions for attaining the higher stages of meditation or *dhyāna*.

2

The Living Language of Colours

THE TRANSFORMATION OF CONSCIOUSNESS which I observed here (and each time I returned to Tibet) was in a certain way similar to that which I experienced during my first stay at Yi-Gah Chö-Ling, though on a bigger scale, because here the connections with the world I had been familiar with were completely severed, and the physical effects of high altitude, climate, and living conditions greatly contributed to this psychological change. The spiritual importance of this change is not lessened by explaining it on the basis of physical reactions. Yoga itself is based on the interaction of physical, spiritual, and psychic phenomena, in so far as the effects of breath-control *(prāṇāyāma)* and bodily postures *(āsana)* are combined with mental concentration, creative imagination, spiritual awareness, and emotional equanimity.

The rarefied air of high altitudes has similar effects as certain exercises of *prāṇāyāma,* because it compels us to regulate our breathing in a particular way, especially when climbing or walking long distances. One has to inhale twice or thrice the quantity of air which one would need at sea-level, and consequently the heart has to perform a much heavier task. On the other hand the weight of one's body is substantially reduced, so that one's muscles seem to lift one almost without effort. But precisely this is a source of danger, because one is not immediately conscious that lungs and heart are at a great disadvantage, and only the fact that one is very soon out of breath, and that the heart begins to race in a frightening manner, reminds one that it is necessary to control one's movements carefully. Tibetans themselves walk very slowly, but at a steady pace, bringing their breath in perfect harmony with their movement. Walking, therefore, becomes almost a kind of conscious *hatha-yoga* or breaching exercise, especially when accompanied by rhythmic recitations of sacred formulas *(mantras),* as is the habit with many Tibetans. This has a very tranquillising and energising effect, as I found from my own experience.

At the same time I realised the tremendous influence of colour upon the human mind. Quite apart from the aesthetic pleasure and beauty it conveyed—which I tried to capture in paintings and sketches—there was something deeper and subtler that contributed to the transformation of consciousness more perhaps than any other single factor. It is for this reason that Tibetan, and in fact all Tantric, meditation gives such great importance to colours.

Colours are the living language of light, the hallmark of conscious reality. The metaphysical significance of colours as exponents and symbols of reality is emphasised in the Bardo Thödol *(The Tibetan Book of the Dead,* as it is commonly known), where transcendental reality is indicated by the experience of various forms of light, represented by brilliant, pure colours, and it is interesting that a serious modern thinker like Aldous Huxley has come to the conclusion that colour is the very 'touchstone of reality'.

According to him, our conceptual abstractions, our intellectually fabricated symbols and images, are colourless, while the given data of reality, either in the form of sense-impressions from the outer world or in the form of archetypal symbols of direct inner experience, are coloured. In fact, the latter 'are far more intensely coloured than the external data. This may be explained, at least in part, by the fact that our perceptions of the external world are habitually clouded by the verbal notions in terms of which we do our thinking. We are for ever attempting to convert things into signs for the most intelligible abstractions of our own invention. But in doing so we rob these things of a great deal of their native thinghood. At the antipodes of the mind we are more or less completely free of language, outside the system of conceptual thought. Consequently our perception of visionary objects possesses all the freshness, all the naked intensity, of experiences which have never been verbalised, never assimilated to lifeless abstraction. Their colour (the hallmark of givenness) shines forth with a brilliance which seems to us preternatural, because it is in fact entirely natural in the sense of being entirely unsophisticated by language or the scientific, philosophical, and utilitarian notions, by means of which we ordinarily re-create the given world in our own dreary human image.'

The Tibetan landscape has 'all the naked intensity' of colour and form which one associates with a preternatural vision or prophetic dream, which distinguishes itself from ordinary dreams by its super-real clarity and vividness of colours. It was precisely in a dream of this kind that for the first time I saw colours of such luminosity and transparence in the form of mountainous islands that rose from a deep blue sea. I was filled with incredible happiness and thought to myself: these must be the paradisical islands of the southern sea, of which I have heard so much. But when later I actually saw some of these lovely palm-fringed islands of the south I found none of those colours I had seen in my dream.

But when I came to Tibet I recognised those colours, and the same happiness came over me as in that unforgettable dream. But why should I have seen those mountains rising out of the deep blue sea? This puzzled me for a long time, until one day we were travelling through a hot, narrow gorge, hemmed in by light yellow rocks which not only intensified the glare of the midday sun but captured its heat to such an extent that one could have imagined travelling somewhere in the tropics or through a gorge in the Sahara, instead of at an altitude of more than 14,000 feet. It was so warm that during a halt by the side of a placidly flowing stream I could not resist the temptation to take off my clothes and enjoy the luxury of a bath and a swim—much to the astonishment of my Ladakhi companions! I felt greatly refreshed, but the effect did not last long, as the gorge became hotter and hotter the farther we proceeded, and even the water of the stream became steadily less until it disappeared in a shallow lemon-yellow lake. After that the gorge became narrower and completely dry—and with it our spirits. We just trudged wearily along, and I was wondering how long we would have to continue in this fashion when suddenly a strange phenomenon stopped me in my tracks. At the far end of the gorge the rock-walls receded, and a radiantly blue object flashed into sight. It was as luminous and as sharply set off from the background as the surface of a cut jewel from its gold setting, and it emanated an intensely blue light, as if it were illuminated from within. It was so utterly unexpected and different from anything I had seen that I simply gasped, unable to find any reasonable explanation or connection with what I saw. I felt so baffled and excited that I called out to my companions, fearing to be the victim of a hallucination: 'Look there! What is that? Look!'

'Tso! Tso! Pangong-Tso!' they shouted, and threw their caps into the air triumphantly, as if they had conquered a mighty pass; and indeed there was a *lha-tse,* a pyramid of scones, left by previous travellers to mark this auspicious spot, from which the first glimpse of the great Pangong Lake could be had. We too added our stones, grateful to be released from the oppressiveness of the gorge. But I still could not believe my eyes. 'Impossible,' I thought. 'This cannot be water. It looks like some unearthly, self-luminous substance!'

But soon we were out of the gorge and its deadening heat, and before us stretched a lake like a sheet of molten lapis lazuli, merging into intense ultramarine in the distance and into radiant cobalt blue and opalescent veronese green towards the nearer shore, fringed with gleaming white beaches, while the mountains that framed this incredible colour display were of golden ochre, Indian red and burnt sienna, with purple shadows. Yes, this was the luminous landscape of my dream, rising out of the blue waters in brilliant sunshine under a deep, cloudless sky!

The mountains to the left had sharp-cut, almost stereometrical forms; those on the opposite side formed a range of softly modelled giants, crowned by eternal snows and mighty glaciers, known as the Pangong Range, running parallel to the fjord-like Pangong and Nyak-Tso Lakes, which form an almost consecutive sheet of water of more than 100 miles length. The two lakes are actually a submerged valley, divided merely by what probably was an ancient rock-fall.

When reaching our next camping-ground at the foot of the snow-range, a little above the lake, I felt so inspired by the colours of the lake and the mountains and the immense rhythm that pervaded this landscape that I forgot hunger and tiredness and immediately returned to the place from where I had the first overwhelming impression of the lake and the glaciers above it. So I walked back a few miles with my drawing-board, papers, and a box of pastels, munching some dry *kulchas*[1] on the way, until I found the spot that I had marked in my mind while passing it, but where I had not dared to delay, as I did not know how far the next camping-place might be. I worked fast and with such enthusiasm that I finished two or three sketches in a short time, keeping in mind that I should be back in camp before sunset. But my excursion almost ended in disaster. Retracing my steps towards the camp, I suddenly found myself confronted by a raging stream that had not been there before! In my eagerness to get to my sketching place I had not noticed that I had crossed several shallow beds of dried-out water-courses. Now the melted waters from the glaciers came rushing down and threatened to cut off my retreat. Knowing that every minute was precious, I splashed through the icy waters, and after thus crossing two or three water-courses in succession I finally reached the camp somewhat out of breath, but happy to have succeeded in capturing something of the unforgettable beauty and freshness of my first impressions of this memorable lake.

---

1. *Kulchas* are a kind of hard, sweetened buns, made of unleavened flour, milk, and sugar, baked in an oven. They can be kept almost indefinitely, being perfectly dry, and therefore useful as an emergency ration. I got a sackful of them prepared in Leh and found them most useful.

3

Dreams and Reminiscences in the Land of the Blue Lake

THE FOLLOWING DAYS we travelled along the shore of the lake at the foot of the snow mountains, whose far-flung slopes gradually flattened out and formed an almost even stretch of land above the lake, interrupted only by dry beds of mountain streams. Very few streams had a continuous flow of water, so that grazing-grounds were few and far between and paradoxically we suffered from lack of water during the greater part of the day, in spite of having miles and miles of water at our feet. But first of all the shore was not always in our reach, as the ground over which we travelled was slightly raised and suddenly broke off into the lake, except for such places where the water-courses from the glaciers had carved out shallow beds, along which one could approach the pebbled or sandy beaches—and secondly, even if one reached the shore, there came a greater surprise: the water was undrinkable because of its high content of magnesium!

This too was the reason for the incredible clarity and colour of the water. The magnesium, though colourless in itself, kept the water absolutely free from organic matter or any form of life, whether plant or fish or crustaceans, and consequently the water was so transparent that on windless days, when the surface of the lake was as smooth as a mirror, it was impossible to see where the water ended and the beach began. I still remember the shock when for the first time I approached the edge of the water, and I suddenly felt its icy touch, because I had not noticed that the pebbles, which looked no different from those on the dry beach, were already under the water. The water was as invisible as the air! Only when it got deeper, the ground assumed a greenish-blue tinge and finally disappeared in the luminous blue that made this lake such a wonder.

The colours of the lake and its surroundings never ceased to fascinate me. In the evenings, when the waters of the glaciers flowed into the lake, they would form lighter streaks on the dark blue surface, while the mountains would glow in orange, red, and purple tints, under a sky of the most sublime gradations of rainbow colours.

The weather suddenly became mild, almost sirocco-like, and one day we crossed a blindingly white and intolerably hot sand desert (mixed with pebbles), stretching for miles between the slopes of the snow mountains and the lake. Though it was in the middle of July, I never expected such heat at an altitude of 14,000 feet. But, as I said before, Tibet is a country of surprises and contrasts: one day one may be in a blizzard and the next in a hot desert or in a sandstorm.

Not long after we had left the 'burning desert' we came upon a lovely oasis of blossoming shrubs and grassland watered by a placidly winding stream that meandered through a wide, slightly undulating plain between the lake and the receding mountains. The blossoms of the shrubs reminded me of heather, both in form and colour, but the stems of the shrubs were sturdy enough to supply us with ample firewood, a luxury which we had not enjoyed for many days, having had to content ourselves with scanty yak-dung that we picked up on the way, or with the roots and twigs of thorny shrubs found near water-courses or in the dry beds. Dry yak-dung was rare, because we were off the beaten track, but even on the caravan route nobody would pass by a precious piece of yak- or horse-dung without picking it up for the evening camp-fire.

The value of yak-dung cannot be easily imagined by those who have never lived in Tibet or in the woodless regions of Central Asia. It is the main fuel of the country and burns almost smokeless with a hot, steady flame. Since I had only as much kerosene as the basin of my primus stove could hold, I could use the latter only in emergency cases or on rare occasions, like in the rock monastery. Since then I had not had a roof over my head, though shortly after crossing the Chang-La we had camped near villages. But after Tankse we had not found any human habitations except for a few huts near a cultivated patch of barley at the foot of the Pangong Range.

Thus fuel was always a major problem and as important as the water and the grazing-grounds for the horses. To find all these necessities of life combined in this uninhabited oasis was a pleasant surprise. So we settled down to a blazing camp-fire in a little depression near the winding stream, protected from wind and cold. It was a most idyllic spot, with a superb view of the snow mountains on the one side and the big fjord-like lake on the other.

I felt so happy and carefree that I decided to camp here for a few days, to explore the surroundings, and to devote myself to painting and sketching, as well as to some quiet spells of meditation. Here in the utter stillness and solitude of nature, far from the haunts of man, under the open sky and surrounded by a dream landscape of 'jewel mountains', I felt at peace with myself and the world.

Strangely, there was no feeling of loneliness in this solitude and no need for talk or outward communication. It was as if consciousness itself was stretched and widened out to such an extent that it included the outer world landscape and space and human beings—those present as well as those with whom one was connected in the past; indeed, the past seemed to rise into the present on its own accord. This latter tendency I observed especially when there was even the slightest increase in humidity, when the air became heavy or sultry, when there was a tendency to cloud formation, and even more so when the sky was overcast.

But even before any visible signs appeared I found that my dreams had a direct connection with the changes of atmosphere, so that I could almost with certainty predict sudden changes of weather. I remembered the popular saying that if you dream of dead people it will rain. I took this to be a mere superstition, as I could not see any reasonable connection between the dead and the rain. But now I observed that whenever I dreamt of a person who was very dear to me and who had been intimately connected with my childhood, but who had died some years ago, rain was to follow exactly within three days. Generally there was not a cloud in the sky and not the slightest indication of any change in temperature or humidity when such a dream occurred, but with unfailing regularity a heavy rainfall, a thunderstorm, or a blizzard would follow. Due to the comparative rarity of rain in this part of the world I observed these facts for the first time during this journey, and from then on I made good use of them. Whenever travelling in Tibet in later years I took notice of my dreams and regulated my itinerary accordingly.

My own explanation for this phenomenon is that our consciousness is sensitive to atmospheric pressure and that with increasing 'heaviness' (whatever it may be due to) our consciousness descends into the deeper layers of our mind, into our subconsciousness, in which the memories of our individual past are stored up. The greater the pressure, the farther we go back into the past, and this is revealed in our dreams by meeting again those persons who were closest to us in our childhood and who, in the majority of cases, passed away by the time our childhood had become a remote remembrance. In the high altitudes of Tibet one not only becomes more sensitive to these things but one is also more conscious of one's dreams. Tibetans themselves rely a great deal on their dream consciousness and they are seldom proved wrong in their judgement.

Besides dreams they have many other methods of contacting the deeper layers of their mind: meditation, trance, certain forms of oracles, and various natural and 'supernatural' (psychic) portents. All these methods have been tried out for millenniums, and their results have been found sufficiently satisfactory to guide people in their daily life. Tibetans would be greatly surprised if one would doubt these facts, which are matters of practical experience and have nothing to do with beliefs or theories. To them the attempts of modern psychologists, who try to 'prove' extrasensory perception by scientific methods, would appear crude and laughable: one might just as well try to prove the existence of light which is visible to all but the blind. The circumstances under which these modern experiments are carried out are in themselves the greatest hindrance to their success. In their attempt at 'objectivity' they exclude the emotional and the spiritually directive elements of the human mind, without which no state of real absorption or concentration can be created. Their very attitude bars the doors of psychic perception.

In Tibet the capacity of concentration and self-observation, as well as our psychic sensitivity, is increased a hundredfold in the vastness, solitude, and silence of nature, which acts like a concave mirror that not only enlarges and reflects our innermost feeling and emotions but concentrates them in *one* focal point: our own consciousness. Thus there is nothing to divert the mind from itself, not even the grandeur of nature, because nature never interferes, but on the contrary stimulates and heightens the activity of the mind. Mind and nature enter into co-operation rather than into competition. The immensity of nature and its timeless rhythm reflect the similar properties of our deepest mind.

It is mostly the effects of other minds that interfere with our consciousness, the quiet scream of inner awareness, of thought and imagination, reflection and contemplation. In the uninhabited or sparsely inhabited regions of the world the mind expands unobstructed and undeflected. Its sensitivity is not blunted by the continuous interference of other mind activities or by the meaningless noise and chatter of modern life, and therefore it can enter into communication with those minds that are spiritually attuned to it, either by affection or by sharing certain experiences of the inner life.

This explains the frequency of telepathic phenomena among the inhabitants of Tibet—not only among the highly trained, but even among the simplest people. I am reminded here of an incident which Sven Hedin reports in one of his travel-books. On his way into the interior of Tibet he had to cross a vast stretch of uninhabited territory with his caravan. Before setting out he met some nomad herdsmen who knew the territory, and with great difficulty he persuaded one of two brothers to act as a guide for his caravan. He was a shy young man and declared that he was not accustomed to travel in a 'crowd' and that he would guide the caravan only under the condition that he would be allowed to go ahead alone, as otherwise he would not be able to concentrate on the landmarks and the direction of the route. Sven Hedin respected his wish, and the caravan followed him without any difficulties or untoward incidents, until one day the young man fell ill and died under inexplicable circumstances. There was no other choice for the caravan but to return the same way they had come. But while they were still several stages away from the place from where they had set out with their young guide his brother came to meet them, and before anybody could tell what had happened he said that he knew that his brother was dead and described the spot and the exact circumstances under which he had died. He had seen it with the mind's eye!

In this case a close relationship favoured the telepathic contact between two individuals. But I remember a case that concerned me personally and in which a third person acted as a transmitter or medium without my co-operation or knowledge. After a year's travelling in Western Tibet without postal communications I was worried about my aged foster-mother, fearing that she might be seriously ill or that she might have died in the meantime. Li Gotami thereupon—without telling me about it—consulted a Tibetan friend of ours, who was well trained in Tantric methods of meditation, to perform a *Mo* or oracle, according to an ancient book of omens in his possession. The answer was that my foster-mother was alive and that there was no cause for worry, but that her legs were swollen and caused her much trouble. I was somewhat sceptical about this answer, because it did not seem to have any connection with any of her former ailments. But a few weeks later I received a letter which proved that the *Mo* had been correct.

Solitude itself seems to produce a similar effect as certain meditational or yogic exercises: it automatically removes distraction by outer influences and thus creates a state of dwelling within oneself, a state of natural concentration. Whatever thought-object comes before one's mind, it takes on a greater reality and plasticity and can be held and contemplated with full attention. The past is telescoped into the present and the present shows itself not as a dividing line between a past that had died and a future that has not yet been born but as a single aspect of the co-existent and continuous body of living experience in four dimensions.

In the detachment of this solitude I could see how little in our life depends on brain-made decisions and how much on apparently insignificant events and impressions which suddenly reveal the inner direction of our essential being. We generally look upon these insignificant impressions and events as 'accidents', happening without apparent cause or connection with ourselves, without noticing that these impressions and events gained importance merely because they set free forces which were at work in us all along, but which we did not notice because our intellectually thought-out plans overshadowed the steady flow of our inner life and the driving forces of our soul.

My childhood dreams hovered about the snow-clad peaks of the Andes and the majestic solitudes of the Bolivian highlands with their clear-cut sculptured mountains which were the haunts of many of my forbears, the birthplace of my mother, and the scene of many adventurous stories of travels by mule and llama caravans with which my grandmother used to regale me to my infinite pleasure, while the other family members around me discussed the affairs of their mines in the mountains of Quechisla; of my grandfather's early days at Cochabamba or the exploits of my great-grandfather, one of the leading generals in the war of liberation and brother-in-arms of Bolivar, for whom he won a decisive victory, which earned him the highest honours and the title of Field Marshal de Montenegro.

However, it was not this that impressed me, but the vastness of those bare mountains of the Bolivian highlands and the secrets they bore in their depths: a hidden world of treasures of gold and silver and bismuth, of which I had seen wonderful specimens and which attracted me more by their beauty than by their value, of which I had no conception. To explore this mysterious world in the depths of the earth, and to live on those enchanted highlands of eternal sunshine and wide horizons, I decided to become a mining-engineer to carry on the family tradition.

But while growing up I discovered that I was not so much interested in the depths of the earth as in the depths of the mind. So, instead of engineering I turned to philosophy. And since philosophy was for me identical with a quest for truth, I was less interested in systems, i.e. in academical forms of philosophical thought, than in its religious expression and realisation. I was deeply moved by Plato's discourses which appealed to me both by their poetic beauty and their religious attitude. Among modern philosophers Schopenhauer had a profound influence upon me, and this led me to the Christian mystics as well as to the Upanishads and to Buddhism.

At the age of eighteen I began to write a comparative study of the three world religions, Christianity, Islam, and Buddhism, in order to clarify my own mind and to decide my own religion, because it did not seem to me reasonable to accept a faith just because my forefathers had followed it or because it was accepted by the society in which I lived. To me religion was a matter of conviction and not merely a matter of belief or convention; and in order to be convinced I had to *know.*

Therefore, in order to find out the merits of these three great religions and the degree in which they were able to convince me of their truths, I set out on a more or less detailed study of their teachings. But since Islam did not seem to add any substantially new ideas to the common tradition of Judaism and Christianity, the former soon dropped out of the contest, and only Christianity and Buddhism remained. At the outset of my study I had felt more or less convinced of the superiority of Christianity (though not of the Christian Church), but the further I proceeded the more I found myself in agreement with Buddhism, until it became clear to me that Buddhism was the only religion I could follow with the fullest conviction. Thus, the book which resulted from my studies in comparative religion was exclusively devoted to the teachings of the Buddha, and I was its convert. In spite of its somewhat immature character the book was published not only in Germany but also in Japan, as I found out on my arrival in Ceylon eight years after its first appearance.

What brought me to Ceylon was the conviction that here I would find the purest tradition of Buddhism and an opportunity to gain deeper experience in meditation and to continue my Pāli studies, which I had begun in my home at Capri as well as at the University of Naples which, thanks to the generosity of King Chulalongkorn of Siam, possessed a complete set of the Pāli Canon in Siamese script.

Ceylon proved indeed fruitful in many respects, and under the friendly guidance of Nyanatiloka Mahāthera, the founder and abbot of the idyllic island monastery of Polgasduwa (near Dodanduwa), who was one of the greatest Pāli scholars of his time, I found ample opportunity to continue my studies and to get first-hand experience of the monastic life and tradition of the Theravāda School of Southern Buddhism. I was greatly impressed by the kindliness of the Sinhalese people and the high standard of discipline and education among the monks. But something was missing—and what it was I discovered only when suddenly a new horizon of religious experience was opened to me at Yi-Gah Chö-Ling, and the great Guru stepped into my life.

Now I could clearly see the pattern of my life and its hidden roots. I could see that this pilgrimage into the unknown was a coming home to the land of my dreams—and that dreams are more real than the plans of our brain, provided they are dreams that mirror the deepest yearnings of our soul, the very centre of our being, and not only our fleeting desires and ambitions which hide behind the reasons of our intellect. How true are Santayana's words:

'It is not wisdom to be only wise—
And on the inner vision dose the eyes—
But it is wisdom to believe the heart.'

Here I was in the land of 'turquoise lakes and golden hills' under the flowering shrubs of an unknown oasis, sitting by the camp-fire with two strange men, the only human beings besides me in the immensity of these uninhabited mountain regions, while our horses were grazing contentedly and their silvery bells tinkled assuringly through the night.

When the moon rose I left the camp-fire and retired to a small clearing among the shrubs, out of sight and earshot from the camp, placed Tomo Géshé's little Buddha-image (which I carried with me in a little shrine) before me on a piece of elevated ground and entered into silent communion with the Guru. If in the previous days my thoughts had often dwelt in the past, now they were fully directed upon the Way that lay before me and the Guide that was ever present. I do not know how long I remained in this happy state of contemplation and inner communion. But suddenly clouds appeared over the glaciers, and I returned to the camp. The next day a mild rain descended upon us like a blessing.

4

Moving Slopes and the Riddle of the Horses' Hoofs

After a day of well-deserved rest near the camp-fire, that kept us comfortable, even though it was raining, the sun broke through again, and I started out to explore the northern end of the lake. Having been absent for a whole day, the sun seemed to be hotter than ever and the cloudless sky even more intensely blue (if that were possible!)—a perfect day for painting.

So I set out, as lightly clad as possible, and with no other burden than my sketching materials. I had had a good breakfast, so that I could dispense with provisions for the excursion, and since my riding-boots were being repaired by my companions, I wore my Indian sandals. It was a wonderful feeling to move so light and carefree through the sunny landscape and the clear crisp air into pathless, untrodden regions, with a feast of colours spread out before me. The wonder of the lake fascinated me as on the first day, and my idea was to move along the eastern shore as far north as possible, in order to get a full view of the great expanse of water and the southern snow mountains along which we had travelled the previous days.

Skirting a promontory I—for the first time—sighted a group of *kyang,* a kind of wild horse which are extremely shy and elusive and move about with the graceful gait of deer. They resemble zebras in size and shape, but not in colour; their heads are bigger than those of horses, in proportion to their body; their coat is light brown, like that of a deer, and their belly is white, which makes them more graceful and slim-looking. They are creatures of wide spaces; they perish in captivity, because they cannot endure the loss of their freedom and refuse to take food gathered by human hands. Thus nobody cries to catch or to domesticate them, nor are they hunted for their meat, since the killing of animals goes against the Buddhist code of morality.

Hunting is not regarded as a sport in Tibet, but a crime, and whenever the slaughter of domestic animals becomes necessary due to scarcity of food during the winter, the herdsman prays for forgiveness from the animals and performs rites for their rebirth in a better state of life. Killing even the lowliest creature is always regarded as an evil and therefore avoided as far as humanly possible under the difficult circumstances of life in Tibet, where fruit and vegetables are almost unknown (except for the fertile, carefully irrigated valleys of Eastern and Central Tibet) and where *tsampa* (roasted barley flour) is the only staple food. Fishing is regarded as particularly offensive, because fish being small (at least as known in Tibet), a great number have to be killed to make a proper meal, and the same holds good for birds. Birds, hares, marmots and other small creatures are therefore exceptionally fearless of human beings, and I remember a case when a hare remained quietly in its lair until I touched it, while birds often walked into our tent to inspect the interior, and little, marmot-like 'tailless rats' popped in and out of the ground to see what was going on in the camp that suddenly had sprung up in their peaceful territory.

But the *kyang* always kept at a respectable distance from human beings, being shy by nature and perhaps being warned by the sight of humans riding on horseback. I was thrilled to see them here for the first time, and, crouching behind a boulder, I observed them for a while before proceeding on my way. In the extensive grasslands around Manasarovar and in many parts of the Chang-Thang they move about in enormous herds of hundreds of animals, and it is a grand sight to see such a herd galloping over the wide undulated plains of the highland.

Skirting the promontory, I descended into an open plain, the greater part of which was covered with a snow-white encrustation, consisting of magnesium crystals and hiding a swamp, reminding me of the treacherous *cliotts* or salt-lakes of the Sahara into which one can walk for a good distance before reaching the actual water, and where people are suddenly swallowed by the muddy ground that unexpectedly gives way under their feet.

I made a wide detour around this swamp and climbed over a range of low hills which still separated me from the shore of the lake. The shore proved to be a boulder-strewn narrow ledge of rock that fell perpendicularly into the lake. There was no place to walk between the boulders. They were so tightly packed that one had to jump from boulder to boulder in order to avoid getting one's feet wedged between them. But I was fresh and eager to get on, and so in spite of these obstacles I covered a good distance along the shore, and the more I proceeded, the more magnificent was the view.

But finally the boulders gave way to a steep, smooth-looking slope of about forty-five degrees that ended abruptly where the ledge broke off into the waters of the lake. I confidently stepped upon the slope, thinking that my troubles would be over, but hardly had I put my feet upon it than the whole slope started to move downwards, being a mixture of sand and rubble in a state of exact and precarious balance, which on the slightest provocacion would turn into a landslide. There was not much time to think, as I was moving inexorably nearer to the precipice and to a plunge into the icy waters of the lake, which would probably have frozen me before I could have swum ashore—apart from the fact that the shore consisted of a sheer rock-face with nothing to hold on to, in order to pull oneself out of the water. I did the only thing that was possible, namely to keep running and jumping forward as quickly as I could before being caught in the momentum of the landslide that rumbled behind me like a pursuing mountain demon hard on my heels. By keeping a diagonal, slightly upward, course, I managed to keep on the level and to reach firm ground on the other side of the moving slopes.

Even the boulder-strewn ledge appeared to me now as a welcome road. At least I could move in safety and at my own pace. But while taking a little rest among the boulders I made a strange discovery: innumerable hoofs of horses were stuck between the boulders and rock debris between them, and not a single one of them was turned upside-down. It looked as if a whole horse caravan or a herd of horses had been literally swept off their feet, leaving only their hoofs behind. But how was this possible? Could an avalanche have done it? But no, there were no snow-peaks above, nor such high mountains in which avalanches could form—quite apart from the fact that in these parts of Tibet snowfall is negligible. Even if a blizzard of unimaginable force could have killed a whole herd of horses and swept away their bodies, their skeletons would certainly be seen in the clear water of the lake, which was so transparent that one could see every pebble on the bottom for a considerable distance right below the place of the catastrophe. But not even a splinter of a bone was visible either in the water or among the stones and boulders! Even if wolves or birds of prey might have devoured the carcasses they could not have done this without leaving a trace. They would have left the skulls or at least the teeth behind! And why should all the hoofs stand upright just broken off at the fetlock? What horror could have caused a whole herd of swift-moving horses to perish in this mysterious fashion?

Whatever it was, I had no time to worry about it, especially as I was eager to find a vantage-point from where I could get an adequate picture of this part of the lake against the snow mountains. So I pushed on until I came to a lovely, almost circular, bay, bordered by a dazzling white beach, against which the water looked like a smooth green-blue opal. On the opposite side of the bay a rocky spur jutted into the lake, providing just the type of vantage-point I had been looking for. But, as so often in Tibet, I underestimated the distance, and though I walked at a good speed, it took me a considerable time before I reached the other side of the bay. While I was painting, big thunder-clouds were rising over the glaciers, but I was too absorbed in my work to pay much attention to them, except as a welcome addition to my composition.

By the time I had finished my painting, the sun had been swallowed by the rising thunder-clouds, and in the gathering darkness I suddenly realised that it was not only due to the clouds that the light was failing, but because the sun was setting. I hurried back along the beach of the bay, but, by the time I had reached the other side, lightning and thunder rolled overhead, the air grew chilly, and the daylight was fading fast.

And then I remembered the moving slopes and the horses that had perished mysteriously just before reaching them. The danger of the moving slopes must have stopped them in their course, while night and storm prevented them from turning back and they were frozen to death. Or were there dangers, even worse than that, of which I knew nothing? The complete disappearance of even their skulls and skeletons down to the tiniest bone could not be explained by the presence of carnivorous animals, for even wolves would not swallow everything, and why should they, when they could gorge themselves on the flesh of a whole herd of horses?

The rough nature of the ground had already convinced me that even before the landslide, which had caused the moving slopes, had occurred, this shore could not have been a possible caravan route; moreover the presence of smaller hoofs showed that there were young ones among the horses, which would not have been included in a caravan unless it was one of people fleeing before an enemy. Whatever it was, I had no time to lose. I had to get over the moving slopes before it was completely dark.

Fortunately the thunder-clouds disappeared as quickly as they had come. The sky was still overcast, but no rain fell and the clouds began to separate. With the last, faintest trace of daylight I reached the moving slopes, and though I was not able to see more than the general outlines of the ground over which I passed, I managed to get across with a supreme effort. I felt like resting and sat down for a short while, to recover my breach, but then I was worried by the thought of wolves and other unseen dangers, especially the danger of falling asleep and exposing myself to the cold of the night with not even a blanket to protect me and no chance to regain my warmth once the chill would have penetrated my body. I was so lightly clad that only movement could keep me warm, and so up I jumped, conscious that it now was a matter of life and death.

I had not eaten anything since the morning, nor had I had a drop of water since leaving camp; and now hunger and thirst began to assail me—especially the latter. What an irony of fate: to have miles and miles of clear water right at my feet and not to be able to find even a drop to quench my thirst. The temptation to take shelter in one of the caves which I had noticed on my way was counteracted by the fear that wolves might lurk in them, and as I had neither matches nor anything that could have served to make a fire, the thought was quickly dismissed. The greatest temptation, however, was the urge to sit down and to rest, and only the thought that once I sat down I would never get up again gave me the determination to move on as long as my legs would support me.

It was no longer possible to pick my way between the boulders that covered the ground for uncounted miles ahead of me; night had completely overtaken me; and yet to my amazement I jumped from boulder to boulder without ever slipping or missing a foothold, in spite of wearing only a pair of flimsy sandals on my bare feet. And then I realised that a strange force had taken over, a consciousness that was no more guided by my eyes or my brain. My limbs moved as in a trance, with an uncanny knowledge of their own, though their movement seemed almost mechanical. I noticed things only like in a dream, somewhat detached. Even my own body had become distant, quasi-detached from my will-power. I was like an arrow that unfailingly pursued its course by the force of its initial impetus, and the only thing I knew was that on no condition must I break the spell that had seized me.

It was only later that I realised what had happened: that unwittingly and under the stress of circumstance and acute danger I had become a *lung-gom-pa,* a trance walker, who, oblivious of all obstacles and fatigue, moves on towards his contemplated aim, hardly touching the ground, which might give a distant observer the impression that the *lung-gom-pa* was borne by the air *(lung),* merely skimming the surface of the earth.

One false step or a single slip on these boulders would have sufficed to break or to sprain a foot, but I never missed a step. I moved on with the certainty of a sleep-walker—though far from being asleep. I do not know how many miles of this boulder-strewn territory I traversed; I only know that finally I found myself on the pass over the low hills with the plain and the magnesium swamp before me, and that by that time a star in the direction of the snow range was visible, so that I could take it as a guiding point in the otherwise featureless expanse before me. I did not dare to divert from this direction and still under the influence of the 'spell' I went right across the swamp without ever breaking through.

But where was the camp? Surely I could not be very far from it, and a camp-fire could easily be seen even from one or two miles' distance. I climbed one of the low shrub-covered hillocks, but nowhere could I see even the smallest glow. Surely my companions would not have allowed the fire to go out or even left the camp in search of me or for any other reason? And what other reason could there be, unless they had been attacked by robbers? They certainly could not have made away with my belongings, leaving me stranded in the wilderness without food and proper clothing and blankets, though nobody in the world could have held them responsible. I simply had walked into the wilderness and never returned! But no, this was nonsense! How could I ever think such a thing! I felt ashamed that such a thought could invade my mind—but being in a state of utter exhaustion I was not able to control my fear. It was more likely that I had missed the direction, and in that case it was best to walk on until I reached the stream and then to follow it up until I reached the camp-site.

Fortunately the direction which I had taken proved to be correct, and when I was almost despairing of ever reaching camp I suddenly saw the glow of the fire in a depression below me. I tried to shout, but my throat was too parched and my voice did not carry far enough to be heard. But the joy of being saved gave me new strength, and a few minutes later I walked into the camp and sank down by the fire, while my companions, happy to have me back, busied themselves around me to give me food and drink. I felt like a lost son come home and never did I enjoy a camp-fire and the company of human beings more than on this memorable night.

Until the present day I have been unable to find a solution to the mystery of the horses' hoofs, though I have told this experience to many people and asked their opinion about it. But for the other, more personal, experience I found a satisfactory explanation when I learned more about the psychic phenomena of *lung-gom,* of which I found the first description in Alexandra David-Neel's book, and further evidence, when many years later I visited (together with Li Gotami) one of the main training centres of this yogic art not far from Shigatse in a side valley of the Nyang-chu, the famous monastery of Nyang-tö Kyi-phug.

5

Trance Walking and *Lung-gom* Training

THE FIRST EYEWITNESS ACCOUNT of a *lung-gom-pa* that reached the West is probably the graphic description which Alexandra David-Neel gave in her famous book *With Mystics and Magicians in Tibet*. One day, while crossing a wide table land, she noticed in the distance a moving black spot which aroused her curiosity, since she was travelling through uninhabited territory, and had not met any human being for almost two weeks. Her field-glasses revealed the moving object to be a man, who 'proceeded at an unusual gait and especially with an extraordinary swiftness'. When he came nearer she 'could clearly see his perfectly calm impassive face and wide-open eyes with their gaze fixed on some invisible far-distant object situated somewhere high up in space. The man did not run. He seemed to lift himself from the ground, proceeding by leaps. It looked as if he had been endowed with the elasticity of a ball and rebounded each time his feet touched the ground. His steps had the regularity of a pendulum.'

When I read this account a few years after my above-related experience I immediately was reminded of what had happened to me on the shores of the Pangong Lake. Her description exactly coincided with my own experience. Beginners in the art of *lung-gom* are often advised to fix their mind not only on a mentally visualised object, namely the aim towards which they want to move, but to keep their eyes fixed on a particular star, which in some cases seems to produce a hypnotic effect. Even in this detail I had unwittingly conformed to the rules, and I clearly reached a condition in which the weight of the body is no more felt and in which the feet seem to be endowed with an instinct of their own, avoiding invisible obstacles and finding footholds, which only a clairvoyant consciousness could have detected in the speed of such a movement and in the darkness of the night.

Alexandra David-Neel thinks that a kind of anaesthesia deadens the sensations that would be produced by knocking against the stones or other obstacles on the way. But this seems not to be the case, otherwise the *lung-gom-pa* would find his feet bruised and swollen afterwards, which apparently is not so, as I have learned from my own experience. Neither can I subscribe to the view that it is due to a remainder of *normal* consciousness, which keeps one aware of the obstacles in one's way. Just on the contrary, it is the noninterference of normal consciousness which ensures the immunity of the trance walker and the instinctive sureness of his movements. There is no greater danger than the sudden awakening to normal consciousness. It is for this reason that the *lung-gom-pa* must avoid speaking or looking about, because the slightest distraction would result in breaking his trance.

The deeper meaning of *lung-gom* is that matter can be mastered by the mind. This is illustrated by the fact that the preparatory exercises are mainly spiritual, i.e. consisting in strict seclusion and mental concentration upon certain elementary forces and their visualised symbols, accompanied by the recitation of mantras, through which certain psychic centres (Skt.: *cakra*) of the body, which are related to those forces by their natural functions, are awakened and activated.

Just as in the *tum-mo* practices, which result in the production of 'psychic heat' (for reference see pp. 159 ff. in *Foundations of Tibetan Mysticism*), the adept has to concentrate upon the element 'fire' in its corresponding psychic centre and in all its phenomenal and essential qualities and psychic implications, so in the case of *lung-gom* the adept is required to concentrate on all the phenomena, aspects, and functions of the vital element air.

Gom (sgom) means meditation, contemplation, concentration of mind and soul upon a certain subject, as well as the gradual emptying of the mind of all subject-object relationship, until a complete identification of subject and object has taken place.

Lung (*rluṅ*) signifies both the elementary state of 'air' (Skt.: *vāyu*) as well as the subtle vital energy or psychic force (Skt. : *prāṅa*). Just as the Greek word *'pneuma'* can signify 'air' as well as 'spirit', so *lung* can be applied to the element 'air' and to those bodily functions which represent the material side of our vital principle, as exemplified by the process of breathing and the faculty of movement, as well as the currents of psychic energy resulting in various states of consciousness.

In combination with *gom*, the word *lung* can only be applied to the *prāṇa* of various meditational practices, connected with the control of vital functions of the human body through the finer forces of the mind. In other words, the *lung-gom-pa* is not a man who has the faculty to fly through the air (a belief that has its origin in the wrong interpretation of the word *lung*), but one who has learned to control his *prāṇa* through the yoga-practice of *prāṇāyāma*, which starts with the simple function of conscious breathing and makes it the basis of a profound spiritual experience, resulting in a transformation of the whole psycho-physical organism and of the very personality of the practitioner. Forces and faculties, which are present in every human individual, are re-channelled and concentrated in a new direction.

Thus *lung-gom* could be aptly rendered with 'concentration on the dynamic vital principle'. It reveals the dynamic nature of our physical organism and of all material states of aggregation—not in the sense of a self-sufficient dynamism, but as something that depends on the cooperation and interaction of various forces and ultimately on the fundamental (and universal) faculties of consciousness. Thus, a direct influence is possible upon the bodily functions and their respective organs, so that a psycho-physical co-operation is established: a parallelism of thought and movement, and a rhythm that gathers all available forces into its service.

If one has reached the point where the transformation of one force or state of materialisation into another one is possible one may produce various effects of an apparently miraculous nature, as, for instance, the transformation of psychic energy into bodily movement (a miracle that we perform on a smaller scale every moment, without being conscious of it), or the transformation of matter into an active state of energy, resulting at the same time in a reduction of weight or the apparent elimination or reduction of the power of gravitation.

In the original system of Buddhist meditation the attainment of magic power is a mere by-product and is looked upon rather as a danger than as a stimulus on the higher path, which aims at liberation and abhors the exhibition of occult forces. The peculiar conditions of Tibet, however, have sometimes made it necessary to make use of these powers to a certain degree, especially when nature placed unsurmountable obstacles in the way of the adept or his desire to be of service to his fellow-beings.

Thus *tum-mo* may at the same time serve as a protection against the excessive cold during the hard Tibetan winters, to which Yogis are exposed in their caves and hermitages high up in the bare mountains, where fuel is almost unobtainable. However, it should be noted that this is far from being the purpose of *tum-mo,* which is purely spiritual, namely the attainment of inner unification or integration, which brings about the state of enlightenment and the wholeness of being.

In a similar way *lung-gom* is only one of the many ways of liberation, though it may under certain circumstances help an individual to move speedily over vast distances, which, in a country where communications are beset with many difficulties, assumes a particular importance. It may happen that people take to this training, spurred by the ambition to obtain spectacular magic powers. But the sacrifice that is demanded of them is so great that anyone who is able to go through the full training must be a man of extraordinary character and spiritual qualities. And such a man, the more seriously he pursues his exercises, will soon lose all his initial pride and ambition, because his whole training is based on the giving up and not on the strengthening of his ego, in which pride and ambition have their origin.

This has been illustrated by many of the popular stories of the famous eighty-four medieval Siddhas (literally: 'Accomplished Ones'), many of whom set out with the idea to acquire supernatural powers for their own benefit, and who in the process of it, or by the time they had realised them, had lost interest in such mundane aims, because they had overcome that very sense of ego which was the source of their desires.

Here only one example, the story of Siddha Kadgapā: There was once a robber, who met a yogi and asked him how he could become invincible. The yogi answered: 'There is a *stūpa* in such and such a place. Go there and circumambulate the sanctuary with the image of Avalokiteśvara for three weeks, reciting the *mantra* and performing the *sādhanā,* which I will give you. If you do this with full devotion and unfailing concentration, without diverting your mind, then at the end of the third week a deadly black snake will emerge from the *stūpa*. You must immediately seize the snake behind the head, and if you have faithfully carried out your *sādhanā,* the snake will not harm you, and you will obtain the power of invincibility.'

The robber thanked the yogi and did as he was told. He devoted himself heart and soul to the indicated exercise, and when the fearful snake finally emerged from the hollow niche of the *stūpa* he seized it behind the head, and lo! he held in his hand the invincible Sword of Wisdom. He had no more use for miraculous powers and became a saint. Since then he has been known as Siddha Kadgapā, 'the Saint with the Sword'.

6

NYANG-TÖ KYI-PHUG

THE MONASTERY OF IMMURED RECLUSES

ALL THAT I SAW and learned at the *lung-gom* training centre of Nyang-tö Kyi-phug *(ñaṅ-stod kyid-phug),* which means 'the Happy Cave in the Upper Nyang Valley' (near Shigatse), confirmed my conviction that the aim of *lung-gom* goes far beyond the attainment of magic powers, like trance walking or levitation, and that this training is certainly not a playground of personal ambition or aggrandisement, because the first thing that is demanded of a prospective *lung-gom-pa* is complete anonymity.

When entering the *ts'hang-khang,* the meditation cubicle, he has as good as died to the world; his name, his family, or even the place from where he came, is not revealed to anybody. He has given up his past, and when after many years he emerges from his cubicle, nothing of his former personality has remained and nobody knows who he was. He is like a new-born being, one who has not only died to his past, but one who has consciously gone through death and has been reborn to a new life, a life purified from all personal attachments and wholly dedicated to the welfare of his fellow-beings.

This is also borne out by the popular belief that *lung-gom* had its origin in a saint's attempt to overcome death by sacrificing his own self.

This saint was the famous historian Buston, who was born near Shigatse in 1289 and was the Great Abbot of the monastery of Shalu, which became the first training centre for *lung-gom.* Not far from this place lived a great magician, known as Yungtön Dorjé Pal, who cried to propitiate the Lord of Death *(gŚinrje,* pron. 'Shinjé'; Skt. *Yama)* in a special ritual in order to persuade him to spare the life of human beings for twelve years. The Lord of Death consented under the condition that somebody would offer his own life as a compensation (the underlying thought being that *one* life offered willingly was worth thousands of lives surrendered under compulsion). None of those present during this fearful ritual were ready to sacrifice themselves, except Buscon (pron. 'Butön'). This revealed to the magician that this saintly man was the only one capable of performing this ritual, and therefore, instead of accepting his offer, he enjoined upon him and his successors the duty to perform the same ceremony every twelve years.

As it was necessary to invite to this ceremony the terrible tutelary deities of the main sanctuaries of the Central Provinces of Tibet, Ü *(dBus)* and Tsang *(gTsaṅ),* and only a messenger who is fearless of death, and able to perform the pilgrimage to these sanctuaries within twenty-four hours, is suitable for this task, the training of *lung-gom* was instituted at Samding and Nyang-tö Kyi-phug, from where the runners were despatched alternately every twelve years.

This is the story which I heard at Kyi-phug and which has also been related by Alexandra David-Neel. I was not able to visit Samding, but some years ago I came across a very moving report by Sven Hedin,[1] in which he describes a cave in a valley 'above Linga and Pesu', in which a Lama was immured, and which he visited on a cold winter day. The cave was at the foot of a rock-wall and was called Samde-phug. It had neither window nor door, but a spring welled up in its interior and its water emerged from a small opening under the wall, which closed the mouth of the cave.

---

1. Published in the magazine *Die Koralle* and also in his book *Abenteuer in Tibet.* My subsequent translation is made from an extract of the original article.

'When three years ago this mysterious Lama Rimpoché had come to Linga, he had taken a vow before the monks of the monastery to go for ever into the darkness. By consulting the holy scriptures, the date of the immurement had been fixed. On that day all the monks assembled to convey him to his grave. Silently and solemnly, like a funeral, the monks moved through the valley, slowly, step by step, as if they wanted to prolong the last minutes in which the unknown hermit could still see sun, light and colours. He knows that he leaves the world for ever, that he will never again see the mountains which hold vigil at his grave. He knows that he will die in the cave, forgotten by all.

'After the entrance of the cave has been walled up, the light is extinguished for him, for ever. He is alone and will never hear a human voice again, only the closed-in echo of his own. But when he says his prayers, there will be nobody who listens to them, and when he calls, nobody will answer. For the brethren, who have buried him alive, he is already dead. The only bond between them and the immured hermit is the duty to supply him with his daily food. A bowl of tea and *tsampa* is daily given him through the little opening under the wall, which is so thick and solidly built that neither a sound nor a ray of light reaches the hermit. The only way to ascertain whether he is alive or dead is to observe whether the food has been consumed or not. If for six days the food remains untouched, the wall has to be broken open. This had already been done in previous cases, as for instance three years ago, when a hermit, who had spent twelve years in the cave, died; and fifteen years ago, at the death of another one, who at the age of twenty entered the cave and lived there for forty years.'

Sven Hedin then pictures to himself the endless years in total darkness, which the immured hermit has to endure. 'He cannot count the days, he only feels the cold of the winter and the milder air of the summer, but soon he forgets to count the years. The only thing he counts are the beads of his rosary and with them his prayers. But finally, after many long years, someone knocks at the entrance to his cave. He opens his arms, to receive the friend for whom he has been waiting so long: it is Death! The blind hermit, who through decenniums had lived in impenetrable darkness, suddenly sees a brilliant light. . . . He is freed from the cycle of life and death.'

This dramatic account haunted me for a long time, and I often wondered whether any human being could possibly endure a life in total darkness and complete absence of fresh air, deprived even of movement—quite apart from the psychological effect of being cut off from all human contact. Could anybody really believe that by shutting out the light of the sun he could find the inner light or attain to Enlightenment? Did not the Buddha himself condemn the extremes of asceticism as much as he condemned the extreme of worldly pleasures?

Physical self-immolation, as a means for attaining one's own salvation, has never been regarded a virtue by Buddhists. And Tibetans, in spite of their belief in supernatural and transcendental powers, show a lot of common sense in their daily life as well as in their religious training methods. They are eminently practical people, and their conception of religion is neither gloomy nor suicidal.

Thu is borne out even in a place like Nyang-tö Kyi-phug, which is known for the seriousness of its practices and the strictness of its rules. Li Gotami and I visited this place in 1947. All that we saw there thoroughly refuted the idea that *lung-gom* has to be practised in complete darkness (as even Mme David-Neel seems to believe[1]) and under inhumanly unhygienic conditions. Quite on the contrary we found to our pleasant surprise that the meditation cubicles, which rose on the slopes of the ascending valley, just above the main temples and shrines of the monastery, were well-kept and built in a most sensible and practical way, as much with a view to preserve the health of body and mind as to ensure the complete silence and seclusion of the hermits. *'Mens sana in corpore sano'*.

Each cubicle was built in such a way as to give access to air, water, and sun, to allow for physical exercise as well as for the contemplation of infinite space, the wide open sky with its heavenly bodies, its wandering clouds and the moods of the seasons. These hermitages were not meant to be places of self-torture or penance, but as abodes of peace and

---

1. 'After their seclusion in darkness for three years, those monks . . . proceed to Shalu where they are immured in one of the grave-like huts. . . .' (*With Mystics and Magicians in Tibet,* Penguin, p. 191.)

undisturbed meditation. Far from being grave-like, they were meant to be places conducive to happiness, as even the name Kyi-phug, 'the happy cave', indicated; and the general impression I had, was such that I felt a strong desire to retire myself one day into one of these cubicles for a longer spell of introspection and unbroken *sādhanā*.

Gomchens were not precluded from taking with them into their cubicle books, images or *thankas,* related to their *sādhanā,* or things connected with their daily rituals, like *vajra,* bell and *damaru,* the usual altar-vessels and butter-lamps, as well as a little *chogtse* on which to place them. From this it became clear that the Gomchen's time would be carefully regulated and fully employed by study, worship, and meditation, interrupted by regular physical exercises, meals, and the necessary little chores in preparing them and in keeping body, place, and utensils clean.

There was a little kitchen with a few pots and pans, to heat the butter-tea which is an indispensable part of the normal Tibetan diet (it is almost

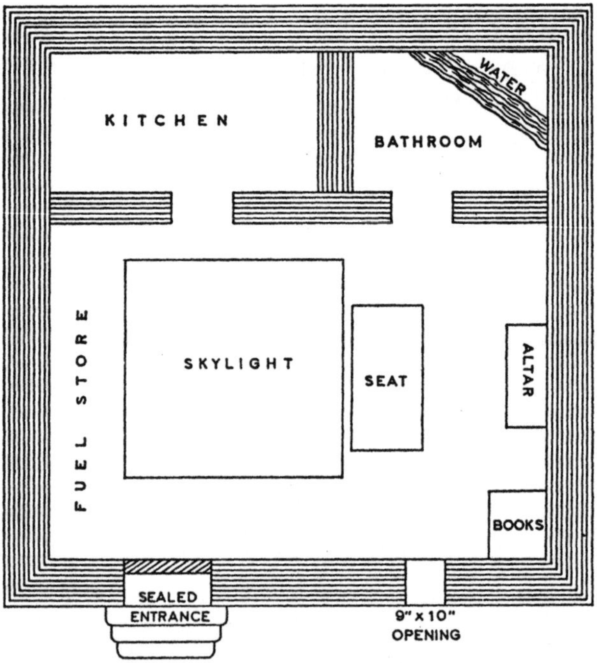

Lung-gom HERMITAGE (GROUND-PLAN)

impossible to swallow dry *tsampa*!) and to prepare simple meals, because devotees often brought merely raw materials which, like other gifts of prepared food, would be placed into the little opening at the bottom of the wall, next to the sealed entrance of the hermitage. Next to the kitchen was a small room, through which the water of a brook had been channelled, providing water for all domestic purposes and serving at the same time as a W.C.

The actual meditation chamber was airy and spacious, with a wide-open skylight. It rather resembled a courtyard, surrounded by a covered gallery, of which one side was wider than the others and served as a sleeping-and-sitting place (indicated by a raised stone or mud platform, on which a mattress or meditation rug could be placed), while the other wall-spaces were used for stacking up fuel, a very important item in a cold climate like that of Tibet, where hot tea is the only way to keep one's body warm in a cold room. Fuel in Tibet is far too precious to be used for heating a room, and in this case the open skylight would have made it impossible anyway. Besides the fuel, which was used in these hermitages, was not the usual yak-dung, in which often worms or beetles are found (and which therefore would not be suitable for one who is engaged in generating love and compassion towards all living beings), but consisted either of brushwood or of a fungus-like woody growth—perhaps a hardened kind of giant moss—that was found in big hemispheric clumps on the surrounding mountain slopes. It was said that this fuel did not contain any animal life.

A ladder led from the 'courtyard', or rather through the skylight, on to the flat roof of the galleries, which thus formed a terrace on which the Gomchen could walk around. This perambulatory, however, was screened from the outside world by a high parapet, so that the Gomchen's meditation and privacy would not be disturbed even while taking exercise.

This perambulatory corresponds to the *chankama* (from Pāli: *caṅkamati,* to pace up and down) of ancient Buddhism, as used even to the present day in the countries of Southern Buddhism (like Ceylon, Burma, and Thailand), where monks are accustomed to pace up and down while meditating or memorising and reciting sacred scriptures. For recluses, practising *lung-gom,* these perambulatories are mainly used to keep physically fit, as they provide the only opportunity for regular walking in the open air.

7

PHYSICAL EXERCISES

OTHER PHYSICAL EXERCISES which are performed during the *lung-gom* training consist in jerking the body up from the meditation-seat with legs crossed and without using the hands. Before each jerk the *lung-gom-pa* fills his lungs with air. By repeating this exercise several times in succession every day during a long period he is able to jump higher and higher, while his body is said to become lighter and lighter. What is important is that deep breathing and physical drill are combined. I have not seen this exercise performed, nor do I remember that it was mentioned at Nyang-tö Kyi-phug, but according to information which Alexandra David-Neel gathered elsewhere in Tibet it appears that these exercises are used as a test for proficiency in *lung-gom*. 'A pit is dug in the ground, its depth being equal to the height of the candidate. Over the pit is built a kind of cupola whose height from the ground level to its highest point again equals that of the candidate. A small aperture is left at the top of the cupola. Now between the man seated cross-legged at the bottom of the pit and that opening, the distance is twice the height of his body. . . . The test consists in jumping crosslegged . . . and coming out through the small opening at the top of the cupola. I have heard Khampas declare that this feat has been performed in their country, but I have not myself witnessed anything like it.'[1]

As I said, I have not found any confirmation of this custom in Nyang-tö Kyi-phug, but strangely enough I found a parallel to it in John Blofeld's description of a Mêng-Goong or tribal magician in a Miao village in Northern Thailand. The magician was seated, facing the shrine of ancestor demons, 'on a bench some three feet high, thumping a drum and intoning a ritual in a voice full of power, but frighteningly inhuman. Now and then, an extraordinary, indeed a really awful, thing would happen. With a frightful scream, he would shoot about four feet into the air and land back upon the bench with such force that it quivered threateningly. Such a movement by a seated man *whose legs never once straightened for the jump* was so uncanny that I actually felt a cold sweat start from my pores.'[2]

This eyewitness account by a well-known and reliable author proves two things: first, that the feat described by Tibetans is not beyond the realm of possibility, as it might appear to a critical reader; and, secondly,

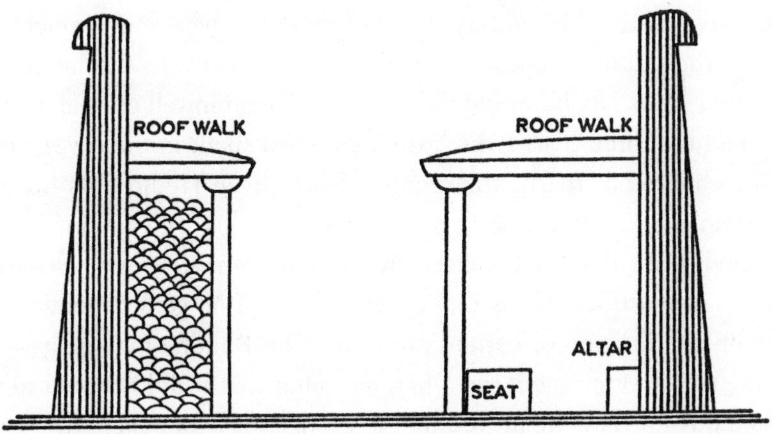

Lung-gom Hermitage (section)

1. *With Mystics and Magicians in Tibet,* Penguin, p. 191.
2. *People of she Sun,* Hutchinson, p. 126.

that more than mere muscle-power is involved in this feat. Tibetans see in it an act of levitation, though only of a momentary nature, made possible through the extreme lightness and will-power of the *lung-gom-pa*.

However that may be, the fact that a similar custom should be found in Eastern Tibet and in Northern Thailand seems to me significant and confirms my impression that the jumping practice is not an original and essential part of the *lung-gom* training but something superimposed upon it. The real origin of *lung-gom* is, as we have mentioned already, the ancient Indian practice of *prāṇāyāma* (an essential feature of both Hindu and Buddhist yoga-systems) in which physical drill never played any role. Nor do those who undergo this training bury themselves alive or take a vow 'to go for ever into darkness'. This is quite foreign to Buddhism, which does not favour 'eternal vows'. There is nothing in the world that is not subject to change or transformation, least of all a human being. Even the vows of monkhood are not 'eternal' or irrevocable. Those who find that they are not suited for a monk's life, or those who feel that they cannot profit by it, are free to return to the normal life in the world. The life in monasteries, hermitages, or in complete seclusion, is a means to an end, and not an end in itself. If, therefore, Sven Hedin reports that his enquiry, whether the monk who daily brought the food to the immured hermit, was able to converse with the latter, was answered with: 'No, he would thereby draw upon himself eternal damnation, and the three years (which the Lama had spent in the cave) would not be counted as merit,' then, quite clearly, Sven Hedin puts his own Christian way of thinking into the mouth of his Tibetan informant.

Buddhism does not believe in 'eternal damnation' and does not regard self-mortification as meritorious, or spiritual gain dependent on vows or the duration of certain exercises. The Buddha himself gave up the life of extreme asceticism when he found that it did not lead to the expected result. And he proved that in a single flash of insight more wisdom may be acquired than in years of self-mortification.

Therefore the length of time to be spent in complete seclusion depends on the capacity and the progress of the practitioner, who is under no compulsion to continue his exercise if his health or his endurance fails. At Nyang-tö Kyi-phug the periods of seclusion are carefully graded.[1] The shortest periods are from one to three months, the middling ones from one to three years, the longest nine years. The latter is regarded as a full course for the attainment of *lung-gom,* though naturally, if the practitioner decides to continue, nobody will prevent him. But in order to prevent frauds and false claims the only entrance to the meditation cubicle is sealed by the authorities of the place, either by the abbot or some high government official, or both; and the seal cannot be broken without the knowledge of the authorities concerned. The longer the period, the greater is the importance that is attached to it.

At the time of my investigation, seven hermits were in retreat at Nyang-tö Kyi-phug. One of them had been shut in there for three years already. He was expected to leave his meditation cubicle in six years.

Nobody is allowed to speak to the *lung-gom-pa* or to see any part of his person. The latter rule is to ensure his complete anonymity. When receiving alms through an opening near the bottom of the wall, next to the sealed entrance, even the hand of the hermit is covered with a sock or a cloth bag, so that he may not be recognised even by a scar or any other particular sign or shape of his hand. The same small opening, which I measured as being 9 in. x 10 in., is said to be used as an exit by the *lung-gom-pa* after completion of his nine years' practice in uninterrupted seclusion and perfect silence.

It is said that his body by that time has become so light and subtle that he can get through an opening not wider than a normal man's span, and that he can move with the speed of a galloping horse, while hardly touching the ground. Due to this he is able to perform the prescribed pilgrimage to all the main shrines and sanctuaries of Central Tibet (Ü-Tsang) within an incredibly short time.

After having performed this pilgrimage the *lung-gom-pa* finds a suitable retreat or hermitage of his own, where he spends the rest of his life, preaching, teaching, meditating, and pursuing his various religious duties in accordance with his own particular *sādhanā* or the requirements

1. Nobody enters on such a venture unless he is adequately prepared by his Guru.

of others. He will bless and inspire all those who come to him, heal the sick, and console those who are in distress. Healing is mainly done through the power of the spirit, either by performing special rites and the laying on of hands, or by the preparation of healing potions or consecrated pills (*ril-bu,* pron. 'ribu'), which play a similar role as the consecrated bread or host in the Eucharist. Healing powers are ascribed to all religious functions, and, therefore, the more saintly a man, the greater is his capacity to heal or to endow consecrated objects with beneficent forces.

8

HEALING POWERS

THE HEALING POWER of saints is not only a Tibetan belief, but a general human experience. Christ, according to the testimony of the Evangelists, was first and foremost a healer (which is the exact equivalent of the German word *'Heiland'*, the most frequent epithet given to Christ), who convinced people not by arguments and sermons but mainly by the power of his saintly personality, which aroused such faith in those who came in contact with him, that they were healed even of long-standing and apparently incurable diseases.

The relationship of faith and healing power is reciprocal. Faith is the capacity to receive; the power of the spirit, the capacity to communicate, to pour out and give from the accumulated fruits of inner experience, that have matured in the stillness of a composed and devoted mind. Healing power and faith are like the positive and the negative pole of the same force, and where the former exists the latter will be aroused as a natural concomitant. But even the reverse is possible: faith may become a power in itself which, like a vacuum, draws all surrounding forces into itself, and thus endows the object or the person with which it is connected with the forces towards which it tends.

Religious leaders depend as much on the faith of their adherents as their adherents depend on the initial inspiration which they receive from their leaders. Once this mutual process has started, it grows like an avalanche. The combined forces of those whose faith is directed towards a religious leader or an incumbent of a high religious office (which normally is due to the outstanding qualities of the individual in question) make him a centre of forces which go far beyond those of his own person or separate individuality. It is for this reason that we should not expect religious leaders taken out of their surroundings and their spiritual and traditional background—like many of the high Lamas who fled from Tibet and are compelled to live in completely uncongenial surroundings, in a kind of spiritual vacuum—to display the same super-individual forces which centred upon them before they were deprived of their natural conditions of life and of the contact of those who had faith in them.

Unless we understand the mutual relationship between faith and spiritual forces we shall regard the healing powers of a saint either as miraculous or as self-deception. But what we call miraculous is nothing but a short cut in the interaction of natural forces, i.e. a direct action from mind to mind, without the usual round-about way via the senses and material agents. Faith merely acts as a conductor, which makes this short cut possible. Just as electricity—which is potentially present everywhere—becomes effective only in the presence of a conductor, so spiritual power becomes effective only in the presence of faith, be it faith in a divine power, or a human Guru, or faith in an ideal or in one's own inner reality.

As long as we are convinced that the mind is not merely a product of physical functions or chemical reactions, but *the* primary fact of life, the builder of the body and not its slave, so long it is only natural to ascribe health to a balanced, harmonious mind and to ascribe diseases to mental disorders or spiritual disharmony. Even the earliest Buddhist scriptures described the mind as the forerunner of all things *(mane pubbaṅgamā dhammā)*, the *conditio sine qua non* of all that exists.

Tibetans, therefore, rather than trying to cure physical symptoms, endeavour to go to the root of all disease by curing the mind. This can be done either by the direct influence of a saintly personality or through certain means which help the transference of power or a stimulation of faith through the medium of consecrated objects, symbols and rites, etc., all of which are intended to guide the mind in a certain direction.

Whether we believe in the psychometric properties of matter in general or the possibility of impressing it with certain qualities through conscious concentration, the fact is that there is a constant interaction between mind and matter, or even between different forms of material aggregation, which, after all, only represent more or less stabilised or 'bound' states of energy. The idea of transubstantiation, therefore, is not only the basis of the Christian Eucharist, but of all rites of consecration, in which certain substances are exposed to the penetrating power of spiritual concentration, as produced in the course of certain magic rites or in the long years of silent meditation to which Gomchens are accustomed in Tibet.

Thus, Tomo Géshé Rimpoché, when emerging from his twelve-year-long period of lonely meditation, had become a healer of such power that the *ribus* (pills) which he distributed freely to all those who came for his blessing were sought after all over Tibet and are nowadays more precious than pearls. When I received three of these *ribus* after my initiation Géshé Tubden Sherab, who had assisted me, begged me to share them with him, and related how in the case of a serious illness, when doctors had been unable to give him relief, he had been cured instantaneously by one of these *ribus.* Not realising at that time the deeper significance of the Guru's gift—thinking of it merely in terms of a medical remedy, of which I did not feel any great need at that time (besides having more faith in Western medicines)—I gave away two of these precious *ribus;* and since it never came to my mind to replace them on later occasions, when I could have asked for them, only one has remained in my possession. It was only many years later that I realised their value.

The following episode may illustrate the importance attached to these *ribus*. When returning from Western Tibet in 1949, together with Li Gotami, we were surprised to find a small but well-equipped Tibetan temple containing a full set of the Sacred Scriptures (*Kanjur* and *Tanjur*) as well as an enormous prayer-wheel, in Rampur, the capital of Bashar State, which was ruled by a Hindu Maharaja. Since the population of Rampur was purely Hindu, we were wondering who could have built and endowed this sanctuary, until we were informed that it was the Maharaja himself who had done it, in the fulfilment of a vow.

This is the story we were told: The Maharaja had been childless for many years, and without an heir his dynasty would have come to an end. Though he had consulted many learned Brahmins and performed various religious rites to propitiate the gods, he had not been blessed with an heir. One day a well-known Lama and his retinue passed through Rampur on a pilgrimage to Mount Kailas, and since his fame had spread wide and far and thousands of people came to have his *darshan*, the Maharaja invited him to his palace and, telling him of his predicament, promised to build a temple for Buddhist pilgrims and to furnish it with a complete set of Tibetan Sacred Scriptures if through the Lama's blessings an heir would be born to the throne.

The Lama promised his help, but he made one condition, namely that the Maharaja would provide him with a place where he could retire for meditation, perform the necessary rites, and prepare the consecrated *ribus* for the Maharaja and his consort. The Maharaja, thereupon, had a special pavilion built in the palace grounds and gave strict orders that nobody should be allowed to approach the pavilion or to disturb the Lama during the performance of his religious rites.

However, one of the servants could not master his curiosity, and in the darkness of night he crept to the door of the pavilion in order to peep through the keyhole and to find out what the Lama was doing there all by himself. Apparently he had heard of the 'wonderworking' *ribus* and wanted to explore the secrets of their composition, as it was said that they contained many precious substances, obtained from supernatural sources. But when he managed to peep inside the pavilion he beheld the Lama, surrounded by a host of super-human beings, celestial as well as demonical, so that he fainted with fright. People found him the next morning at the foot of the steps leading to the entrance of the pavilion. When he came to himself he was raving as if in a fever and died within a few hours. After this, nobody dared to approach the pavilion, and for many days and nights the Lama was absorbed in his devotions. Only the sounds of bell and *damaru* and of the Lama's sonorous incantations were heard from time to time.

On the appointed day the Lama emerged from the pavilion, gave his blessings and the consecrated *ribus* to the Maharaja and his consort—and before the year was out an heir was born to them. In gratitude to the saintly Lama, the Maharaja fulfilled his vow and built the promised temple. He sent a special delegation to Tibet to have the Sacred Scriptures printed and to fetch the necessary altar-vessels and whatever else was necessary for the completion of the temple and the performance of religious services.

After having paid a visit to the temple, we were inspecting the beautiful Tibetan pavilion in the palace grounds, in which the Lama had lived during his retreat. We asked the caretaker, who showed us around, whether he remembered the name of the Lama. His answer was: 'Tomo Géshé Rimpoché.'

All along the road from Tibet we heard miraculous stories about the pilgrimage of Tomo Géshé Rimpoché, who had given new faith and hope to thousands of people, and who had healed the sick and encouraged the downtrodden. In the village of Poo, on the Tibetan frontier, a dying girl was brought to him on a stretcher. She had been ill for a long time and her condition was such that her people were afraid to carry her, lest she might die on the way. However, the villagers had such faith in the powers of Tomo Géshé that they persuaded the girl's parents to take the risk. When they arrived with the stretcher at the Lama's place almost the whole village was assembled there.

Under their very eyes, at the command of Tomo Géshé, the girl opened her eyes, got up from the stretcher, and after having received the blessings of the Lama she walked out of the house as if she had never been ill. The girl was still alive during our stay at Poo, and numerous eyewitnesses vouchsafed for the truth of this event. We had no reason to doubt these reports—even if Tomo Géshé had not been our own Guru—because there was hardly a place through which he had passed during that memorable pilgrimage where people did not speak about him with veneration and glowing eyes—though many long years had passed since then—and the Guru himself had given up his body in the meantime.

Though popular imagination may have woven a veil of legends over many of the actual events, the fact of his healing powers and the tremendous impact of his personality upon the people stood out clearly and unmistakably from all the stories that came to our ears. Even during his lifetime he had become a legend, but to all those who had come into actual contact with him it became clear that there is more truth in the legends growing around a saint's life than our critical intellect may suspect, and that even in our times saints are walking the face of the earth—just as in the day of Buddha Śākyamuni or Christ, Mohammed or St. Francis of Assisi.

The example of Tomo Géshé Rimpoché shows convincingly that even those who go through the most severe practices of yoga training, living in complete solitude for years on end, do not thereby lose their inner bonds with their fellow-beings, nor their functions and usefulness in human society. Indeed, they played a far greater role and had a deeper influence on the spiritual life of Tibet than those who were exclusively engaged in verbal teaching or literary work.

In Tibet the function of a religious teacher is not so much the proclamation of a doctrine or the elucidation of the commonly accepted teachings of traditional Buddhism but the demonstration that the highest religious aims can be realised and that the ways towards their attainment are practicable. Even a silent hermit may act like a beacon of spiritual light in the darkness of ignorance and illusion. The very fact of his existence, the very fact that he *can* exist in the light of his own inner realisation, is sufficient to give courage and confidence to others.

Solitary confinement is regarded as the greatest punishment for the average individual. The untrained mind breaks down under the weight of prolonged confinement in solitude. Those who emerge unscathed from such an ordeal prove that they possess an unusual reserve of strength. Such strength, however, is not a matter of physical or mental robustness, but of a spiritual self-sufficiency that presupposes an unusually rich and active mind and a discipline that can only be acquired through a long and careful training.

Tibetans, therefore, are right when they show greater trust and respect to those who have proved their moral and spiritual strength in a solitary life of meditation and religious practice than to those who are merely good speakers or clever intellects. Only a man who knows how to unlock the treasures of the inner world can dare to renounce the outer one. To do this he must have the key that unlocks these treasures, and this key consists in the practice of his *sādhanā,* in which he has been trained under the guidance of his Guru.

Through the Guru's *mantra* he remains in touch with him and with the hierarchy of his spiritual predecessors; through his *sādhanā* he enters into contact with the inner world. And slowly, bit by bit, this inner world unfolds itself, takes on greater and greater reality, and finally surrounds him like a celestial *maṇḍala,* in whose centre he experiences a bliss that surpasses all the pleasures of the world which he left outside his cubicle or his cave.

There is no time for him to be idle. His days are filled—not in passive waiting for death or for visions to come—but in the creation, consolidation, and re-integration of a new world, built from the universal and ever-present form-elements of a deeper and vaster reality. In the process of this creative activity the adept frees himself from the last traces of attachment or clinging to any particular form or *'Gestalt',* because the whole orchestra of creative possibilities is at his disposal, and as little as a great conductor will cling to any phase of his creations—because he is their master and can produce them whenever he will—so the adept will know himself as the sovereign creator of all forms and at the same time the silent centre of the universe.

9

The Hermit Abbot of Lachen

FROM THE FOREGOING chapters it will be clear that the deepest sources of inspiration are not the big monasteries or the great monastic colleges and universities (like Sera, Drepung, and Ganden, the greatest seats of learning in Tibet), but the humble hermitages, tucked away in the folds and cracks of mighty mountains, or in lonely valleys and in inaccessible canyons, or perched on high cliffs like eagles' nests, or scattered over the solitudes of remote highlands and along the shores of placid lakes, far away from the tracks of caravans and the noise of trading camps and market-towns.

It was in these hermitages that saints and sages of Tibet found their inspiration, and it is to these hermitages that those who want to tread the path of wisdom and liberation return again and again. It is for this reason that every monastery possesses a number of isolated cubicles for meditation, as well as mountain retreats (*ri-khrod,* pron. 'ritö') and hermitages.

The greatest hermit of Tibet was the poet-saint and yogi Milarepa (Mi-la-ras-pa), who spent the larger part of his life in caves and in the most inaccessible mountain fastnesses—and up to the present day his followers (in the Kargyütpa Order) lay greater stress on silence and meditation than on book knowledge and learned discussions. His life is perhaps the best example for the profound influence that even the most unworldly hermit may exert upon the world at large. His contributions to the cultural and religious life of Tibet are unrivalled in their originality and spontaneity, their beauty and their sense of dedication.

An outstanding example among modern hermits is the Abbot of Lachen, better known as 'the Gomchen of Lachen', who had his hermitage on the border between Northern Sikkim and Tibet. The Earl of Ronaldshay (later Marquis of Zetland), a former Governor of Bengal, has written admiringly about the Gomchen: 'Over a period of twenty-six years he had been in the habit of retiring from the world from time to time and living a life of solitary meditation in a remote cave—high up and difficult of access, among the cliffs of an inhospitable mountain tract above the path to Thangu. One of those periodic retirements from the world had been extended over a period of five years, during which time he had seen no human being and had kept body and soul together on a minimum of food.'

This was written almost thirty years ago, in the book *Lands of the Thunderbolt,* in which the Earl of Ronaldshay describes his conversation with the Gomchen, from which he had the impression that the latter had reached the state of liberation. 'This at least is certain', he added, 'the motive which impels men to leave their fellows, and for years on end, spurning the weakness of the flesh, to live a life of solitary confinement, must be an extraordinary powerful one. That such lives excite admiration and respect is equally certain.'

People may ask whether such tremendous effort and achievement would not have benefited the world more if the hermit had returned to the haunts of man and propagated the wisdom which he had acquired. This would have been in keeping with the example of many other spiritual leaders. But the hermit's way was different.

One day a Western scholar approached his cave and asked to be admitted as a *chela* (disciple). The hermit pointed to another cave in the vicinity and answered: 'Only if you will stay in that cave for three years without a break.' The *chela* accepted this condition and stayed on for three years, enduring patiently the hardships and utter isolation of three Himalayan winters with arctic temperatures.

The *chela* was none other than the famous French Orientalist and explorer Alexandra David-Neel, whose books on Tibet were so outstanding that they were translated into all the major languages of the world. The profound knowledge that informed these books, which for the first time gave an objective account of hitherto unknown spiritual practices and psychic phenomena, were the direct outcome of these three years of study and meditation under the Great Hermit, who thus—with unfailing certainty—had chosen the right medium for broadcasting his message over the entire world, without himself ever leaving his far-off retreat among the snows of the Himalayas. With this 'message' I do not mean a message of any personal nature or the propagation of any particular doctrine, but a message which opened the eyes of the world to the hitherto hidden spiritual treasures of Tibetan religious culture. If the Gomchen had not had this aim at heart he would never have consented to be Alexandra David-Neel's Guru and to spend three years in teaching her all that which enabled her to enter Tibet and its inner life. One of the main gains of her life in the solitude of those years has been expressed by her in the following significant words: 'Mind and senses develop their sensibility in this contemplative life made up of continual observations and reflections. Does one become a visionary or, rather, is it not that one has been blind until then?'

This is really the crux of the matter: the contemplative hermit, far from closing his eyes and being dead to the world, opens them and becomes wide awake; far from blunting his senses, he develops a higher awareness and a deeper insight into the real nature of the world and of his own mind. And this shows him that it is as foolish to run *away* from the world as to run *after* the world: both extremes having their root in the illusion that the 'world' is something separate from ourselves. It is this lesson which the Gomchen taught his disciple, a lesson which in the philosophical language of Buddhism is based on the mystery of *śūnyatā*, the inconceivable nature of the Plenum-Void. It is the same lesson which he taught me—though in a very different way—when I visited him in his mountain retreat near Thangu, at an altitude of about 13,000 feet in the Central Himalayas. The Maharaja of Sikkim, whose guest I was during my stay in Sikkim in 1937, had been kind enough to give me his own men and horses, to equip my little caravan with all necessary provisions, and to allow me to make use of all rest-houses and monasteries in which I might choose to stay on my journey to the northern extremity of his realm in order to meet the Great Hermit. It had been my ardent desire to meet him, and as he was already over seventy years old, I felt that there was no time to lose. I did not mind a two weeks' journey on horseback through the most mountainous region of the world (Sikkim is said to have the greatest number of mountains above 24,000 feet compared to any other area in the world of similar size), if thereby I would have a chance to meet face to face a man who had such a profound influence on the spiritual life of his country. I even did not mind the risk of finding his hermitage closed against any visitor, as it happened so often when he was engaged in a long period of meditation. A further risk was that the winter was fast approaching, and, indeed, the day before I had set out on the last stage of the journey a heavy snowfall had almost blocked the road. I was warned to wait until yaks could be procured, since the horses might not be able to negotiate the snow-drifts. But I was impatient of further delay, feeling that it was a matter of now or never, and so I pushed on and succeeded in getting through, in spite of all obstacles.

I put up in a horribly cold and draughty wooden rest-house not far below the hermitage of the Gomchen, and since it was too cold and too late to do anything else, I retired as soon as possible, hoping to meet the hermit in the course of the next morning.

But before I could fall asleep a strange thing happened: I had the sensation that somebody took possession of my consciousness, my will-power and my body—that I had no more control over my thoughts, but that somebody else was thinking them—and that, slowly but surely, I was losing my own identity. And then I realised that it could be none other than the hermit, who, by directing his attention upon me, had entered my body and taken possession of it, probably quite unintentionally, due to the power of his concentration and my own lack of resistance in the moment while I was hovering between the waking and the sleeping state. There was nothing aggressive in his presence—on the contrary, it gave me some kind of satisfaction and a sense of wonder to yield to its irresistible magnetism and growing power.

I felt like a meteor, drawn into the orbit of a bigger celestial body—until it dawned upon me that once I allowed myself to 'fall' without reserve, the impact would be my inevitable end. And then, suddenly, a terror seized me, the terror that neither this body nor this mind would be mine any more, the terror of losing my own identity for good, and of being pushed out of my own body, irrevocably: the indescribable, inexpressible fear of emptiness—to be blown out like a candle—to fall into the Nameless Void, a void from which there could be no return!

And with a last effort of self-preservation, by the very strength of this terror, I jerked myself from my bed on to my feet and, struggling tenaciously against the power that still seemed to hold me, I lit a candle, grabbed my drawing-board and a piece of charcoal (which I always kept handy during the journey), and, in order to assure myself of my own reality, I started frantically to draw a self-portrait in front of my shaving-mirror. No matter that the temperature in the room was below freezing-point—I had to do something and do it quickly! And as I got into the work the strange power left me! When the sketch was finished I had regained my self-control, went to bed, and slept peacefully until next morning.

After breakfast I climbed up to the hermitage, where the Gomchen received me with a friendly smile. After exchanging the usual polite questions and sipping hot Tibetan butter-tea, which he poured into my wooden cup from the eternally simmering teapot, I told him how deeply I was impressed by his *chela's* works, and that I had often wondered how she had been able to endure the hardships of an anchorite's life for so many years. He beamed when I mentioned her name, enquired about her whereabouts, and brought out an old yellowed newspaper cutting with Alexandra David-Neel's picture on it, recalling the time of her discipleship and praising her endurance and strength of character.

He asked me about my own Guru, and when he learned that it was Tomo Géshé Rimpoché (who at that time had already passed away), he took my Guru's small Buddha-image, which I had been showing him, from my hands and reverently placed it on his head. 'He was a great Lama,' he said, 'a very great Lama!'

When I told him about my earlier training in Ceylon he laughingly pointed to his pigtail and asked me what the Buddhists in the South would think of him, since he had never shaved his head and had been a married man throughout his life, though his wife had died many years ago. 'Well,' I said, joining in his laughter, 'even the Buddha had a wife and child and never shaved his head; and yet he attained Enlightenment within the same life! I But you are right—most people judge by appearances and external circumstances. They do not know that it is not the robe or the shaven head but the overcoming of selfish desires that make a saint.'

'And the knowledge that springs from the experience of ultimate reality in meditation,' the Gomchen added. 'Mere goodness and morality without wisdom is as useless as knowledge without goodness.'

This brought us to the subject of meditation and its various methods and experiences, and in this connection I was almost on the point of mentioning the happenings of the previous night. But as I felt slightly ashamed of my terror, when faced with the experience of falling into the abysmal void, I let the opportunity pass and merely asked him to write some suggestions in my meditation booklet, which for many years had served me as a kind of breviary during my journeys.

He hesitated a moment, saying that he was old and that his hand was no more steady, but then, suddenly taking a bamboo-pen and dipping it into his home-made ink, he filled a page with Tibetan characters.

'There!' he said. 'Here is your subject for meditation: *The Eighteen Kinds of Voidness!'*

So he was aware of what had happened to me the previous night and what I had tried to hide! I was deeply moved. And when leaving the Great Hermit, after having received his blessings, I felt that I had not only met him in the flesh but in the spirit: in a manner which revealed both his spiritual power and his human kindness.

I was never to see him again—for he soon followed my own Guru. But whenever I contemplate the self-portrait which I did on that memorable night I know that it is not only myself but the Hermit as well—and that, though it seems to have my features, it looks at me with the eyes of him who had realised the Great Void.

Thus my journey had not been in vain, and I returned with gratitude in my heart—both towards the Gomchen as well as towards the Maharaja, who had made this journey possible for me and who, in doing so, expressed his own high esteem and veneration for the Great Hermit. I shall never forget the peace of his hermitage amidst the eternal snows and the lesson he taught me: that we cannot face the Great Void before we have the strength and the greatness to fill it with our entire being. Then the Void is not the negation merely of our limited personality, but the Plenum-Void which includes, embraces, and nourishes it, like the womb of space in which the light moves eternally without ever being lost.

10

Miraculous Escape and Floating Lights

Before returning to Gangtok I visited the Maharaja's monastery of Podang. The old abbot, a man with a remarkably beautiful and spiritualised face, remembered Alexandra David-Neel from the time she had stayed in this monastery. I occupied the same room in which she had lived and where a strange voice had warned the young Maharaja (the predecessor of the Maharaja Tashi Namgyal, who ruled at that time) of his impending end and the failure of his intended religious reforms. Like many young men with Westernised ideas, he felt it his duty to free his country from what he thought mere superstitions, without realising that this would only have resulted in the disruption of all traditional values.

That these were still alive, though perhaps hidden under the weeds of popular beliefs and customs (as only natural in a country inhabited to the greater part by primitive jungle-folk), became apparent to me when meeting the learned Bermiak Rimpoché, the brother of the Maharaja's private secretary, the Kazi of Bermiak. Both the Rimpoché and his brother (with whom I have been connected through bonds of friendship for many years) convinced me that if any religious reform was necessary in their country it could only spring from a reassessment of those cultural and traditional values upon which Tibetan Buddhism was based, but never through the introduction of alien ways of thinking, even though they might be nearer to the historical sources of Buddhism. But historical facts and considerations never play any decisive role in religious life, which depends far more on experience and creative imagination than on abstract 'truths' and logical thoughts. The legendary figure of the Buddha, as conceived in the minds of poets and devotees, the very image of the Buddha, as created by countless generations of artists and as a result of inner vision and contemplation, has had a far greater influence on the development and life of Buddhism than all philosophical theories which tried to interpret religious experience in terms of rational thinking, systems, and laws. Such interpretations were not without value; on the contrary, they are a necessity for the thinking mind, whose function it is to experience and reason.

On the way to Podang my trip almost came to a bad end. During the steep ascent to the monastery through tropical jungle I had dismounted from my horse, a lovely white steed, which, as the syce had told me, was the Maharaja's own riding horse, and had it led behind me together with the horse of my personal attendant (cook-bearer) who had likewise dismounted. The path was narrow, leading along yawning precipices and deep gorges. I therefore had warned the syce to be careful and to lead the horses one behind the other. For some time everything went smoothly and I enjoyed the wild scenery of rocks and jungle, but when the path made a turn at a particularly precipitous corner, and I was just about to give another warning to the syce, I found, when looking back, that the horses were walking side by side. But before I could open my mouth the horse which was on the inner side of the bend pushed the Maharaja's white horse over the edge.

I was almost frozen with terror when I saw the white form disappear into the gorge, and the cries of the syce confirmed my worst fears—the horse was lost! I rushed back to the spot from where it had fallen, steeling myself for the horrible sight of the poor creature's mangled body at the bottom of the gorge. What would the Maharaja say and what would happen to the syce, through whose negligence all this had happened? Weeping and lamenting, he had meanwhile started to climb into the gorge and I myself hurried after him. Halfway down we saw the white body of the horse caught in a clump of bamboo and precariously dangling over the lower part of the precipice. It did not stir, as if conscious that one wrong movement would hurtle it to its death—or was it that the legs were broken? The suspense until we reached the place was almost unbearable, and equally indescribable was our relief and joy when we found that the creature was hale and hearty, and not a limb was broken or hurt. We all felt that a miracle had happened—and it was almost as great a miracle that we succeeded in getting the horse off from its precarious perch and out of the gorge. With a prayer of thanks in our hearts we continued our ascent, and when the monks of Podang heard what had happened they praised the invisible protectors who had so obviously saved us from disaster.

On my return to Gangtok, where the Maharaja had put the Maharani's residence, Dilkusha, at my disposal, since the Maharani was staying in her retreat a few miles outside Gantok, I utilised the opportunity to study many valuable details of Tibetan art and ritual in the beautiful new temple near the Palace, as well as to have certain text copied from manuscripts and block-prints at Enché Gompa. The monks in both these places were very friendly and helpful. I also had special recommendations from Enché Kazi, a Sikkimese nobleman, to whose family estate the last-mentioned monastery and temple belonged.

I had lived in his house as a guest during my first stay at Gangtok in 1932 during my first short trip to Tibet. Both he and his wife had been very kind to me and had accepted me in their house as if I were a member of their family. It was on this occasion that I learned that in this very same house Lama Yongden had lived and served as a young boy, thus earning his livelihood and his education, since he came from a poor family. Enché Kazi and his wife were greatly surprised when I told them of Yongden's career as a Lama and traveller and the fame he had earned as a collaborator and co-author with Mme David-Neel. It was in Enché

Kazi's house that she had met him and decided to take him with her with the Kazi's consent. It was a decision that completely changed Yongden's as well as her own life and helped to make Tibet known to millions of readers all over the world. Future events showed that Enche Kazi's house was indeed a place in which destinies were shaped.

On the day of my departure from Gangtok, the Maharaja had arranged for an early lunch on the veranda of his palace, and I was delighted to find that the table was laid only for the two of us, and that thus I had an opportunity of having an informal and quiet talk with His Highness on religious matters. It was a lovely day, and while looking out over the valleys and mountains, spread out before us in all their dazzling beauty, I pointed to a far-away range of hills, where I had observed bright lights moving about at great speed during the previous night, when sitting on the veranda of Dilkusha.

'I never knew that there was a motorable road in those hills,' I said, 'or is it that a new road is under construction there?'

The Maharaja looked at me with surprise.

'What makes you think so? There is no road whatever, nor is there any project to build one. The only motorable road that exists in my country is the one by which you came from the Tista Valley.'

I then told His Highness about the swift-moving lights, which I had seen gliding over that range and which I had taken for the headlights of motor-vehicles.

The Maharaja smiled, and then, lowering his voice, he said: 'Many strange things happen here, and I generally do not like to speak about them to outsiders, because they would only think me superstitious. But since you have seen it with your own eyes, I may tell you that these lights have no human origin. They move about over the most difficult ground with an ease and speed that no human being could attain, apparently floating in the air. Nobody has yet been able to explain their nature, and I myself have no theory about them, though the people of my country believe them to be a kind of spirit. However that may be, the fact is that I have seen them moving right through the palace grounds towards the site where now the temple stands. This was always a sanctified place, and some people say that there had also been a cremation-place or a cemetery here.'

Feeling that the Maharaja had touched on something that meant more to him than he liked to say, I did not press him further, confining myself to the assurance that, far from ridiculing the beliefs of the people, I respected their attitude in trying to give a higher significance to the many inexplicable phenomena that surround us, instead of looking upon them as meaningless mechanical processes devoid of any connection with animated life. Why should physical laws be regarded as an antithesis of conscious life if our own corporeality shows itself as a compromise of spiritual and physical forces, of matter and mind, of the laws of nature and the freedom of the individual? Our consciousness makes use of electric currents in nerves and brain, thoughts emit vibrations similar to those of wireless transmitters and can be received over vast distances by sensitive conscious organisms. Do we really know what electricity is? By knowing the laws according to which it acts and by making use of them we still do not know the origin or the real nature of this force, which ultimately may be the very source of life, light, and consciousness, the divine power and mover of all that exists. It is the ultimate mystery of protons, neutrons, and electrons of modern science, before which the human intellect stands as helpless as the primitive tribesman before the visible phenomena of nature. We certainly have no reason to look down upon the animistic beliefs of primitive man, which only express what the poets of all times have felt: that nature is not a dead mechanism, but vibrant with life, with the same life that becomes vocal in our thoughts and emotions.

The phenomenon of floating lights has also been observed on the sacred mountain of Wu T'ai Shan in China, whose Tibetan name is Ri-bo-rtse-lnga, 'the mountain of the five peaks', dedicated to the Embodiment of Wisdom, the Dhyāni-Bodhisattva Mañjuśrī. On the southern peak of this mountain there is a tower from which pilgrims can have an unimpeded view. However, this tower is not meant to admire the landscape, but to give the pilgrims an opportunity to witness a strange phenomenon, which many people suppose to be a manifestation of the Bodhisattva himself.

A vivid description of this phenomenon has been given by John Blofeld, who spent many months on the sacred mountain: 'We reached the highest temple during the late afternoon and gazed with great interest at a small tower built upon the topmost pinnacle about a hundred feet above us. One of the monks asked us to pay particular attention to the fact that the windows of this tower overlooked mile upon mile of empty space. Shortly after midnight, a monk, carrying a lantern, stepped into our room and cried: "The Bodhisattva has appeared!" The ascent to the door of the tower occupied less than a minute. As each one entered the little room and came face to face with the window beyond, he gave a shout of surprise, as though all our hours of talk had not sufficiently prepared us for what we now saw. There in the great open spaces beyond the window, apparently not more than one or two hundred yards away, innumerable balls of fire floated majestically past. We could not judge their size, for nobody knew how far away they were. Where they came from, what they were, and where they went after fading from sight in the West nobody could tell. Fluffy balls of orange-coloured fire, moving through space, unhurried and majestic—truly a fitting manifestation of divinity!"[1]

---

1. *The Wheel of Life,* Rider & Co. (London, 1959), p. 549 f.

PART THREE

Death and Rebirth

I

The Guru's Passing Away

Returning from Gangtok, I stayed in Tomo Géshé Rimpoché's private apartments at Yi-Gah Chö-Ling. It was as if time had stood still in the little shrine-room which I inhabited and in which nothing had changed since my first meeting with the Guru. His seat, with his heavy cloak carefully arranged on it in an upright position, looked as if he had just stepped out of it, and on the *chogtse* in front of the seat stood his jade cup filled with tea, together with his ritual implements, such as *vajra,* bell, and rice-vessel. The central butter-lamp before the carved shrine with the golden image of Dölma burned with its steady, timeless flame, which Kachenla, undeterred by age and cheerful as ever, tended with loving care.

To him the Guru was ever present, and daily he would prepare his seat, shake and refold his robe, fill up his teacup (before he would sip his own tea), polish and replenish the water-bowls and butter-lamps, light the incense-sticks, recite the formulas of worship and dedication, and sit in silent meditation before the shrines, thus performing all the duties of a religious life and of a devoted disciple. Serving the Guru was to him the highest form of divine service—it was equal to serving the Buddha.

Not a speck of dust was allowed to settle on the seats and *chogtses* or on the carvings of the shrines and altars. The floor looked like a mirror, and the *thankas* and the lovely brocades, in which they were mounted, had lost none of their softly vibrating colours. The handwoven rugs on the low seats, the wall-hangings above them, the dark brown cloth that was stretched across the ceiling, and the silken canopies above the Guru's seat and the main shrines, edged by rainbow-coloured volants, gave me the feeling of being in the tent or 'yurt' of a nomad-patriarch or ruler of old, somewhere in Central Asia—far away from our present world and time. I could feel in this room the traditions of a millennium, intensified and sublimated through the personality that filled this place with its living presence.

A similar feeling had assailed me during our last meeting at Sarnath, when the whole place had been turned into a Tibetan encampment, and at night the camping-ground under the mango-trees was illuminated with countless oil-lamps in honour of Tomo Géshé and his retinue. He himself was staying in a big tent in the centre of the mango-grove, and in the soft light of the oil-lamps and the glow of camp-fires, whose smoke was hanging like transparent veils between the trees and the tents, the grove seemed to me transformed into an oasis far away in the heart of Asia, with a caravan of pilgrims resting after a long desert journey. It was indeed one of the last stages in the Guru's life-journey—a leavetaking from the sacred places of the Buddha's earthly career. It was Tomo Géshé's last pilgrimage to India in 1935-6, accompanied by many of his disciples and received everywhere with great enthusiasm, though he himself shunned all personal honours and public attention.

When passing through Calcutta on his way back to Yi-Gah Chö-Ling and to Tibet, the papers in Calcutta carried the following report: 'A famous Lama, who ranks fourth after the Dalai Lama, is staying in Calcutta at present. The Venerable Geshey Rim-po-che is on his way to Tibet after completing his pilgrimage to the Buddhist sacred places in

North India. Supernatural powers are ascribed to the seventy-one-year-old Lama. He spends the greater part of his time reading the sacred texts, discoursing with his disciples, or being absorbed in meditation. He shuns the public, hardly ever leaves his room, and is said never to sleep. He is accompanied by a retinue of forty Lamas. They visited Sarnath, Gaya, and Rajgir. In Sarnath he and his retinue dwelled in tents.'

The idea that Tomo Géshé never slept was caused by the fact that—as I mentioned before—he never used to lie down, but remained in the posture of meditation all through the night, thus never losing control over his body even in sleep, which, according to the highest form of meditational practice, becomes a natural continuation of *sādhanā* on a different level of consciousness. Though there is no doubt that Tomo Géshé's spiritual powers were far above those of the ordinary (i.e. untrained) man, he would have protested against the term 'supernatural' and still more against giving publicity to such things. In fact, when reporters tried to satisfy their curiosity about magic powers and mystic rituals in Tibetan Buddhism he broke off the conversation, pointing out that these things would not help them in understanding the essential teachings of the Buddha.

Thus the reporters had to content themselves with the externals of the pilgrimage, which was organised and led by Sardar Bahadur Ladenla, who had served the thirteenth Dalai Lama in various capacities and had been given by him the rank of General. They mentioned that Tomo Géshé and Ladenla had gilded the Buddha-image in the new temple of Sarnath as an act of devotion, and that the Maharaja of Bhutan had sent with them a beautifully worked canopy of silver for the image.

I found this newspaper report in the diaries of Baron von Veltheim-Ostrau, who personally paid a visit to Tomo Géshé Rimpoché during his stay in Calcutta on the 2nd of February 1936. Due to the many visitors who tried to see the Lama, he was not able to talk to him. 'In the midst of people's goings and comings he [the Lama] was the only resting pole. He was seated on a rug, smiling and silent. The old man made an extremely dignified impression, ripe with knowledge and wisdom, like one who was already approaching the state of transfiguration.'

And this, indeed, was the case, because the ultimate phase in Tomo Géshé's life and his conscious transition into a new one, which took place the following year, was truly a 'state of transfiguration', a triumph over death.

Kachenla told me all that had happened during the Guru's last days; and later on, in 1947 during a visit at Dungkar, Tomo Géshé's main monastery in the Tomo Valley of South Tibet, we heard the details about his passing away from those who had been present. The Guru had made it known that he would soon leave his body, which had become a burden to him. 'But,' he said, 'there is no reason for you to feel sad. I do not forsake you, nor my work for the Dharma; but instead of dragging on in an old body, I shall conic back in a new one. I promise to return to you. You may look out for me within three or four years.'

Not long after this announcement he retired for a longer spell of meditation and gave instructions to be left undisturbed, though he remained in his usual quarters within the monastery. He soon entered a state of deep absorption and remained in it for many days. But when ten days had passed, and the Guru was still sitting motionless on his seat, his attendants began to be worried. One of them held a mirror near to his face, and when it was found that the surface of the mirror remained unclouded they realised that he had stopped breathing: he had left his body during his meditation and had consciously passed over the threshold between life and death—or, more correctly, between one life and another.

He had left his body, before death could snatch it away from him, and directed his consciousness towards a new germ of life, that would carry on the impetus of his will and form itself into a new instrument of the attainment of his ultimate aim and the fulfilment of his Bodhisattva Vow, which might be summarised in these words: 'Whatever be the highest perfection of the human mind, may I realise it for the benefit of all living beings. Even though I may have to take upon myself all the sufferings of the world, I will not forsake my aim and my fellow-creatures in order to win salvation for myself only.'

This vow is based on a deep understanding of the root of suffering and its cure. The root of suffering is man's egohood, which separates him from his fellow-beings and from the sources of reality. How can he overcome this suffering? 'Basically, there can only be two answers. One is to overcome separateness and to find unity by *regression* to the state of unity which existed before awareness ever arose, that is, before man was born. The other answer is to be *fully born,* to develop one s awareness, one's reason, one's capacity to love, to such a point that one transcends one's own egocentric involvement, and arrives at a new harmony, at a new oneness with the world.'[1]

The former is the way of the average Hindu mystic, especially the strict Vedantin, who wishes to return to the oneness of the uncreated *(brahman),* to dissolve his individual soul in the All-Soul. The latter is the way of the Bodhisattva, the way towards Buddhahood. The first is the way of asceticism and world-negation (world illusion), the second is the way of life-acceptance (of individual values) and world-transcendence, or world-transformation—because whether the world is experienced as *saṁsāra* or *nirvāṇa* depends on the spiritual development or state of realisation of the experiencing subject; it is not a quality of the world. It is for this reason that in the Mahāyāna, and even more so in the Vajrayāna of Tibet, *saṁsāra* is equated with *nirvāṇa.*

The purpose of Buddhist meditation, therefore, is not merely to sink back into the 'uncreated' state, into a state of complete tranquillisation with a vacant mind; it is not a regression into the 'unconscious' or an exploration of the past, but a process of *transformation,* of *transcendence,* in which we become fully conscious of the present, of the infinite powers and possibilities of the mind, in order to become masters of our own destiny, by cultivating those qualities which lead to the realisation of our timeless nature: to enlightenment. Thus, instead of contemplating a past that we cannot change, upon which we cannot have any more the slightest influence, meditation serves to sow the seeds of final liberation and to build already *now* the bodies of future perfection in the image of our highest ideals.

---

1. Erich Fromm, *Zen Buddism aid Psychoanalysis.* Allen & Unwin (London, 1960) p. 87.

2

TULKU

THE CREATION OF the 'image' of our highest ideals is the real 'magic', namely the power that acts, forms, and transforms. An ideal, therefore, can only act if it is represented by a symbol—not merely a conventional sign or a mere allegory, but a valid, living symbol that can be visualised, experienced, felt, and realised by our whole being. It is for this reason that Tibetan Buddhism lays such stress on visualisation of the symbols of Buddhahood—which are as numerous as its qualities—on the contemplation of images, *maṇḍalas, mantras,* etc. All these things are not so much objects of worship but aids, instruments of visualisation, through which the *sādhaka* becomes one with his ideal, is transformed into it, becomes its embodiment.

This is what first and foremost a *'tulku'* is meant to be. He is not a 'phantom',[1] nor an *'avatār'* of a god or a transcendental being that takes on human form. If, for instance, the Dalai Lama is regarded to be the

1. A translation based on a blindly philological interpretation of the Tibetan term *'sprul',* which means the power of transformation, the creative power of the mind, which can result in the formation of ephemeral phantom-forms as well as in material reality. Even this reality is 'real' only in the context of time, i.e. only in a relative sense.

tulku of Avalokiteśvara, it does not mean that a divine being, or a Buddha or Bodhisattva, has descended from heaven and appears in the shape of man, hut rather that a divine idea has been realised in a human being to such an extent that it has become its living embodiment. And having thus overcome the limitations of a merely individual existence by realising its universal background, or, as we might say, its eternal source, a *tulku* reaches beyond the frontiers of death by establishing a conscious continuity between his consecutive lives.

This continuity enables him not only to utilise the fruits of his former knowledge and experience but to proceed consequently on his chosen path in the pursuit of enlightenment and in the service of his fellow-beings. According to the law of Karma none of our actions and thoughts is lost. Each of them leaves its imprint on our character, and the sum total of one life creates the basis for the next. But as long as people are not conscious of this continuity they will act only in conformity with their momentary necessities, desires, and petty aims, identifying themselves with their present personality and span of life, thus floundering from existence to existence without direction and therefore without a chance of ever breaking the chain reaction of cause and effect.

Only if we realise that it is in our hands to bridge the chasm of death and to determine and direct the course of our future life in such a way that we can pursue or accomplish in it what we regard our highest task, then only can we give depth and perspective to our present existence and to our spiritual aspirations. The torn and tortured human being of our time, who knows neither his infinite past, nor the infinity of his future, because he has lost the connection with his timeless being, is like a man suffering from incurable amnesia, a mental disease which deprives him of the continuity of his consciousness and therefore of the capacity to act consistently and in accordance with his true nature. Such a man really dies, because he identifies himself with his momentary existence.

There is a well-known spiritual exercise in Tibet, practised by those who have been initiated into the Bardo-teachings (concerning the intermediate states of consciousness between life and death or between death and rebirth), which has the purpose of penetrating into the centre of our being, into which consciousness retreats in the moment of physical death, thus anticipating the experience of the transition from one life to another. It is not a question of calling up the past or anticipating the future, it has nothing to do with the remembrance of former lives or the divination of a future existence, it is the full recognition of that which is *present* already and in which the germs of future possibilities are contained. He who recognises them in their true nature obtains mastery over their hidden forces and can direct them in such a way that in the moment of death, when they are freed from their bodily bonds, they will maintain the given direction and ensure the conscious continuity of their directing impulse by projecting it into a new vessel of life.

While the ordinary, i.e. untrained, man is overtaken and overpowered by death, those who have brought both body and mind under control are capable of withdrawing from the body on their own accord, without undergoing the suffering of a physical death-struggle; in fact, without losing control of their body even in this decisive moment.

This was demonstrated in the case of Tomo Géshé's passing away by the fact that his body remained unchanged and erect in the posture of meditation even after he had left it. Nobody knows the exact day on which this happened. It may have been several days before the mirror was held before his face, because even after that the body remained in the same position for several weeks, as testified also by Mr. H. E. Richardson, the British Envoy to Lhasa at that time. A few weeks after he had heard of Tomo Géshé's death he was passing through the valley in which Dungkar Monastery is situated, and as he had known the Rimpoché during his lifetime, he interrupted his journey and rode up to the Gompa, which stands on an isolated hill in the middle of the fertile valley. He was very politely greeted by the abbot, who, before he could even express his condolences, told him that the Rimpoché was glad to receive him. Somewhat taken aback and wondering whether he had perhaps been misinformed about Tomo Géshé's passing away, he followed the abbot to the Rimpoché's private apartments. How great was his surprise when entering the room to find Tomo Géshé sitting in his usual seat. Before he could give vent to his astonishment he realised that it was only the Rimpoché's body, though the abbot seemed to have a different idea about it, since he acted exactly as if he were in the living presence of the Rimpoché. Announcing Mr. Richardson's visit, he asked the latter to be seated and said—as if repeating the words of the Rimpoché's inaudible voice: 'The Rimpoché welcomes you and asks: have you had a good journey, and are you in good health?' And in this way a complete conversation ensued between the Rimpoché and Mr. Richardson, while tea was served, and everything seemed to be as usual, so that the visitor almost began to doubt his own senses. It was a most fantastic experience, and if Li and I had not heard it from Mr. Richardson's own lips, when we met at Gyantse a few years later, I would have found this difficult to believe.

It is hardly necessary to mention that it was not the abbot's intention to pretend to be in mediumistic contact with Tomo Géshé's spirit. He was simply acting in accordance with his conviction of the Guru's presence. As long as the sacred vessel of the Guru's mind—in the form of his body, which apparently was still controlled and kept upright by the power of his will—was present, the abbot had to treat it with the same respect which had been due to it during his lifetime.

It may be difficult for the Westerner to put himself into the feelings of a pious Tibetan, and still more to understand the attitude of those to whom life and death are not contradictory opposites, but only two sides of the same reality. It is due to this that Tibetans show far less fear of death than most other people. The necromantic aspects of prehistoric religions and their survival in certain traditions and rituals of Tibetan Buddhism—in which the symbols of death, like skulls, skeletons, corpses, and all aspects of decay and dissolution, are impressed upon the human mind—are not means to create disgust for life but means to gain control over the dark forces which represent the reverse side of life. We have to make ourselves familiar with them, because they have power over us only as long as we fear them. To propitiate the dark forces does not mean to pacify them or to bribe them, but to give them a place in our own mind, to fit them into the order of the universe of our experience, to accept them as a necessary part of reality, which teaches us not to get attached to any particular form of appearance and thus liberates us from bodily bondage.

I do not know how long the body of the Guru remained in his seat. I only remember that the Abbot of Dungkar and all who had been present stressed the fact that the body had shown no signs of decay and that many weeks (if not months) had passed before the entombment took place.

When a person has attained a high degree of realisation or, as we may say, saintliness, it is assumed that the material components of the body have been transformed to a certain degree by being saturated with psychic forces, which continue to exert a beneficial influence on their surroundings, and especially on those who open themselves to those influences on account of their devotional attitude and sincere faith. The same forces are believed to retard the natural decay of the body—a fact that has been observed also among the saints of other religions (even under the most unfavourable circumstances in tropical climates, as in the case of St Francis Xavier of Goa). The world-wide belief in the value of relics is based on such facts as well as on the above-mentioned belief in the psychometric qualities of matter under the impact of great spiritual forces.

It is for this reason that the bodies of saints and great Lamas (like the Dalai and Panchen Lamas) are not cremated or otherwise disposed of, but preserved in reliquaries of gold and silver in the form of *chortens*. Such a *chorten* was built for Tomo Géshé too, and its magnificence is as much a monument to Tomo Géshé's spiritual attainments as to the love and veneration in which the people of Tibet held him. As soon as his passing away became known, thousands of people from near and far streamed to Dungkar Gompa to pay their last respects and to bring gifts of gold and silver and precious stones as a contribution to the memory of the great Guru. Even the poorest insisted on adding their share: some of them would give their turquoise ear-ornaments, or their rings and silver bangles, others their coral beads and necklaces; some would even give their silver charm-boxes studded with precious stones—nothing was too good or too great a sacrifice for such a great cause: to create a worthy shrine, which would remind future generations of the great Guru and would make them partake of his spirit's lingering presence. The people's enthusiasm seemed to know no bounds. The amount of gifts in the form of valuables, money, and ornaments was so great that a two-storey-high *chorten* of silver was built, embossed with golden scroll work, studded with coral, turquoise, onyx, agate, lapis-lazuli, garnet, topaz, and amethyst and the like. The best gold- and silversmiths were employed to create a work of great beauty and perfection.

The lower part of the *chorten* was big enough to form a room, in which the mummified body of Tomo Géshé could be enthroned in full regalia and with all his ritual implements on a little table *(chogtse)* before him, as in life. The *chorten* was housed in a specially built high-ceilinged hall, the walls of which were covered with beautiful frescoes of Buddhas, Bodhisattvas, and saints, among them the famous Eighty-four Accomplished Ones (Siddhas).

Before the body was prepared[1] for the final installation in the *chorten* a stylised yet life-like gilt statue was modelled after the actual body and features of the Guru by one of the traditional image-makers, and a replica was placed in the Lhakhang of each of Tomo Géshé's main monasteries, below and at the side of the central Maitreya statue, which he himself had erected during his lifetime. He is represented in the *Dharma-desana-mudrā,* the gesture of 'showing the Dharma': the right hand is raised with the palm outwards, like in Amoghasiddhi's gesture of fearlessness and blessing, but thumb and forefinger are joined to form a circle—it is the gesture that indicates the highest form of blessing, the gift of truth, from which fearlessness is born.

---

1. The Tibetan method of mummification consists in draining all liquids from the body by keeping it for some time in a container closely packed with salt. In order to clean the inner organs, quicksilver is poured through the mouth. After the body is dried (in the posture of meditation) it is covered with bandages to ensure its steadiness and to give a grounding for a coating of clay or lacquer and gold, which converts it into a statue and makes it impervious to climatic influences.

3

REBIRTH

TOME GÉSHÉ RIMPOCHÉ had promised to return to his monastery and to his pupils in due time, and his promise came true. Little, however, did I think that his rebirth would take place in the very house in which I had been staying as a guest during my first trip to Tibet, the very same house which I revisited during my pilgrimage to the Great Hermit: the house of Enché Kazi at Gangtok. It was from his own mouth that I learned the details of Tomo Géshé's rebirth and of his discovery a few years later with the help of the great State Oracle in Lhasa.

Knowing Enché Kazi as a sincere and deeply religious man, I can vouchsafe for the truthfulness of his report of which Li Gotami also was a witness. In spite of the fact that he had reason to be proud of being the father of a *Tulku,* his story was tinged with sadness, because he had lost his wife soon after the child was born,[1] and a few years later, when it

1. It is a common belief in Tibet that a *Tulku's* mother generally dies soon after his birth, and I remember several cases where this was so—the present Dalai Lama being a great exception. Also the mother of Buddha Śākyamuni, Queen Maya, died a few days after she had given birth to the future Buddha.

became apparent that his son was none other than the rebirth of Tomo Géshé, he had to give up his only child. It was only in the face of overwhelming evidence and for the sake of the boy's happiness, who himself wanted to 'return to his monastery, that the father finally gave in and allowed him to be taken to Dungkar Gompa.

The Maharaja himself had pleaded with the father not to interfere with the boy's higher destiny, which was clearly indicated by the findings of the Great Oracle of Nächung and confirmed by the boy's own utterances and behaviour. The latter had always insisted that he was not Sikkimese but Tibetan, and when his father called him *'pu-chung'* (little son) he protested, saying that his name was Jigmé (the Fearless One). This was exactly the name which the Oracle at Lhasa had mentioned as the name under which Tomo Géshé would be reborn.

The fact that the State Oracle had been invoked shows how much importance was attached to the finding of Tomo Géshé's rebirth. Apparently the local oracle at Dungkar had not been able to give a clear indication or had advised the authorities to seek further clarification from Nächung. The latter, indeed, had been most specific by pointing out not only the direction where the child would be found but by giving a detailed description of the town and the locality in which he was born. From all these details it became clear that the town could only be Gangtok. Furthermore, the year in which the boy was born and the exact age of the father and the mother was given, as well as a description of the house in which they lived and of the trees that grew in the garden. Two fruit-trees, which stood in front of the house, were particularly pointed out as a characteristic feature of the place.

Thus, a delegation of monk-officials was sent to Gangtok, and armed with all these details they found the boy, who was then about four years old. As soon as the monks approached the house and entered the garden, the boy called out: 'Father, my people have come to take me back to my Gompa!' And he ran to meet them, jumping with joy—rather to the embarrassment of the father, who was not yet prepared to give up his only son. But the latter pleaded with his father to let him go, and when the monks spread out before him various monastic articles, like rosaries, *vajras,* bells, teacups, wooden bowls, *damarus,* and other things which are in daily use in religious rituals, he immediately picked out those objects which had belonged to him in his previous life, rejecting all those which had been deliberately mixed up with them—though some of them looked far more attractive than the genuine articles.

The father, who saw all these proofs and remembered the many signs of the boy's extraordinary intelligence and unusual behaviour which had often surprised him, was finally convinced and—though it was with a heavy heart—he finally gave his consent that the boy should go with the delegation to his monastery in Tibet.

On his journey to Dungkar Gompa the party met the Amchi, the Tibetan doctor who had treated Tomo Géshé during the last years of his life, and the boy, recognising him, called out: 'O Amchi, don't you know me? Don't you remember that you treated me when I was sick in my previous body?'

Also in Dungkar he recognised some of the older monks and, what was most remarkable, the little dog who had been his special favourite in the last days of his previous life recognised him immediately and was beside himself with joy at being reunited with his beloved master.

Thus Tomo Géshé had fulfilled his promise, and people again streamed from near and far to Dungkar Gompa to pay their respects to the Guru and to receive his blessings. The little boy impressed everybody with his self-assured and dignified behaviour when he sat on his throne in the great hall of the temple, conducting rituals, presiding over the recitations on festive occasions, or receiving pilgrims and blessing them—while otherwise he was natural and spontaneous like any other boy of his age. But during religious functions it was as if through the innocently pure and transparent features of the child the face of a man, mature in years and wisdom, could be seen. And soon it became clear that he had not forgotten the knowledge which he had acquired in his previous life. His education was nothing but a rehearsal of his former knowledge, and he progressed so quickly that soon there was nothing left that his tutors at Dungkar could teach him. Thus, at the age of seven he was sent to Sera, one of the great monastic universities near Lhasa, for higher studies and for obtaining again his degree of Doctor of Divinity (Géshé).

All this may appear incredible to the critical Westerner, and I admit that I myself would have found it difficult to believe had I not come across similar cases, which not only proved that the idea of rebirth was more than a mere theory or an unfounded belief, but equally demonstrated the possibility of remembering important aspects or achievements of former lives. The scientist who only believes in physical heredity never asks himself what the fact of heredity actually means. It is the principle of preservation and continuity of acquired characteristics which finally results in the faculty of conscious remembrance and conscious direction under the guidance of organised knowledge, i.e. through co-ordinated experience. Heredity, in other words, is only another name for memory, the stabilising principle and the counter-force of dissolution and impermanence. Whether we call memory a spiritual or a material property or a biological principle is beside the point, because 'material', 'biological', and 'spiritual' signify only different levels on which the same force operates or manifests itself. All that matters is that it is both a form-preserving as well as a form-creating force, the connecting link between the past and the future, which finally manifests itself in the experience of the timeless present and of conscious existence. The simultaneousness of preservation and creation is achieved in the process of continuous transformation, in which the essential elements or form-principles remain present like an ideal nucleus out of which new forms crystallise according to inherent laws and under the influence of external stimuli.

If, as is obvious, no physical or purely materialistic or scientific explanation is possible, and we have to admit that an unknown force is the agent that forms and determines the conception, formation, and development of a new physical body and its consciousness, according to the inherent directive impulse of that force—then nothing could be a more natural explanation than to ascribe this impulse to an already existing individualised consciousness, which in the moment of its release from its bodily basis (as in death) or from the dominance of physical functions (as in states of trance, or deep absorption and concentration) seizes the still undifferentiated, pliable, and receptive germ of life as the material basis of a new individual organism. Even if we want to take into account physical heredity, since the parents of a new being provide the 'material' out of which the new organism is formed, this would not contradict its capacity to respond to the impulse of a conscious force, especially if the latter is in tune with the qualities of the former or the circumstances under which the 'material' originated. It is not the material on which an organism feeds, or which it takes from its surroundings to build up its bodily frame, which determines its nature, but the formative force of consciousness (in its widest sense), which transforms the crude material. It goes without saying that there must also be a certain affinity between the assimilating organism and the material of which it makes use. If heredity would proceed in a purely biological manner through permutations of chromosomes and the like there would be no point in the development of an individual consciousness, capable of reflective thought and higher reason and the awareness of its own existence. The instinct of an animal would serve its purpose far better, and any mental development beyond this level would appear meaningless. 'Due to his reflecting mind, man has been lifted above the animal world and demonstrates through his mind that nature in him has put a high premium on the development of consciousness' (C. G. Jung). Indeed, the whole gigantic process of biological development through millions of years seems to have had no other purpose than to create the necessary conditions for the manifestation of higher consciousness.

To the Buddhist consciousness is *the* central factor, from which all other things proceed and without which we would neither have a notion of our own existence nor of a world around us. Whether the 'world around us' is a projection of our consciousness or something that exists in itself, and only appears to us in the form in which we experience it, is of secondary importance. It does not change the fact that it is our consciousness which by its selective faculties of perception and co-ordination determines the type of world in which we live. A different kind of consciousness would create a different world around us, whatever the existing—or non-existing—raw material of the universe may be. It is only in our consciousness that we get at the root of it, and only through our consciousness can we act upon it. We cannot change the world other than through our consciousness—which *is* the world as well as that which transcends it: *saṁsāra* and *nirvāṇa,* bondage and liberation.

Consciousness is based on two functions: awareness and the storing up (or preservation) of the fruits of experience, which we call memory. Consciousness as a storehouse of experience by far outweighs consciousness as awareness. While the latter is momentary and more or less limited to one object, the former is universal and not affected by time, persisting even while we are not aware of it. It is for this reason that the *Vijñānavādins* defined the deepest consciousness as *ālaya-vijñāna* or 'store-consciousness', in which not only the experiences of our present life, but those of all our 'ancestors', reaching back into the infinity of time and space, are preserved, and which therefore is ultimately a consciousness of universal character, connecting the individual with all that exists or ever has been in existence or may come into existence again.[1]

Consciousness is a living stream which cannot be caught in the vessel of a narrow ego, because its nature is that of movement, of flowing; and flow means continuity as well as the relationship between two levels or two poles. Without this polarity there can be no movement, no life, no awareness—and without continuity no meaningful relationship. The greater the distance or the difference between these two levels or poles, the more powerful is the stream or the force that results. The highest consciousness is the product of the widest range of experience: the amplitude between the poles of universality and individuality.

The average consciousness, however, is confined to the narrow circle of temporal aims and desires, so that the great flow is hampered and diverted, its energy scattered and the resulting light of awareness dimmed. When individuality thus loses its conscious relationship with universality and tries to become an end in itself by clinging to its momentary existence, the illusion of a changeless separate ego is created, the flow

---

1. Mere awareness without relationship to former experience, without the process of identification and co-ordination, is as futile as a merely automatic reaction (as found in lower forms of life). Systems of meditation, which claim to practise 'mere awareness', are pure self-deception, because it is impossible to be fully conscious of anything, without reference to previous experience; and even, if this were possible, no spiritual or any other gain would result from it! It would merely be a temporary regression into a state of vegetative or animal-like existence which, if persisted in, would lead to a state of mental stagnation and unjustified self-complacency.

is arrested, and stagnation sets in. The cure for this is not the suppression of individuality but the realisation that individuality is not the same as egohood (in the above-mentioned sense) and that change, which is a natural and necessary condition of life, is not arbitrary or meaningless but proceeds according to an inherent and universal law, which ensures the continuity and inner stability of movement.

Individuality is not only the necessary and complementary opposite of universality but the focal point through which alone universality can be experienced. The suppression of individuality, the philosophical or religious denial of its value or importance, can only lead to a state of complete indifference and dissolution, which may be a liberation from suffering, but a purely negative one, as it deprives us of the highest experience towards which the process of individuation seems to aim: the experience of perfect enlightenment or Buddhahood in which the universality of our true being is realised.

Merely to 'merge into the whole' like the 'drop into the sea', without having *realised* that wholeness, is only a poetical way of accepting annihilation and evading the problem that the fact of our individuality poses. Why should the universe evolve individualised forms of life and consciousness if this were not consistent with or inherent in the very spirit or nature of the universe? The question remains the same whether we see the universe with the eyes of a scientist, as an objective universe of physical forces, or with the eyes of a Buddhist, as an emanation or projection of a spiritual force, subjectively experienced as an all-embracing universal 'store-consciousness' (*ālaya-vijñāna*). The very fact of our individual existence must have a meaningful place in the order of the universe and cannot be brushed aside as a deplorable accident or a mere illusion—whose illusion? one might ask.

However, more important than our intellectual reasoning are the observable facts which—long before any explanations were offered by either religion, philosophy, or psychology—led to the conviction not only of a survival of individual consciousness beyond death in some higher or lower realms beyond our own but of a rebirth in this our human world. I will, therefore, relate two outstanding cases that came under my personal observation.

4

U Khanti, the Seer of Mandalay Hill

In the year 1929, during a pilgrimage in Burma, I was staying for some time at Mandalay together with the Venerable Nyanatiloka Mahāthera of the Island Hermitage near Dodanduwa in Ceylon, where I had undergone my novitiate as a Brahmachari. Nyanatiloka Thera had come to Burma a short time after my arrival at Rangoon to pay his last respects to his old Guru, U Kumara Mahāthera, who had just passed away in the little monastery of Kyundaw Kyaung, where Nyanatiloka had received his ordination twenty-six years before. The body of the revered teacher was kept in a dragon-protected richly adorned teakwood sarcophagus filled with honey to preserve the body until the preparations for the cremation had been completed. Since this might take a year or more in accordance with Burmese custom, it was not possible for us to wait for this opportunity, and therefore Nyanatiloka decided to join me during a part of my pilgrimage upcountry. After travelling for about two weeks on a trading steamer on the Irrawaddy, visiting on the way the ruined city of Pagan, with its thousands of temples and pagodas, we finally reached Mandalay, which we made our headquarters for the time being in order to visit the many places of religious and historical interest in and around the town.

The most sacred place of Mandalay is a rocky hill which rises steeply on the outskirts of the town from the otherwise flat country. The hill is covered with temples, pagodas, and innumerable smaller shrines and sanctuaries, connected by a long flight of roofed stairs, which lead from the foot to the top of the hill. One of the most remarkable sights, however, when approaching the hill, is two groups of hundreds of small pagodas (altogether more than one and a half thousand!) presided over by a big central pagoda in each group.

The origin of these enormous building activities goes back to King Mindon Min, who reigned over Burma from 1851 till 1878. Inspired by a dream, he abandoned his former capital Amarapura and founded Mandalay, which he adorned with magnificent palaces and religious monuments. Being an ardent Buddhist, he wanted to follow in the footsteps of a former king, who had caused the teachings of the Buddha to be inscribed on golden tablets, which were housed in a beautiful temple. This, however, only aroused the cupidity of the neighbouring Chinese, who invaded the country and carried away the golden tablets. King Mindon Min, therefore, decided to have the sacred texts carved on heavy marble slabs, which would attract neither invaders nor thieves, and which would preserve the teachings of the Buddha in their purity for all coming generations. At the same time they should be freely accessible to all people who wanted to know the word of the Buddha—not only scholars and priests but also the common man. For this reason each single slab was housed in a separate open shrine, a miniature pagoda-like temple, in which people could study undisturbed any part of the innumerable sacred texts not only in the original Pāli, but also in Burmese transcription.

Thus the King built the Kuthawdaw Pagoda, surrounded by 799 smaller pagodas, each executed with the same meticulous detail, housing the complete canonical texts *(Tipitaka)*. A similar 'city of pagodas' was to be built for the even more numerous commentaries of the sacred scriptures, but the King died before this work could be started. His successor, King Thibaw, was more interested in his sumptuous court and his numerous concubines, and was soon overthrown by the British, who annexed his kingdom. Thus, King Mindon Min's work was forgotten, and even the sanctuaries on the Mandalay Hill fell into disrepair. Pilgrims hardly dared to approach them because of robbers who often waylaid them on the deserted hill.

But one day a lonely pilgrim, whose heart burned with the pure flame of faith, felt so deeply grieved at seeing the desecration and decay of this place—which, according to Burmese belief, was once visited by the Buddha himself, that he decided to devote his life to the sacred hill and not to leave it until it had been restored to its former glory. Though he had no worldly possessions beyond his begging-bowl and the dark red robes of an ascetic, he had implicit faith in the powers of the spirit, and without worrying over the ways and means to achieve his purpose he sat down on the summit of the hill, in the shelter of one of the dilapidated sanctuaries, and devoted himself to meditation, unconcerned for his safety or his livelihood. Nobody could rob him, because he possessed nothing worth robbing. On the contrary, the pilgrims who saw him engaged in silent meditation began to bring gifts of food. When no pilgrims came he went hungry, when food was offered he ate. But slowly more and more people were encouraged and attracted to visit the sacred hill, when the news spread that a hermit lived on its top among the ruins of ancient shrines.

His mere presence seemed to re-sanctify the so-long-deserted place and soon people offered their help to repair the shrines and even to build new ones, as well as places where pilgrims could rest and meditate. Thus, temples, statues, halls, and pavilions, and covered stairways connecting them, grew up one after another, and the more the work proceeded, the more means were put in the hands of him who possessed nothing, but who seemed to command all the riches of the world. Not content with having restored the Mandalay Hill to its old glory and sanctity, he soon started on an even more ambitious undertaking; to complete the work, which King Mindon Min had not been able to accomplish in his lifetime: by having a complete set of the Great Commentaries to the

Holy Scriptures of Buddhism engraved on marble slabs and by building a second 'city of pagodas', even bigger than that of the Kuthawdaw, in which to house them.

After having accomplished this gigantic task, U Khanti, the Hermit of Mandalay Hill, who by now was known as Mahā-Yathi, the 'Great Rishi' (or 'Seer'), decided that it was not sufficient to preserve the sacred scriptures in stone and to make them accessible to those who could visit the pagoda shrines, but that they should be made accessible to the whole world by printing the complete canonical and important post-canonical literature of Buddhism. This was so enormous a task that no publisher or printer could have undertaken or financed such a venture. But the Great Rishi was undaunted. His power seemed to be limitless. Within a short time he was able to build his own up-to-date printing press at the foot of the hill, and at the time Nyanatiloka Thera and myself were staying at Mandalay an enormous amount of books, covering almost the whole of the above-mentioned literature, had been published in well-printed and neatly bound volumes. Even in Ceylon, with its more advanced book production, many of the important Pāli texts, especially those of the Abhidhamma, dealing with the philosophical and psychological aspects of the Buddhist doctrine, were not available in printed form in those days.

After hearing of U Khanti's achievements we naturally were anxious to meet him, and so one mormng we set out to pay a visit to the Rishi of the Mandalay Hill. We lived outside the town at a considerable distance from the sacred hill, so that we had to take a tonga (a two-wheeled horse-cart) to reach our destination. But when we arrived there we were informed that the 'Yathi' (Rishi) had left in the early morning for a place some twenty to twenty-five miles distant in order to supervise the restoration of an ancient Buddhist monument.

It goes without saying that we felt greatly disappointed, especially as it was uncertain whether we could find another opportunity of meeting him, because we had a rather busy programme before us.

Reluctantly we climbed back into our tonga, but hardly had the horse turned, when a motor-car came from the opposite direction, stopped right before the entrance of the covered staircase leading to the crest of the hill, and a tall red-robed figure emerged from the car. There was something incredibly impressive in the appearance and the quiet movements of this noble figure, unhurried and self-assured with the natural dignity of a born king or a great leader of men. We immediately felt: this must be the Great Rishi—and without hesitation we stopped the tonga, got out again, and went back to the gate, where we were told to our great joy that, against all expectations, U Khanti had suddenly returned, and that we would be able to see him. We were led into an open pavilion, and there, surrounded by a number of Bhikkhus and other attendants, the Great Rishi received us. Again I could not help feeling how his personality stood out from all the others who were present, and how he, who was not an ordained member of the Bhikkhu Sangha (the orthodox Order of Theravāda Monks), commanded respect even from those who regarded themselves the exclusive custodians of the Buddhadharma and superior in ecclesiastical rank. He received us smilingly and with great politeness, bowing to Nyanatiloka as an Elder (Thera) of the Sangha, and invited us to sit down, while giving orders to his attendants, who served us with tea and sweets. In the meantime he answered questions from his secretaries, who from time to time approached him with papers or asked for instructions, but all this went on so quietly and unobtrusively that it never seemed to interrupt his attention towards us or to disturb the flow of our conversation. He was greatly interested in the activities of the International Buddhist Union, of which Nyanatiloka was the President and I myself the General Secretary. When speaking about our plans to make the 'Island Hermitage' of Dodanduwa into an international centre of Buddhist culture and the necessity to make Buddhist literature more accessible to the world, I was just about to mention our special interest in the Abhidhamma literature and our difficulties in procuring the necessary books. But before I could make any such remarks he turned to one of his attendants, who thereupon disappeared in the direction of a building nearby, which, as we later realised, housed his press and his bookbinding department. Within a few minutes some servants appeared with stacks of books in their arms. 'Here is a present for you,' the Rishi said with a smile, and motioned the servants to spread the books out before us. How can I describe our surprise! They were exactly the volumes which were missing in our Dodanduwa library: a complete set of Abhidhamma texts! We were absolutely overwhelmed and almost speechless at the promptness with which the 'Yathi' had divined our secret wish and his kindness at presenting us with such a valuable gift.

When he saw our joy he offered us also the other sets of books which he had printed in his press—all of them beautifully bound with gold-embossed leather backs—but they were too many to take with us in our tonga—and so they were sent to our place on the following day. As I see from old newspaper cuttings of those memorable days in Mandalay, we received books to the value of more than 700 Rs., a sum which today would amount to not less than 3,000 Rs.! This was indeed a gift worthy of a king, and we were moved beyond words.

After we had taken leave from the Rishi, some Bhikkhus of his entourage accompanied us through the innumerable sanctuaries of the hill, which gave us an idea of the magnitude of the work that had been accomplished here and which yet was only a fraction of the activities of this remarkable man. In the course of our conversation, one of the Bhikkhus told us that the 'Yathi' had left Mandalay Hill in the early morning in order to supervise the building activities at a distant place, as we had been informed on our arrival. But in the middle of his inspection work he suddenly announced that he had to return immediately to Mandalay, as there were some people who had come from far away to see him. And without further delay he got into his car and asked the driver to go as fast as possible. And, as if he had forseen it, he arrived exactly at the moment we were about to leave!

Now we realised that our meeting was not merely accidental, and when we told the Bhikkhu how surprised we had been when the Rishi gave us exactly those books which we had had in mind—before we even could mention them—he said in a voice, vibrant with emotion and deep conviction: 'Don't you know who he is? He is the rebirth of King Mindon Min!'

I must confess that I had no doubt that it was so. In fact, it only confirmed what I had felt from the first moment I set eyes upon the noble figure of the Rishi. There was something royal in his bearing, something that commanded respect, if not veneration. His appearance, his deeds, and his whole personality were to me a greater proof than what factual investigations could have produced. His life and his actions showed unmistakably that he possessed unusual psychic and spiritual powers, among which the remembrance of his former birth and the aspirations of his previous life seemed to be the driving force of his personality, a force that gave a heightened meaning to his present existence. To him the knowledge of the past was not a dead weight or a hindrance but a greater incentive to act and something that aroused his sense of responsibility for the completion of a task which had been left unfinished. It was like the fulfilment of the vow of a Boddhisattva, who retains the continuity of his consciousness over many lives and deaths on account of an aim that is bigger than the horizon of a single human existence. It is our higher aspirations and our ultimate aim that make us immortal—not the permanence of an immutable separate soul, whose very sameness would exclude us from life and growth and from the infinite adventure of the spirit and condemn us for ever to the prison of our own limitations.

5

Maung Tun Kyaing

Sooner than I expected I came across a second case of pre-natal remembrance which was even more remarkable, because it offered ample means of verification—though for my own person it matters little whether we can prove the fact of rebirth or not, as it seems to me the most obvious and natural thing in the world, in accordance with reason, fitting into the evolutionary tendencies of all organic life, as the discoveries of biology and depth-psychology have revealed.

It was in Maymyo, the summer capital of Burma in the northern Shan States, where Nyanatiloka Thera and myself had gone to escape the heat of Mandalay, that we heard of a little boy whose name was Maung Tun Kyaing and who was in full possession of his pre-natal remembrance and knowledge, so that even the Governor of Burma (Sir Henry Butler) had called him to his Residency in Maymyo in order to convince himself of the truth of this extraordinary phenomenon. The little boy created such a favourable impression upon the Governor and all who were present during that memorable interview that he was encouraged to visit even the prisons all over the country, so that he might bring light and hope to those who were in the greatest darkness. Since then he was moving from place to place, and thousands of people were listening to him wherever he went.

However, his present whereabouts were not known, and as I had decided to continue my journey northwards through Upper Burma and from there into China (Yunnan), I took leave from Ven. Nyanatiloka, returned to Mandalay, and travelled up the Irrawaddy to Bhamo, from where the caravan route into Yunnan started. I put up in a *kyaung* (monastery) near the so-called Bell Pagoda and was housed in a spacious temple hall, where I set up my camp-bed for the night. It gave me a somewhat eerie feeling to find myself alone in the night with three silent marble Buddha statues smiling down upon me in a strange place, among strange people. There was nobody who knew English in that monastery. Before retiring I had tried to find out what the time was in order to set my watch, which had stopped because I had forgotten to wind it. But nobody seemed to be able to give me any information. Consequently I had no idea how long I had slept when I woke up the next morning and found people coming into the hall. They carried buckets full of water, and before I could quite grasp where I was and what they wanted they rushed towards the Buddha-images and with several well-aimed throws emptied the buckets over them, as if the temple was on fire. I had no idea what was the purpose of this strange performance and expected any moment to share the fate of the Buddha-images, when to my great relief the people left as unexpectedly as they had come, without taking the least notice of me.

It was only afterwards that I learned that this was the day of the water festival, on which it is customary to 'bathe' the Buddha-images as well as to throw water at each other in the streets—only those in yellow robes being exempted. Only this had saved me from a cold douche, apparently. At any rate, I thought it expedient to get up and be prepared for further developments. These came soon in the form of a watchmaker, who explained that he had been sent for to repair my watch. The poor fellow had come all the way from the town to this out-of-the-way monastery because he had been told that my watch was out of order.

When I cleared up the misunderstanding and convinced him that my watch was in perfect working order he had a good laugh and assured me that he did not mind having come all the distance, since it had given him the opportunity of making my acquaintance. I, on my part, assured him that I was equally pleased to have found somebody who knew English.

In the meantime tea was brought, and we settled down to a friendly talk, in the course of which I mentioned what I had heard about Maung Tun Kyaing, wondering whether I might have a chance to meet him one day. 'Why,' said the watchmaker, 'there is nothing simpler than that. Maung Tun Kyaing is just here in Bhamo and will be preaching in a neighbouring monastery today.'

'What a strange coincidence!' I exclaimed, 'that my way should have brought me here exactly on this day without having the slightest indication that Maung Tun Kyaing was even in this part of the country. It seems that my mere wish was sufficient to bring about its fulfilment.'

'Surely it is the right wish,' he said, 'that draws us to the right place. Nothing of importance happens accidentally in our life. I am sure that even our meeting here, though due to a misunderstanding, was not merely accidental, but a necessary link to bring about the fulfilment of your wish.'

'I agree with you,' I said, 'and I am certainly most grateful to you for having come here and having given me this information.'

When I arrived at the monastery where Maung Tun Kyaing was staying he was addressing a vast audience that filled the entire courtyard in front of the temple. It was an astonishing sight to see a small boy speaking with the ease and self-assurance of a practised speaker, his face radiant with happiness and his voice clear and melodious like a bell. Though I could not understand a word, it was a joy to hear this voice, that seemed to come straight from the depth of his heart like the song of a bird.

After the sermon, to which all present had listened with spellbound attention, I was introduced to the little boy, who was accompanied by his father and his younger brother. Both the boys were clad in yellow robes, though they did not yet officially belong to the Sangha, being below the age of admission. Maung Tun Kyaing looked to me hardly more than six years old, and his younger brother about five. But I was told that Maung Tun Kyaing was eight years old, while his brother was seven. But what a difference between the two! The younger brother looked like any other normal child of about that age; Maung Tun Kyaing, however, was of exceptional beauty. I have seldom seen such absolute purity and radiance in a human face, combined with an expression of uncommon intelligence and alertness. He was not in the least embarrassed when I examined the various auspicious signs of his body, which the father pointed out and the interpreter explained to me in detail. To all my questions the boy answered without hesitation and in perfect naturalness.

His story, mostly told by his father, a simple, very sincere man, was verified by Maung Tun Kyaing and all who were present, monks as well as laymen, and seemed to me the most interesting and significant verification of the idea of rebirth and the fact of pre-natal remembrance. Fortunately I had taken with me notepaper and pencil, so that I was able to take notes of all important details of the interview, which now lies thirty-four years back. Consulting my notes, this is the story of Maung Tun Kyaing as it emerged from this interview: He was the son of very poor, illiterate mat-weavers. When he was four years old the father took him and his younger brother to a fair in a neighbouring village. On their way they met a man with a bundle of sugar-cane, which he wanted to sell at the fair. Seeing the two little boys and realising that the father was too poor to buy anything, he offered a piece of cane to each boy. But while the smaller one greedily put the cane into his mouth, Maung Tun Kyaing exhorted him not to eat before having expressed his gratitude to the giver in form of a blessing. (‘*Sukhi hotu*’—‘May he be happy!’—is the appropriate Pāli formula, used by monks.) While admonishing him thus, it was as if the gates of his memory were suddenly opened, and he asked his father to lift him on to his shoulders, because he wanted to preach to the people on the virtue of giving (the first of the ‘ten great virtues’ of the Buddhist religion). The father, good-humouredly, lifted him up on to his shoulders, thinking it nothing more than a childish whim. But to his and the bystanders’ surprise the little boy began to preach a most beautiful sermon on the blessedness of giving, as even a religious teacher could not have done better. The people in the street began to crowd around the little preacher, and the father was bewildered at the sudden change that had come over his little boy. The latter, however, was undaunted and said, after he had finished his sermon: 'Come, Father, let us go to my Khyaung.'

'What do you mean by your Khyaung?'

'The monastery over there; don't you know?'

'I don't remember that you have ever been there,' retorted the father, 'but nevertheless let us go and see it.'

When they arrived at the monastery they met an elderly monk, who in fact was the abbot of the Khyaung; but Maung Tun Kyaing seemed to be absorbed in thoughts and simply looked at him without observing the customary forms of greeting, so that the father scolded him and said: 'Will you not pay your respects to the venerable Thera?' Whereupon the boy greeted the monk as if he were his equal—instead of prostrating himself in the prescribed manner.

'Don't you know who I am?' asked the abbot.

'Certainly I know!' said the boy without the slightest hesitation. And when the Thera looked at him in surprise the boy mentioned the Thera's name.

'How do you know? Did somebody tell you?'

'No,' said the boy. 'Don't you remember me? I was your teacher, U Pandeissa.'

The abbot was taken aback, but in order to test him he asked the boy: 'If that is so, what was my name before I entered the Order? If you know it you may whisper it into my ear.'[1]

---

1. Once a person enters the Order, he enters a new life, receives a new name, and never uses his former one again. To address a member of the Sangha by his former lay-name would be an insult, and even to ask him about it and his family would be disrespectful, because one who has entered the 'family of the Enlightened Ones' can no longer be regarded from the point of view of blood relationship, social background, caste, or class, all of which he has left behind. In this connection it may be recalled that when the five ascetics, who had abandoned the Buddha before his enlightenment, because he had given up his extreme self-mortification, ventured to address the Buddha by his family name, he rebuked them for doing so.

The boy did so. And when the Thera heard his name, which nobody knew, except those who had grown old with him and had known him intimately, he fell at the boy's feet, touched the ground with his forehead, and exclaimed with tears in his eyes: 'Now I know, you are indeed my teacher!'

And he took him, together with his father and his little brother, into the monastery, where Maung Tun Kyaing pointed out the room which he had occupied in the eastern wing of the building, the place where he used to meditate, the particular image before which he used to light candles and incense, and many other details which the old Thera remembered. After all, it was not so many years ago that U Pandeissa had been the abbot of Yunkhyaung, as the monastery was called.

The most significant thing, however, was that Maung Tun Kyaing not only remembered the general circumstances of his previous life but that he had retained even his former knowledge. When the Thera showed him some of the ancient Pāli scriptures the boy proved to be able to read and to understand them, though he had never had any schooling and had been brought up in a home where nobody knew how to write or read—let alone the knowledge of Pāli. If there had been any doubt about his pre-natal remembrances here was a clear proof.

When the father and the two children were about to return to their village, which was situated on the bank of the same river (the Irrawaddy, if I remember rightly) as the monastery, the abbot suggested that they should take one of the boats which belonged to Yunkhyaung. They went down to the river, and as there were several boats to choose from, the abbot asked Maung Tun Kyaing which of them he would like to use, and without hesitation the boy pointed out one of them, which he said was his own.

Burmese boats are generally painted with vivid colours and with eyes on their prow, giving them the individuality of a living being, in accordance with the animistic beliefs of ancient Burma, that all things possess a life of their own or are the abodes of spirits ('Nats'). But as he who knows the 'name' of a thing thus animated and identified with the indwelling Nat gets power over it, the name is not revealed to strangers, and therefore not painted on the boat. The name is only known to the owner and his family or his friends.

The abbot, therefore, said: 'You claim that this is your boat, but do you know its name?' The boy immediately mentioned the correct name.

After all these proofs nobody doubted that Maung Tun Kyaing was the rebirth of U Pandeissa, the former abbot of Yunkhyaung, and everybody wanted to hear him preach. From all sides he received invitations and his people were afraid that his health might break down under the strain, but he said: 'The Buddha spent innumerable lives in self-sacrificing deeds, striving to attain enlightenment. I too, therefore, should not spare any pains in striving after Buddhahood. Only by attaining the highest aim can I work for the benefit of all living beings.'

His sermons were so inspiring that people by the thousands came to hear and to see him, and once it so happened that a monastery collapsed under the weight of the crowd–but fortunately without killing anybody, because monasteries in Burma are mostly built of wood, resting on high stilts, and when the structure gave way there was still enough time for the people to get out.

Soon Maung Tun Kyaing's fame reached the ears of the Governor of Burma, who at that time was Sir Henry Butler. While in his summer residence at Maymyo he sent for the boy in order to convince himself whether the stories, which he had heard about Maung Tun Kyaing's extraordinary gifts and his remembrance of his former life, were true.

Maung Tun Kyaing not only acquitted himself most creditably but gave a masterful exposition of the religious tenets of Buddhism, and Sir Henry was so pleased with the little boy that he presented him with a box of sweets and a hundred-rupee note. Neither Maung Tun Kyaing nor his father had probably even seen such a big note or possessed such a sum—but the boy refused to accept it—because, as he said, he could not sell the Dharma and, besides, Buddhist monks are not allowed to accept money. But he explained that he could accept the sweets, as the rules allowed a Bhikkhu to take food that was offered to him. Though these rules were not yet binding on Maung Tun Kyaing, who on account of his young age could not yet be a member of the Buddhist Order, he inwardly regarded himself a Bhikkhu, as he had been in his previous life and as he would continue to be in this.

Maung Tun Kyaing, however, also wanted to give a present to the Governor, and the only thing he possessed was his rosary. He carefully unwound it from his wrist and handed it over to Sir Henry, who was greatly touched by this gesture and smilingly accepted the gift. 'But now you must tell me how to use this rosary,' he said, whereupon Maung Tun Kyaing explained: 'This is to meditate on the three marks of existence, *"anicca"* (impermanence), *"dukkha"* (suffering), and *"anattā"* (egolessness).' And then he explained the meaning of these three words in detail.

To hear these profound truths from the mouth of a little child greatly impressed the Governor. How was it possible that a little boy at the age of four could speak with the wisdom of an old man? And he spoke not like one who had been taught to repeat words which he himself could not yet fully understand—on the contrary, he spoke with such conviction and sincerity that Sir Henry was visibly moved and encouraged the boy to bring his message to all the people of Burma. 'You should go from one end of the country to the other,' he said, 'and preach to high and low, even to the prisoners in the jails, because nobody could touch the heart of the people deeper than you. Even the hardest criminal would melt in the presence of such genuine faith and sincere goodwill.'

And thus it happened that even the gates of the jails were opened to Maung Tun Kyaing, and wherever he went he inspired the people with new religious fervour, strengthening their convictions and filling them with fresh life.

6

The Mind that Conquers Death

After having met and talked to Maung Tun Kyaing and his father, as well as to many others who were intimately acquainted with them, I could understand the tremendous effect which Maung Tun Kyaing's words and presence had upon the people. And it struck me as significant that again—as in the case of the Great Rishi of Mandalay Hill—it was the Bodhisattva-Ideal, the *directedness*[1] towards a spiritual goal, which alone can convert consciousness into a one-pointed, unified vital force that had spanned the chasm of death and had given the impetus that

1. *Directed* consciousness, according to Buddhist psychology, is that which has 'entered the *stream*' towards liberation or enlightenment, in which its universal nature is realised. Undirected consciousness allows itself to be driven hither and thither by blind urges and external sense-stimuli. On account of its dependence upon the external world, it is called mundane consciousness *(lokiya),* while directed consciousness is called supramundane (*lokuttara*). The justification of the term 'directed' is borne out by the fact that the transition from worldly to supra-worldly consciousness is called 'entry into the stream' (*sotāpatti*) and that one who finds himself in this phase of development is called '*sotāpanna*' (one who has entered the stream). (Cf. my *The Psychological Attitude of Early Buddhist Philosophy,* Rider & Co. (London, 1961), p. 80.)

linked one life to the other in an ever-widening awareness of its responsibility and its all-embracing aim.

This linking up of lives was not achieved by clinging to the past or by a morbid curiosity about former existences by means of hypnotic trances or other abnormal psychic states, but by the forward-looking purposefulness of a directed mind, based on the insight and realisation of the universal nature of consciousness, rather than on the personal aspects of an individual past. The latter may appear automatically before the mind's eye in the process of meditation, especially in states of deep absorption, but they should never be pursued for their own sake.

As an example I may mention here the Buddha's experience, which led to his final enlightenment, and in which his awareness in ever-widening circles, beginning with the remembrance of his former lives (but without giving undue importance to their individual features), proceeds to the realisation of how living beings come into existence, how they appear in ever new forms and conditions, according to their inborn or acquired tendencies, their subconscious desires and their conscious actions—and after having thus traced life to its very origins, he observed the origination and dissolution of whole world-systems in endless cycles of materialisation and reintegration, following each other like a cosmic systole and diastole.

Only in such a cosmic vision can the individual path be seen in its proper perspective, from which it derives both its meaning and its value. Unless this perspective has been established, either mentally or through direct experience, pre-natal remembrances would prove to be only a burden, a useless and unnecessary encumbrance of the mind. It would nullify the very justification of death, namely its faculty of freeing us not only from a worn-out body, but even more so from an overcrowded intellect, from the rut of habits, of hardened opinions and prejudices, from the accumulations of inessential memory details, which bind us to the past and prevent any fresh approach to the problems of the present, stifling our awareness and spontaneity *vis-à-vis* new situations and wider relationships.

Directedness and spontaneity of consciousness may appear to be mutually exclusive, for which reason some of our modern apostles of 'spontaneous living' and 'intuitive thought' deceive themselves and others with the idea that any form of logical thought, of purposefulness, intention, or spiritual direction—in fact any form of striving to overcome one's limitations, be it through meditation or any other practices—are all forms of preconceived ideas with which we violate our intuitive genius. All this is very attractive to those who need a fashionable excuse for not exerting themselves, for merely drifting through life, mistaking whims and unpredictable behaviour for signs of spontaneity, laziness for a sign of detachment, and indifference towards moral values or towards the weal and woe of others for a sign of equanimity.

But the seeming contradiction between concentration and intuition, between directedness and spontaneity, is only due to thoughtless generalisations which have no foundation in experience or reality. Reality, therefore, seems paradox in terms of such abstract terminology, as, for instance, if we practise 'one-pointedness' or concentration in order to arrive at universality and all-inclusiveness (the very opposite of 'one-pointedness'), or if we have first to achieve individuality before we can experience universality.

We have to turn from a wayward, chaotic consciousness, from a mind that is agitated or diverted by all kinds of ephemeral objects and illusions, to a directed, i.e. co-ordinated, harmonised consciousness, which is not directed towards any particular point or limited object, but which consists so-to-say in the integration of all directions and points. 'One-pointedness' (*ekagratā*) does not necessarily mean 'to be directed towards something' (towards one particular object), but rather to be mentally and spiritually unified, like the rays of the sun in one focus. The focus of a lens is not directed towards anything: it simply unites the scattered rays of the sun and re-creates the *complete* picture of the sun in *one* point; and this point, though it has no extension in space, does not abrogate the infinity of each ray which passes though it. Here we have the practical demonstration of the paradox, how the finite (the point) and the infinite (the rays) can be combined and co-exist.

The 'one-pointedness' of our consciousness is similar to the focalisation of a lens: it can be utilised for bringing a particular object into focus, or for the focalisation of consciousness itself, by excluding any particular object and just letting consciousness rest in itself, integrated in its own awareness. In such a state one is not 'holding on to anything' or 'concentrating on anything', the mind is completely free from object-awareness or from the interference of will-power or intellectual activity.

For most people, however, it is necessary first to free themselves from the multiplicity of objects and sense-impressions by concentrating or focussing their attention on *one* object, and when they have thus succeeded in eliminating all outer and inner disturbances, then even this object can be dropped—or rather it disappears by itself by losing its 'object'-character the moment the meditator has become one with it—and the state of intuitive receptiveness and perception has been attained, a state in which we are no more bound by forms and objects or by aims and intentions.

Meditation in Buddhism comprises both the preliminary states of thinking and reflecting and concentrating on a chosen subject (*parikrama bhāvanā*) as well as the states of attainment of complete integration (*appanā bhāvanā*) and intuitive awareness or spiritual vision (*dhyāna*). Intuition, however, is based on repeated experience, and experience is based on practice. Only when practice has led to a complete mastery of any subject or any technique, so that they no more require our conscious attention, only then is it possible to rely on our intuition and to act spontaneously and effortlessly like a virtuoso, who masters his instrument (including his mind) to such an extent that he can compose or improvise with complete freedom without ever violating the laws on which the harmony of his creation is based.

Just as lower organisms serve as building materials for higher ones, so also the stored-up experiences of the subconscious or automatic functions serve the higher purposes of the mind. Living cells turn into hard bones to support the structure of the body; and most of the bodily functions, like heart-beat, digestion, breathing, etc., have become automatic. If all these functions were dependent on our conscious effort all our energies and our attention would be absorbed by them, and no intellectual or spiritual life would be possible. As little, therefore, as we should attempt to reverse automatic functions into conscious ones, should we attempt to revive the details of previous existences, from which repeated deaths have freed us, by converting the experience-value of each life into a quality of our character or an ability of our mind. Only those remembrances, which through the very force of their meaningfulness and direction towards an aim have retained their value, can have significance for our present life, and perhaps for our future ones too—provided the aim, or the idea that inspired us, was wide enough to include a future beyond the span of one lifetime.

7

The Case of Shanti Devi

THE DIRECTEDNESS OF our consciousness, however, is not only dependent on the strength of our spiritual aim but to a certain extent on the intenseness of our emotions, especially when these are connected with a religious aim, a sacred duty, or a deep human relationship, based on a pure and selfless love. If such emotions are very strong at the moment of death they may result in carrying their remembrances consciously into the next following life, where they will be particularly vivid in early childhood, before new impressions and experiences can replace them.

A case of this type came to my knowledge in the winter of 1935–6. A little girl named Shanti Devi, who lived in Delhi with her parents, insisted that she was married and that her husband, Kedarnath Chaubey, together with her son, were staying at Muttra, a town about 80 miles distant from Delhi. When the girl first began to talk in this way she was barely three years old and nobody took much notice of it, assuming that it was just playful childish talk, imitating grown-ups. But when the girl was about eight years old, and still persisted in her talk about husband and son, her grand-uncle, Professor Kischen Chand, began to suspect that there was more to it than childish imagination. He found out that in the very locality of Muttra described by Shanti there was indeed a person answering to the name of Kedarnath Chaubey. The Professor lost no time in getting in touch with him and related all that the girl had said. The news came rather as a shock, as Kedarnath had married again in the meantime; and there was also the fear that someone might be playing a trick upon him and the Professor. As, however, all the facts were fitting, he finally agreed to meet Shanti at her parents' house.

On the 13th of November 1935 Kedarnath Chaubey with his second wife and his ten-year-old son arrived in Delhi. Shanti had not been informed of their coming. As soon, however, as she entered the room in which her parents and their visitors were assembled she recognised Kedarnath as her husband and the boy as her son. She embraced the child with tears in her eyes, using the very terms of endearment which her former husband remembered so well. If there had been any doubt in his mind as to Shanti's identity the last trace of it was removed. She also reminded her former husband of small intimate occurrences, known only to him and to her. The proof was complete.

Now other people too became interested in the case, and Deshbandhu Gupta, the President of the All-Indian Newspaper Editors' Conference and Member of Parliament, took up further investigations in order to convince himself of the truth of Shanti's alleged pre-natal memories. He therefore took her to Muttra and asked her to show him and to the others who accompanied them the way to her former home. They took a tonga and Shanti led the party with absolute assurance through the many narrow lanes and winding roads of the town to the very house where she had lived with her husband. But she at once remarked that the colour of the house had been changed. 'I remember that it was painted yellow, not white, as it is now!' she exclaimed. This was correct. Kedarnath had left the house after her death, and the new residents had painted it white. Kedarnath thereupon took the party to his new residence, and afterwards Shanti led them to her former mother's house. There too she immediately noticed certain changes. 'There was a well in the garden,' she said, 'what has happened to it?' She pointed out where it had been, and when the place was dug up, the well was found under a big stone slab covered with earth. She also recognised her former parents and her former father-in-law, an old Brahmin, bent with age. Shanti's remembrances had proved correct in every detail.

She would have liked to stay with her former son, but she realised that she could not take him away from his father; and as to her former husband she knew that she could have no more claims upon him, since he had married again.

Thus, the realisation dawned upon her that the bonds of marriage and motherhood cannot be maintained beyond death, whose very function it is to free us from those bonds and the sufferings of separation and remembrance, without destroying whatever we may have gained by our capacity to love and to serve others, so that we may meet those whom we loved under new conditions and in new forms, without being encumbered by the limitations of former relationships and the memories of an irretrievable past. And this realisation made her turn to the more permanent values of a spiritual life in which all our loves and longings are sublimated into a deeper sense of compassion for all that lives: into the faculty to share the joys and sorrows of all with whom life brings us into contact.

Shanti Devi has never married again, but she dedicated her life to the service of others. She became a highly qualified teacher in a Delhi high school. Friends who know her personally told me that she leads an intensely religious life and plans to found an *ashram,* where she can devote herself completely to her *sādhanā* and to those who share her religious ideals.

Now, one might ask, why do such things happen so often in the East and not in the West? My answer is that they happen as often in the West as in the East; the only difference is that the West does not pay any attention to them, because they do not fit into the mental attitude of the average Westerner, whose religion teaches him that entirely new beings come into existence at birth, and that those same beings, who were non-existent before their physical conception, would go on existing for eternity ever after, while those who have discarded this view as being inconsistent with logic and common sense have generally come to the opposite conclusion, namely that beings which did not exist before birth (or conception) will also not exist after death, thus equating living beings with their physical existence and denying any possibility of pre-natal existence or survival after death, except in the form of physical heredity. But if we examine this mechanism of physical heredity we soon discover that the combinations and permutations of chromosomes, etc., are not sufficient to explain either the transference of an infinity of hereditary details, nor the distinct uniqueness of each individual—even if it has originated from the same hereditary material (as in the case of children from the same parents)—which shows that an individual is not only the sum total of the qualities of its progenitors. Very clearly an unknown factor is involved in the formation of a new physical organism, a directing creative force beyond all possibilities of observation or scientific analysis, a principle that cannot be reduced to a mathematical formula or a mechanistic theory. 'The real difficulty for the mechanistic theory is that we are forced, on the one hand, to postulate that the germ-plasm is a mechanism of enormous complexity and definiteness, and, on the other, that this mechanism, in spite of its absolute definiteness and complexity, can divide and combine with other similar mechanisms, and can do so to an absolutely indefinite extent without alteration of its structure . . . The mechanistic theory of heredity is not only unproven; it is impossible. It involves such absurdities that no intelligent person who has thoroughly realised its meaning and implications can continue to hold it' (J. S. Haldane).

Yet in spite of these absurdities of current scientific idea, which are as unsatisfactory from a spiritual point of view as the former religious beliefs from a logical point of view, the average Westerner clings to his prejudice against the idea of reincarnation and thus fails to observe the ample proofs that are daily offered to him in various forms and through many phenomena which until now have remained inexplicable.

Among the latter the phenomenon of child prodigies defies all laws of science as well as of current psychology. No amount of scientific knowledge can explain the spontaneous knowledge and even technical skill of such children. Unless we admit the possibility of remembrances from skills and experiences or knowledge acquired in a former existence there is no reasonable explanation for such phenomena. A genius does not fall from heaven, but is, as all other things in this world, the product of a long evolution of trial and failure and final success through long practice and experience. How otherwise could one explain that a barely four-year-old child could master spontaneously the intricacies of a complicated musical instrument like the spinet, and the even more intricate and subtle rules of musical composition, without having been taught or trained, as it happened in the case of Mozart, Beethoven, and other prodigies. Mozart composed minuets at this early age and gave public performances at the age of seven at the court of the Empress Maria Thérèsa and in many other places. Beethoven, even before he had reached the age of four, had already composed three sonatas. He too gave concerts at the age of eight. Handel, Brahms, Dvořák, Chopin, and other great composers and musicians performed similar feats to perfection at an incredibly early age.

Many such cases could also be quoted from the fields of literature, mathematics, and other sciences. Voltaire at the age of three knew by heart all of Lafontaine's fables and Stuart Mill at the same age mastered the Greek language and at six he wrote a history of Rome. William Thomson (Lord Kelvin) at the age of eight or nine solved mathematical problems without the aid of grown-ups and at ten he entered the university. One could multiply such examples *ad infinitum*.

In addition to this, new evidence of pre-natal remembrances has been found in recent times by means of hypnosis. The results were all the more astonishing as they had not been expected or intended. They were merely a by-product of medical treatment, in which hypnosis was used for different purposes. The most outstanding of these cases was that of Edgar Cayce, an American, born in Kentucky in 1877, who later on became the founder of the well-known Cayce Foundation at Virginia Beach (Virginia). In his youth he had lost his speech on account of a psychosomatic constriction of the throat. After all known medical remedies and methods of treatment had proved ineffective he agreed to be treated by a hypnotist, who put him into a deep trance. And here it happened that not only his voice returned but apparently also his former knowledge of medicine, because during his trance he was able to give a correct diagnosis of his case and to describe in detail the necessary treatment in professional terms, though in his waking state he knew nothing of these things.

The treatment which he had revealed in his trance was so successful that other people too came to him for advice when professional doctors were at their wits' end. Again it was a great success, and his prescriptions were of such technical perfection and ingenuity that only a man of vast medical and pharmaceutical experience could have formulated them. Some of his remedies were entirely unknown to the professional world and contained ingredients and combinations that had never been used before. But the cures which he effected through them proved the correctness of his prescriptions. More and more people came to him for help, and he helped them without ever accepting any fees, probably because he felt this strange faculty of his as a gift from heaven. He had no knowledge of Eastern doctrines of rebirth or of a universal store-consciousness or of meditational practices to induce trances. Yet after a short time he found out that he could put himself into a trance state without the help of a hypnotist. He had discovered the secret to dive into his subliminal depth-consciousness at will.

Once while he was in trance he was asked whether reincarnation was a fact, and without hesitation he answered in the affirmative. When, after he had returned to his normal state of mind, he was told about it he felt greatly upset, because he feared that the idea of reincarnation was incompatible with his Christian beliefs and that perhaps he was in the grip of some evil power. It was only after penetrating deeper into this matter through his trances, as well as through informing himself of the main ideas of Eastern teachings, that he set aside his fears and consented to continue to use his gifts for the benefit of all those who sought his help. Their numbers, however, were steadily increasing; and since he was able to treat even people who lived far away, his work finally spread over the whole of the United States and even to foreign countries. Edgar Cayce died in 1945, leaving behind him a big and prosperous institution to carry on his work and the ideas which inspired it. Though Cayce might never have heard of a Bodhisattva, he certainly acted like one, and perhaps it was this hidden quality in him which enabled him to make use of his pre-natal knowledge.

Though modem psychology is slowly catching up with the East by recognising the 'unconscious' part of our psyche (which perhaps would be better called our *depth-consciousness)* as the repository of various types of pre-natal remembrances (individual, collective, racial, universal), more or less corresponding to the Buddhist idea of the *ālaya-vijñāna,* it has not yet dared to admit the possibility of a conscious connection between consecutive forms of existence in the development of a self-perpetuating individual consciousness. In other words, it has not yet dared to recognise the possibility of rebirth. Due to this, even such cases as the above-quoted assume the character of either freakish or miraculous, but in any case 'abnormal', occurrences, due to which they lose their general significance for the human world. A phenomenon that cannot be integrated into the general aspect of the world or brought into relationship with other constituents of our experience can neither be evaluated nor utilised as a step towards a deeper understanding of the world and of ourselves.

There certainly is no dearth of facts or reasons for the justification of the idea of rebirth and the possibility of pre-natal remembrances. Even in observing the behaviour and the spontaneous talk and imagination of children at an early age, we would probably find that there are as many cases of pre-natal remembrance in the West as in the East. We seldom realise how much of what we call 'imagination' is a faint echo of remembrances—just as our dreams have their roots not only in the events of our present life but very often in the deeper layers of our 'depth-consciousness' in which the remembrances of our pre-natal past (which widens out the farther we descend, so as finally to include remembrances and experiences of a supra-individual, universal nature), are preserved in the form of archetypal 'pictures' and symbols.

But prejudice is the greatest enemy of objective observation and creative thought, while an awareness of yet unexplored possibilities will open our minds to new perspectives which reveal new facts. Then suddenly phenomena which seemed to be unconnected with the rest of our world and our experiences, and thus inexplicable in any natural way, fall into place, so that finally we wonder how we could pass by them without recognising their real significance or perhaps without seeing them at all.

Even by accepting the idea of rebirth or consciousness-survival as a theory or working hypothesis, an enormous amount of factual material, whose existence we failed to observe, would disclose itself before our very eyes and give to our life a new dimension of reality and a deeper meaning.

8

A Message from the Past

FOR MYSELF REBIRTH is neither a theory, nor a belief, but an experience. This experience came to me towards the end of my childhood—however, in a way that I was not able to recognise its nature. It was only much later (at the age of about twenty-one) that I realised the actual source of what I had taken for a product of my youthful imagination. I was living at that time on the island of Capri, and among my friends there was the son of a well-known local landscape painter. This friend, as well as his mother, were great devotees of Padre Pio, in whom the miracle of St Francis of Assisi had repeated itself: he had received the stigmata, and though he had done everything possible to conceal the fact that the wounds of his hands began bleeding during every Friday Mass, he had not been able to prevent the news of his miracle from spreading through the whole of Italy. People in Capri were greatly impressed by this occurrence, and among the more sophisticated it led to a new interest in occult powers and current theories about them.

One day my friend told me that he and his mother and a few others were holding spiritistic seances, and he invited me to take part in them. As a Buddhist I did not hold a high opinion about such things—not because I denied the possibility of occult powers, but because I found the theories as well as the practices of spiritists crude and unsatisfactory. On the other hand I welcomed the opportunity to gain some factual knowledge in this matter. So I accepted the invitation and attended one of these seances.

We all sat around a heavy table in a softly lit room, keeping our hands spread out before us on the table, lightly touching its surface in the prescribed manner, and when the table began to move, one of the participants proposed to put questions about the former lives of those present. The answers were, as often in such cases, too vague to be of much interest and besides beyond any possibility of verification. When the questioner enquired about my past the table tapped out a name that was obviously Latin, and nobody among those present had ever heard it. I too was puzzled, though I had a faint remembrance of having casually read the name in a bibliography as being the pseudonym of a comparatively lesser-known author, whose actual name I could not recall. Anyway, I did not take this answer seriously, nor was I impressed by the whole procedure, because it seemed to me unlikely that any intelligent being, whether in the form of a 'spirit' or any other conscious entity, should stoop to answer idle questions of this kind and to communicate them in such a primitive and clumsy manner. If they wanted to contact human beings they certainly would be able to discover more adequate means of communication. It seemed to me more likely that the forces invoked by such means were none other than those of the participants' subconsciousness. It therefore seemed to me unlikely that through them anything could be revealed that was not already in them, i.e. in their subconscious or unconscious psyche. About the latter, however, I had not yet a clear conception, as I was not yet familiar with the idea of the *ālaya-vijñāna*. I therefore dismissed the matter and gave it no further thought.

Some time later I happened to read to another friend of mine, a young German archaeologist, a story which I had written in my childhood and which I had conceived as part of a mystic novel, in which my religious convictions and inner experiences were symbolically expressed.

My friend was a few years older than myself and I greatly valued his knowledge of art and literature and his mature judgement.

After I had been reading for sonic time he suddenly stopped me and exclaimed: 'Where did you get this from? Did you ever read—' and there he mentioned the same name that had puzzled me and the other participants of the aforementioned seance.

'Now, this is funny,' I said, 'this is the second time that I hear this name.' And then I told him how it had turned up in that seance.

My friend thereupon explained to me that this author had written a similar novel, but had never finished it, because he died young, suffering from the same ailment that had led me to a sanatorium in the Swiss Tessin, where we first had met. Not only the background of my story and the ideas expressed in it were similar to those of this author, but even the style, the imagery, the symbols, and the use of certain typical phrases.

I was surprised and assured my friend that I had never read a word of this author. And this was no wonder, because, as I learned now, he had died a century ago and was not popular enough to be included in the normal high-school curriculum. Greatly impressed by my friend's words, I decided to order the works to which he had referred. But before I could get them (since they were not available in Italian bookshops) another strange thing happened.

One day I was invited to a birthday party, where, as usual in Capri, people of various nationalities were present. Among them was a German scholar who had just arrived on the island for a short stay and whom I had not met before. When entering the room where the party was held I noticed an expression of utter surprise on the face of the newcomer, and even after I had been introduced to him I felt constantly his gaze upon me.

A few days later I met the hostess again and asked her: 'Who was the gentleman to whom you introduced me during your party? I wonder why he stared at me all the time. I never met him before and do not remember even his name.'

'Oh, you mean Dr. So-and-so! Well, he has left already. But I can tell you what interested him so much in you. He is writing the biography and editing the works of a German mystic writer and poet who died a century or so ago. When you entered he could hardly master his surprise—as he told me later on—because the similarity between you and the only existing portrait of the poet from the time when he was about your age is so striking that it almost gave him a shock.'

But a further surprise was in store for me. When the books I had ordered finally were in my hands I recognised not only substantial parts of 'my story' but found certain passages *literally identical* with my own childhood writings! And the more I read, the more I began to realise that I read my own innermost thoughts and feelings, expressed in exactly the words and images which I myself was wont to use. But it was not only the world of my imagination which I found mirrored in every detail; there was something even more important, because it related to what I had conceived as my present life-work, the outline of a morphology of human thought and culture, resulting in a magic vision of the universe. I myself had drawn up such a plan with youthful optimism and had started to work on it in various fields (art, archaeology, religion, psychology, philosophy, etc.), hoping to collect and to co-ordinate the necessary material in the course of my life. But soon I found that the frame of the plan was too wide and that even a lifetime would not be sufficient to complete such an encyclopaedic work. Thus I was finally forced to confine myself only to such subjects for which I was best qualified by temperament, training, and inclination. Looking back upon my life, I now know that this was the right thing to do, and that what is left will be continued or accomplished in another life.

It is this certainty which fills me with confidence and peace, and allows me to concentrate unhurriedly on whatever task the present demands. No work of importance, that one's heart is bent upon with single-minded devotion, will remain unfinished. This is what Tibet has taught me, where the saints and Siddhas of old kept on returning through ever new incarnations, in ever new forms until the present day—thus confirming what first came to me as a faint remembrance or message from the past and grew in the pursuance of a distant aim into an inner certainty.

It is not my ideal to be reborn for ever in this world, but neither do I believe that we can abandon it before we have fulfilled our task in it—a task which we may have taken upon ourselves in some remote past, and from which we cannot run away like cowards.

I knew that it was something greater than merely the desire to escape from the dangers and troubles of life that prompted me when I chose to lead a monk's life for twenty years, though I did not bind myself to the vows of the Bhikshu Sangha and its innumerable rules. I have never believed in them—as little as the Buddha did, who merely said 'Come' to those who wanted to follow him, without ever using the sterile formulas of a stereotyped ordination questionnaire, and who was ready to free the Sangha from the accumulated dross of petty rules, as reported in the Mahāparinibbāna-Sutta of the Dīgha-Nikāya.

When I chose the way of a lone and homeless pilgrim (*'Anagarika'* means a 'Homeless One') I did so in the conscious pursuance of an aim that allowed me neither to make myself 'at home' in the security of a monastic community nor in the comforts of a householder's life. Mine was the way of the Siddhas: the way of individual experience and responsibility, inspired and supported by the living contact between Guru and Chela though the direct transference of power in the act of initiation—which is more than a mere routine ritual of prescribed formulas or a set of prearranged questions and answers, but depends as much on the Guru's spiritual powers or attainments *(siddhi)* as on the Chela's preparedness or receptivity. While an ordination can be performed, irrespective of the attainments of those who perform the ritual, initiation can only be given by one who has himself realised the power which he wants to bestow, and can be received only by those who have sincere faith and an earnest desire for truth.

It is for this reason that in the Vajrayāna initiation is valued higher than ordination, as may be seen from the famous biography of Tibet's poet-saint Milarepa, who for the sake of being granted initiation by Marpa, his great Guru, underwent years of toil and suffering. While Milarepa was a Yogi of high accomplishments and a celibate (though he never entered the Bhikshu Sangha, nor did he ever wear the robes of this

Order, preferring the simple, undyed cotton cloth, for which reason he was called Repa, 'the Cotton Clad'), his Guru was a married man, but one of the greatest initiates of his time, being a pupil of the Mahāsiddha Naropa. The latter had been one of the leading lights of the Buddhist University of Vikramasīla in Bengal, a Brahmin by birth, and an honoured member of the Bhikshu Sangha. But in spite of all his learning and his virtuous life, he had not attained realisation! When he met Tilopa, a wandering Yogi and teacher of the Mahāmudrā doctrine, who had attained the state of liberation, Naropa renounced his honoured position and his monastic robe, in order to follow the Siddha and to be initiated into the Mahāmudrā doctrine, and its mystic meditation. The following words of Tilopa may give an indication of its nature:

'When mind has no place where it can stop (and become limited) the Mahāmudrā [lit. 'the Great Attitude'] is present. By cultivating such an attitude one attains supreme enlightenment.'[1]

In other words, the Mahāmudrā is the *universal attitude* of the mind, which by nature is infinite and all-embracing. Therefore Tilopa says: 'The jewel-casket of original mind, free from selfish passions, shines like the [infinite] sky.'[2]

Thus the Siddhas had rediscovered the direct way of spontaneous awareness and realisation of the universal depth-consciousness, which had been buried under the masses of scholastic learning, abstract philosophical speculation, hair-splitting arguments, and monastic rules, in which virtue was not the natural product of higher knowledge but of mere negation. The self-complacency of negative virtues was a greater hindrance on the way towards enlightenment than the passions themselves, which, through insight into the real nature of the mind, could be transformed and sublimated into the forces of liberation. This is the key to the seemingly paradoxical saying of Tilopa: 'The true nature of passions has turned out to be the sublime knowledge of emancipation.' Only a man

1. *Mahāmudrapadeśa* ('Tib. *Phyag-rgya-chen-pohi-man-nag*).

2. *Acintaya-mahāmudrā* (Tib.: *Phyag-rgya-chen-po-bsam-gyis-mi-khyab-pa*). Quoted by H. V. Guenther in *Origin and Spirit of the Vajrayāna* (Stepping Stones, Kalimpong).

who is capable of great passions is capable of great deeds and great accomplishments in the realm of the spirit. Only a man who had gone through the fire of suffering and despair, like Milarepa, could have accomplished the highest aim within a lifetime.

It was the protest of the Siddhas of India, the mystics and sages of Tibet, the Ch'an Patriarchs of China and the Zen Masters of Japan, that rejuvenated the religious life of Buddhism and freed it from the shackles of mediocrity and routine and widened its scope beyond the confines of an exclusively monastic ideal—because, as Lin Yutang rightly says: 'The human desire to see only one phase of the truth which we happen to perceive, and to develop and elevate it into a perfect logical system, is one reason why our philosophy is bound to grow stranger to life. He who talks about truth injures it thereby; he who tries to prove it thereby maims and distorts it; he who gives it a label and a school of thought kills it; and he who declares himself a believer buries it.'

PART FOUR

Southern and Central Tibet

I

New Beginnings: Ajo Rimpoché

SINCE MY JOURNEY to the highlands of Western Tibet (Chang-Thang) and Ladakh, from which I had brought back a complete set of tracings of the Eighty-Four Siddhas as well as of various Tibetan temple frescoes, my interest in the mystic path of the Siddhas, their teachings, their partly historical, partly legendary biographies and their iconography had steadily grown—and with it my determination to visit the temples of Lotsava Rinchen Zangpo in the deserted capital of the ancient Kingdom of Gugé, where I hoped to find the remnants of Tibet's earliest and most accomplished tradition of religious art.

Six years had passed since the vision in the ancient rock monastery on the way to the Chang-Thang had opened my eyes to the importance of creative visualisation in the process of meditation, and therewith the role of religious art which, far beyond all aesthetic values, contained the key to the secrets of *maṇḍalas,* the unfoldment of spiritual vision, the meaning of *sādhanā* (meditative practice), and the parallelism between the inner world of man and the universe around him.

I had utilised these six years by studying the religious life and literature of Tibet, collecting all possible information about Rinchen Zangpo's work and his role in the restoration and stabilisation of Buddhism in Western Tibet after the fail of Langdarma. But in the midst of my preparations for a new journey to Western Tibet the Second World War broke out and shattered all my hopes for a speedy realisation of my plans.

Tsaparang seemed to have receded into an unreachable distance. But in the meantime I had found an ally for my plan in Li Gotami, who joined my work and my life after many years of friendship, inspired by our common faith in Buddhism and her particular interest in Tibetan art. We had first met at Rabindranath Tagore's International University, Santiniketan, Bengal, where I was a lecturer in the postgraduate department, and where she studied Indian Art for twelve years (first under Nandalal Bose, and later under Abanindranath Tagore) as well as the techniques of Tibetan fresco and thanka painting under Tibetan artists, while I introduced her to the intricacies of Tibetan iconography and religious thought, which finally led her to join with me the Kargyütpa Order as my wife (*gSang-yum*) and companion in the Dharma (*dharma-sāhinī*). Tomo Géshé Rimpoché seemed to have foreseen this, because he had given her his blessings during his last visit to Sarnath and prophesied— when she asked him whether she would be successful in her art—that she would achieve great success if she would devote herself to the Buddha-Dharma.

Our religious marriage was performed by Ajo Rimpoché, who presided over the Monastery of Tsé-Chöling in the Chumbi Valley. A Lama friend of mine of many years standing had introduced us to this venerable patriarch, who at that time was eighty-four years old and known as a great master of meditation (*gom-chen*)[1] The reverence which he commanded in Southern Tibet, as well as in Sikkim and Bhutan, was reflected in the magnificent two-storeyed temple which he built with the willing help and contributions of his numerous devotees. Though he had lavished a fortune worthy of a king on the buildings, statues, frescoes, collections of religious books, and

1. When he was 105 years old he had the distinction of being the first Lama to receive the Indian Prime Minister, Jawaharlal Nehru, on Tibetan soil during the latter's journey to Bhutan, which at that time was only accessible through the Chumbi Valley of Southern Tibet.

precious thankas, he himself had no personal possessions and lived in a tiny wooden cottage below the temple buildings in utmost simplicity.

Like the Hermit Abbot of Lachen and many of the Siddhas before him, he was a married man, and his wife was a real 'Damema' (*bdag-med-ma*), which means 'the Selfless One', as Marpa's wife was called, a mother to all who came within the charmed circle of her and her Guru-husband's life. Ajo Rimpoché was one of the successive reincarnations of the Siddha Dombi-Heruka of the eighth century A.D., who had renounced a throne in order to lead a life of meditation in the solitude of the forest, where finally after many years he attained realisation and became a Siddha. And as at that time he had returned to his people as a spiritual guide and a living example of his realisation, he became a teacher of men in many subsequent reincarnations, ever mindful of his vow not to abandon the world as long as living beings were in need of his help. To receive his blessings and initiation into one of his particular *sādhanās* was an experience that gave a new impetus to our spiritual life.

There could not have been a more perfect continuation of the inspiration and guidance I had received from Tomo Géshé Rimpoché. In fact, it seemed to me as if all subsequent initiations into various meditative practices and teachings of the Vajrayāna (the 'Diamond Vehicle'), which we received in the course of the next two years of our pilgrimage in Southern, Central, and Western Tibet, were part of a complete system of interrelated meditational experiences, which crystallised into a perfect *maṇḍala,* a magic circle, containing all the major aspects of Tibet's religious life.

Strangely enough, it was during my first stay at Yi-Gah Chö-Ling that a Sikkimese friend had presented me with a thanka, containing the main symbols of this *maṇḍala:* Buddha Śākyamuni in the centre; above him Amitābha, the embodiment of Infinite Light; below him Padmasambhava, the revealer of the Bardo Thödol and of the mystic teachings of the 'Direct Path'. The two upper corners of the thanka were occupied by Mañjuśrī, the embodiment of Transcendental Wisdom, and Tārā (Tib.: 'Dölma'), 'the Saviouress' (the active counterpart to the Transcendental Knowledge of Mañjuśrī)—while Avalokiteśvara, the embodiment of Compassion, and Vajrapāṇi, the powerful Protector of the Dharma and the

Master of its Mystic Teachings, filled the corresponding lower corners.

Just as the Buddha Śākyamuni, as the Ādi-guru (or first teacher) of our era, occupies the central position in this thanka, so the first Guru always occupies a central position in the Chela's heart. But this does not preclude him from sitting at the feet of other teachers who might benefit him in the absence of his Tsawai Lama (lit. 'Root Lama'), because there is no competition between real Gurus, just as there is no competition between different aspects of reality or truth. Each teacher can only reveal what he himself has experienced, or realised, of what he himself has become the embodiment. No single teacher can exhaust all aspects of truth or of ultimate reality; and even if this were possible each teacher has his own individual approach towards this ultimate aim, and it depends not only on the accomplishments of the Guru, but equally on the character and capabilities of the pupil, which particular methods are helpful to him. As the ultimate aim of all methods is the same, there can be no contradiction or disharmony between them, though it would be foolish to jump from the one to the other without having attained a certain measure in any of them.

A real Guru's initiation is beyond the divisions of sects and creeds: it is the awakening to our own inner reality which, once glimpsed, determines our further course of development and our actions in life without the enforcements of outer rules. Initiation, therefore, is the greatest gift a Guru can bestow, a gift that is regarded infinitely more precious than any formal ordination on entering the state of monkhood (or any other organised religious society), which can be performed at any time, without demanding any spiritual qualification, neither of those who perform it, nor of those who receive it—provided the candidate is willing to obey the prescribed rules and is not barred by mental, moral, or physical deficiencies.

A Guru can give only as much as he has realised himself, and in order to transmit his own experience he must be able to renew or to re-create it each time he performs the Wangkur *(dbang-bskur)* rite. This requires an extensive preparation—not just an intellectual one, like that of a school or university teacher, who prepares himself by assembling all relevant data on his subject and by mapping out a logical way of presenting those data in the most convincing way—the preparation of a religious teacher consists in putting himself in touch with the deepest sources of spiritual power through intense meditation, during which he *becomes* the embodiment of the force or quality which he wants to transmit. Such a preparation may take days or weeks, according to the nature of the forces involved and the more or less intricate character of their creative symbols which have to be awakened in the consciousness of the recipient who on his part is required to prepare himself by purifying his mind and directing his attention to the teachings, ideas, or aims of the sought-for initiation.

Without this double preparedness of Guru and Chela the rite of initiation would be a mere farce, and no really great teacher will ever lend himself to such a thing. As long as the tradition of Tibet was unbroken, and its guardians and promoters lived in the security of their age-old traditions, upheld by institutions and by a society in which the values they represented were understood and respected, the temptation to lower the standard or the conditions under which initiations were to be granted was hardly present. But after the terrible holocaust and the religious persecution which followed the Chinese invasion of Tibet all bonds with the past were broken, and those who fled were thrown into an unfamiliar world, where all that had been sacred and infallible truth to them was neither known nor recognised. And thus, partly from a desire to spread the Dharma and partly from the wish to justify their position as religious leaders or ecclesiastical dignitaries, many of them felt justified to perform such rites even for those who had no knowledge of their meaning, in the hope that at least some spiritual benefit might come to the recipients of these rites as long as it awakened or strengthened their faith. In this way a rite that originally was meant to confer initiation into a profound spiritual experience became devoid of its essential meaning, and all that was left was a gesture of blessing, which might lead those who are not conversant with the traditional background to the conclusion that this is all there is to it.

The 'transference of the power of Amitāyus, the Buddha of Infinite Life', for instance, is used as a communal rite (known as '*Tsé-wang*') in a similar way as the communion in the Catholic Church, or as a certain type of paritta-ceremony in Theravāda Buddhism, in which the 'life-giving' water is sanctified and charged with the forces of mantric invocations, recited by a group of monks or lay-devotees, and given to those who are ailing or in danger of death.

The *tsé-wang* of Amitāyus (*tse-dpag-med*), however, can be turned into a proper rite of initiation (*wang-kur*)—what it was originally meant to be—if the initiator prepares the Chela for the conscious participation and understanding of the details and symbols of the ritual.[1] As a result the initiate in the course of time is enabled to invoke the life-giving forces of Amitāyus for himself and others, by practising the *sādhanā* of Amitāyus and by transforming his mantric formula into the visual and spiritual unfoldment of all those properties of which Amitāyus is the embodiment, until the devotee realises these qualities within himself and has become a true vessel of them. Only when he has achieved this can he transmit the spiritual forces engendered by this realisation.

Ajo Rimpoché was one of those rare masters who were fully conscious of these facts. He spared no pains in preparing himself and every smallest detail for the initiation he bestowed upon us. The initiation altar itself was a work of art, built up with meticulous care, according to the rules of religious tradition, in which beauty is the natural and spontaneous outcome of its indwelling spirit—and not of an intended aesthetic effect. The self-conscious element of an art that is divorced from life or meaning is unknown in Tibet. The altar represented a perfect *maṇḍala* of significant symbols, and Ajo Rimpoché explained their meaning and function, so that we could fully understand their significance and the part they played in the ritual. But what we appreciated most was the way in which he instructed us in the details and technique of the particular type of meditation and creative visualisation into which we were initiated and which we were to practise daily with the *mantras* bestowed upon us. It is only from the standpoint of creative visualisation *(dhyāna)*, guided and sustained by the living power of the inner sound *(mantra)* and crystallising into the universal order of a *maṇḍala*, that we can understand the significance of religious art in Tibet and especially the meaning of thankas and frescoes.

---

1. *Any 'wang'* given without religious instructions and guidance (as to *sādhanā*) is not an initiation and cannot establish a *guru-chela* relationship.

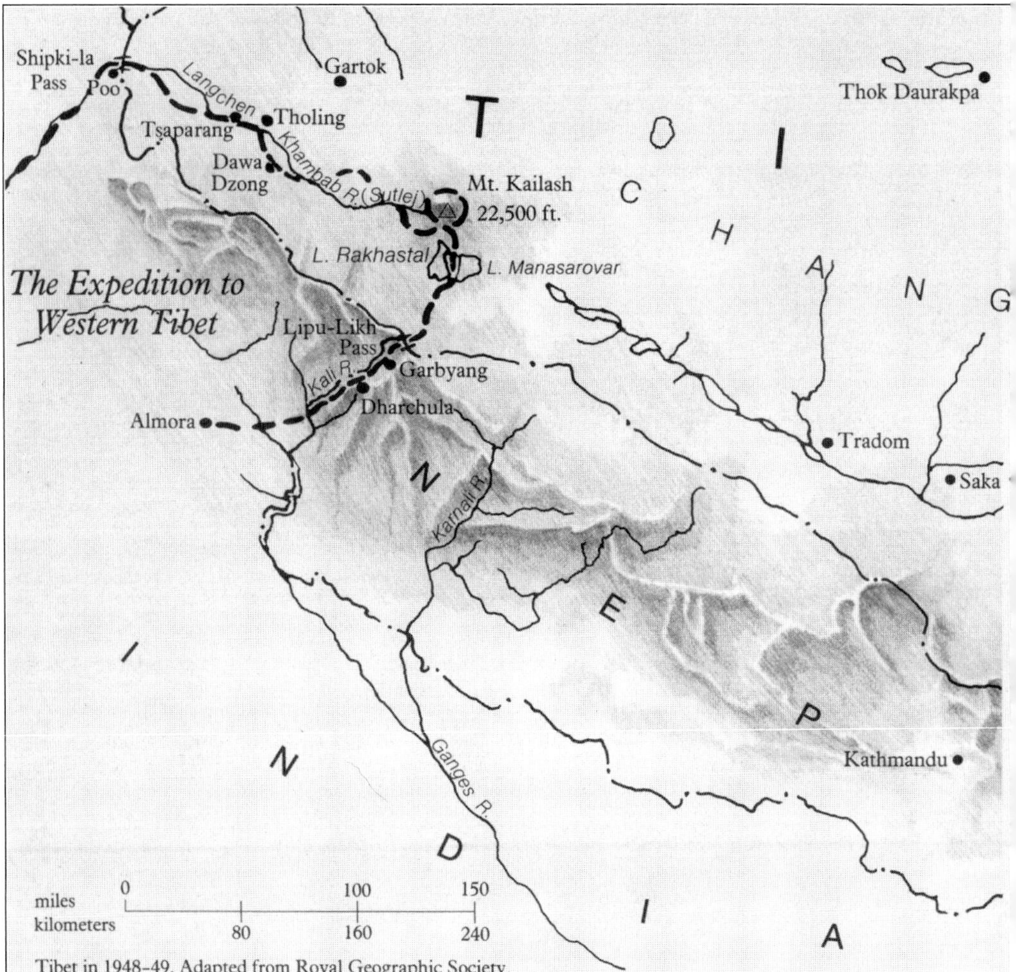

Tibet in 1948–49. Adapted from Royal Geographic Society.

Preceeding page: Lama Govinda in Tibet, Tsang Province

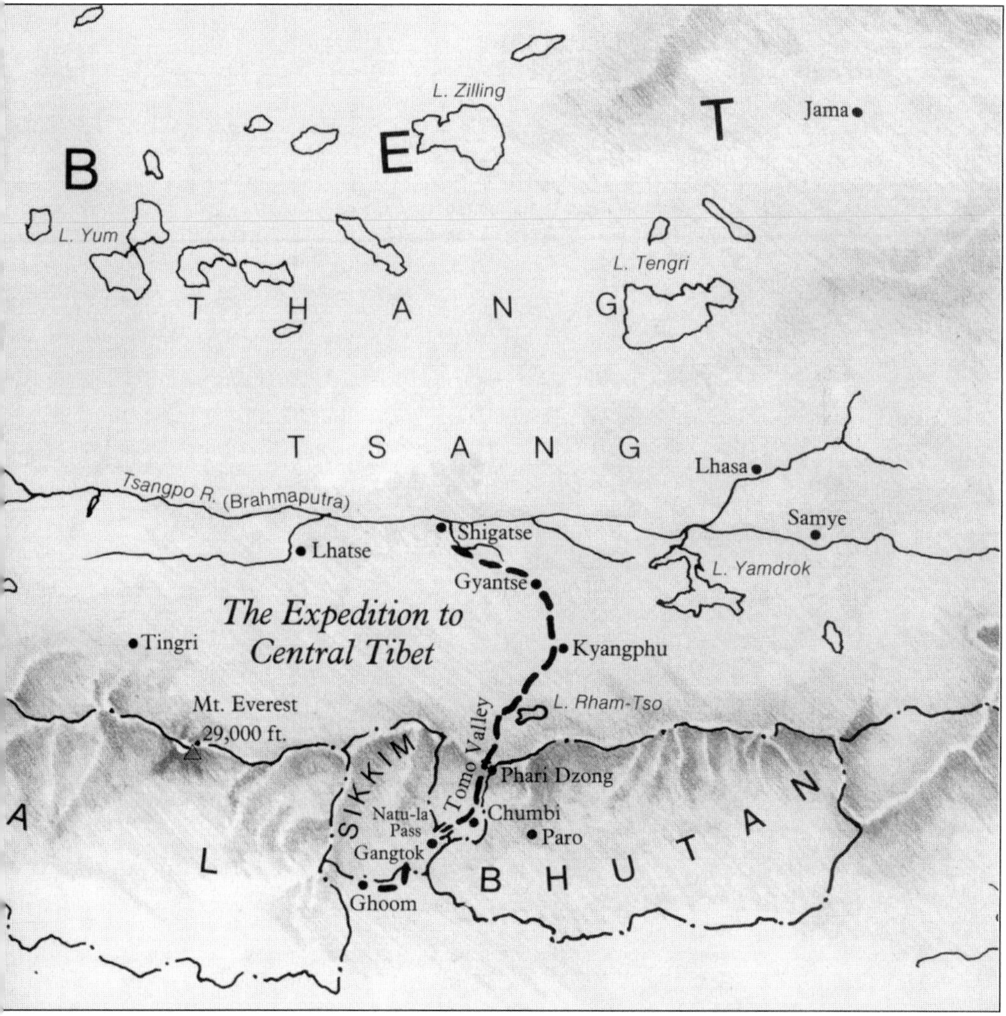

Map of Govinda's expedition to Western Tibet

Above: Tibetan Nomad Couple, Western Tibet (*See pp. 80-81*)

Right: Lama Scholar of Ganden, Rizong Pordah Monastery, Phari Dzong

Facing page: Dhyāni-Buddha Vairocana, Iwang Temple, Tsang Province (*See pp.* 30, 32, 34, 274, 295, 304, 368)

Right: Anjorepa Rimpoche, Tse Choling Monastery (*See pp.* 232-34)

Below: Traditional Tibetan Stag Dance, Tse Choling Monastery

Right: Wealthy Tibetan
Woman in Lhasa, Gyantse

Left: The Kumbum From Above,
Gyantse (*See pp.* 237-41)

Crossing the Kali River in the Himalayas, Kumaon (*See pp.* 272-79)

Facing page: En Route on Dolma Pass, Kailash Parikrams (*See pp.* 295)

Left: Old Beggar, Gyantse, Central Tibet

Below: Lama Govinda, peforming pūja at the shores of Lake Nanasarova (*See pp.* 274-75 *and* 286-88)

Above: Canyon Landscape en Route to Tholing (*See pp. 312-13*)

Left: Bandit, Western Tibet

Facing page: In the Ruins of Tsparang (*See pp. 329-30*)

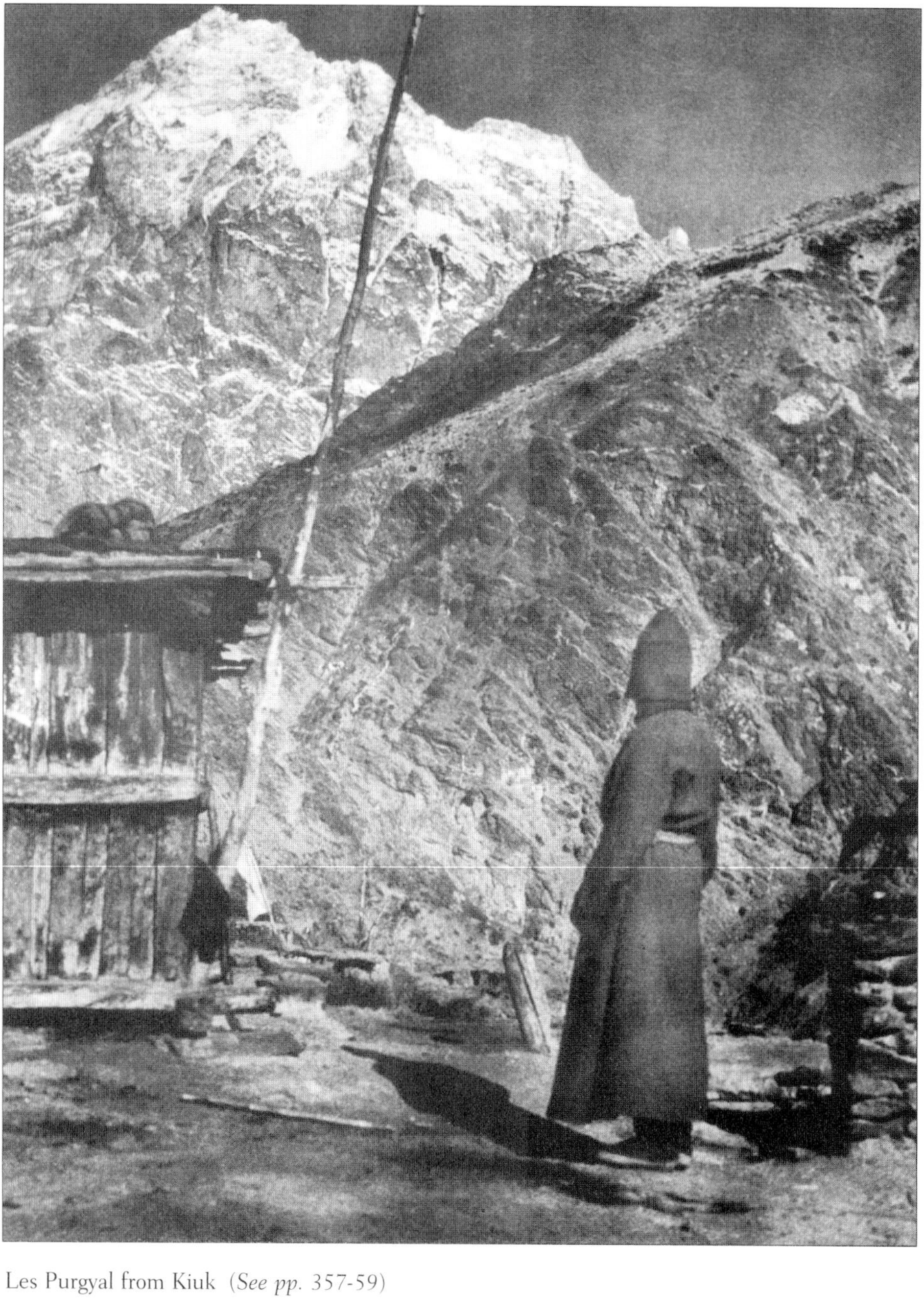

Les Purgyal from Kiuk (*See pp.* 357-59)

2

Interlude at Dungkar Gompa

SINCE THE TIME of the passing away of Tomo Géshé Rimpoché I had not felt a similar upsurge of religious emotion and the feeling of deep relationship which characterises the bonds between Guru and Chela; in fact, Ajo Rimpoché was not replacing my first Guru, but became another link connecting him with me, by strengthening and completing what I had received during my apprenticeship at Yi-Gah Chö-Ling. And here I must also remember with gratitude the impetus which we received from my Guru-bhai,[1] the abbot of Dungkar Gompa, who administered Tomo Géshé's chief monastery during his absence and the minority of his reincarnation, who at that time was studying at Sera near Lhasa. His hospitality and kindness during our stay at Dungkar Gompa were both touching and reassuring, because it demonstrated the tolerance and the mutual respect that exists between the different branches of Buddhist tradition in Tibet, where all initiates are honoured, irrespective of the sect or school to which they belong.

---

1. 'Guru-bhai' means a religious brother having the same Guru.

We were given a beautiful little Lhakhang, a kind of private chapel, as used by incarnate Lamas or high dignitaries—as our dwelling-place. But since, according to the rules of the Gelugpa Order (which maintains strict celibacy), no woman can stay overnight within the walls of the monastery, Li Gotami was offered for the nights a little room in an outhouse just at the entrance of the monastery. The Nyerpa (steward) very innocently said to us: 'Anila[1] need not be afraid to be alone; she will sleep with the Lama to whom the room belongs.' Before any misunderstanding could occur I assured the Nyerpa that I would stay there myself with Anila during the night, as it would be too difficult to separate our luggage, and that only during the daytime would we stay in the Lhakhang. The Nyerpa, naturally, had meant no offence, because in Tibet, where dwelling space is limited and the climate cold, it is customary for pilgrims or travellers of both sexes to spend the night together in any available room without the slightest embarrassment.

A short time later we had an opportunity to observe this for ourselves. The room in which we used to sleep had a kind of flimsy wooden partition open at one end and more a symbolical than factual barrier between the two parts of the room, which remained, anyway, open to view. The Lama whose guests we were during the nights slept on one side of the partition, while we occupied the other. He was a very kind and considerate person, who respected our privacy and made us feel quite at home in our little nook.

During the days of the Losar (the Tibetan New Year Festival), however, crowds of people from the Tomo- and Amo-chu Valleys congregated at the monastery, and all those whose homes were too far away to return there for the night remained in the Gompa, while their women-folk spent the nights in the available outhouses. In this way we and our good host found our quarters invaded by a lot of women, who without further ado spread themselves on every available bit of floor-space on both sides of the partition.

During our later travels we had more opportunities to observe the naturalness and the unrestricted hospitality of Tibetans, to whom prud-

---

1. Polite address of a nun or a Lama's wife.

ery is unknown, so that women without the slightest embarrassment would undress down to the waist in order to wash their hair and the upper part of their body on warm summer days, and some of them would even work in the fields during harvest-time, stripped to the waist, when the sun got uncomfortably hot in the valleys.

It goes without saying that this applies mainly to the common people and not to the more sophisticated Lhasa society, with whom we came in contact during our prolonged stay at Gyantse, where for some time we inhabited the beautifully decorated Yabshi-Pünkhang, a palatial building of one of the aristocratic families of Lhasa, connected by marriage with the royal house of Sikkim. On the whole one can say that the position of women in Tibet was very high. They played a leading role in all walks of life, except political, governmental, or ecclesiastical affairs, which in the Tibetan theocracy were closely interwoven.

Women were managing business and family property, they generally were the inheritors of family holdings, which were not to be divided, but had to be passed on intact from generation to generation, thus preventing the fragmentation and depreciation of the already scarce arable land, mostly depending on artificial irrigation. It was mainly due to these economic reasons that Tibetans had to find ways and means to keep the population strictly in proportion to the existing sources of livelihood. This was achieved partly by the system of polyandry—which prevailed mainly in the desert-like regions of Western and Northern Tibet—partly by the custom that at least one son of a family, and very often a daughter too, would join a monastery as a monk or a nun respectively.

Both monks and nuns were highly respected, especially those who had acquired some degree of learning or proficiency in meditation and in the performance of religious rituals. Among Tibetans knowledge was almost as highly prized as sanctity, and very often both were combined to a remarkable degree. Among the Gelugpas (the only exclusively celibate sect of Tibetan Buddhism) intellectual knowledge, based on the study of traditional religious literature, including history, logic, philosophy, poetry, and in certain cases also medicine and astrology, was given particular prominence, while among the Kargyütpus proficiency in meditation and spiritual experience was regarded as more important than book-knowledge and the art of debating. While the Gelugpas had to qualify themselves through a long course of studies in one of the monastic universities (like Drepung, Ganden, or Sera), the highest qualification of a Kargyütpa consisted in his ability to spend long periods in complete seclusion in caves, hermitages, meditation chambers, etc., during which he could put into practice what he had learned from his Guru and through the study of a limited number of religious texts which served as a guide for his particular *sādhanā*.

3

The Two Siddhas of Tsé-Chöling

It was as a Gomchen and as a teacher in meditation that Ajo Rimpoché had gained his prominence and had finally become recognised as the spiritual head of the monastery, whose abbot had died many years before and whose small Tulku (who at our time was about nine years old) now looked upon him for guidance until the time of his maturity, when again he would take over the full responsibilities as abbot of Tsé-Chöling. Ajo Rimpoché was one of the Repas or 'Cotton-Clad' followers of Milarepa, who did not wear the usual dark red robe of a monk, but a white shawl *(zen)* with broad red stripes; and like Milarepa he had not cut his hair, but wore it coiled up on his head. In his ears he wore the white, spiral-shaped conch-rings of the wandering ascetics *(rnal-ḥbyor-pa)* or Yogi-Siddhas of old.

Also the young Tulku was the reincarnation of one of the ancient Siddhas, namely of Saraha, who had been one of the great mystic poets of his time (seventh century A.D.). But in contrast to Ajo Rimpoché he wore the usual monastic robes; and his personal tutor, a scholarly and extremely kindhearted man who looked after the little boy with the tenderness of a mother, was a fully ordained Gelong *(bhikshu)*. Also the Umdzé, the leader of the choir, who assisted Ajo Rimpoché during our initiation, was a Gelong, while the majority of the inmates of the monastery were married people, who wore the usual red monastic robe, but lived with their families in separate little houses, scattered around the Gompa. They assembled in the main Lhakhang for religious services, which on festival days were presided over by the small Tulku of Saraha, who in spite of his tender age performed his high office with great dignity and composure.

It was strange to see how in this little boy childlike innocence and age-old wisdom seemed to be combined, and how the child in him could suddenly change into the behaviour of a wise old man, or again revert to the naturalness of a lively little boy. His tutor told us that he rapidly regained his former knowledge, reciting whole books by heart, and the Umdzé gave us a detailed account of how he found his way back to his former monastery.

He was born in a village just below Dungkar Gompa and as soon as he was able to speak he began to talk about a monastery on a hill, where he had lived as a monk. When he persisted in this talk, people took it for granted that he meant Dungkar Gompa, which could be seen from his village, but he resolutely rejected this suggestion. By chance the Umdzé of Tsé-Chöling heard about this boy, who was then between three and four years of age, and since the Tulku of Tsé-Chöling had not yet been discovered, the Umdzé, accompanied by some senior monks, went to the village where the little boy lived and, without revealing the purpose of their visit, they managed to meet him and to get into talk with him while he was playing about the house. Tibetans love children, and there was nothing exceptional in the friendly interest that some travelling monks might take in a little boy. The Umdzé carried with him a bag with ritual articles, as most Lamas do, when on a journey, and among these articles there were also some that had been used by the former abbot of Tsé-Chöling. Under some pretext or other the Umdzé opened the bag and allowed the boy to examine its contents, taking out one thing after another. When seeing the interest with which the boy contemplated each object, he asked him if he would like to have some of them, and what he would choose. Without hesitation the boy picked out a slightly damaged bell, though there was another undamaged one of the same type. 'Why do you want that old thing,' asked the Umdzé, 'when there is a much better one? Won't you have the nice new one?'

'No,' said the boy, 'I would rather have my old bell.'

'How do you know this is *your* bell?' asked the Umdzé with some surprise.

'Because one day it fell down and got chipped at the rim,' and saying this the boy turned the bell upside-down and showed the Umdzé that a tiny piece of metal was missing in the inner rim. The incident which the boy had mentioned was later on confirmed by the former abbot's old servant, who was still alive. He also confirmed the boy's observation that in the rosary which the boy had recognised as his own, a turquoise which had formed the end of the 108 beads was missing. Every single object that had belonged to the former abbot was immediately recognised by the boy, who firmly rejected all other things, though many of them were identical in shape.

The most remarkable thing, however, happened when the little boy, who was now accepted as the Tulku of the former abbot, was brought back to Tsé-Chöling. When entering the Labrang (as the abbot's residence is called) he said: 'This is not the place I used to live in. I remember it was on top of a hill.' He was correct, the Labrang in which the old abbot had lived and passed away had been higher up on a spur above the present monastery, but a fire had destroyed the building which, like most houses in this part of Tibet, was a structure of half stone half wood, surmounted by a wide roof of wooden shingles, weighed down with stones, similar to the chalets of the Austrian or Swiss Alps with which the surrounding landscape had much similarity.

Like at Dungkar Gompa we were given a beautiful Lhakhang for the duration of our stay at Tsé-Chöling, but in accordance with the more liberal attitude of the Kargyütpa Order, which embraced both married and celibate Lamas and Trapas, Li Gotami was not required to leave the precincts of the monastery at night, and thus both of us stayed together in the spacious shrine-room, in which a life-size statue of Padmasambhava was enthroned as the central figure, flanked by the numerous volumes of his and his followers' esoteric teachings. They are known as Termas (*gTer-ma* means 'treasure'), because like treasures they had been hidden underground or in caves during times of danger and persecution or—as tradition says—until the time was ripe for their understanding and rediscovery by later adepts of the ancient mystic lore. The Bardo Thödol *(Bar-do Thos-grol),* which has become famous as one of the great works of religious world-literature under the title *The Tibetan Book of the Dead,* is one of the Termas.

That Ajo Rimpoché had accommodated us in one of the chief sanctuaries of Tsé-Chöling was more than merely a sign of hospitality and trust: it meant that he had accepted us not only as honoured guests but as members of his spiritual community. We were touched at the thought that while the Guru himself lived in a bare room of his modest little cottage, we were housed in a spacious pillared and richly decorated Lhakhang, fit for a king rather than for two humble Chelas.

One side of the Lhakhang was formed by a single long window, stretching from one wall to the other, made of small glass panes, like a glassed-in veranda, so that one had a free view over the spacious courtyard and the buildings of the monastery which rose in tiers on the gentle slope of the mountainside between tall fir trees, *chortens,* and prayer-flags. We could see the Labrang, where the little Tulku lived in a lovely shrine-room covered with precious thankas, and we could also see his tutor's little bungalow, that looked like a doll's house with its elegantly fashioned woodwork and bright colours.

In the evening the tutor and the little Tulku would walk around the *chortens* and temple buildings, reciting their prayers, rosaries in hand: the tutor walking gravely ahead and the little boy cheerfully trailing behind. Sometimes he would be more interested in the birds or in a little puppy that crossed his way and had to be picked up and caressed—and then the tutor would suddenly turn back and gently remind him of his prayers, though one could see that he could quite understand a little boy's attraction for birds and puppies and his urge to play. He certainly was an understanding man, and we never saw him being harsh, though we knew that the education of a Tulku was generally much more strict than that of other novices.

Saraha Tulku was in every respect an extraordinary boy, and even if we had not known that he was a Tulku we would have easily picked him out from a crowd of ordinary boys by his exceptionally intelligent face, his bright eyes, and his gentle and yet natural behaviour. When he sat on his raised seat during a ceremony in the temple he was entirely the 'Rimpoché'; and when he received us in his private Lhakhang he did this with a charming mixture of dignity and hidden curiosity. When Li Gotami made a portrait of him in his lovely shrine-room against a row of beautiful thankas and surrounded by ritual objects, as befitting his ecclesiastical rank, he showed keen interest in the progress of her work and lost all his initial shyness, enjoying the newness of the situation and chit-chatting freely whenever there was a pause in the work. At the same time he proved to be an excellent model, sitting motionlessly in the same posture as long as the work required, without the slightest sign of impatience or tiredness.

One day, after a heavy snowfall, while we were admiring the view from our Lhakhang window, we suddenly saw some naked figures emerging from the Labrang, joyfully jumping about in the fresh snow and finally rolling in it as if in a white feather bed, while we were fairly shivering in our big but unheated 'royal abode'. The naked figures were no others but our little Tulku and two other boys of his age, who greatly enjoyed themselves in the snow. After having rolled in the snow they would quickly retire into the Labrang—probably to warm themselves—and then they would emerge anew to repeat the same performance over and over again until they had had their fill.

We were glad to see that with all learning and discipline, bodily training and youthful play were not neglected in the boys' education, and that there was no prudery in spite of the religious nature of their upbringing. We suppose that these snow-sports had something to do with preparing the boys—and especially the Tulku—for the training in Tummo, during which they must prove their capacity to resist cold by producing their own psychic heat through the mastery of body and mind in Yogic exercises. However, since we did not know whether we would cause embarrassment on mentioning that we had observed the boys in their playful enjoyment, we refrained from questioning the tutor or discussing the matter with any of the other inmates of the monastery.

We also found plenty of work to do besides our devotional practices, as there were books to study, notes to be taken, woodcuts to be printed and some outstanding frescoes to be copied or traced in outline. I was specially interested and delighted to find that the main upper Lhakhang (opposite our own), which was dedicated to Vajradhara *(Dorjé-Chang),* the Ādibuddha of the Kargyütpas (corresponding to Küntu-Zangpo, Skt. *Samantabhadra,* of the Nyingmapas), was decorated with excellent frescoes of the Eighty-Four Siddhas. This gave me another opportunity of collecting further tracings and notes, a valuable addition to my former work on this important iconographical and historical subject.

Also outside the monastery there was plenty to do in the way of sketching and photographing. We certainly had not a dull moment, and in between we had ample opportunities of discussing religious questions with Ajo Rimpoché, the Umdzé, the little Tulku's learned tutor (Gergen) and some of the Trapas. Outstanding among the latter was the Konyer *(sgo-nyer),* who was in charge of the main Lhakhangs, performing the daily offerings of water, light, and incense, and keeping everything clean and shining. He did this conscientiously, as a sacred duty, and with such devotion that he had developed a permanent swelling on his forehead from knocking it on the ground during his daily prostrations before the many images of Buddhas and Bodhisattvas, saints and Gurus, and the terrifying embodiments of the mighty protectors or tutelary deities of the faithful, the Yidams, the Masters of super-human mysteries, like Mahākāla or Vajrabhairava (Tib.: *Dorjé-hjigs-byed),* Kālacakra, Hevajra, Yeshé-Gombo, Demchog *(bDe-mchog,* Skt.: *Mahāsukha)* and others. The latter is one of the special Yidams of the Kargyütpas (though in equally high esteem with the Gelugpas and other sects, being the main symbol of one of the most profound meditational systems—to which I myself devoted a year of intense study), and it was for this reason that a special Lhakhang, adjoining that of Padmasambhava, in which we lived, had been dedicated to Demchog and the great *maṇḍala* of his deities.

At Dungkar Gompa we even found a complete plastic model of this *maṇḍala* with all its intricate details and all the 164 deities minutely executed. Unfortunately the model, which was placed in a corner of the main temple hall, was encased in a framework of wood and glass, which made it difficult to study the details and impossible to take a satisfactory photograph.

4

Lengthening Shadows

At Dungkar we had hoped to meet Tomo Géshé's little Tulku, who was about the same age as Saraha's at Tsé-Chöling. But on our first visit in 1947 he was still at Sera, where in spite of his tender age he had been sent for higher education, having successfully absorbed all the studies that his tutors at Dungkar had to offer him. All learning was merely a remembering and brushing up of his previous life's knowledge. But there had recently been disturbances at Sera in the wake of a political upheaval, due to an attempt on the life of the Regent, who headed the government of Tibet during the Dalai Lama's minority, and the people in Dungkar, as also Tomo Géshé's father in Gangtok, were worried as it was impossible to get a clear picture of the situation and it was thought to be perhaps better to call him back, unless conditions became more safe. Everything seemed to be shrouded in mystery, and the farther we proceeded into Tibet the more mysterious it became.

At Phari we found the palace of Reting Rimpoché sealed and empty (except for a giant mastiff, who almost tore us to bits when we approached the courtyard to have a look at the place). Reting Rimpoché had been the previous Regent, who had discovered the present Dalai Lama and had resigned the regentship under political pressure a few years before. One day—it was in April 1947—a bomb of Chinese make exploded when a parcel addressed to his successor was opened by a curious servant, and immediately the suspicion fell upon Reting Rimpoché, who was accused of conspiracy against the new Regent and of being in league with the pro-Chinese faction of the Tashi Lama, who had fled to China many years before in a conflict with the regime of the thirteenth Dalai Lama.

Summoned to Lhasa, the Reting Rimpoché—against the warnings and entreaties of his monks—had accepted the challenge, but while awaiting his trial in the Potala he suddenly died. According to what we were told, he was found dead one morning in the apartments to which he was confined, sitting in the posture of meditation and without any sign of violent death. His teacup, however, was found embedded in one of the hardwood pillars of his room, and, what was more, the teacup had been turned inside-out! Nobody could explain how this could have happened, but all were convinced that it was due to the Rimpoché's spiritual power. It was said that he had gone into a trance and consciously left his body, or, as others said, that he had willed himself to die.

What actually had happened, and whether the Rimpoché had really been guilty, never became known. The common people, as well as those members of the aristocracy with whom we came in contact, seemed to think him innocent, though foreign observers in Lhasa were inclined towards the opposite opinion. But it was characteristic of the general attitude of Tibetans that even though the government had arrested the Rimpoché and confiscated his estates his framed photographs were displayed in prominent places in almost every house that we visited, and also in many shops.

To the average Tibetan it seemed unthinkable that a Tulku, who had been the ruler of Tibet for many years, who had been instrumental in discovering the fourteenth Dalai Lama due to his spiritual vision, and who had renounced power on his own accord, because a significant dream had indicated that it was time for him to retire from the world—that such a man should be guilty of a common crime. Reting Rimpoché, the head of one of the oldest monasteries (*Rva-sgreng,* pron. 'Reting'), founded by Atīsha's famous disciple Bromston (born in 1002), had been recommended for the regentship by the thirteenth Dalai Lama himself, shortly before his death, though Reting Rimpoché was only twenty-three years old at that time and of delicate frame. He seemed to have been a mixture of mystic vision and worldly ambition, according to what people who had known him told us. Apparently he was torn between two worlds. His tragic end remains for ever the secret of the Potala.

When the news of it reached Reting Gompa the whole monastery rose in rebellion and overpowered the government guards who had occupied it during the Rimpoché's absence. Thereupon a military force was sent from Lhasa, and in the ensuing fight the monastery was destroyed, while the surviving monks fled all over the country.

But this was not yet the end of the tragic events. Reting Rimpoché had been a graduate of Sera, one of the biggest and most powerful monasteries of the Gelugpas, only three miles from Lhasa. Enraged by the happenings at Reting, a section of the monks of Sera rose against the government, and only after a bombardment by artillery was peace restored, though the causes of unrest were still existent and it seemed as if future events had already thrown their shadows over this otherwise so peaceful land.

These were the conditions which agitated the minds of all those who feared for the safety of the little Tulku of Tomo Géshé Rimpoché at Sera.

In the meantime we were occupied with our studies in the great monasteries and temples of Gyantse—the Pal-khorlo Chöde and especially the Kumbum, the 'Temple of the Hundred Thousand Buddhas'—while awaiting our Lamyig (an official pass entitling one to transport facilities and basic provisions while travelling in Tibet) and our authorisation to work in the ancient monasteries and temples of Rinchen Zangpo in Western Tibet. We were too busy to give much attention to political affairs, and, moreover, we had given an undertaking to the political officer at Gangtok not to divulge any information about inner political events in Tibet. So we left things well alone, avoiding any expression of opinion and taking no sides—neither for nor against Reting Rimpoché—though *one* thing we could see very clearly, namely that power and religion could not go together in the long run, and that the greatest danger for Tibet lay in the accumulation of power in those monasteries in which thousands of monks were living together as in an ant-heap and where the most precious thing of a truly religious life was lost: the peace of solitude and the integrity and freedom of the individual.

Even in the great monastic city which dominated the secular town of Gyantse we could see the deterioration of standards which is inevitable wherever human beings are crowded together, and we all the more appreciated the wisdom of Milarepa and his followers, who preferred lonely retreats and small religious communities to vast institutions of learning, where book-knowledge became more important than the formation of character and the development of wisdom and compassion.

In the past the Sakyapas, who took their name from Sa-skya ('tawny earth') Monastery south-west of Shigatse (founded A.D. 1071), had become the most powerful religious organisation and finally became the rulers of the whole of Tibet. The political power, however, was the very cause of their downfall, because force creates counter-forces. They were finally overthrown by the Gelugpas, who, with the consolidation of the Dalai Lamas in Lhasa, took over both the spiritual and the temporal power in Tibet. Their monasteries grew into cities in which up to 10,000 monks were residing.

They reminded one of the ancient monastic universities of Nālanda and Vikramaśīla, which centralised the religious and cultural life of Buddhism to such an extent that they offered an easy target to the Mohammedan invaders, who by the destruction of these powerful institutions annihilated the Buddhist religion in India, while Hinduism that was neither centralised nor dependent on monastic organisations survived, because its tradition was carried on within the intimate circles of priestly families or pious householders, and by independent individuals who chose the life of wandering ascetics or formed themselves into small groups of Chelas around a Guru. Even the destruction of temples cannot destroy a religion in which every house has its own little shrine and where in every family there is at least one who is able to carry on the religious tradition.

It was only a few years later, shortly after we had left Tibet, that history repeated itself: the great monasteries of Tibet became the first target of the communist invaders, and if Buddhism is to survive at all in Tibet it will be only in hidden hermitages, far away from towns and trade-routes, and in those families in which religious life does not depend on monastic organisations and institutions, but where the flame of faith is handed down from generation to generation, as I have seen especially among Nyingmapas, Kargyütpas, and other smaller groups of Tibetan Buddhists, following strictly the personal Guru-Chela tradition in preference to the mass education in big monastic institutions.

As I said, the events of the future threw their shadows ahead. The withdrawal of the British from India, and the fear that China might try again to claim overlordship over Tibet, created a feeling of uncertainty—though at that time nobody thought that the danger would come from the communists, who were still fighting the Kuomintang—and it probably was for this reason that the government of Tibet did not dare to judge Reting Rimpoché in an open trial or to reveal the facts and their political implications.

We ourselves had almost forgotten these events and it seemed that Sera had settled down to its normal peaceful life, since no further news had been received from there. Moreover, during the festive season in autumn, everybody, from the Regent down to the smallest official, from the Dalai Lama down to the simplest Trapa, and from the most prominent citizens down to the humblest servant, enjoyed a variety of public entertainments: mystery-plays in the monasteries, theatrical performances of religious legends (like stories concerning the former lives of the Buddha) by professional actors in the courtyards of big family mansions (but open to all and sundry without entrance fee), picnic-parties in richly decorated tents at beauty spots around the town or near monastic mountain retreats, and last but not least, popular horse-racing, arrow-shooting, folk-dances and similar amusements, enjoyed by rich and poor. The Tibetan has as great a zest for life and pleasure as for religion, and he knows how to combine the two and thus to 'make the best of both worlds'.[1]

1. That the Tibetan lives in constant fear of demons is one of those silly remarks which have been repeated *ad nauseam* by those who know nothing of Tibetan mentality or those who need an excuse for trying to convert Tibetans to their own brand of superstitions.

But soon the intense cold of the approaching winter put a stop to most outdoor entertainments, and everybody went about in fur caps and winter clothing, though the sun was as radiant as ever and the skies like deep blue velvet. But the ground and the ponds were frozen, and even the swift-flowing river was bordered with ice.

It was then that we heard a rumour that the little Tulku of Tomo Géshé had left Sera and was on his way home to Dungkar. He was expected to break his journey at Gyantse and to rest there for a few days before proceeding to his monastery. But so often had we heard such rumours that we did not give them much credence, especially since peace seemed to have been restored at Sera.

One day we were returning from the 'Temple of the Hundred Thousand Buddhas' (Kumbum), where I was copying inscriptions and fresco details of iconographic interest, while Li Gotami took photographs of some of the most beautiful statues (of which some were reproduced in my *Foundations of Tibetan Mysticism*). It was a particularly cold and windy day, and we were muffled up in our heavy Tibetan clothes like everybody else. While hurrying through the main bazaar, which we had to cross daily on our way to and from the walled monastic city, we saw two or three monks coming from the opposite direction apparently on their way to the Pal-khorlo Chöde. One of the Trapas carried a little boy on his shoulder, who like him was clad in the usual dark red monastic robes. We would probably have passed the group without taking any notice of them had it not been for the unusual behaviour of the little boy, who suddenly straightened himself, raised his head, and looked at us intensely, as if stirred by a sudden impulse or surprise—while neither the monk who carried him, nor those who accompanied him, took the slightest notice of us. In fact, we were indistinguishable from other Tibetans in the street, and our eyes, which might have given us away as foreigners, were hidden behind dark glasses. The latter were very popular among Tibetans as a protection against the glaring sun as much as against the penetrating particles of sand and dust during windy days and sandstorms. When passing us the boy seemed to get more agitated, turning round in the arms of the monk who carried him and looking at us with undisguised attention—as if trying to remember somebody whom he knew, but whom he could not identify. Now it was our turn to be puzzled—and suddenly it came to us like a flash that the little boy might be the Tulku of Tomo Géshé Rimpoché.

But in the meantime we had left the group already a good distance behind us, and though Li urged me to turn back and to run after them, I somehow felt that this was not only against Tibetan etiquette, but more so that this was not the place nor the time for such a momentous meeting. To stop them in the middle of the bazaar in the icy wind, with a crowd of curious onlookers—no, this was not how I would like to meet my old Guru—even though he was in the disguise of a mere child. I wanted this to take place in quiet surroundings and in silence, so that I would be able to listen to my own heart and to the spontaneous reaction of the little Tulku. No, I would not have liked to desecrate this precious moment by vulgar curiosity and empty polite talk!

We therefore decided first to make sure that we had not been mistaken in our surmise and to find out the place where the little Tulku was staying, so that we could pay him a visit early next morning. I was deeply stirred at the thought of our meeting, and we both wondered whether the boy would be able to recall the past clearly enough in order to re-establish the old contact. After all, he was already nine years old, and the impressions and experiences of his new life would certainly have replaced most of his pre-natal remembrances.

We hurried back to our quarters, and soon we found out that it was indeed Tomo Géshé's Tulku whom we had met on his way to the temple. But when next morning we went out to meet him we were informed that he and his party had left before sunrise!

We were deeply disappointed, but we consoled ourselves with the thought that we would meet him certainly at Dungkar on our return journey, and that there we would not only have the opportunity of a quiet talk but of living for some time in his own surroundings and in daily contact with him.

5

Mystery-plays

How differently things turn out from what we expect! When a few months later we arrived at the Monastery of the White Conch, Tomo Géshé Rimpoché had left for a tour of his monasteries in the Darjeeling district, and by the time we got back to India he had returned again to Sera, which people thought safe enough now—not suspecting the terrible fate that hung over this place and the untold sufferings it would bring to the young Tulku. However, I will relate these happenings in a later chapter and confine myself first to the events nearer at hand.

Due to various reasons we stayed several months longer at Gyantse than intended, but our time was well spent and we took the opportunity to visit numerous monasteries and mountain retreats *(ri-khrod,* pron. 'ritö') in the nearer and farther surroundings, besides making as thorough a study of the famous Kumbum as possible within the time at our disposal (the amount of iconographic material contained in it could not have been exhausted in a lifetime!) and attending many religious ceremonies and festivals, including the famous monastic dances and mystery-plays with all their splendour of gorgeously brocaded costumes, the fantastic vivacity of their masks, their magic gestures and movements and the sonorous musical accompaniment, in which the voices of divine and demoniac powers seemed to contend with each other in a vast arena of soaring mountains and monumental architecture.

I had attended similar performances at Yi-Gah Chö-Ling, Hemis, and a number of smaller places—the most impressive at Hemis (Ladakh), where the mystery-plays continued for three days in succession and where thousands of people, who had come from near and far (many of them trekking for many days to attend the festival), camped in and around the monastery, situated in a wild mountain scenery of fantastic beauty. Here, where people in those days had not yet come in touch with the outer world, where people had never seen a vehicle on wheels, where the mere mention of railways or steamships aroused an incredulous smile, and where aeroplanes or the like had never been heard of—it was here that one could see and participate in the feelings which these mystery-plays aroused.

They were far from being merely theatrical performances: they were the coming to life of a higher reality through magic rites, in which beings from the spiritual world were propitiated and invited to manifest themselves in the bearers of their symbols, who for the time being divested themselves of their own personality, by going through a ritual of purification and making themselves instruments and vessels of the divine powers which their masks represented. These masks, which seemed to take on a life of their own under the strong Tibetan sun and in the measured rhythmic movements of their bearers, were not only of a benevolently 'divine' nature but embodied likewise the terrible guises which those powers assumed in the outer world as well as in the human heart: the powers of death and destruction, the terrors of the great unknown, the powers of demoniacal fury and hellish illusion, of fearful spectres and sneering demons of doubt, which assail us on our way from birth to death and from death to rebirth, until we have learned to face life and death with the courage that only the compassion for our fellow-beings and insight into the true nature of phenomena can give us. Unless we are able to recognise all these fearful and terrifying appearances as emanations of our own mind and transformations of the force that will ultimately lead us towards enlightenment we shall wander endlessly in the rounds of birth and death, as it is said in the *Bardo Thödol (The Tibetan Book of the Dead)*.

Thus the mystery-plays of Tibet are the representations of this supernatural, or better, super-human world that manifests itself in the human soul and would overpower it if no adequate expression could be found. The mystery-plays of ancient Egypt as well as those of the Dionysian cult sprang from the same source. And just as in Greece the theatre developed from the mystic Dionysian dances, so the Tibetan religious plays had their origin in the ritual dances of the magicians, in which symbolical gestures (*mudrā*) and incantations (*mantra*) served the purpose of warding off evil and creating beneficial influences.

As with the Greeks the performance takes place in the middle of the audience. There is no separate or elevated stage, but the plays are performed in the main courtyard of the monastery, which is generally surrounded by galleries in which the most prominent people are seated, while the others are crowded in the remaining space in the courtyard and on all the available roofs round about. The imposing architecture, the gorgeously decorated galleries and the colourful gay crowd form a natural and most beautiful setting, which is as inseparable from the dances as the architecture from the landscape and the spectators from the performers. The very fact that the latter were not separated from the spectators by a stage, but moved through and within the crowd, emphasises the oneness of spectators and performers in an experience in which the boundaries between the natural and the supernatural, the profane and the sacred, have been eliminated, so that the spectators become as much a part of the play as the actors, participating in and fully responding to the magic, mind-created reality of a higher dimension. Their expectancy and implicit faith, their spontaneous reactions and emotions, seem to create a kind of integrated consciousness, in which performers and spectators are merged and lifted up to a level of spiritual experience that otherwise would have been unattainable and inaccessible to them.

What an unforgettable sight to see the super-human figures of saints and of celestial and demoniacal beings emerge from the dark cave-like portals of the main temple, majestically descending the long flight of steps down to the courtyard, accompanied by the thundering blasts of twelve-foot-long horns and the slow rhythm of deep kettle-drums. Thousands of people who occupy every inch of ground round the open space in the centre of the courtyard, as well as the open verandas, balconies, and roofs of the adjoining buildings, hold their breath in spellbound silence. Step by step the awe-inspiring figures descend: under the multi-coloured royal umbrella Padmasambhava himself, the great apostle and master of all magic arts, followed by the various forms and incarnations which he assumed in his multifarious activities in the service of mankind: as Buddha-Śākyamuni, as king, as scholar, as Yogi, as monk, and in his terrible forms: as the subduer of demons and protector of the Sacred Law, etc. In measured dance-steps and with mystic gestures they circle the open space around the tall prayer-flag in the centre of the courtyard, while the rhythmically swelling and ebbing sounds of a full monastic orchestra mingle with the recitation of holy scriptures and prayers, invoking the blessings of Buddhas and saints and glorifying their deeds and words. Clouds of incense rise to heaven and the air vibrates with the deep voices of giant trombones and drums.

But while those awe-inspiring figures solemnly wheel around, the almost unbearable tension and exaltation, which has gripped the spectators, is suddenly relieved by the appearance of two grotesquely grinning masks, whose bearers are aping the movements of the sacred dancers and seem to mock the Buddhas and even the terrifying Defenders of the Faith. They are weaving in and out of the solemn circle, gaping into the faces of the dancers, as if defying and ridiculing both the divine and the demoniacal powers. These, however, seem to take no notice and move on with unperturbed dignity.

The effect is astonishing: far from destroying the atmosphere of wonder and sacredness, the juxtaposition of the sublime and the ridiculous rather seems to deepen the sense of reality, in which the highest and the lowest have their place and condition each other, thus giving perspective and proportion to our conception of the world and of ourselves.

By experiencing the opposite pole of reality simultaneously, we actually intensify them. They are like the counterpoints in a musical composition: they widen the amplitude of our emotional response by creating a kind of inner space through the distance of simultaneously experienced opposites. The wider the amplitude, the greater the depth or intensity of our experience. Tragedy and comedy are for ever interwoven in the events of our life, seriousness and a sense of humour do not exclude each other; on the contrary, they constitute and indicate the fulness and completeness of human experience and the capacity to see the relativity of all things and all 'truths' and especially of our own position.

The Buddha's sense of humour—which is so evident in many of his discourses—is closely bound up with his sense of compassion: both are born from an understanding of greater connections, from an insight into the interrelatedness of all things and all living beings and the chain reactions of cause and effect. His smile is the expression of one who can see the 'wondrous play of ignorance and knowledge' against its universal background and its deeper meaning. Only thus is it possible not to be overpowered by the misery of the world or by our own sense of righteousness that judges and condemns what is not in accordance with our own understanding and divides the world into good and bad. A man with a sense of humour cannot but be compassionate in his heart, because his sense of proportion allows him to see things in their proper perspective.

In the Tibetan mystery-plays all states of existence are present: the worlds of gods and men, of animal-headed monsters and hungry spirits, the spectres of death and annihilation and the human and super-human incarnations of love and compassion, through which all forms of existence are freed from their limitations and reunited with that greater life that encompasses all.

The struggle between the forces of light and darkness, between the divine and the demonic, between the titanic forces of decay and dissolution and the innate urge for eternal life—this struggle is depicted both on the historical as well as on the timeless plane of the human soul. The coming of Padmasambhava and his victory over the black magicians and the host of evil spirits, whom the latter tried to appease with bloody sacrifices, both human and animal, is the main subject of the first day's performance in the monasteries of the Old Schools (Nyingma, Kargyüd, and Sakya), while the Gelugpas depict the slaying of King Langdarma in the bow-and-arrow dance of the hermit, who appears in the guise of a black magician, attired in the robes and the black skull-surmounted hat of the Bön priests, as described in the historical appendix of this book.

More important, however, than the historical allusions are those related to *The Tibetan Book of the Dead* (*Bardo Thödol*), Padmasambhava's greatest work, which makes it clear that all the gods and demons, the forces of light and darkness, are within us, and that those who want to conquer the Lord of Death will have to meet him and to recognise him in the midst of life. Then Death will appear as the revealer of the ultimate mystery of life, who under the guise of the terrible bull-headed King of Death, and accompanied by all the frightful spectres that a terrified human conscience can conjure up, slays the demon of egohood and selfishness and thus performs the only sacrifice that the Buddha recognises: the sacrifice of one's own 'ego'. The Lord of Death *(yama-rāja)* is none other than the Great Compassionate One, Avalokiteśvara. Thus the bloody sacrifices of the past were replaced by that of our own little self that has held us in bondage for aeons and will keep us in the unceasing rounds of birth and death until we have grown beyond it and freed ourselves from its clutches.

Padmasambhava, one of the wisest teachers of all time, thus gave a new meaning to the magic ritual that had been handed down by the Bön priests from times immemorial, when sacrifices of blood seemed to be the only way to appease the gods and the dark powers of the universe that threatened man's very existence. Now the human heart had become the stage of the universe, and instead of a living human being or an animal, the effigy of a man, made of coloured dough, was carried into the arena by skeleton-like cemetery ghouls, who performed a wild dance around it, until the Lord of Death and his frightful retinue appeared on the scene and drove them away.

And now follows the most dramatic and significant part of the sacred dances (forming the highlight of the second day of the mystery-play of the Old Schools): the Lord of Death, wearing the dark blue mask of a three-eyed, skull-crowned bull of frightful size and appearance—a blood-filled skull-bowl in one hand and swinging a broad-bladed battle-sword in the other—dances with ever-quickening steps and increasing ferocity around the prostrate human figure in the centre of the court-yard, until he whirls around at such speed that his features become a mere blur and his sword a bundle of flashes. The drums accelerate their rhythm to a crescendo of thunder—and at that moment the sword strikes the effigy, dismembers it, and scatters the parts in all directions. Now a wild scramble ensues, in which the host of demons pick up the scattered parts of the effigy and, after having devoured some morsels of it, throw the remainder into the air and among the spectators, who like-wise take part in the sacrificial feast.

It is difficult to give an idea of the realistic and at the same time fan-tastic effect of this intermingling of the natural and the supernatural. The masks—over-life-sized and expressively stylised in form and colour—seem to be animated in the most uncanny way and more real than the human beings who wear them or the spectators who have completely surrendered themselves to the spirit of the play. All of them participate in an experience that transcends their present state of existence and seems to lift them beyond the frontiers of death: where the gates of all the worlds and forms of rebirth are opened, and where at the same time the path that leads beyond them appears before the inner eye or is felt as an upsurge of longing towards the ultimate aim of liberation and enlightenment.

Now performers and spectators are welded into one and have both become active participants in a magic rite, which initiates them into one of the most ancient mysteries which is the origin of all religious life and the beginning of the awakening of man.

6

The State Oracle of Nächung

The mystery of death was the greatest challenge to the human mind and the birth of religion. It was through death that man became *conscious* of life. A great biologist (Lecomte de Noüy) once said that 'the greatest invention of Nature is death'. In other words: even from a biological point of view, death is not a negation of life, but one of the means to add a new dimension to life and thus to raise it to a higher level.

Unbroken physical continuity is a characteristic property of the lowest organisms, the most primitive and undeveloped forms of life, because physical continuity fetters the organism to the rigid laws of matter and the dictates of once-established patterns, whose inherent repetitiveness prevents any deviation from the norm and thus becomes the greatest stumbling block in the way of development and further evolution.

Death, on the other hand, is the characteristic feature of the higher forms of existence, which achieve the survival of acquired properties and experiences through a new form of propagation, that relies no more on division, but on *integration,* no more on a merely physical, but on a psychic, continuity, capable of building a new organism according to its own individual impetus—unhampered by the rigid accumulations of obsolete or worn-out material form-elements.

Similar to the transition from a purely physical to a predominantly psychic survival and continuity is the next step, which so far has only been achieved by the most highly developed individuals: it is the step from the unconscious to the conscious (and finally to the consciously directed) survival through the art of spiritual projection (*powa*).

However, before man could visualise the possibility of this step, he had already realised the importance of death as a key to the mysteries of a greater life. Out of this realisation grew the cult of the dead, the earliest form of religion. It stimulated man to build the first *enduring* monuments of architecture (in contrast to the frail and transitory dwellings for the living); monuments that were not the outcome of necessity and want, of momentary needs or temporal utility, but of a will towards eternity, a spiritual urge that pointed towards a reality beyond temporal existence.

Thus the origin of religion was not the *fear* of death, but the recognition of death as the great transformer and initiator into the true nature of man's innermost being. The fear of death could only originate at a time when human consciousness had hardened into an extreme form of individualism, based on the illusion of being a permanent entity, a self-existing soul or ego that separates one being from the other, and living beings from dead things: thus drawing a line between life and death, a line that finally becomes a boundary, an impenetrable wall, towards which life rushes headlong—only to be annihilated in the impact.

But at a time when human beings had not yet lost the connection with their origins and their surroundings, in a world in which man was still in touch with the subtle forces of nature, the spirits of the departed, the realms of gods and demons, in short: in a world in which there was nothing that could be conceived as lifeless, death was not the contradiction to life, but a phase in the movement of life's pendulum, a turning-point, like birth. The pendulum swings from birth to death and back from death to birth.

The movement of life's pendulum, however, is not confined to one plane only; it can swing on an infinite number of planes, move in all dimensions of consciousness, according to its inherent momentum or according to the conscious impetus that it may receive in that infinitesimally small fraction of timelessness at its turning-point, that is, between death and rebirth, or between one realm of existence and another. It is this timeless 'moment', in which those who have learnt to look inwards, who have practised introspection and developed their inner vision through *sādhanā* and *dhyāna,* will be able to perceive the realms of existence open or adequate to them, and to direct their mind consciously towards the plane that offers the greatest chances for the realisation of their highest aspirations, as explained in the *Bardo Thödol*.

These various realms to which we normally have access only at the turning-point of our life, i.e. at the moment of death, can be contacted also by inducing artificially a state of catalepsy or suspended animation, in which man goes temporarily through the process of death, relinquishing the dominion over his body and the consciousness of his own individuality. This is a state of trance, which can be created either by autohypnosis or by certain yogic practices or through powerful rituals, in which inner and outer stimuli combine to release super-individual forces, normally dormant in the deeper layers of the human psyche and not accessible to the intellect.

These rituals, which were known to the magicians, shamans, and 'sorcerers' of old, i.e. people who had power over the human mind and the key to its hidden forces, were retained even after the advent of Buddhism in Tibet, though modified sufficiently to fit into the general frame of Buddhist ideas and traditions. Padmasambhava, himself a great master of this secret science, made wise use of it and thus fought the Bön shamans, who tried to prevent the spread of Buddhism in Tibet with their own weapons. At the same time he respected the local deities and incorporated them into the Buddhist system as 'Protectors of the Sacred Law'—just as Buddha Śākyamuni had done with the Hindu deities of his time.

These Protectors (Skt.: *dharmapāla,* Tib. *chos-skyong*) were invoked in a special temple at Samyé, Tibet's oldest monastery, which had been built by Padmasambhava. In this temple the high priest or Chöjé (*chos-rjé*) was said to be possessed by the ancient gods or guardian spirits of

Tibet whenever the elaborate liturgical service in their honour was performed. On these occasions the Chöjé fell into a trance, during which the gods spoke through him and answered the questions that were submitted to them during the ritual. Thus the oracle of Samyé was established.

Strangely enough, the Gelugpas—who were the farthest removed from the tradition of the ancient Nyingmapas and who are generally supposed to have reduced the elements of magic ritual, which had been taken over from pre-Buddhist times—not only took over the oracle-tradition from Samyé but raised it to the level of a state institution. This happened under the great fifth Dalai Lama, when the Gelugpas were at the peak of their power. It was at this time that the Nächung (*gNas-chung*) Oracle was attached to the famous monastery of Drepung (*hbras-spungs*) and recognised as the State Oracle of Tibet. It was regarded as the highest authority and its advice was sought whenever there was a difficulty in finding the reincarnation or Tulku (*sprul-sku*) of a high Lama (as in the case of the Dalai Lama and of Tomo Géshé Rimpoché), or whenever a political decision of great importance was to be made. Even the Dalai Lamas were guided by the pronouncements of the Great Oracle, whose predictions proved to be of astonishing accuracy.

The institution of oracles, however, did not remain confined to Nächung. Many of the more important Gelugpa monasteries had their own oracles, whose high priests occupied an important place in the religious hierarchy. But all of them had to be confirmed by the State Oracle, after having gone through a strict training and a gruelling test. Special temples were devoted to their rituals, and everything that was connected with them was of such magnificence that they could vie with the most beautiful shrines of Tibet. Like the main temple of Lhasa (the so-called 'Jokhang') and the chapel of the Dalai Lamas on top of the Potala, the sanctuary of Nächung is covered with a golden roof.

The name Nächung (*gNas-chung*) literally means 'Small Place', and its origin is explained in a popular story. A mighty magician, who lived in the upper reaches of the Kyi-chu (*sKyid-chu*)—the river that flows past Lhasa—forced a powerful spirit into a small box, which he threw into the river. When the box floated past the monastery of Drepung, one of its monks, who happened to be in the valley below the monastery, saw the box, and wondering what it might contain, he pulled it out of the river and opened it. At that moment the spirit escaped from his 'narrow confinement' (*gNas-chung*) with a terrifying noise, and assuming the form of a dove, flew towards a small grove and took his abode in it. In order to propitiate the spirit and to prevent him from doing harm, a sanctuary was built on the spot where the dove had alighted, and since that time the officiating Lama of that temple became possessed by the spirit, whenever the latter was invoked.

However, the fact that the Nächung Oracle is possessed not only by one but by six deities or Protectors (*chos-skyong*) clearly indicates that it has its origin in the ancient oracle of Samyé. The above-mentioned legend was probably meant to hide this fact at a time when the power of the Gelugpas was replacing the influence of the older schools. The well-meant reforms, the systematisation of tradition and the centralisation of spiritual and temporal power, could not succeed without the sanction and inclusion of older traditions, whose knowledge and ability to deal with psychic or super-human powers had won them the confidence and the support of the people.

This must have been the motive that caused the fifth Dalai Lama to reestablish the oracles in their former importance and to give them an honoured position within the Gelugpa Order, by equipping these sanctuaries in the most magnificent way. As if to placate the dark and untamed powers of a primordial world, the place and every object connected with the secret ritual had to be of the purest and most precious materials and in strict accordance with the rules of an age-old magic symbolism. All ritual implements were of gold or silver, adorned with precious stones, the walls were covered with frescoes, painted with gold on a black background, and a band of mantric inscriptions in raised golden letters in the sacred mystic script of the tenth or eleventh century (*lantsa*) encircled the sanctuary in which the divine or demoniacal forces were to manifest themselves. The golden throne of the oracle, on a raised platform between red-lacquered pillars, was beautifully carved and richly decorated with gems, like coral, onyx, turquoise, garnet, amethyst, agate, etc. Life-size images of the six Spirit-Kings, fierce, awe-inspiring, daemonical figures, wielding various weapons, guarded the sanctuary. Replicas of these weapons were placed before the oracle-priest during his trance, and the weapon seized by him indicated which of the six tutelary spirits or 'Protectors of the Sacred Law' had taken possession of his body, transforming him into the living image of the invoked deity, who now spoke through his mouth.

Nobody, who has not witnessed this transformation, can imagine the weird, almost frightening effect of it; because what happens here seems to contradict all laws of reason: a man changing before your very eyes into another being, taking on a different personality, physically and mentally. His features completely change, and his head as well as his body seem to grow in size—the latter developing a super-human strength, equal to that of half a dozen men. If ever there has been the materialisation of a 'spirit' in broad daylight—here it is. It is the materialisation of forces which—much as our intellect tries to deny or explain them away—can be seen and felt by all who are present during these rites. The whole atmosphere of the sanctuary seems to be changed with an irresistible power, which communicates itself even to the most detached observer.

Whatever may be the explanation of these phenomena, one thing is sure: here is no deception, no mere make-believe (which, indeed, would go beyond human endurance), but a psychic reality, a last survival of a tradition that reaches back into the dawn of humanity. Tibet is (or was) probably the last country in which the knowledge of these primeval psychic forces had not only been preserved, but in which the dangers inherent in them had been mastered and directed into safe channels, due to the wisdom and the tactful guidance of Buddhist saints and sages. Though the origin of these traditions and rituals has nothing to do with Buddhism, Buddhists could not afford to disregard them, as long as they played a vital role in the spiritual life of the people. However unpalatable certain aspects of reality may be, they have to be faced as facts and met at their own level. Problems cannot be solved by disapproval but only by facing them.

7

The Oracle of Dungkar Gompa

DURING OUR FIRST VISIT to Dungkar, Li Gotami and myself had been admiring the beautiful oracle-temple *(chökyong-lhakhang)* with its magnificent golden throne and its fierce images and frescoes. But we had not been able to get any information about its functions, nor whether the oracle-priest was in residence or on what occasions he would go into trance. We had the feeling that the young Trapa, who showed us around, was reluctant to speak about these things and that—since we had only recently arrived from the outside world beyond the passes and were not yet known to him—he obeyed the usual rules of secrecy which apply to the cult of the fierce and terrible powers.

But there were so many other things that occupied our attention that we did not press him. Moreover, we had been so warmly received by the abbot and the other inmates of the monastery, that we felt sure nothing would be hidden from us in the long run. The abbot was glad to find in me a brother disciple (guru-bhai) of Tomo Géshé Rimpoché and insisted that we should stay at Dungkar for a longer time on our return from Central Tibet. We gladly accepted this invitation, because we felt that the spirit of Tomo Géshé was still pervading the whole place and was alive in the minds of all who dwelled here. This showed itself in the kindliness of the monks, the sense of order and cleanliness that prevailed everywhere, the discipline without harshness that governed the monastic life, and the courtesy that was shown to us by all, from the highest to the lowest. All religious duties were meticulously observed, everybody went about his appointed task, and the little boys who received their education in the monastery seemed to be happy and well treated. Sometimes Lobonla, as the abbot was called, would wobble along holding one little tot with each hand, and whenever the little ones would feel homesick, he would console them like a good mother. Lobonla himself was not in good health, and he moved about with difficulty, partly due to arthritis or rheumatism and partly because of his heavy bulk.

We were, therefore, all the more touched when on our return Lobonla and a group of senior monks received us with great cordiality at the main entrance of the Gompa. In spite of his difficulty in climbing steps (and staircases in Tibet are generally very steep) Lobonla insisted on showing us personally to our quarters and entertaining us there with tea and sweet Tibetan bread.

The day after our arrival was the great Prayer Festival (*mon-lam*), and from all neighbouring valleys people were streaming towards the monastery, while the monks were busy with preparations for the main celebration, which was to take place in the evening and during the night. In the morning the Pratimoksha ceremony (confession), in which only Gelongs (Bhikshus) take part, was celebrated in the main temple. We therefore remained in our private chapel.

Shortly before noon we heard from the Chökyong Temple the booming of kettle-drums and saw a crowd pressing forward towards its entrance. Wondering whether some important function was taking place there or that perhaps the Oracle was in action, we hurried down to the courtyard, dived into the crowd and following the maelstrom of humanity we found ourselves soon pushed up the steps of the temple into the vestibule and finally into the hall of the sanctuary. Before we knew how it happened we stood before the throne of the Great Oracle!

It was all so utterly fantastic and surprising that we could only stare at the majestic figure that occupied the golden throne and was clad in magnificent brocades and crowned by a jewel-studded golden tiara with the three eyes of the all-seeing spirit. A shining golden breast-plate, the magic mirror, engraved with the sacred syllable 'HRĪ', was suspended from his neck. Like a vision of one of the legendary emperors of old, a mighty ruler of a vanished world, resplendent with all the attributes of power, the figure was of almost super-human size and appearance, and for a moment we wondered whether it was a statue or a living giant. At this moment the full orchestra of *radongs* and clarinets, cymbals and kettle-drums rose to a crescendo, while the deep voices of a choir of monks chanted invocations to the powerful protectors, punctuating their recitation with bells and *damarus.* Clouds of fragrant smoke rose from various censers, and the crowd stood in petrified attention, everybody's eyes riveted upon the majestic figure on the golden throne. His eyes were closed; his feet, in big ceremonial Tibetan boots, were firmly planted before him on the ground.

But suddenly a tremor seemed to pass through them, as if emanating from the ground, and slowly increasing in intensity, until his legs were trembling violently and his body was seized by convulsive movements, apparently gripped by a current of tremendous power rising up within him and filling his mortal frame. It was as if the dark powers from the depth of the earth, the chthonic powers that governed humanity before the dawn of history, had seized his body and threatened to burst it. It was a frightful sight, this struggle between the human body and the unknown power that was taking possession of it, until the mortal man was transformed into a being of another world. Even his facial features had changed completely and seemed to have become that of another person, nay, of a terrifying deity.

Now one of the senior monks, the Master of the Protocol, steps upon the raised platform and approaches the throne in order to present the questions which the deity is expected to answer. The questions were previously written on bits of paper and tightly folded. The Master of the Protocol is waving each of them before the spirit-eyes of the Oracle's tiara, while a number of sturdy monk-attendants hold and support the swaying body of the oracle-priest. But hardly has the Master of the Protocol stepped back from the dais when—like a giant roused to action—the oracle-priest jumps up, hurling his attendants aside with superhuman strength, and launching forward from his throne, he grasps a sword from a collection of ritual weapons at the foot of the platform, and, as if fighting an invisible enemy, the blade flashes in all directions with incredible speed and force. It is a terrifying spectacle, which holds everybody spellbound in spite of the fear that the sword may descend upon the crowd before the throne and that human heads may fly in the blind fury of battle, in an unbridled dance of destruction let loose by powers beyond human control.

Those nearest to the throne shrink back in horror; but before anything can happen, five or six of the monk-attendants—selected for their strength—try to take hold of the frenzied figure of the oracle-priest, in order to draw him back upon the throne. But the latter does not seem to notice them, and for some time they are tossed about like mere children, until by the sheer weight of their bodies they succeed in moving the struggling giant back upon his throne, where finally he collapses, utterly exhausted, breathing heavily, with sweat running down his unnaturally bloated face and foaming at the mouth, uttering strange sounds, as if trying to speak.

Now the Master of the Protocol steps forward again, with a writing-board in his hand. Bending down near to the mouth of the oracle-priest, he takes down the words that finally form themselves on his lips. While the message of the Oracle is being written down, a hushed silence prevails, except for the subdued voices of psalmodising monks in the background. Though the fierceness of the deity seems to have abated, its power still pervades the entire hall of the temple, submerging all individual thoughts and feelings in the awareness of its presence. Only utter surrender can appease the unseen power that dominates all minds and can break the hypnotic ban that has gripped each and everybody in the congregation, and now the people surge forward and throw themselves at the feet of the Oracle to pay homage to the Sacred Protector of the

Law and to receive his blessings. We ourselves could feel how we were lifted out of our own consciousness and seized by an upsurge of uncontrollable emotion, so that we threw ourselves like the others at the feet of the Oracle, oblivious of anything else around us, except the reality of a power beyond our understanding.

The oracle-priest slowly recovers. Monks support him on both sides. A chalice with tea is put to his lips, and he sips a little to revive himself. From the background sounds the hum of reciting monks. The rhythm of drums and cymbals is slow and quiet, and the excitement of the crowd has ebbed away.

However, soon the rhythm is accelerated, the music grows in volume, the voices in urgency, and after some time the oracle-priest falls into trance again and is seized by another of the six Spirit-Kings, as revealed by the weapon which he chooses when the trance has reached its climax. I do not remember how many of the trances we witnessed or how many had gone before we entered the temple. I only know that all the six Chökyongs took possession of the oracle-priest or Chösjé *(chos-rjé)* one after another, and that at the end of each trance he was stretched out as if dead and finally had to be carried away in an unconscious state. How any human body could endure for hours on end the terrible strain of such violent trance-states was more than we could understand. Surely nobody could endure this unless he was genuinely seized in a state of deep trance; and nobody would expose himself to the danger of relinquishing his body to an unknown power, unless he was convinced of the necessity or the value of his sacrifice; because this it was: the crucifixion of a human being, sacrificed on the altar of primeval powers in the service of a higher ideal to which even those powers had to submit for the welfare and guidance of men, who still were struggling in the meshes of samsaric life.

8

The Life Story of an Oracle-Priest

NO GREATER CONTRAST could be imagined than that between the tense and overpowering atmosphere that prevailed in the sombre Chiökyong Temple during the invocation of the Oracle and the festival of the first full moon on the fifteenth day of the new Tibetan year *(co-lnga-mchod-pa chen-po),* which was celebrated in the evening of the same day and continued until late into the night. Here the Buddha reigned supreme, and happiness was reflected on all faces. Since the early morning elaborate preparations had been going on, creating a sense of joyful expectation and a festive mood, similar to that of Christmas Eve in Western countries. The similarity was heightened by the fact that the celebrations took place during a winter night (February) in the warm and cheerfiul light of more than a thousand butter-lamps in the big courtyard of the monastery, which had been turned into a vast hall, having been covered with a temporary roof of tent-canvas, to keep out the snow which had started to fall in the afternoon. The whole two-storeyed front of the main temple was hidden under an enormous silk-appliqué thanka, fastened under the eaves of the roof and reaching almost to the ground. The central figure of this thanka was the Buddha Śākyamuni, benignly smiling down upon the large congregation of monks and the happy and colourful crowd of men and women, clad in their best garments and decked out with all their traditional jewellery. In front of this thanka a huge altar had been erected, on which hundreds of butter-lamps were burning, illuminating an elaborate structure of highly artistic decorations and offerings, representing flowers, fruits, animals, gods, and human beings, as well as many auspicious religious symbols, flanked by golden dragons—all beautifully modelled, down to the smallest detail, and delicately coloured, as if made of the finest porcelain. But, as we discovered later, all thus—except for the dragons—was made of butter!

The monks who recited the Monlam Prayers were arranged in three groups, forming three sides of a rectangular open space before the altar. In the centre of the row facing the altar was the empty throne of Tomo Géshé Rimpoché with his robes folded upright on their cushions, and to the left of it was the raised seat of Lobonla, the present abbot. But where was the Chöjé? We looked around among the rows of the monks, but we could not discover him. Immediately the prayers were over, we asked some of the monks whether the Chöjé did not take part in the prayers, whereupon one of them pointed to a monk standing near us and said: 'Here he is! Did you not recognise him?' Indeed, we had not, and at first we could hardly believe that this simple Trapa could be the same person whom we had seen on the golden throne of the Oracle only a few hours before!

But during the following weeks we often enjoyed his company and learned to know him as a kind-hearted and humble man. We soon were on friendly terms with him, and this enabled us to learn much about his life, his training as Chöjé *(chos-rjé)* or High Priest of the Oracle, and his own inner attitude towards the strange phenomena which manifested themselves through him.

However, during this memorable night we had no opportunity of approaching him, and we enjoyed to the full this 'festival of lights' with its prayers and blessings for the welfare of all living beings, so similar in spirit to that of Christmas with its feelings of joy and goodwill and innocent revelry. The latter came towards midnight at the end of the religious celebration and consisted of a rider-dance, in which colourfully costumed and masked young men were prancing about on hobby-horses, which they handled so well that every movement was true to life and that one had to make an effort to realise that the riders were not seated on real horses. The heads of the hobby-horses were realistically made of wood or papier-mâché while a cloth-covered bamboo structure suggested the body of the horse and hid the legs of the dancer. It was amusing and beautiful to observe this scene of youthful enjoyment, and it seemed to be the most natural thing to see the giant figure of the Buddha smiling down upon the scene. How far away was all this from the deadly pessimism that Westerners associate with the teachings of the Buddha! It was a perfect ending to a perfect day during which we had traversed the whole gamut of human emotions.

The crowd slowly melted away, most of the people remaining within the precincts of the monastery during the night. Most of the men were housed in the monastery proper, while women and children were accommodated in the outhouses. All of them appeared like one big family, rich and poor, clergy and laity; all of them were united through the strong bond of faith in the common destiny of man and the supreme power of the Enlightened Ones. It is this that enables the Tibetan to stand up against the demoniacal powers and dangers of an unseen world and to meet them fearlessly. We were fortunate in being able to discuss with the Chöjé himself many of the questions which were uppermost in our mind after the experience of the Oracle.

On the following day he paid us a visit in our private chapel. He was still suffering from the after-effects of his trance and complained that his whole body was hurting. He asked whether we had any medicine to relieve the pain, and we gave him some aspirin, which he gladly accepted. But to our surprise he refused to take tea or anything to eat, because, as he explained, it was his rule never to accept food or even tea prepared by others. He lived on a very simple and strictly vegetarian diet and prepared everything with his own hands, because he had to be exceedingly careful to preserve the purity and perfect balance of his body. Any mistake in his diet, any uncleanliness in body or mind, could have fatal consequences, and only by a life of austerity, devotion, and discipline could he protect himself from the dangers to which anybody who offered his body to the Spirit-Kings of the Great Oracle would be exposed.

Our first question was whether he remembered any of the answers that had come through him during the previous day's invocation of the Oracle. 'No,' he said, 'I know nothing of what happens during the trance. But when I come back to my normal state my whole body is in pain and I feel completely exhausted. It always takes days for me to recover.'

'But what made you accept the position of a Chöjé, if it is so dangerous and painful? Was it that you had any natural inclination towards spiritual things or mediumistic abilities?'

'Oh no, not in the least! I had a wife and children and earned my livelihood as a muleteer on the caravan route between Sikkim and Lhasa. I was a very simple man and I had no ambitions. In fact, my comrades looked down upon me, because I was shabbily clothed and did not care for cleanliness. I led a rough life, but I was quite happy, though I was poor and could neither read nor write. I had a little house at Phari, where I lived with my family when I was not on tour. And it was there that one day I fell ill. Nobody knew what it was, and I got worse and worse, until I was so weak that my wife thought I would die and called a Lama to read the prayers and to prepare me for death. But while the Lama recited the invocations to the powerful Protectors of the Sacred Law, the Chökyongs, I was suddenly possessed by them—though I myself knew nothing about it, nor about the contents of the recitation—and when I came to, the Lama told me that my life would be saved if I were willing to serve the Chökyongs, who had chosen me as their vehicle. However, I did not want to leave my wife and my children. But the Lama told me: "If you die, you will have to leave wife and children too: but if you will serve the higher powers, you will not only save your life, but your wife and your children will not have to starve." My wife agreed that the Lama was right, and so I gave in and promised to dedicate my life to the Dharma, and especially to the Great Protectors, if they would save me from death. From the moment I had taken the vow, I became better and soon recovered completely. But whenever those invocations were recited I fell into trance and was seized by the divine powers.'

'Did you go through a special training before you were appointed to the Great Oracle; or had you to pass certain tests, before being recognised as Chöjé?'

'Indeed! To make sure that my case was genuine and neither imagination nor fraud, I was sent to Lhasa and confronted with the Great Oracle of Nächung. We were made to sit side by side during the invocation, and only after various trials and a careful observation of all symptoms was I admitted as a candidate for the priesthood of the Oracle. I had to take the vows of celibacy and observe all the rules of the Vinaya. From then on I wore monastic robes and was given special tutors, who taught me to read and write and instructed me in the Scriptures. I had to observe special rules of cleanliness and diet. My life was completely changed and more strictly regulated than that of an ordinary monk, because the smallest transgression or mistake in my conduct might make me vulnerable and lead to my destruction by the very powers to whom I had devoted myself, to whom I had surrendered my body and my life. It was only after a long and severe training that I was finally declared fit and was sent to Dungkar Gompa, where the throne of the Oracle had become vacant. And I have been here ever since.'

The thought that this intelligent, polite, refined-looking monk, who behaved with the quiet self-assurance of a born aristocrat, could ever have been an ordinary mule-driver was something that we could not imagine. But people who had known him previously confirmed it and told us that he had not only been an ordinary muleteer but one who was exceptionally uncouth and rough, so that he was an object of ridicule. When he returned from Nächung his former associates could not recognise him, and everybody who had known him before wondered how such a complete transformation was possible.

A few days later we were invited by him to tea in his private apartments. He was a most charming host, and we admired not only his perfect manners, but even more so the meticulous cleanliness and orderliness of his rooms and his little kitchen with its gleaming copper utensils, in which he prepared his food.

The longer we knew this man, the more we liked him. He was neither proud nor bigoted and was ever ready to help us in our studies. In fact, he was more open-minded than most Tibetans towards research work, and he allowed me to make tracings of inscriptions in the Oracle Temple; and what was more: he allowed Li to photograph and to sketch him in his full regalia on the golden Throne of the Oracle, a unique favour, never granted to anybody else before.

9

MAGIC AS METHOD AND PRACTICAL KNOWLEDGE

WHAT IMPRESSED US particularly was the objective attitude and almost scientific precision with which Tibetans handle occult matters and psychic phenomena, which in Western countries are either products of sentimentality, morbid curiosity, or superstitious beliefs, as demonstrated by most spiritist seances, which mainly rely on neurotics or 'psychic' women, who are abnormally sensitive and therefore prone to all sorts of subconscious influences and illusions. Tibetans, on the contrary, seem to avoid abnormally sensitive or 'psychic' types and prefer to train perfectly normal, robust individuals, who neither boast of special 'spirituality' nor of psychic faculties and are not prompted by personal ambition.

Hugh Richardson, the British Envoy to Lhasa (mentioned before), told us an extraordinarily interesting case of a Lhasa aristocrat, a man who was known as a very jolly and sociable person, who one fine day, to his and everybody's surprise, was appointed to succeed the High Priest of the State Oracle of Nächung. He had never shown any spiritual leanings nor any mediumistic faculties, but was a healthy man in his best years, who enjoyed life like anybody else. As the appointment had been made through a pronouncement of the State Oracle, it could not easily be disregarded, and so the gentleman submitted to the demands of the Oracle. He gave up his former position (as far as I remember, he held an administrative post in the government service), retired to Nächung, where he was initiated into the mysteries of the Great Oracle, and on the day of his formal installation he promptly fell into trance and was seized by the presiding spirits of the temple. Mr. Richardson, who had known him well for many years, told us that the change that had taken place in this man was so extraordinary that one could hardly believe him to be the same person. But nobody knew what had happened to him during his initiation that had brought about this extraordinary transformation.

It is certain that here forces are at play about which we know nothing yet and whose functions have remained the secret of the few institutions which have preserved some of the most ancient traditions of religious magic.

Another strange feature of these Oracles is their connection with nature. Not only are they connected with certain localities in which terrestrial forces seem to be concentrated, but it also appears that they have a certain influence over or relationship to natural events. Some of them are therefore invoked in times of natural calamities, as for instance in the case of severe droughts and failing harvests, or of blizzards and hailstorms. Though it is difficult to see the connections between psychic phenomena and climatic conditions, I could not help observing that the claims of Tibetan 'weather-makers'—their predictions (in form of yearly forecasts) as well as the effects of their magic rituals—were justified by facts, or on so great a number of strange 'coincidences', that it is difficult to think of them as products of mere chance. It is also hard to believe that people should persist for centuries in keeping up such institutions and relying on such magic performances, if the results had not justified their existence.

As an example I may mention here the Oracle of Gadong, situated in a side valley of the Kyi-chu, about four hours' ride to the south of Lhasa. This Oracle is said to have special power over the weather. The well-known traveller and writer Amaury de Riencourt was allowed to witness an important invocation of this Oracle (though disguised in monastic robes) during his stay at Lhasa as the guest of the British-Indian Mission there. There had been a long period of exceptionally dry weather, so that the crops were perishing and the country was threatened by famine. In this calamity the Gadong Oracle was invoked. Riencourt's eyewitness report deserves special attention for its detached objectivity and careful observation. Being a newcomer and unacquainted with Tibetan Buddhism, he was neither spiritually nor emotionally involved in the things that happened in his presence. But the facts which he witnessed were sufficient to impress him profoundly. The first thing that completely took him by surprise was the visible transformation of the Oracle Priest: 'Very gradually, blood appeared to withdraw from his changing features and his flesh looked as if it were melting away. While the thudding and shrilling of the music went on, I saw with stupefaction the bone structure of his face protrude as if it were becoming a death mask, a mere skull covered with thin grey skin. It was an unbelievable and petrifying metamorphosis of Dr. Jekyll into Mr. Hyde . . . I was stunned, stupefied by this weird ceremony, not so much by the colourful pomp as by some indefinable conviction that I had seen a real occult performance.' But his greatest surprise came when he was about to retire the same night after the invocation: 'Rain was pouring down in bucketfuls and thunder was rolling up the entire valley of Lhasa.' He concludes his report by saying: 'I had begun to understand by now that there is more to psychic forces than meets the eye of Western man. The performances of the Oracles had opened to me the gates of a new and entrancing world which the Tibetans have explored thoroughly—a world which lies between the higher forms of religious research and the everyday preoccupations of earthly life: the mysterious world of magic and psychic forces, the universe of Yoga and of what lies beyond death.'[1]

As mentioned before, all these things have intrinsically nothing to do with Buddhism, and also Tibetans regard them more in the way of natural phenomena of which they make use, just as a Westerner makes use of electricity, without connecting this equally mysterious force with

1. Amaury de Riencourt, *Lost World,* Victor Gollancz (London, 1951), pp. 245 ff.

his religious beliefs by attributing it to a personal god or a cosmic intelligence. Though to the Tibetan there is no difference between the realm of nature and the realm of the mind, he recognises the difference between the mundane and the supramundane, between worldly and religious activities, without, on the other hand, excluding the interaction of both in a realm between these extremes. It all depends on the degree in which one is conscious of the inner relationship between the many, apparently disconnected, phenomena, by discovering the common laws that govern their activities.

A magician, therefore, according to Tibetan ideas, is not necessarily a particularly religious man, but rather one who knows how to make use of the laws that govern the parallelism of psychic and cosmic forces. If he is a religious man, he will use his knowledge for the benefit of all beings, if he is not, he will use them only for the benefit of himself, or those who are of use to him. It is this that distinguishes 'white' from 'black' magic, though both are based on the same principles. Like science, magic powers are neither good nor bad in themselves: it entirely depends on the use we make of them.

PART FIVE

Return to Western Tibet

I

The Sacred Mountain

THERE ARE MOUNTAINS which are just mountains and there are mountains with personality. The personality of a mountain is more than merely a strange shape that makes it different from others—just as a strangely shaped face or strange actions do not make an individual into a personality.

Personality consists in the power to influence others, and this power is due to consistency, harmony, and one-pointedness of character. If these qualities are present in an individual, in their highest perfection, then this individual is a fit leader of humanity, either as a ruler, a thinker, or a saint, and we recognise him as a vessel of divine power. If these qualities are present in a mountain we recognise it as a vessel of cosmic power, and we call it a sacred mountain.

The power of such a mountain is so great and yet so subtle that, without compulsion, people are drawn to it from near and far, as if by the force of some invisible magnet; and they will undergo untold hardships and privations in their inexplicable urge to approach and to worship the centre of this sacred power. Nobody has conferred the title of sacredness on such a mountain, and yet everybody recognises it; nobody has to defend its claim, because nobody doubts it; nobody has to organise its worship, because people are overwhelmed by the mere presence of such a mountain and cannot express their feelings other than by worship.

This worshipful or religious attitude is not impressed by scientific facts, like figures of altitude, which are foremost in the mind of modern man. Nor is it motivated by the urge to 'conquer' the mountain. Instead of conquering it, the religious-minded man prefers to be conquered by the mountain. He opens his soul to its spirit and allows it to take possession of him, because only he who is *inspired* or 'possessed' by the divine spirit can partake in its nature. While the modern man is driven by ambition and the glorification of his own ego to climb an outstanding mountain and to be the first on top of it, the devotee is more interested in his spiritual uplift than in the physical feat of climbing. To him the mountain is a divine symbol, and as little as he would put his foot upon a sacred image, so little would he dare to put his foot on the summit of a sacred mountain.

To see the greatness of a mountain, one must keep one's distance; to understand its form, one must move around it; to experience its moods, one must see it at sunrise and sunset, at noon and at midnight, in sun and in rain, in snow and in storm, in summer and in winter and in all the other seasons. He who can see the mountain like this comes near to the life of the mountain, a life that is as intense and varied as that of a human being. Mountains grow and decay, they breathe and pulsate with life. They attract and collect invisible energies from their surroundings: the forces of the air, of the water, of electricity and magnetism; they create winds, clouds, thunderstorms, rains, waterfalls, and rivers. They fill their surroundings with active life and give shelter and food to innumerable beings. Such is the greatness of mighty mountains.

But even among the mightiest there are some of such outstanding character and position that they become symbols of the highest aspirations of humanity, as expressed in ancient civilisations and religions, milestones of the eternal quest for perfection and ultimate realisation, signposts that point beyond our earthly concerns towards the infinity of a universe from which we have originated and to which we belong.

In the dust-filled valleys and low plains of our daily existence we have forgotten our connections with stars and suns; and therefore we need the presence of these mighty signposts and milestones to shake us up and arouse us from the slumber of self-complacency. Not many are there who hear the call or feel the urge to rise from under their thick blanket of petty self-interests, of money-making or pleasure-hunting, but the few whom the call has reached, and in whom the longing for greater things is still awake, form a steady stream of pilgrims who keep alive the tradition and knowledge of these sources of inspiration.

Thus it is that above all the sacred mountains of the world the fame of Kailas has spread and inspired human beings since times immemorial. There is no other mountain comparable to Kailas, because it forms the hub of the two most important ancient civilisations of the world, whose traditions remained intact for thousands of years: India and China. To Hindus and Buddhists alike Kailas is the centre of the universe. It is called Meru or Sumeru, according to the oldest Sanskrit tradition, and is regarded to be not only the physical but the metaphysical centre of the world. And as our psycho-physical organism is a microcosmic replica of the universe, Meru is represented by the spinal cord in our nervous system; and just as the various centres (Skt.: *cakra*) of consciousness are supported by and connected with the spinal cord (Skt.: *meru-danda*), from which they branch out like many-petalled lotus-blossoms, in the same way Mount Meru forms the axis of the various planes of supramundane worlds. And as the psycho-physical microcosm of man is crowned by the highest centre of consciousness, the thousand-petalled lotus of the mind (Skt.: *sahasrara cakra*), so Meru or Kailas is surmounted by the

ABOVE AND BELOW: ELEVATIONS OF KAILAS

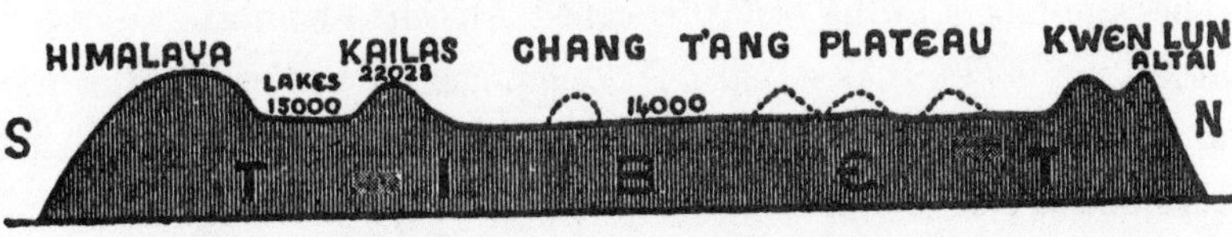

invisible temple of the highest transcendental powers, which to each devotee appear in the form that symbolises to him the highest reality. Thus to Hindus Kailas is the seat of Shiva, while to Buddhists it represents a gigantic Maṇḍala of Dhyāni-Buddhas and Bodhisattvas, as described in the famous Demchog Tantra: the 'Maṇḍala of Highest Bliss'.

This is not the place to go into the metaphysical or psychological intricacies of Hinduism and Tantric Buddhism. The question, however, which spontaneously comes to everybody's mind is: why or how was it that of all the mighty mountains of the Himalayan and Transhimalayan regions this very peak was thus honoured and by common consent recognised as the centre of the world?

A glance at the map, which shows the position of Kailas on the highest elevation of the Tibetan highland and its relationship to the river system of the Indo-Tibetan region, will give an immediate explanation. Kailas forms the spire of the 'Roof of the World', as the Tibetan plateau is called, and radiating from it, like the spokes from the hub of a wheel, a number of mighty rivers take their course towards the east, the west, the north-west, and the south. These rivers are the Brahmaputra, the Indus, the Sutlej, and the Karnali. All these rivers have their source in the Kailas-Manasarovar region, which forms the highest tier of the Tibetan plateau.

In ancient scriptures these rivers are described as outlets from the Manasarovar Lake at the foot of Mount Kailas, and they are said to encircle the sacred area seven times before flowing in the various directions, thus paying homage to the throne of the gods, according to the ancient rite of circumambulation (Skt.: *pradakshina*). The Tibetans call the Brahmaputra, the source of which is in the east of the Kailas-Manasarovar region, 'Tamchog-Khambab': the river 'flowing out of a horse's mouth'. The Sutlej, whose source is in the west, is called 'Langchen-Khambab', i.e. the river 'flowing out of an elephant's mouth'. The Indus, whose source is in the north of Kailas, is called 'Sengé-Khambab', i.e. the river 'flowing out of a lion's mouth'; and the Karnali in the south (which becomes the Gogra in the plains) is called 'Magcha-Khambab', i.e. the river 'flowing out of a peacock's mouth'. These animals are the 'vehicles' or throne-symbols of four of the Dhyāni-Buddhas. The river names thus indicate that they are regarded as parts of a universal *maṇḍala,* of which Kailas is the centre.

It is through these rivers that the religious and cultural relations between Tibet and India are established. This is specially apparent in the case of the Indus and the Brahmaputra, which, like two gigantic arms emerging from the Kailas-Manasarovar region, embrace the entirety of the Himalayas and the whole of the Indian subcontinent, the Indus flowing into the Arabian Sea in the west, the Brahmaputra into the Bay of Bengal in the east.

In actual fact not all the four rivers have their sources at the slopes of Kailas or in Manasarovar, but their valleys lead towards the plateau which is dominated by Kailas, thus making this mountain the signpost of the crossroads which connect the south, the north, the east, and the west.

Take away a few thousand feet from the altitude of Mount Everest, or of any of the other famous big mountains of the Himalayas, and nothing outstanding would remain of them; they would simply disappear from the map and merge into the myriad of unknown or unnoticed peaks and mountain massifs. But even if one would take away a few thousand feet of Mount Kailas it still would retain its importance, its unique central position in the general pattern of mountain ranges and the river systems of Tibet and India.

The mountain stands so completely isolated in the centre of the Transhimalayan range that it is possible to circumambulate it within two or three days: and its shape is so regular as if it were the dome of a gigantic temple, rising above a number of equally architectural forms of bastions and temple-shaped mountains which form its base. And as every Indian temple has its sacred water-tank, so at the southern foot of Kailas there are two sacred lakes, Manasarovar and Rakastal, of which the former is shaped like the sun and represents the forces of light, while the other is curved like the crescent moon and represents the hidden forces of the night, which—as long as they are not recognised in their true nature and directed into their proper channels—appear as the demonic powers of darkness. These ideas are also expressed in the names of the two lakes. 'Manas' (Skt.) means mind or consciousness: the seat of the forces of cognition, of light, and finally of enlightenment. 'Rakas' or, more correctly, 'Rakshas', means demon, so that Rakastal means 'Lake of the Demons'.

The solar and lunar symbolism of the sacred lakes is illustrated in

Tibetan pictures, like the one on page 278, by showing the sun-disk in the sky above the circular shape of Manasarovar, and the waning moon above the crescent-shaped Rakastal.

These sun and moon symbols are used in every Tibetan scroll-painting *(thang-ka)* in which Buddhas, deities, or saints are depicted. Sun and moon signify the two streams or currents of psychic energy, which move upwards to the right and to the left of the central channel or 'median nerve' of the spinal column. In Yogic meditation these two currents are integrated in the central channel and rise through it from one psychic centre or level of consciousness to the other, until the integrated stream reaches the highest multi-dimensional level of an enlightened consciousness. As Mount Kailas corresponds to the spinal column, it represents the axis of the spiritual universe, rising through innumerable world-planes (indicated by the actual horizontal stratification of the mountain, which is as regular and distinct as that of an Indian temple), from the human to the highest divine level, while the two lakes are looked upon as the reservoirs of the two streams of psychic energy.[1]

Our picture (p. 278) also shows that Manasarovar is on a higher level than Rakastal, which is geographically correct and coincides with the fact that the former represents the highest, the latter the lowest (but equally important) *cakra* or centre of psychic force. The one is the root and foundation of all our inner forces, the other the blossom and fruit of realisation. The one stands at the beginning, the other at the end of spiritual evolution.

It is for this reason that according to the oldest Buddhist tradition the descent of the Bodhisattva into his last life—in the fulfilment of his vow to attain final enlightenment, or Buddhahood—is connected with Manasarovar. According to this tradition, Queen Maya dreamt that the couch on which she rested was borne by the guardian gods to the Anotatta Lake (the Pāli name for Manasarovar) and was bathed in its sacred waters, whereupon all human impurities were removed from her, so that the future Buddha could enter her womb. He descended from the direction of Mount Kailas, appear-

1. Details about the currents and centres of psychic energy may be read in my *Foundations of Tibetan Mysticism.*

ing like a white elephant in a cloud. This shows that even from the very beginnings of Buddhism, Kailas and Manasarovar were held in the highest esteem and that the Buddhists fully shared in a tradition which goes back to Vedic times, if not to the very beginnings of human civilisation.

According to Hindu tradition it was Brahma himself who created Manasarovar and the divine Jambu tree which—though invisible to human eyes—grows in its centre. For this reason our world was called 'Jambudvipa' by the ancients; and it is said that due to the fruits of this divine tree the waters of Manasarovar are turned into a life-giving elixir. The Tree of Life in the Lake of Supreme Consciousness—what a profound symbolism, and how reminiscent of the Tree of Knowledge in the biblical story of the Paradise! Certainly there is no place on earth more exalted and worthy to be identified with it than the Kailas-Manasarovar region, which the Tibetans call 'the navel of Jambudvipa [our human world], the centre of all countries, the roof of the earth, the land of jewels and gold, the source of the four great rivers, dominated by the crystal pagoda of Kailas and adorned by the magic turquoise disk of Manasarovar'.

The place from where the pilgrim starts his circumambulation of Mount Kailas is seen in our picture as a deep cleft or gorge to the left of the sacred mountain. It is the entrance to the western 'Valley of Amitābha'. The pass to the right of Kailas, which is marked by a small stone pyramid (below the sun-disk), is the Dölma-La, the pass of Tārā, the highest point (18,600 feet) on the pilgrim's route. The dark triangle below it is a small lake, called Gaurikund by the Hindus and Thugjé-chempoi Tso, 'the Lake of the Great Compassionate One', by the Buddhists. We shall hear more about these places when dealing with the *parikrarna,* the pilgrimage around the sacred mountain, in the third chapter.

The Tibetan original of our illustration contained many more details which, however, had to be sacrificed for the sake of clarity and in keeping with our purpose, i.e. to provide an ideal view of the Kailas-Manasarovar region, as seen from the direction of the Gurla Pass, from which the pilgrim approaches the holy land, and which is the only place from where both the two lakes and Kailas can be seen simultaneously. The proportions of the picture are not those of optical but of mental perspective, as seen by the mind's eye. However, the forms, though stylised, are more true to reality than any photograph with its unavoidable distortions of angles and foreshortening of masses.

It is interesting to note that even the geographical position of the two lakes corresponds to their relationship to light and darkness, day and night. Manasarovar is in the east, at the beginning of the day, Rakastal in the west, at the beginning of the night. In Tibetan Manasarovar is called 'Tso Mapham', the lake of the invincible forces of the Buddhas (who are also called 'Victors'), while Rakastal is called

BRUSH DRAWING OF A TIBETAN THANKA-PAINTING

'Langag Tso' or, more correctly, 'Lha-nag-Tso', the Lake of the Dark Deities.

Consequently the Tso Mapham is surrounded by a number of monasteries and retreats, while the other lake is completely deserted of human habitation, and in spite of its scenic beauty a strange and uncanny atmosphere seems to hover over it. Though it is held in fear, it is as sacred as its sister-lake, because even those powers which appear to us terrifying and destructive, or hidden in the darkness of the depth, are as divine as those which we worship as embodiments of light and goodness.

The interrelationship of these forces—solar and lunar energy, conscious and subconscious forces, the principles of light and darkness, male and female energies, action and contemplation, emptiness and form—is the great discovery of Tantric philosophy. He who realises its truth is fit to worship the awe-inspiring Master of Kailas, whether he sees him in the form of Shiva, the destroyer of this world of illusion, or in the form of Demchog, who like Shiva tears asunder the elephant-hide of ignorance and whose twelve arms signify the twelve links of the formula of dependent origination, taught by the Buddha Śākyamuni.

Only he who has contemplated the divine in its most awe-inspiring form, who has dared to look into the unveiled face of truth without being overwhelmed or frightened—only such a person will be able to bear the powerful silence and solitude of Kailas and its sacred lakes, and endure the dangers and hardships which are the price one has to pay for being admitted to the divine presence on the most sacred spot on earth. But those who have given up comfort and security and the care for their own lives are rewarded by an indescribable feeling of bliss, of supreme happiness (as symbolised by Demchog, Skt.: Mahāsukha). Their mental faculties seem to be heightened, their awareness and spiritual sensitivity infinitely increased, their consciousness reaching out into a new dimension, so that many of them see wonderful visions and hear strange voices and fall into trance-like states, in which all their former obstructions and difficulties disappear like in a flash of light that suddenly lights up what was hidden hitherto. It is as if their individual consciousness, which obscured or distorted their views or their conception of the world were receding and giving place to an all-embracing cosmic consciousness.

2

The Land of the Gods

In order to understand the full significance of Mount Kailas and its extraordinary surroundings one has to see it not only geographically, culturally, or historically but first and foremost through the eyes of a pilgrim. In order to do this, we have to divest ourselves of the narrow confines of our personality and especially from the intellectual prejudices of Western education, because the experiences with which we are dealing here are too great and timeless to fit the stage of a purely personal occurrence or a description of accidental happenings. On our way to the sacred mountain Li Gotami and I felt ourselves merely as a link in the eternal chain of pilgrims, who since times immemorial travelled the lonely and perilous paths of an untamed mountain world and the limitless spaces of the Tibetan highland. The only thing that appeared significant to us, was our taking part in that supra-personal experience which surpassed by far all individual thoughts and feelings and raised us to a new level of awareness.

So let us follow the nameless pilgrim: Imagine him leaving the fertile plains of India and toiling for some 200–300 miles over endless mountain ranges, through steaming hot valleys and over cold, cloud-covered passes, fording wild mountain streams, where a slip of the foot means certain death, or crossing the thundering abyss of a torrential river, clinging precariously to a shaky reed-rope of uncertain age. Imagine him travelling through gorges, where stones are falling from invisible heights and where waterfalls seem to rush down straight from the clouds. Imagine him negotiating overhanging cliffs on narrow mountain paths and sharp-edged rock-ledges which cut into his sore and tired feet. Imagine all this, and see him finally on the top of the Lipulekh Pass, wrapped in the icy mists of its perpetual summer cloud-cap.

Suddenly the clouds lift and the pilgrim looks down the other side into a country of eternal sunshine, with mountains that have nothing of that sombre heaviness of the Himalayas, but seem to be made of the purest, almost transparent, pastel colours: yellow, orange, red, purple, set into a deep blue velvet sky. The contrast is so surprising that the pilgrim almost forgets the dark, heavy clouds still threateningly hanging over his head and breathing their icy air upon him.

However, he soon gets down into the wide open valley, and only now realises fully the difference of the world he left behind from the world he has entered: the valleys which he left were lined with sombre fir-forests, the ground was covered with grass, moss and ferns, flowers and shrubs; dark rocks were towering above the green valley and were lost in the heavy monsoon clouds which hid the snow-peaks; while here the vivid colours and the chiselled forms of rocks and mountains stand out in brilliant clearness, divested of any trace of vegetation, like the world on the first day of creation when only heaven and earth were facing each other in primeval purity.

Farther down the valley, along the winding river, there appear green patches of grassland and small yellow fields of barley, which form a striking contrast to the otherwise barren landscape. They are almost an anachronism, so to say, foreshadowing a stage in the development of creation which should appear millions of years later, as it is not yet existent in the surrounding nature.

Human habitations appear, and they are as strange as the landscape: plain cubic forms, huddled together, and behind them the huge rock-bastions of a table mountain, with cave-dwellings built into the rock-face and with castles and monasteries on its summit.

It all looks weird and forbidding and as antediluvian as the landscape. And high above all this rise in the background the dazzling snow-peaks of the Gurla Mandhata Range. Very different from the rugged peaks of the Himalaya in the south, the Mandhata Range forms one plastically moulded massif which if it could be seen from the air would appear in the form of an immense swastika. The broad central ridges are covered with one solid cap of snow and ice, extending without a break for some twenty miles, while between the arms of the swastika huge glaciers find their way downwards.

It is this vast range which separates the district and valley of Purang from the Kailas-Manasarovar region. Thus, the pilgrim has to skirt the wide slopes of the Swastika Mountain, until in a steady ascent he has reached the Gurla Pass which leads over one of the prolonged arms of the swastika.

There are no more difficulties in the form of natural obstacles, but as so often where nature is kind and gentle, man is not. The power of the Tibetan Governor of Purang does not reach farther than the inhabited part of the valley. Once the pilgrim is out of that region, he is a fair prey of robbers who waylay the lonely traveller or the unarmed caravan with impunity. The rumours and gruesome reports which come to the ears of the pilgrim in Purang are such that only those who have courage and faith will proceed farther, while the timid ones will either have to wait until they find others with whom they can join up for protection or they will have to be satisfied with visiting the sanctuaries in the lower valley of Purang, leading into Nepal.

However, this will hardly be the case with any of the numerous Hindu sanyasins who year after year go on this greatest and holiest of all pilgrimages and who for the sake of their faith undergo untold hardships and privations. It is difficult enough, even for those who can afford to hire horses or yaks to carry tents and provisions, etc., and who themselves can ride for the greater part of the journey. But those who possess nothing but what they carry on their own backs, who travel without protection against rain and wind, snow and freezing cold nights—to say nothing of protection against robbers and many unforeseen dangers—those courageous pilgrims deserve our highest admiration. Many of them never return, and those who do have given proof of supreme faith and endurance. They return to their country with shining eyes, enriched by an experience which all through their life will be a source of strength and inspiration, because they have been face to face with the Eternal, they have seen the Land of the Gods.

Anybody who has looked down from the Gurla Pass upon the Kailas-Manasarovar region can testify that this is not an exaggerated expression. Already one day's march before reaching this pass, at the western flank of the Swastika Mountain, there appears over the softly undulated hills, which are the continuation of one arm of the swastika, something that looks like the rising full moon in the dark blue sky; it is the shining ice-dome of Kailas!

It looks so unreal, so utterly beyond all earthly things, that the pilgrim forgets all his worries and fears, and is filled with but one desire: to reach the pass and to reassure himself of the reality of this wondrous apparition. His feet seem to have grown wings, they have lost all their tiredness. The rhythm of *mantras* and songs is on his lips, and only one thought lives in his mind, the thought of the great *Darshan,* the sacred vision, of which he has just had the first glimpse.

Now no evil powers can have any more influence; the vision he has seen, nobody can ever take from him. He is suddenly filled with such perfect confidence and inner security that he feels as if he were surrounded by a magic armour which no outer force can break or destroy.

Thus he reaches the last camping-place before the final ascent to the pass. He spends the night happily at the foot of a glacier, from which a crystal-clear brook emerges, watering a lovely green carpet of welcome grazing-ground, studded with sturdy, fuel-giving shrubs and little flowers. It is one of those natural camping-grounds where everything seems to welcome the tired wanderer; where sparkling water invites him to drink, where there is food for yaks and horses, fuel for a friendly camp-fire, and soft ground to rest upon, protected by near hillsides and rocks.

With dawn the pilgrim is up again and, after a simple meal, he starts for the final ascent, vibrating with inner joy and expectancy. Today is the dawn of the great day when, for the first time, he will behold the Land of the Gods, the day when he will cross the threshold of the Promised Land and realise the aspiration of a lifetime.

And yet when the pass is reached, and he finally stands on the sacred threshold, all his expectations are surpassed. Who can put into words the immensity of space? Who can put into words a landscape that breathes this immensity?—where vast blue lakes, set in emerald-green pastures and golden foothills, are seen against a distant range of snow mountains, in the centre of which rises the dazzling dome of Kailas, the 'Jewel of the Snows', as the Tibetans call the holy mountain.

Indeed, it dominates the whole vast landscape, which is spread out at the feet of the pilgrim like a map. The clarity of the air is such that the eye can see for more than a hundred miles, and every form and colour appears clear and distinct, as if seen by eyes endowed with the super-human perception of infra-red rays.

It certainly is one of the most inspiring views of this earth, a view, indeed, which makes the beholder wonder whether it is of this world or a dreamlike vision of the next. An immense peace lies over this divine landscape and fills the heart of the pilgrim, making him immune to all personal concerns, because, as in a dream, he feels one with his vision. He has gained the equanimity of one who knows that nothing can happen to him other than what belongs to him already from eternity.

There is no more need even for any 'armour', because he is both the dragon and the knight, the slayer and the slain, the demon and the God. And while the pilgrim touches the holy ground with his forehead and adds a few more stones to those heaped up by previous pilgrims, in token of their devotion and happiness to have been granted the realisation of their life's dream, there is only one prayer in his mind: 'May I never forget it! May I ever be able to keep this realisation alive within me!' And again and again he will touch the ground with his forehead, circumambulate the pyramids of stones of which each stone signifies a prayer and a blessing of those who preceded him—whose brotherhood he has entered today.

There are many religious Orders in this world, Orders with rules and regulations, with dogmas and rituals, with vows and initiations. But the brotherhood of those who have performed the pilgrimage to Kailas, who have gone through the trials of dangers and hardships, and were rewarded with the glorious vision of the sacred land, has received an initiation of the most profound nature. The invisible bond which unites them needs no vows, no dogmas, and no rituals. It consists in their common experience, the lasting effect of which is stronger than any man-made rules and distinctions.

Thus the pilgrim slowly descends into the Land of the Gods; but he is no more the lonely, frightened individual of previous days; he feels himself in the company of a host of invisible companions—the spiritual brotherhood of fellow-pilgrims—and surrounded by the many subtle influences which seem to hover over this region, and which, in accordance with the various religious traditions, have been described as the presence of Gods, or Buddhas and Bodhisattvas.

How little does modern humanity know of these things! How childish the efforts of those who think it below their intellectual dignity to admit the reality of spiritual powers and try to explain them away with high-sounding scientific phrases, or by discarding any experience of such realities as superstitions and hallucinations. As if the last word of science were also the last word of truth, and as if there was no other reality than that of science! Science is admirable in its own realm, but it is applicable as little to spiritual phenomenon as to any creative form of art.

Due to our exclusive concentration upon and cultivation of our intellectual faculties we have neglected and, to a great extent, lost our psychic sensitivity. Therefore, to speak of deities, Gods, Buddhas, and Bodhisattvas in any other sense than that of poetical or metaphorical usage is to expose oneself to the charge of superstition. Yet to the pilgrim they are real enough to make him immune to dangers, and to raise him beyond the fear of death and suffering, which neither poetical artistry nor scientific knowledge can achieve.

It is necessary to keep these facts in mind if we wish to understand and appreciate the experiences of the pilgrim.

The excitement of the first impact between him and his new surroundings is gradually giving place to an exalted serenity.

While Kailas, 'The Jewel of the Snows', is disappearing behind a cap of cumulus clouds, which are gathering around its dome with the progress of the sun and its increasing warmth, the sacred lakes become the almost exclusive centre of the pilgrim's attention. He cannot stop admiring their radiating blueness and wondering at the strange play of nature which seems to impress him with all the symbols of ancient tradition—behind him the Mountain of the Swastika (the symbol of eternal creativeness), in front of him the two lakes, of which Rakastal (the lake of the terrifying deities of darkness) appears to the left in the form of a crescent, while the round shape of Manasarovar, to the right, is reminiscent of the sun (the Lord of the Day and the peaceful deities of light).

This combination of signs is one of the favourite Tibetan symbols, shown like this:

The sign of the swastika, moreover, is repeated on the southern side of Kailas. First it appears as a mighty cross which divides the ice-dome into four quarters. When coming nearer, the smaller arms or 'hooks' of the swastika become visible (especially the horizontal ones).

Within a few hours after leaving the Gurla Pass the pilgrim reaches the shores of Manasarovar and experiences the glories of his first sunset over the sacred waters. The blue of the lake changes into Veronese green near the beach and appears deep ultramarine in its centre. The light, evening clouds are aflame with all the colours of fire. They are low and are swiftly moving and changing. Sometimes they seem to burst like fireworks, cascading in fiery streams into the now purple waters of the lake, or shooting up like rockets and dissolving into a rain of fire.

And while the pilgrim, spellbound and overawed, watches this divine spectacle, the animals come out of their dwelling-places to watch the stranger. Birds come fearlessly to his feet, little creatures come out of their holes to greet the pilgrim, hares sit up with cocked long ears, scrutinising him with astonishment, and even *kyangs* (a kind of wild horse, resembling a zebra in stature, but of plain brown colour with a white belly) graze peacefully and undisturbed in his vicinity.

It is the unwritten law that nobody is allowed to kill or to hurt the animals inhabiting this region, and, as if the animals were conscious of their divine protection, they behave as they were supposed to behave in a long-forgotten paradise. And the pilgrim, who since the beginning of this day has moved as if in a dream, from wonder to wonder, begins to realise that if there is a paradise anywhere in this world it is here.

According to Tibetan belief, which is shared by most of the Indian pilgrims, the very water of Manasarovar, as well as its colourful sands and pebbles and some strange variety of fish, is said to have medicinal properties of some kind of magic healing power. Naturally, nobody would think of catching or killing the fish or the numerous wildfowl *(haṁsa)* which inhabit the lake, but during great storms the waves dash against the shores with such force that many fish are thrown upon the beach, where they die and dry up, so that pilgrims can pick them up and take them away as a much coveted medicine.

The low hills and plains around the lakes are covered with low shrubs and miles and miles of pastures, where thousands of *kyangs* and yaks, as well as the flocks of sheep and goats of the nomads, find welcome grazing-grounds.

Also, among the plants of this region are many herbs of medicinal value and others which can be used as incense and which are highly valued for their wonderful fragrance. All these things are regarded as '*prasāds*', as the gifts of the gods to the pilgrim. There are many other '*prasāds*', each of them pertaining to a particular locality.

Among the pebbles of Manasarovar there is a dark red variety which is as smooth as silk to the touch, beautifully polished, and shaped by the action of the waters through hundreds of thousands of years. They are not too hard, so that they can be scraped with a knife. Tibetans mix the stone-flour thus obtained with milk, and use it as a medicine as well as a charm in all kinds of afflictions.

On the eastern side of the lake are the so-called jewelled sands, composed of 'five varieties of precious substances', which have been described traditionally as turquoise, coral, crystal, gold, and silver. Whatever they are, they certainly look very beautiful, scintillating in many colours, and they are peculiar in that they are found only for a short stretch along the eastern coast, and that they are astonishingly heavy. In spite of this they are only found as a thin layer on top of other sands.

On the western shore of Manasarovar, especially on the narrow isthmus between Manasarovar and Rakastal, there are the 'golden sands'. They are of the most lovely orange-yellow colour, and actual gold has been found among them. The biggest find, so far, was a lump as big as a dog, and the place where it was found is still called 'Serkyi' ('the golden dog').

However, the Tibetans, like the ancient Incas of Peru—with whom they have many characteristics in common—are of the opinion that any gold found in this sacred soil belongs to the gods, and should not be misused by greedy men. So it happened that when the lump of gold of the size of a dog was unearthed nobody dared to keep it, and it was therefore sent to the Dalai Lama at Lhasa. When the Dalai Lama, however, came to know that it was taken from the Land of the Gods he immediately sent it back and had it buried again at the spot where it was found. Nowadays only a small mound remains of the *stūpa* which was erected there in commemoration of 'the golden dog'.

The *'prasāds'*, which nature offers freely to the pilgrim, are certainly more valuable than any amount of gold which—if Lhasa had fallen into the temptation of prospecting and digging for it—would have turned the Land of the Gods into a hell of infernal greed and murderous passion. Though robbers may lurk at the approaches to the holy land, and even enter it in the guise of harmless pilgrims or travellers, they at least abstain from deliberate killing on the sacred soil and in the presence of powers which, even if they cannot understand them, they at least fear and respect.

3

The Last Trial

After so many weeks, if not months, of trudging through narrow valleys and gorges and cloud-covered mountains it seems almost unbelievable to the pilgrim to look over miles and miles of open water, surrounded by green plains, soft hillocks, and shining snow-peaks in the distance, under a clear sunny sky. He is filled with unspeakable happiness and continues his journey after many a deep drink from the sacred waters of Manasarovar, which is like nectar to both his mind and body.

In the shelter of hills the sun burns almost with a summerly heat, which one hardly expects at 15,000-foot altitude. Only in the shade the coolness and crispness of the air remind the pilgrim where he is, and warn him of the possibility of a sudden hail or snowstorm which might unexpectedly sweep down from the icy walls of the Himalayan range in the south.

The approach of such a storm, however, is a spectacle which in itself is of such grandeur that even the temporary inconvenience to the pilgrim cannot preclude him from admiring the majestic beauty of the unloosed elements of nature. The change of the whole landscape and its colours is sudden and surprising, as if it were all a magic play.

Due to the altitude and its pure, rarefied air, all colour contrasts are incredibly heightened, distances are eradicated, space becomes telescoped and at the same time intensified.

A mountain range, twenty miles away, suddenly turns indigo-blue, and seems to race towards you like a big dark wave, not more than five miles away. The ultramarine-blue waters of Manasarovar turn into a purplish hue in the centre and bottle-green towards the shores. Cloud-shadows are flitting over the agitated waters, and soon the whole lake looks like a huge opal in which all colours fight for supremacy. Clouds piled upon snow mountains look like mountains piled upon clouds, because the contours and formations of the mountains merge into darkness, and the clouds stand clear-edged and super-plastic in the sky.

But the pilgrim is irresistibly drawn towards the ultimate goal of his pilgrimage, the mysterious Kailas, the hidden Jewel of the Snows. Only in the morning and in the evening hours does its dome become entirely visible and free from clouds, and thus, morning and evening, the pilgrim reverently bows down in the direction of the sacred mountain, repeating his *mantras* and calling up all the forces of light inhabiting this cosmic *Maṇḍala*.

When crossing the isthmus between the two lakes he looks back for the last time upon the sunny Manasarovar, and soon finds himself near the northern shore of Rakastal. A strange, uncanny atmosphere seems to hover over the placid blue waters of the long, comparatively narrow lake, an atmosphere of utter loneliness and severity, which never occurred to him on the shores of Manasarovar.

It is difficult to find an explanation for it, because the landscape surrounding Rakastal is of superb beauty—the soft, red-brown hill at both sides and the mighty, snow-covered massif of the Gurla Mandhata (the Swastika Mountain) give an impressive and colourful frame to the deep blue lake. And yet a feeling of sadness weighs down the beauty, and the very inexplicability of it makes it all the more uncanny. Apparently others have felt the same, and this feeling must have been so strong that nobody dared to build monasteries or hermitages, as on the shores of

Manasarovar. There are mysteries which man is called upon to unveil, and there are others which are meant to be felt, but not to be touched, whose secrecy must be respected. Rakastal is one of these.

Much has been told and written about Manasarovar, but hardly anything is known about Rakastal. And yet it is Rakastal which receives the waters that come directly from Mount Kailas, and there is even a communication between Manasarovar and Rakastal, so that, when the waters of the Manasarovar (the surface of which is fifty feet higher) flow over they find an outlet through a channel which leads to Rakastal.

This is regarded as a very auspicious event, portending better conditions in the world, but characteristically this has not happened for many years, and the channel has almost completely dried up, so that the pilgrim can cross it without even wetting his feet. Tibetans are rather worried about this and fear that worse times, of which the already increasing insecurity gives them a foretaste, are yet to come.

The pilgrim now has to traverse the vast plain between the northern shores of Rakastal and the foot of Mount Kailas. This wide, grassy plain, which looks as friendly and innocent as a summer meadow, is the meeting place of many caravan routes from east and west, north and south, and is therefore the favourite haunt of robbers and invading tribes of nomads from the northern steppes (Chang-Thang). Besides this, the plain is intersected by dozens of swift-flowing streams and many treacherous swamps, in which the pilgrim may get stuck if he tries to cut straight across the country in order to avoid the danger of being waylaid on the caravan routes.

But he keeps his mind and his eyes fixed on the sparkling Jewel of the Snows, which is now straight before him, completely dominating the landscape. After fording the last shallow river, the plain rises in a gentle slope towards the foothills of Kailas, whose dome now disappears behind them, while the red buildings of a monastery and the white dots of many tents around it come into sight.

Camp-fires of pilgrims, traders, beggars, and nomads welcome the pilgrim into this haven of safety. It is strange to be again in human society, agreeable to be able to replenish the scanty provisions—but his heart is still with the silent solitudes of the lost paradise, the hallowed shores of Manasarovar, while his mind is eagerly looking forward to initiation into the mysteries of Kailas.

He experiences again that joyful tension of the night before crossing the threshold of the Land of the Gods at the Gurla Pass, but at the same time he feels that the days which lie ahead of him will tax his strength and endurance, both mentally and physically.

Nobody can approach the Throne of the Gods, or penetrate the *Maṇḍala* of Shiva or Demchog, or whatever name he likes to give to the mystery of ultimate reality, without risking his life—and perhaps even the sanity of his mind. He who performs the Parikrama, the ritual circumambulation of the holy mountain, with a perfectly devoted and concentrated mind goes through a full cycle of life and death.

He approaches the mountain from the golden plains of the south, from the noon of life, in the vigour and full experience of life. He enters the red valley of Amitābha in the mild light of the sinking sun, goes through the portals of death between the dark northern and the multicoloured eastern valleys when ascending the formidable Dölma-La, the Pass of Tārā, the Saviouress—and he descends, as a new-born being, into the green valley of Aksobya on the east of Kailas, where the poet-saint Milarepa composed his hymns, and from where the pilgrim again emerges into the open, sunny plains of the south, assigned to the Dhyāni-Buddha Ratnasambhava, whose colour is that of gold.

The pilgrim who actually walked over the 'golden sands' in the south feels that here he is moving through a gigantic *Maṇḍala,* miraculously created by nature, in which colours and shapes speak to him in the symbolic language in which the experiences of meditation have been handed down from the dawn of humanity.

Entering the narrow valley on the western flank of Kailas, the place assigned to Amitābha, whose colour is red, he finds himself in a canyon of red rocks, the structure of which is so architectural in appearance that the pilgrim feels as if he is walking between rows of gigantic temples. They are adorned with elaborate rock-cornices, pillars, and ledges, and high above them there appears suddenly the dazzling ice-dome of Kailas.

Its shape is remarkably regular, as if it had been sculptured out of one immense block of ice, and towards the west two deep hollows, like the eyeholes of a perfectly shaped white skull, look mysteriously down upon the pilgrim, who is thus reminded of the terrible aspects of Shiva and Demchog (Mahāsukha) who are both adorned with skulls, symbolising the wisdom of *śūnyatā,* the realisation of the emptiness and transitoriness of all phenomena.

Buddhist monks and hermits, who wanted to contemplate this aspect of the sacred mountain, built a small cave-monastery in the opposite rock-face, on which it appears to the pilgrim like a swallow's nest. Before the valley turns to the north-east is a rock rising thousands of feet sheer from the bottom of the valley, shaped like the sacred Nandi bull, with its head raised towards the summit of Kailas, as if looking lovingly at its master.

Reaching the northern side of the mountain, the colour of the rocks and the structure of the foothills abruptly change. They seem to be composed of a predominantly dark conglomeration of stones, which deprives them of the clear-cut architectural quality of the rocks and mountains lining the red valley of Amitābha.

But there is one outstanding feature which makes up for these shortcomings: the foothills suddenly step aside and give the pilgrim the full view of Kailas in all its grandeur. The view is absolutely overwhelming, and, according to the scriptures, it is on this spot that those who are initiated into the rituals and meditations of the respective Tantras should perform their devotional practices on the great *Maṇḍala* of Supreme Bliss.

Those who do so are favoured not only with the *'darshan'* of the holy mountain in the indescribable beauty of a gigantic domed temple of perfect symmetry and breathtaking splendour, but also with a splendid vision *(darshan)* of their *Ishta-devata,* the deity or ideal of their heart, be it in the divine forms of Shiva and Parvati, or of Buddhas and Bodhisattvas, or any other significant symbol connected with this place and its compelling atmosphere.

Sometimes thunder-clouds and blizzards envelop the holy mountain, and the pilgrim has to wait for days until the fury of the elements has abated and the veil of whirling clouds has been drawn aside. Then the mountain will suddenly appear in all its pristine purity, with its dazzling white dome, its blue-green ice-falls, violet-blue shadows and dark purplish rock-faces, a spectacle so overpowering as to defy words.

The mountain is so near that it seems to the pilgrim as if he could just walk over and touch it—and at the same time it is intangible in its ethereal beauty, as if it were beyond the realm of matter, a celestial temple with a dome of crystal or diamond. And, indeed, to the devotee it is a celestial temple, the throne of the gods, the seat and centre of cosmic powers, the axis or hub which connects the earth with the universe, the super-antenna for the influx and outflow of the spiritual energies of our planet.

What the pilgrim sees with his naked eyes is only the sub-structure and emanation of something much more grand and far-reaching. To the Tibetan the mountain is inhabited and surrounded by thousands of meditating Buddhas and Bodhisattvas, radiating peace and bliss, and sowing the seeds of light into the hearts of those who want to liberate themselves from the darkness of greed, hatred, and ignorance.

The two hills between which Khang Rimpoché (Kailas) appears are called the hills of Vajrapāṇi and Mañjuśrī, i.e. they are regarded as the seats of the Wielder of the Diamond Sceptre (commonly translated as 'thunderbolt'), who fights against the powers of darkness and decay—the diamond being the symbol of the indestructible—and of the Bodhisattva of learning and active wisdom, who, with the flaming sword of knowledge, cuts through the knots of ignorance and prejudice.

At his side is the hill of Avalokiteśvara, the Boddhisattva of compassion, the Patron of Tibet, while next to the hill of Vajrapāṇi, on the north-eastern side of Kailas, rises the hill of Dölma (Tārā), who is said to have been born out of a tear of Avalokiteśvara when he grieved over the suffering of this world. These hills stand like sentinels (like four pyramids) at both sides of Kailas, seen from this main place of worship.

While experiencing all these wonders, the pilgrim leaves the sacred spot like one whose whole being is in a stare of ecstasy and transformation. But this transformation cannot be successfully completed so long as he carries about his old ego. He has to go through the gates of death before entering the valley of Akṣobhya on the east, where he will be reborn to start a new life. This is his last trial.

While climbing up to the high pass of Dölma, which separates the northern from the eastern valley, he comes to the place where he beholds the Mirror of the King of Death (Yama), in which all his past deeds are reflected. On this spot he lies down between huge boulders in the position of a dying man. He closes his eyes and faces the judgement of Yama, the judgement of his own conscience in the remembrance of his former deeds. And with them he remembers all those who were dear to him and who died before him, all those whose love he was unable to repay; and he prays for their happiness in whatever form they may have been reborn. And as a token of this he leaves little relics of their earthly days on this hallowed spot—a small piece of cloth, a strand of hair, a pinch of ashes from the funeral pyre, or whatever he could preserve for this last service to his beloved dead.

After he has thus made peace with the past and has gone through the gates of death he crosses the threshold of his new life on the snow-covered pass of the all-merciful mother Dölma. And lo, at his feet there is a lake of the purest emerald colour (which is the colour of Dölma or Tārā) in the midst of rocks and snows. In Tibetan it is called the Lake of Mercy while Hindus call it Gaurikund. In it the pilgrim receives his first baptism as a new-born being.

Now he has passed his last trial, and all anxieties and hardships are over. Many a pilgrim has died from exertion on the ascent to the terrific altitude of nearly 19,000 feet, where a blizzard can freeze a man within a few minutes and where every gasp of breath has to be husbanded as if it were the elixir of life. But death is not feared by the devotee who dies in the presence of the gods on the most sacred soil; because he will die in the most exalted moment of his life, thus realising his highest aspiration.

The friendly valley of the eastern Dhyāni-Buddha, Akṣobhya, welcomes the pilgrim with lovely green camping-grounds and silvery streams of crystal-clear water. As a last remembrance of past trials he sees a strange upright rock, in the shape of an axe, on his way down to the valley. It is the emblem of the King of Death, and it is called the axe of Karma. To the pious pilgrim it has lost its power through the mercy of Tārā, the Saviouress, because mercy is stronger than Karma; it washes away our past deeds in the tears of compassion for all suffering beings. Sharing the suffering of all leaves no place for one's own suffering, and finally results in one's growing beyond one's own little ego.

This has been taught by the Buddha as well as by many of his followers and especially by Tibet's great poet-saint, Milarepa, of whom many remembrances still live in the Eastern Valley, especially in the cave of Dzundulphug. In this cave he sang and meditated, and the pilgrim is shown the imprint of his hand on the ceiling of the cave, which now forms the sanctuary of a little monastic hermitage.

The story goes that Milarepa found the cave too low and pushed the rock ceiling up with his bare hand. But his force was such that the ceiling went up too high, so that the cave became too cold and draughty in winter. So he went on top of the rock and pressed it down with one foot until it was in the proper position. Up to the present day an imprint of his foot is visible on the top of the rock.

Another little story is told about him in connection with a Bön priest, a black magician of the pre-Buddhist faith of Tibet. He challenged Milarepa that through his magic power he would be able to reach the summit of Mount Kailas. Milarepa replied that he could do the same. 'Let us see,' said the magician, 'who will reach it first'—and he started to climb up.

It was very early in the morning, the sun had not yet risen, and Milarepa said that he would rest a little. Those who had been present when the magician had challenged him grew worried and implored him to hurry after his adversary. Milarepa, however, was unruffled and did not move from the spot.

The magician had almost reached the top of Kailas, and was jeering at Milarepa, when the first ray of the sun touched the summit of the holy mountain. This was the moment for which Milarepa had been waiting. Through the mighty power of his concentration he immediately became one with that ray, and before the magician realised what had happened the figure of Milarepa appeared on top of Kailas. 'Hallo!' he called out to the magician, who was panting and puffing below him, 'don't exert yourself!' and the magician, who saw himself defeated, got such a shock that he dropped his magic drum *(damaru)*.

It leaped down in big bounds, and each time it bounced against the ice-dome of Kailas it emitted a loud tone and left a deep cut on the surface of the dome. 'Tang—tang—tang,' it went, to the great hilarity of all onlookers. And up to the present day a perpendicular line of stair-like impressions are to be seen, forming the vertical axis of the big swastika on the southern face of the dome of Kailas.

Many such stories, full of humour and religious significance, have grown up around the figure of Milarepa. But he himself was an historical personality of great charm and achievements, who left the greatest poetical legacy of Tibet in his 'Hundred Thousand Songs'. His life was perhaps the most remarkable that any saint has ever lived. He went through all the depths and heights of human existence, and after the most dramatic struggles he finally attained realisation. He was not only a follower of the Buddha, but he himself attained to Buddhahood. This is all the more significant and encouraging as his life is well authenticised, in spite of numerous legendary stories which grew up around his personality later on.

He was lucky enough to have a learned and capable disciple, who wrote down the songs and became at the same time his biographer. His name was Rechung. Thus Milarepa's message has been kept alive by his spiritual descendants, the patriarchs and followers of the Kargyütpa Sect. Both the monasteries at the northern and eastern ideas of Kailas belong to this sect and are hallowed by the remembrance of Milarepa.

Strange as it sounds, Hindu pilgrims generally identify Milarepa with Shava, probably because both are depicted as ascetics with long hair and lean bodies of white colour. In the case of Milarepa this white is sometimes greenish, because it is said that due to his living mainly on nettles during the years of his hermit life in the wilderness of the snow-mountains his body took on a greenish tinge. He used to boil these nettles in an earthen pot which was his only earthly possession. One day even this pot broke, but Milarepa, instead of grieving over this loss, composed a hymn in which he said: 'Even this earthen pot has become a Guru to me, it has taught me the law of the impermanence of all worldly things and freed me from my last attachment to them.'

It is interesting to note that nettles are still eaten by the poor, and they abound and thrive especially in the surroundings of Kailas.

So, on his way round the holy mountain, the pilgrim is constantly reminded of Milarepa when passing by luxuriantly growing patches of nettles. And many a pilgrim will sing one of Milarepa's songs, popular all over Tibet, in praise of the solitudes and the life of renunciation, or in praise of the Buddha and his Guru, Marpa, The Translator.

And thus the pilgrim passes through the last part of the Eastern Valley which is like a fairyland of colours. Some of the rocks are flaming red, others dark blue and green, and next to them vivid orange and light yellow ones. It is as if, before leaving Kailas, the pilgrim were presented with samples of all the varieties of coloured rocks which he admired during the Parikrama.

Finally, he emerges from the valley into the open plains until he reaches again the starting-point of the Parikrama, at the little monastery of Tarchen. While passing numerous *maṇi-walls,* composed of thousands of stones upon which pious devotees have carved the mantra *Oṁ maṇi padme Hūṁ*, in praise of the Buddha Avalokiteśvara, who is the Jewel (*maṇi*) which should reside in the Lotus (*padma*) of the devotee's heart, the pilgrim adds his own stones in gratitude for what this pilgrimage has given to him, and as a blessing to the pilgrims who will come after him: '*Sukhe Bhavantu!*' (May they be happy!)

4

A Bön Monastery

Li and I were still filled with the presence of Kailas when after a day's journey to the west we came to a place which stood out from the rest of the landscape by its vivid red colour, as if it had been marked by nature as a hallowed spot. And, indeed, it was a place of great sanctity, that once every year came to life during an important religious festival, commemorating the birth of Śākyamuni Buddha in the full-moon night of June. On this night a wondrous sight is seen by those who are present: the full moon rises like a fiery dome over the icy crest of Kailas, and as the moonbeams trace the outline of the sacred mountain on the red slope, 'heaven' and 'earth' are connected, and as if the realm of divine beings, inhabiting the 'Throne of the Gods', were projected in a flood of light into the world of man. The Enlightened Ones and their retinue are believed to descend on the rays of the moon and assemble on the red carpet of earth to bless the faithful by their luminous presence. It is like a rite of transcendental communion, a rite subtler than any man-made ritual, a truly universal Mass, in which the light is the body and the life-blood of the divine, the human heart the chalice.[1]

1. This is probably the origin of the popular belief that once every year all the Buddhas and Bodhisattvas assemble in a remote valley on the Tibetan highland.

The very soil on which this 'mass' is celebrated every year is hallowed, and when we camped there for one night we experienced an extraordinary sense of profound peace and bliss. In the morning each of us collected a handful of the red earth as a remembrance of the sacred spot and as a last farewell gift of Kailas.

Four days after we had left Kailas we entered a deep valley, bordered by perpendicular rock-walls. The floor of the valley was flat and green, and a shallow river, the beginning of the Langchen-Khambab, wound its leisurely way through it. Towards evening we saw the gleaming white walls of a monastery, standing out against a dark rock-face pierced with the caves and galleries of rock-dwellings. The whole scene was reminiscent of the Valley of the Kings near Thebes, with its cubic Egyptian temple structures at the foot of bare table mountains, whose rock-walls contained numerous galleries with the tombs of the Pharaohs. The only thing that surprised us was the apparent newness and neatness of the whitewashed, red-bordered buildings, which rose like a fortress out of the lonely, otherwise uninhabited, valley.

The leader of our caravan of eight yaks (we had to carry provisions for a year's travel in the wilderness with scant chances of replacing our stores) told us that the monastery had been rebuilt recently, because a few years before during the incursions of Mohammedan raiders from Turkestan the Gompa had been pillaged and burnt, and the inmates had either been killed or ill-treated. The abbot himself had been stripped naked and beaten, but left alive. After the destruction of the monastery he had taken refuge in the cave-dwellings and ancient meditation chambers above the Gompa, and there he had remained even after the buildings had been restored.

We had looked forward to being comfortably housed in one of the monastery buildings, but contrary to our expectations nothing stirred when we approached the Gompa—a most unusual thing in a country where people never hide their curiosity and where the arrival of a caravan is an important event. Not even a dog barked, and that could only mean that the place was uninhabited. So we pitched our tents outside the walls near the river and prepared for the night.

The next morning we sent our caravan leader to the abbot in order to announce our visit, and after we had received his reply we were led up a narrow path to the foot of the rock-face, from where a staircase led inside the rock, until we came to a trapdoor which was opened at our approach, and after a few further steps we found ourselves in a well-lit cave in front of the abbot. He was seated on a high throne, framed by a decorative wooden arch. The whole structure reminded me somewhat of a concierge's box with a counter-window and was in strange contrast with the neolithic style of a cave-dwelling. The walls of the cave were covered with minutely executed frescoes of innumerable miniature Buddha-figures which, as we discovered only after a closer inspection, proved to be a tapestry of colour reproductions, printed on small paper sheets and skilfully pasted on the walls of the cave. The same prints had been used over and over again, but the repetition of the same figures in regular sequences rather heightened the decorative effect and were quite in keeping with the traditional frescoes of the 'Thousand Buddhas', seen in many of the ancient temples and grottoes. The mellow light that came through the open window of the cave helped to harmonise the colours, so that one could mistake them at first sight for original frescoes. The abbot, in spite of the rather theatrical setting, was a simply dressed middle-aged man with an intelligent face and dignified behaviour.

After exchanging the customary pleasantries and sipping some buttered tea we finally came to the main point of our visit, namely the necessity of getting transport for the next stage of our journey, since the caravan that had brought us here was to return to Purang, from where we had started almost a month ago. Generally people are reluctant to venture beyond the territory with which they are familiar and it is therefore necessary to assemble a new team of people and animals for every stage of the journey, which generally means from one inhabited place to another. In the sparsely inhabited parts of Western Tibet this may mean anything from a few days to one or two weeks' distance, and once one has reached the end of the stage, the people are anxious to return home with their animals as quickly as possible, without waiting whether or when the travellers may be able to find further transport.

The abbot, though friendly, declared that he could not supply us with transport, as there were neither yaks nor men available in this season, and when we pointed out that we held a Lamyig from Lhasa, which entitled us to transport and food supplies at the local prices, and when we showed him the document, he laughed derisively, as if it was a big joke, and we felt that his attitude changed from friendliness to defiance. Apparently he wanted to show us that he would not take any orders from the Lhasa authorities. We began to wonder what might be the reason for his antagonism against Lhasa and so we tried to appeal to his sense of religious duty to help us in our predicament. But he declared that the few able-bodied people at his disposal and their yaks were busy with the harvest somewhere down in the valley, and that he could not do anything about it. We could feel that there was no point in pressing our demand and showed instead of this our admiration for the artistic way in which he had decorated the walls of his cave. It was then that we learned that he had been several times to India and that on these occasions he had ordered a number of paintings to be reproduced. He also had some important texts of the Sacred Scriptures printed there and showed us some specimens. Though the titles looked familiar to me, they contained strange names and *mantras,* which made me doubt whether these could be Buddhist texts. But since I had no chance to inspect them more closely, I thought it wiser to keep my doubts to myself and merely to express my admiration for the good work he had done for the propagation of the Dharma and for the high quality of the colour reproductions. Apparently he had spent large sums to get all these things done, and I could not help wondering how a man living in a lonely cave in the wilderness of these remote mountain-tracts could have collected the funds not only to rebuild his monastery, but to engage in cultural and literary work of this kind. Only a man of high reputation and far-reaching influence could achieve all this. But who were his followers and where were his disciples? Except for a few nuns who, as we were told, lived in some of the other caves, there was nobody around anywhere. All the more were we keen to see the monastery and when we mentioned this he readily agreed to instruct the Konyer (caretaker) to open the gates and to show us round.

So we took our leave and returned to our tent, while our caravan people packed up their belongings and left in a hurry—as if afraid to have us on their hands. Even money could not induce them to go farther, and so we were left alone between the ominous-looking rock-face and the deserted monastery. It all seemed very weird to us. A big well-built monastery without a living soul in it, an abbot and a few nuns hiding in caves, and nobody around who could give us any information or assistance. And stranger still was the fact that the abbot had not offered us shelter in the monastery, though he knew that we were Buddhist pilgrims—or was it precisely because of this?

The next day the Konyer came to our tent and, though we were reluctant to leave it without a guard, we followed him to the Gompa, trusting that anyway no human beings were around, who might take the opportunity to steal our precious stores or any other useful things in our equipment, which would be an irreplaceable loss.

When approaching the Gompa we observed outside and right in front of it a low, long building that seemed to contain a row of narrow cells. From the position we might have concluded that it was a kind of outer sanctuary, like a *maṇi-wall,* placed there for circumambulation. But to our surprise we were told that it was a row of latrines, which were used on festival days by the pilgrims and worshippers camping outside the monastery. This was certainly a very praiseworthy innovation and showed the abbot's appreciation for modern hygiene. But we still could not help wondering why this structure had been placed just in the front centre of the Gompa. Or was it perhaps a symbolical way of saying that 'cleanliness is godliness'?

Our next surprise was that the Konyer led us in an anti-clockwise direction around the monastery, which in any other place would have been regarded as highly improper, if not an insult to the sanctuary.

Since it is only the Bön-pos who reverse the direction of the circumambulation or who pass a shrine or a sacred place (as for instance Mount Kailas) with the left shoulder towards it, our suspicion that the abbot was not a Buddhist but a Bön-po was confirmed, and when we entered the main temple our last doubt vanished, because everything we saw seemed to be a reversal or at least a distortion of Buddhist tradition. Thus the swastika sign of the Bön-pos points to the left, while the Buddhist one points to the right. On the other hand the Bön-pos have copied almost every feature of Buddhist iconography. They have their own Buddhas and Bodhisattvas, their own fierce 'Protectors' and deities of sky and earth; their names are different, but otherwise they are hardly distinguishable from their corresponding Buddhist originals. The same can be said of the Bön-Scriptures, which are more or less an imitation of the Buddhist ones, sometimes even bearing the same titles (like the Prañāpāramitā texts), but ascribing them to different authors, giving them a different setting and different *mantras* (instead of *'Oṁ maṇi padme hūṁ hrī'*, for instance, *'Om ma-tri-mu-ye-sa-le-du'*). The main deities of the Bön-pos were originally those of the sky, the embodiments of space and light, of infinity and purity; thus it was easy to identify them with the Buddhist system of Dhyāni-Buddhas and to take over the complete symbolism of Buddhist tradition (thrones, animal vehicles, gestures, body-colours, haloes; implements like *vajra* and bell, sword and hook, spear and arrow, skull-bowl and magic dagger, etc.). The impact of Buddhism upon Bönism was so overpowering that the latter could only survive by adopting Buddhist methods and interpreting its doctrine in Buddhist terminology, so that Bönism, as it survives today, is hardly more than an off-shoot of Buddhism, or merely another sect of Lamaism. This seems to be how the common man in Tibet feels about it, as we could see from the way in which our caravan people spoke to us about this monastery. It never appeared to them as non-Buddhist, but merely as 'different' from the other better-known sects; and this was the main reason that made us reluctant to think of it as a Bön-monastery, though the province of Shang-Shung, in which it is situated, is known as the original home of the Bön-pos.

Before entering the main Lhakhang we observed among the frescoes of the porch the familiar 'Wheel of Life'. But instead of the usual twelve divisions with the pictorial representations of the twelve links of the Buddhist formula of Dependent Origination *(pratītyasamutpada)* there were thirteen divisions, the additional one depicting the state of *samādhi* or *dhyāna* in the form of a meditating Buddha-like figure, inserted between 'death' and the beginning of a new incarnation.

Entering the assembly hall of the Lhakhang, we expected to find ourselves facing the main image. Instead of this we were facing an empty wall with the throne of the abbot in its centre. The wall, however, did not cover the whole width of the hall, but left two narrow passages to the right and to the left that gave access to a corridor behind the wall which contained a row of over-life-size statues of what appeared to us images of the five Dhyāni-Buddhas. But their gestures did not fit their colours, nor were the symbolical animals of their thrones in accordance with them, nor were their emblems. A figure that looked like Amitābha, for instance, had white as its body-colour, instead of red, and was seated on an elephant throne, instead of peacock throne, and his name was 'Shen-lha Ö-kar' *(gShen-lha ḥod-dkar),* 'the God Shen of the White Light'. We had to crane our necks in order to see the images properly, because only a narrow passage was left between the statues and the wall screening them from the main hall. Why the images were screened from the hall and the congregation, and why they were placed behind the abbot's seat, remained a riddle to us. But there were so many strange things in this place, that it was not possible to go into further details unless we were forced to stay here for a longer time, which we fervently hoped would not be the case.

However, we were impressed by the neatness and solidity of the buildings, which had the compactness of a fortress and reflected the power of a well-trained mind. But what moved him to rebuild this place, if there was nobody to live in it and if he himself preferred to remain in his cave? And where was the community that could support and maintain such a monastery in this remote valley? All these questions moved us while we were returning to our tent. We had hardly reached it when we saw a dog dashing out of it—and found to our dismay that the food we had prepared for the day was gone!

The lesson was not lost upon us, and we never left the tent alone again. Though this was a great handicap, because it meant that we could never go out together, we found sufficient subjects for sketching and photographing around our tent—apart from the many little chores that regularly crop up on rest days—to keep us busy for one or two days more. Yet we began to feel worried, wondering how long our enforced stay here would last, because we could ill afford to waste our precious time, and our equally precious stores, without getting nearer the main object of our journey: the ruins of the ancient city of Tsaparang and the temples of Rinchen Zangpo. We had already spent a year in Central Tibet in order to secure the permission of the Lhasa authorities for a proper study of the temples and monasteries founded by or attributed to Rinchen Zangpo, belonging to the period of the tenth and eleventh centuries A.D. (roughly 750–1050) and it was essential to do as much work as possible before the onslaught of the winter and before political events could upset our plans.

However, our patience was finally rewarded by the unexpected visit of the abbot to our tent. We welcomed him warmly, and now he seemed to be an entirely different man. His proud aloofness and the slightly sarcastic smile with which he had listened to our demands and perused our Lamyig had given place to a friendly expression and a genuine solicitude for our difficulties. We on our part stressed the fact that we were dependent on his kindness and that we would be grateful for any help he could give us. We did not mention the Lhasa authorities nor the Lamyig again, but told him that we had been greatly impressed by all that we had seen during our visit to his Gompa, and now he began to open out and promised to send us a number of yaks and some people who could look after them and who knew the difficult territory ahead of us. We had imagined—judging from the maps—that we could travel comfortably over green meadows or shrubland along the banks of the Langchen-Kharnbab, as we had done on the last stage before getting here. But now the abbot explained to us that the river flowed through a deep, inaccessible gorge, and that by following the course of the river we would have to cross innumerable deeply intersecting ravines and side valleys, formed by generally dry water-courses, which with every rainfall would turn into raging torrents within a matter of minutes. He therefore advised us to travel over the highland, following the ridge of the mountain range to the north that separates the Gartok Valley from that of the Langchen-Khambab. This meant that we had to give up the idea of visiting one or two ancient monasteries of Shang-Shung, in which we might have found more information about the origin of Bön, but the danger of further delay was too great, and so we resisted the temptation and followed the abbot's advice. There was also another advantage in avoiding inhabited places: it gave us an opportunity to cover a bigger distance in one leap without changing the caravan.

The abbot was as good as his word, and the next day two men came and offered their yaks and their services. They were rather old and decrepit-looking, and we noticed that both of them were limping. But they told us that all the younger and stronger people were engaged in harvesting and that therefore they had reluctantly agreed to come with us at the Rimpoché's request. After inspecting our luggage and assessing the number of yaks we required, we finally came to terms with them—though at a considerably higher price than we had bargained for. But there was no other choice, since we could not risk further delay.

We started the following morning and were glad to be on the move again. The whole day we were travelling uphill. There was no track and the two old fellows, limping along and from time to time consulting each other, did not seem to be quite sure as to the direction or their whereabouts. Towards evening we reached the endlessly undulating ridge of the mountain range, here and there strewn with enormous boulders, as if giants had scattered them in the fury of battle. There was no recognisable landmark anywhere, and finally we realised that our caravan leaders had lost their bearings altogether. Everybody was exhausted, and this was aggravated by the altitude of more than 16,000 feet, but there was no chance of pitching camp, because there was not a drop of water to be found anywhere.

Our caravan had been increased by a wandering Trapa and a little girl of about twelve years, who claimed to be a nun and had attached herself to the caravan in the hope of food and warmth by the camp-fire. It had become bitterly cold and neither a rock-shelter nor any shrubs for fuel were in sight; and everybody's throat was parched after the incessant climb under a merciless sun, which had only lost its fierceness with the approaching evening.

On the eastern horizon we got a last glimpse of the white dome of Kailas, while the southern horizon was filled by the glittering snows of the Himalayas, dominated by what appeared like a second Kailas, the sacred mountain of the Menla-Buddhas (the Great 'Healers': *bcom-ldan-ḥdas-sman-bla*), called Khang-men. It was a magnificent, breathtaking view, that made us feel as if we were floating high above the world on a petrified sea of softly swelling and ebbing mountain waves.

But, alas, we were too exhausted to enjoy this view for long, and when finally we found a trickle of water between an outcrop of tumbled boulders we had hardly sufficient strength left to pitch our tent, to prepare some hot tea, and to eat some dry chapaties, which we had prepared the evening before. Li had got fever and could hardly eat, and in the night we were shivering with cold, in spite of keeping on all our clothes and wrapping ourselves in all available blankets. The water which we had collected in a basin for the morning was solidly frozen and the bottle with the sacred water of Manasarovar had burst! This was our first taste of what was in store for us in the winter, if we delayed too long.

Our men, the Trapa, and the little beggar-girl seemed to be none the worse for having spent the night without shelter or cover, and we could not help admiring them. As soon as the sun had risen, the Trapa performed the ceremony of offering water and light, while reciting prayers and blessings for all living beings. As his bell rang out in the crisp morning air and the sun rose victoriously over the far-off mountains, we too forgot the rigours of the night and were filled with the joy of a new day.

5

The Valley of the Moon Castle

A FEW DAYS LATER, when emerging at the rock-gate of Kojomor from the lonely highlands, everybody heaved a sigh of relief at leaving the inhospitable wilds for warmer and flatter regions. We looked down upon a vast expanse of gently rolling lowlands, bordered by the snows of the Himalayas in the south, and we imagined that now we would be able to travel along the Langchen-Khambab without further obstacles. But hardly had we reached what seemed to be the floor of the vast valley when suddenly we found ourselves at the edge of a plateau, looking down into a labyrinth of canyons, thousands of feet deep. We felt that we had come to the very end of the world and that there was no other choice left but to turn back. How could our heavily loaded yaks and horses ever negotiate the sheer, almost perpendicular, walls of these canyons, which were so deep that we could not even see their bottoms? And how should we ever get out of this labyrinth, which stretched from horizon to horizon and might take days or even weeks to traverse? But before these questions could be answered the first men and pack-animals had already disappeared into a gap at the edge of the plateau, through which a narrow path led down into the nether world, into the gaping bowels of the earth. The 'path' was only discernible to experienced caravan leaders who were familiar with the terrain—and even these people seemed to rely on some sixth sense, especially when suddenly the faint track disappeared in the debris of disintegrating rocks and boulders or in steep sand-falls (generally at exactly forty-five degrees), on which the whole caravan, fully loaded pack-animals included, would slide down in the pious hope of being arrested in time before they reached the next perpendicular rock-face. Woe to the bold traveller who should try to cross these regions without a guide! Even if he were lucky enough to descend into one of these canyons without losing either his life or his luggage, it would be much more difficult for him to get out again.

I still remember how during our first camp at the bottom of one of these canyons we tried to guess how the caravan would proceed the next morning. After thoroughly examining the surroundings, we came to the conclusion that, since we were encircled by sheer cliffs on all sides, we could only get out by wading along in the water of the shallow but swift-flowing stream, until we reached an opening in the cliffs or an intersecting side valley However, the next morning we climbed—yaks and all—over the very cliff that we had ruled out as the most inaccessible of all! How we did it is still a miracle to me. But somehow we succeeded in finding footholds here and there, pulling up the animals one by one, and finally emerging on a narrow ledge, which jutted out from an almost perpendicular rock-wall and was interrupted by occasional sand-falls that started to move as soon as one set foot on them.

Fortunately we soon came on safer ground, but when after some hours' travelling we reached the actual canyon of the Langchen-Khambab, we were faced by a long, swaying rope-bridge. Its main support was two steel-cables, hanging side by side, and upon them short planks and sticks were fastened with ropes and wires. There was nothing to hold on to, neither a rail nor even a single rope to steady oneself. The yaks had to be unloaded and every piece of luggage had to be carried separately over the bridge that was precariously swaying more than a hundred feet above the swirling, icy-cold waters of the river. After all the luggage had been dumped on the other side the yaks were supposed to cross the bridge one by one, but they wisely refused to step on the shaky planks—and we wondered how we could get out of this dilemma. But our people proved to be more resourceful than we expected. They managed to get the yaks down to the river-bank, drive them into the water and to direct them with shouts and stone-throwing to swim across the river. The current was so strong in the middle of the river that we were afraid the animals would be swept downstream, where the steep banks would have made it impossible for them to get out of the water. But thanks to the stone-throwing the yaks were prevented from turning downstream and safely reached the other bank. Finally we ourselves had to cross the bridge, and we did so with our hearts in our mouths. No wonder that innumerable prayer-flags and strips of cloth adorn all the bridges of Tibet! People rely more on the strength of their prayers than on that of the bridge. At any rate it seems safer to commend oneself into the hands of higher powers and to be prepared for the worst.

In spite of all these dangers and troubles we were richly rewarded by the indescribable grandeur of the canyon country which unfolded itself in all its fantastic beauty the deeper we penetrated into this region. Here the mountain scenery is more than merely a landscape. It is architecture in the highest sense. It is of awe-inspiring monumentality, for which the word 'beautiful' would be far too weak, because it is overpowering by the immensity and abstract purity of its millionfold repeated forms that integrate themselves into a vast rhythm, a symphony in stone, without beginning or end.

One's first reaction is that this cannot be the work of nature only, the result of a mere play of blind forces, but rather the consciously composed work of a super-artist, on a scale so vast that it staggers the human mind and takes away one's breath. What is so surprising, however, is not the variety of forms but the precision and architectural regularity with which certain motifs and patterns are repeated and gradually integrated into bigger units in an ever-ascending rhythm, till the whole vast scene thunders in the upsurge of one overpowering movement.

Thus, whole mountain ranges have been transformed into rows of gigantic temples with minutely sculptured cornices, recesses, pillared galleries, bundles of bulging cones, intersected by delicate ledges, crowned with spires, domes, pinnacles, and many other architectural forms.

Some of these mountains look like the most elaborately carved Hindu temples in the styles of Khajuraho, Bhuvaneshvar, or Konarak, others like South Indian gopurams, others again like Gothic cathedrals or fairy-tale castles with innumerable spires and towers.

Due to the rarefied air of these altitudes, every detail is clearly defined and visible even from very great distances, while colours attain a brightness and purity unknown at lower levels. The shadows themselves appear in luminous colours, and the generally cloudless Tibetan sky forms a deep blue backdrop, against which the rocks stand out in fierce yellows and reds and all shades of copper and ochre, changing to all the colours of the rainbow at the magic hour of sunset.

How the wonders of this Tibetan canyon country, covering hundreds of square miles, could have remained unknown to the world is almost as surprising as seeing them with one's own eyes. And it is all the more astonishing since these Tibetan canyons offer an additional attraction to their natural beauty: the hidden treasures of a great past, which comes upon the traveller like the revelation of a magic world, in which dreams have been turned into reality under the spell of secret spiritual forces that reigned over this country for almost a millennium and still pervade it in a subtle way. Here the castles of the Holy Grail, the imaginary troglodite cities of the moon, the mountain fastnesses of medieval knights, the cave sanctuaries of secret cults, with their treasure of art and ancient manuscripts, come to life.

Indeed, they do not belong merely to the past. The lofty hermitages of pious anchorites, clinging to the rocks like swallows' nests, and the proud monasteries and temples on mountain-tops or in secluded valleys, still keep the flame of faith and ancient tradition alive.

Yet this is a dying country, a country slowly crumbling into dust, like those regions of Central Asia which a thousand years ago were flourishing centres of civilisation and which have turned into deserts, like the

Gobi or the Takla Makan. Western Tibet, and especially the region of Ngari Khorsum, which even less than a thousand years ago was able to support a substantial population and a highly developed civilisation, is nowadays almost denuded of human life except for a few oasis-like settlements where irrigation permits the cultivation of barley or wheat.

The gradual desiccation of Western Tibet springs probably from the same causes that created the deserts of Central Asia. Geologists tell us that the Himalayas are steadily rising and that consequently the regions beyond their mountain bastions get less and less rainbearing clouds. Many of the big glaciers on the Tibetan side of the Himalayas and in the interior of Tibet are, according to them, remnants of the last glacial age, since the present annual rate of snowfall does not suffice to explain their existence.

Large regions of Tibet, therefore, live on the ice reserves stored up from prehistoric times, and when these reserves are exhausted the country will turn into a perfect desert, for even now the rainfall is not sufficient for the cultivation of crops or for the growth of trees. One may wonder how erosion can be such a prominent feature in the Tibetan landscape if rain and snowfall are so insignificant. The answer is that the differences in temperature between day and night, sunlight and shadow, are so great that they can crack the hardest rocks and reduce the mightiest boulders to sand. Under these conditions even occasional showers, or the waters of melting snow, together with the fierce winds which sweep over the higher altitudes at certain seasons, are sufficient to complete the work on a grand scale.

How comparatively quickly the process of desiccation and the creation of desert-like conditions takes place can be understood when one realises that only 600–700 years ago certain species of big conifers used to grow in regions where nowadays trees are as unknown as in the antarctic—or when one comes upon the ruins of cities and mighty castles, which even 500 years ago must have been teeming with life and activity, supported by fertile districts and provinces and a flourishing population. They were the abodes of kings and scholars, feudal lords and rich traders, skilful artists and craftsmen, who could bestow their gifts and talents upon temples and monasteries, libraries and religious monuments. We read in Tibetan chronicles of images of silver and gold, and we can believe that these reports were no exaggerations when we see the amount of gold that was used in the plating of temple-roofs, in the gilding of large clay and metal images, and in the decoration of temple halls and their extensive frescoes, in which gold was lavishly employed. As in the days of the ancient Inca Empire, where gold was regarded as the exclusive property of the Sun-God, so in ancient Tibet gold was thought to be fit only for the glorification of Buddhas and Bodhisattvas and their teachings, which sometimes were actually written in gold and silver, and illuminated with miniatures on a gold ground.

It is difficult to imagine the religious fervour of those times, which transformed the inaccessible wilderness of mountains and canyons into a paradise of peace and culture, in which matters of the spirit were regarded as more important than worldly power and possessions, and where half the population could dedicate itself to a life of contemplation or to the pursuit of culture for the benefit of all, without suffering from want.

When James Hilton in his famous novel *The Lost Horizon* described the 'Valley of the Blue Moon' he was not so far from reality as he himself or his readers might have thought. There was a time when in the far-off canyons of Western Tibet there was many a hidden 'Valley of the Blue Moon' where thousands of feet below the surface of the surrounding highlands, accessible only through some narrow rock-clefts and gorges, known only to the local inhabitants, there were flower-bedecked gardens, surrounded by trees and fields of golden wheat and fertile pastures, through which, like silver veins, flowed the water of crystal-clear mountain streams. There were lofty temples, monasteries and castles, rising from the surrounding rock-pinnacles, and thousands of neatly carved cave-dwellings, in which people lived comfortably, without encroaching on the valuable, fertile soil. They lived in a climate of eternal sunshine, protected from the cold winds of the highlands and from the ambitions and the restlessness of the outer world.

On our way to Tsaparang we had the good luck to be stranded in one such valley, aptly called the Valley of the Moon Castle (Dawa-

Dzong). The caravan that had brought us was in such a hurry to return that before we could even find out whether there was a chance of further transport we were left alone in the strange valley without a living soul anywhere in sight. The caravan people did not even care to camp for the night, but simply dumped our luggage (and ourselves) near a shallow stream at the bottom of a wide canyon, surrounded by fantastic rock formations which rose before us like the bastions and towers of a primeval giant fortress.

By the time we had set up our tent, stowed away our numerous bags and boxes, unpacked our camping equipment, and prepared our evening meal, the sun had set and the world shrank to the space of our four sheets of canvas. The darkness that enveloped us was like a protective cloak, and when we woke up next morning and looked around, the idea of being stranded here for an uncertain time did not upset us in the least; in fact we were inwardly rejoicing at having an opportunity to explore and to sketch this incredible place, which looked more like an illustration of Jules Verne's *Journey to the Moon* than anything seen on this earth.

It may be that others might have felt oppressed by the loneliness and strangeness of the place, but to us it was just paradise: an enchanted world of rock formations which had crystallised into huge towers, shooting up thousands of feet into the deep blue sky, like a magic fence around an oasis, kept green by the waters of springs and mountain brooks. A great number of these nature-created towers had been transformed into dwellings—nay into veritable 'skyscrapers'—by the people who had lived here many hundreds of years ago. They had ingeniously hollowed out these rock-towers from within, honeycombing them with caves, one above the other, connected by inner staircases and passages, and lit up by small window-like openings. Groups of smaller rocks were rounded like beehives and served as single cave apartments. A number of cubic buildings between them seemed to be the remnants of monastic settlements, of which the main buildings stood on the rest of a rocky spur, jutting out into the valley and dividing it into three arms.

The centre of the crest was crowned with temples, *stūpas (chorten)*, monasteries, and the ruins of ancient castles, whence one could get a beautiful view into the valley, bordered by phalanxes of rock-towers rising up, row after row, like organ-pipes and perforated by hundreds and hundreds of cave-dwellings and their windows.

The greatest surprise, however, was to find the main temple not only intact but actually covered with a golden roof that gleamed in the wilderness of rocks and ruins like a forgotten jewel—a reminder and symbol of the splendour and the faith of a past age, in which this valley was inhabited by thousands of people and ruled by wise and pious kings. The remnants of ancient frescoes showed that this temple had been built towards the end of the tenth century—almost a thousand years ago.

Now, except for a few herdsmen, who grazed their sheep and goats on the green pastures of the valley, we seemed to be the only human beings around that deserted city of troglodytes.

What a powerful silence! What an overwhelming loneliness! A silence which was full of the voices of the past, a loneliness that was alive with the presence of countless generations of those who had built and inhabited this ancient city. A great many of the caves had served as meditation chambers and as permanent abodes of hermits and monks, so that the whole place was saturated with a spirit of religious devotion and a life of contemplation. The very rocks appeared as in an upsurge of ecstasy.

Like a magnetised piece of steel, which retains its magnetic force for a very long time, in the same way this place seemed to have retained an atmosphere of spiritual power and serenity, so that one forgot all cares and fears and was filled with a deep sense of peace and happiness.

We had been camping here already for a week, but time seemed to stand still in the valley of the Moon Castle, so that we were quite oblivious of its passage. We had been told that Dawa-Dzong was the seat of a Dzongpön, a governor of a district or a province. But his 'Dzong' (his 'fortress' or 'castle') consisted of nothing but a little house, tucked away in a grove of willows in the main canyon at the foot of the ruined city, which was hidden in a side canyon, whose entrance was barred formerly by a strong wall, now mostly in ruins. To our disappointment the Dzongpön was on tour in his district, and nobody knew when he would return, not even his wife, who was alone in the house with one or two servants.

When we told her our transport problem she assured us that she would gladly help, but that the yaks were grazing in the highlands and there was nobody to catch them and to bring them down, since her husband had taken his men with him. According to Tibetan custom a Dzongpön always travels with an armed escort, not only as a matter of safety but more as a matter of prestige. So we had to resign ourselves to an indefinite delay—though this time we did not mind it so much.

One evening, when returning from a sketching excursion, while Li was guarding the tent (we took it in turns), an old Lama emerged from one of the half-ruined buildings near the golden-roofed temple. He greeted me with a friendly smile, though probably no less surprised to meet a stranger than I was.

After a few words of greeting we slowly circumambulated the temple, from time to time setting in motion the prayer cylinders fixed here and there into small recesses in the outer walls of the building. Behind the cylinders pious hands had stuffed loose pages of old manuscripts, which apparently had been picked up among the debris of crumbling temple buildings or *stūpas,* since it is the custom never to destroy or to deface even the smallest fragment of the holy scriptures.

'You are a Lama,' the old man suddenly said to me, as if thinking aloud, 'but not from this part of the country. Are you able to read our holy scriptures?'

'Certainly I am.'

'Then read what is written here'—and he pulled out a manuscript hidden behind one of the prayer cylinders.

I read: 'I will act for the good and the welfare of all living beings, whose numbers are as infinite as the expanse of the sky, so that, by following the path of love and compassion, I may attain to perfect enlightenment.'

The old Lama's face lit up and he looked straight into my eyes, saying, as he grasped both my hands, like one who has found a long-lost brother: 'We are travelling on the same path!'

No more words were necessary—and while the rocks were lit up by the sinking sun, like fiery sentinels, I hastened towards the little tent in the valley below.

Arriving there, Li told me that a messenger had come during my absence, to let us know that the yaks for which we had been waiting so long had been finally secured and would be reaching us within a day or two.

This was good news—but with a sudden sadness we realised that never again would we see the golden roof of that ancient sanctuary, where for a thousand years pious monks had followed the path of light, and where I had found a friend—a nameless friend and companion in the spirit—whose smile would always be present in my memory of the profound peace and happiness we found in this enchanted valley.

6

Arrival at Tsaparang

After the Valley of the Moon Castle and the awe-inspiring canyons on the way to Tholing we feared that Tsaparang would perhaps come as an anticlimax or at least as something that could not compete with the natural wonders through which we had passed. But when, on the last lap of our journey—while emerging from a gorge and turning the spur of a mountain—we suddenly beheld the lofty castles of the ancient city of Tsaparang, which seemed to be carved out of the solid rock of an isolated, monolithic mountain peak, we gasped with wonder and could hardly believe our eyes.

As if woven of light the city stood against the evening sky, enhaloed by a rainbow, which made the scene as unbelievable as a *fata morgana*. We almost feared that the scene before us might disappear as suddenly as it had sprung up before our eyes, but it remained there as solid as the rock on which it was built. Even the rainbow—in itself a rare phenomenon in an almost rainless country like Western Tibet—remained steady for quite a long time, centred around the towering city like an emanation of its hidden treasures of golden images and luminous colours, in which the wisdom and the visions of a glorious past were enshrined.

To see our goal after two long years of pilgrimage and uncertainties, and more than ten years of painstaking preparation, and moreover to see it enhaloed and transfigured like this, appeared to us more than a mere coincidence: it was a foreboding of greater things to come, of discoveries of far-reaching importance and of a work that might well occupy us for the remainder of our lives. It was a pledge for the ultimate success of our efforts and a confirmation of our faith in the guidance of those powers that had led us here.

We reached the abandoned city in the evening and took shelter in a crude stone hut that had been built in front of a cave, in which the only permanent inhabitants of this former capital of the kingdom of Gugé were living: a shepherd with his wife and child, who served as a caretaker of the three remaining temples that had survived the ravages of time. His name was Wangdu, and since he was miserably poor, he was glad to have an opportunity to earn a little money by supplying us with water, brushwood, and milk. So we settled down in the little stone hut, whose interior was so rough and dark that it gave us the feeling of living in a half-finished cave. But the mere thought of being in Tsaparang transformed this miserable hovel for us into a most acceptable dwelling-place.

On that memorable first evening—it was on the 2nd October 1948—I wrote in my diary: 'It was my dream for many long years to see Tsaparang and to save its crumbling treasures of art and religious tradition from oblivion. For ten years I have been striving towards this aim, against heavy odds and against the sound opinions of others, who thought I was chasing after castles in the air. Now the dream has come true—and now I begin to understand another dream I had more than thirty years ago: I dreamt of a wooden tower that stood on a mountain-top. It was an old tower, and wind and weather had peeled off its paint. I felt sad when I saw this, because I recognised the tower as that from which I had often admired the beautiful landscape, in which I spent my boyhood days. Suddenly I saw the Buddha coming towards me, carrying a pail with paint and brushes. Before I could give expression to my surprise, he handed me the pail and the brushes and said: "Continue and preserve this work of mine!" A great happiness came over me, and suddenly I understood that this tower of vision was the symbol of the Dharma, which the Buddha had erected for all those who want to see beyond the narrow horizon of their mundane world. But what I did not know at that time was that it was actually through brush and colour that I was meant to serve the Buddha-dharma and to save some of its most beautiful monuments from oblivion.'

And still less did I know that I would have a gifted and eager helper in the form of Li Gotami, who like me was devoted to the Enlightened Ones and inspired by the great works of Buddhist art, of which Ajanta and Tsaparang seemed to be the noblest and most accomplished. Only people to whom the spiritual life was more important than material comfort, to whom the teachings of the Buddha was a greater possession than worldly goods and political power, could have achieved such works, which transformed barren nature into a manifestation of inner vision and crude matter into representations of transcendental reality.

We felt overwhelmed by the power of this reality when on the following day we entered the halls of the two big temples, the White and the Red Lhakhang (as they were called according to the colour of their outer walls), which had remained intact amidst all the destruction. The over-life-size golden images, gleaming amidst the warm colours of the frescoed walls, were more alive than anything we had seen before of this kind; in fact, they embodied the very spirit of this deserted city: the only thing that time had not been able to touch. Even the conquering hordes that caused the downfall of Tsaparang had shrunk from defiling the silent majesty of these images. Yet it was apparent to us that even these last remnants of former glory were doomed, as we could see from the cracks in the walls and leaks in the roofs of these two temples. Parts of the frescoes had already been obliterated by rain-water or the water of melting snow seeping here and there through the roof, and some of the images in the White Temple (which were made of hardened clay, coated with gold) were badly damaged.

The frescoes were of the highest quality we had ever seen in or outside Tibet. They covered the walls from the dado (about two and three-quarter feet from the floor) right up to the high ceiling. They were lavishly encrusted with gold and minutely executed, even in the darkest corners or high up beyond the normal reach of human sight, and even behind the big statues. In spite of the minute execution of details, some of the fresco-figures were of gigantic size. Between them middle-sized and smaller ones would fill the space, while some places were covered with miniatures not bigger than a thumb-nail and yet containing figures, complete in every detail, though only discernible through a magnifying glass. It soon became clear to us that these paintings were done as an act of devotion, irrespective of whether they would be seen or not; they were more than merely decorations: they were prayers and meditations in line and colour.

And as we traced as many of these frescoes as time and opportunity allowed, we began to experience the magic of these lines, which enshrined the heart-beat and the living devotion of the artists who had dedicated themselves to this work. Merely to trace these delicate lines accurately demanded the most intense concentration, and it was a strange sensation to relive the feelings and emotions of people who had lived almost a millennium before us. It was like entering their very bodies and personalities, their thoughts and feelings, and thus reliving their innermost life. It showed that not only inner emotion can be expressed by outer movement—be it in the form of brush-lines or in the movements of dance, gestures, *mudrās* and *āsanas*—but that equally the faithful repetition of such outer movements could induce emotions and experiences similar to those which originally created those movements.

Thus, while becoming more and more absorbed by our work, we seemed to relinquish our own identity, taking on the personalities of those who had dedicated themselves to a similar task centuries ago. Maybe we ourselves were the rebirths of some of those artists, and this inner connection had drawn us back to the place of our former activities. Every day, for three months, before starting our work, we would perform our *pūjā* with light and water offerings (signifying consciousness and life) and recite the formulas of refuge and self-dedication at the feet of the golden Buddhas. And with every day their presence would become more and more powerful, until it filled us with a perpetual inspiration, so that we forgot hunger and cold and all other hardships and lived in a kind of trance that enabled us to work from sunrise to sunset almost without interruption and with a minimum of food.

As time passed the cold became more and more intense, especially inside the temples, into which the sun could not penetrate. When filling the seven altar-bowls with water from the morning *pūjā*, the first bowl would already be solidly frozen by the time the last one was being filled, though it took hardly five seconds to fill each bowl. The temple walls were so cold that it became almost impossible to touch them without suffering excruciating pain, so that even tracing became a torture. Li had to keep her bottle of Chinese ink inside her *amphag* to prevent it from freezing and had to breathe from time to time on her brush to thaw the ink which tended to get solid after a few strokes. This was particularly annoying, especially during the last days of our stay when every minute counted; and I remember once when she wept in despair on account of the excessive cold that made it almost impossible for her to hold the brush, her tears were frozen before they could reach the floor and bounced up from it as beads of ice with a thud.

As I worked on the bigger figures of Dhyāni-Buddhas and Bodhisattvas, I was able to work with pencil and conté on a less transparent and slightly more rough-surfaced paper; but I had to battle with the disadvantage that the greater part of my subjects were higher up on the walls and that I had to build a rough kind of scaffolding on pyramids of stone blocks (collected from the debris outside the temples), which had to be dismantled and rebuilt at least once or twice every day according to the progress of my work. It was a back-breaking job, and balancing precariously on top of this pyramid or on the rungs of a roughly made ladder, inserted into and kept together by the stones of the pyramid, I soon found my feet getting frozen, so that I had to climb down from time to time to get my circulation going and to warm up in the sunshine outside. We also had to thaw out our hands there, by placing them on the iron bands, with which the temple doors were fortified and which caught and intensified the warmth of the sun to a remarkable degree.

Another difficulty was the lack or rather the uneven distribution of light in the Lhakhangs. Tibetan temples are built in such a way that the light falls directly upon the main image through a window high up on the opposite side or through a kind of skylight between the lower and the raised central roof. In this way the reflection from the golden face and body of the statue fills the temple with a mild light, sufficient to admire the frescoes and the other objects in the hall, but not for the drawing or painting of small details. Moreover, the light thus reflected from the central image is not stationary but highlights different parts of the temple at different times, according to the position of the sun. On account of this we had to follow the light from one place to another or to reflect it with white sheets into dark corners or places where the pillars, supporting the roof, obstructed the light.

Often one had to abandon the work on which one was engaged and rush to another part of the hall or even to another temple where the light was just favourable, and this process had to be repeated until all the details of each panel were traced and recorded. Photography under these circumstances was particularly difficult, and even Li, a one-time Associate of the Royal Photographic Society of Great Britain, who took all the photographs in these temples, had a hard and sometimes nerve-racking time, because we had no flashbulbs nor any other modern appliances. In those days photographic material was very scarce, colour films were not available, and we had to be glad to get ordinary films for our good old cameras, which had served us well for one or two decades. Li's little Kodak No. I, series 3, with its old-fashioned bellows, but an excellent lens, certainly proved its value (as the results have shown), though it required exceedingly long exposures (without a light-meter!), for which Li had an unfailing 'hunch' and which brought out the plastic values of statues far better than any flashlight could have done. However, some of the frescoes were so unevenly lit that it was impossible to get good results. Even the statues could only be photographed with the help of skilfully placed reflectors and after day-long observations of the different light-effects. The photographs of these statues are, next to our fresco tracings, the most valuable records of our Tsaparang Expedition.

Among the frescoes of Tsaparang, those representing the life of Buddha Śākyamuni are the most remarkable and beautiful. They are the oldest and most complete frescoes of the Buddha's life that have come to light hitherto. Even Ajanta, which until now held the pride of place in the world of Buddhist painting, has almost only scenes from the legendary lives of the Buddha's previous incarnations and very few scenes that can be related to the life of Śākyamuni. All the more were we thrilled to find the frescoes of Tsaparang so complete and with few exceptions in such excellent condition. Even the passage of centuries had not been able to dim their rich colours or to efface their delicate line-work. The colours looked as fresh as if they had been painted in our lifetime and not eight or nine hundred years ago.

The life of the Buddha was depicted in each of the two main temples, called the White and the Red Temple *(lha-khang dkar-po* and *lha-khang dmar-po).* The White Temple (so called because its outer walls were whitewashed) was the older of the two, and contained a colossal, rather archaic-looking statue of Śākyamuni made of beaten and heavily gilt metal sheets. The apsis in which the statue was housed was decorated with finely executed frescoes, depicting the life of the Buddha. The different scenes were interwoven in such a way that various incidents would appear in one and the same composition. The space of each composition was determined by the available wall-surface on both sides of the apsis. Unfortunately half of them were washed away by rain- or snow-water on account of a badly leaking roof.

In the Red Temple, however (so called because its outer walls were painted dark red), nearly all the frescoes were intact, and those that were missing or in poor condition were just the ones which had escaped destruction in the White Temple. This was extremely lucky, as it enabled us to get a complete record of the traditional pictorial representation of the life of the Buddha.

I will not go here into the details of these frescoes, since they will be the subject of a separate publication, in which Li Gotami's faithful tracings and colour-renderings will be reproduced. While she was occupied with the panels of the Life of the Buddha, I worked alternately (according to the conditions of light) on the big figures above them, as well as on the frescoes of the White Temple, which represented two sets of Dhyāni-Buddhas, each of whom was surrounded by a retinue of twelve figures, symbolising different aspects of meditation: altogether 130 figures, out of which sixty-five were set into floral designs, while the other half was set into highly decorative architectural backgrounds.

The monumental Buddha-figures in the frescoes of the Red Temple (above the Life of the Buddha series) would have been of less interest, due to their rather stylised and conventional forms (more or less adhering to the same pattern, so that they distinguished themselves only by their different *mudrās* and the colour of their faces), had it not been for the elaborate decoration of their thrones, which contained a wealth of Buddhist symbols, woven into charming arabesques and architectural designs. These thrones alone would justify a book on Buddhist symbology!

With all these treasures of beauty spread around us, we worked from morning to evening, obsessed with the premonition that we would probably be the last people from outside Tibet who had the privilege to see and to record these unique works of art, and that one day our tracings and photographs would be all that is left of them. We were particularly privileged, since probably never before in the history of Tibet had an official permission been given, to make tracings directly off the walls of such religiously and historically important sanctuaries. We strained to the limits of our capacity to trace every line with the utmost accuracy and to record the colours as faithfully as possible. As to the latter, we were helped by pieces of painted stucco that had fallen from damaged frescoes and which now served us as a colour-key and enabled us to reproduce the frescoes in their original colours, according to our systematic and detailed notations on each of our fresco tracings.

7

Critical Days

We felt confident that if we were allowed to work without disturbance or interference from outside for a long enough time (but not less than three or four months) we could bring back a complete and authentic record of almost all the important frescoes. But at the same time we were only too conscious of the fact that our activities would sooner or later arouse the suspicion of the provincial authorities or of simple-minded people, who could not understand the reason for our prolonged stay in the desolate ruins of a deserted city or the nature of our work, and who therefore might fear that we were agents of a foreign power (China in particular) or that we were engaged in some sort of black magic or treasure-hunting. The ancient monuments of Tibet were always regarded as the repositories of secret forces, on which the safety and prosperity of the country depended. Nobody was worried if they decayed and fell to pieces—this was the natural way of all things—as long as those powers were not disturbed or revealed to those who might utilise them for their own purposes.

The first inkling of trouble came to us in the second week of our stay at Tsaparang with the arrival of a nun, who—as we soon found out—was a member of the household of the provincial governor, the Dzongpön of

Tsaparang, who, however, had his permanent residence in Shangsha, several days' journey away from Tsaparang, which he visited only once or twice a year on his official tour of inspection and tax-collection. A modest building, not far from our cave-like dwelling, served him as temporary headquarters during his brief visits. It was here that the nun had put up, and this invested her with some sort of prestige and authority.

She surprised us while we were at work in one of the temples. She had come there in the company of a Trapa, who was in charge of the Chamba Lhakhang (the Temple of Maitreya) a short distance below the ruined city. The nun began to question us in a somewhat haughty manner, which made us suspect that she had probably been sent out to Tsaparang to spy on us and to report to the Dzongpön about our activities. We tried to explain to her the nature of our work, but she did not seem to understand its purpose and finally declared that if we tried to continue with it, she would see to it that we would no longer be supplied with water and fuel (in the form of brush-wood), which until now had been fetched daily from the valley by Wangdu. This would have meant the end of our stay in Tsaparang! We showed her the authorisation from the Lhasa Government, which allowed us to work and to study in the temples and monasteris of Rinchen Zangpo without let and hindrance and without any time-limit, but we could see that even this did not allay her suspicions. How did we get such an exceptional authorisation? And who knew whether the document was genuine?

At this moment my thoughts turned to Tomo Géshé. Who else could come to our rescue but the Guru who had set me on the path that had led us to Tsaparang and whose name had opened so many doors to us and removed so many obstacles! It was in my capacity of being a personal Chela of Tomo Géshé Rimpoché that I had applied to the Lhasa authorities for permission to work at Tsaparang. Though I did not expect that a simple nun in this remote corner of Tibet would have heard of Tomo Géshé I mentioned that he was our Guru and that we both had been staying at Dungkar Gompa only last year.

When she heard this, her whole attitude changed and she explained: 'I myself come from Dungkar and Tomo Géshé Rimpoché is my Tsawai Lama! How wonderful!'

Now the ice was broken, and when we mentioned the names of various inmates of Dungkar Gompa, whom she too knew, personal contact was finally established and we invited her to come to our quarters at Wangdu's cave, where we showed her the photographs which Li had taken at Dungkar. Now that she could convince herself with her own eyes of the truth of our words, no doubts remained, and when I showed her Tomo Géshé's seal underneath the little image, which I had received from him and which I always carried with me, she reverently bowed down to receive the Guru's blessings.

This incident was a timely warning, as it had shown us how precarious our situation was. We therefore continued our work with an even greater sense of urgency than before, and took greater precautions to keep our activities as secret as possible. Fortunately it happened very rarely that travellers passed through Tsaparang, as it was off the main caravan route, which ran along the other side of the valley of the Lanchen-Khambab. But whenever it happened, we could either hear or see the people, before they were able to climb up to our temples, and in the meantime we could pack away our working materials and devote ourselves to other studies, which rendered us less conspicuous.

We had experienced similar difficulties in Gyantse. Though the Labrangtse (the administrator of the monastic town) had given us permission to study, to sketch, and to take photographs in the temples and monasteries under his jurisdiction, he was greatly afraid of the reactions of the common people, who might regard the tracing of frescoes as sacrilegious, because one could not avoid putting one's hand upon the faces of Buddhas and other sacred personages while tracing them. A Buddha-image (or that of a great saint or a Bodhisattva), whether in the form of a painting or of a statue, becomes an object of veneration from the moment the eyes are opened (by inserting the pupils) with appropriate *mantras,* by which the image becomes imbued with 'life' and spiritual significance.

Tibetans are particularly careful where sanctuaries of powerful tutelary deities are concerned. They look upon them like modern nations would look upon a nuclear power-plant, on which the security and strength of the country may depend and from which outsiders are kept away, for their own security as well as for that of the nation, and they try to keep these installations secret. To Tibetans, likewise, certain sanctuaries of their powerful protectors are of similar importance, and they are hidden from the eyes and guarded from the interference of those who are neither initiated nor engaged in their service, because the powers invoked in these sanctuaries demand a very precise ritual and knowledge of *sādhanā,* so that any disregard or ignorance in this direction might bring about calamities.

As an example I may mention an experience we had during our stay at Tholing, the greatest and historically most important monastery of Western Tibet, founded by Rinchen Zangpo under the patronage of the Kings of Gugé. It was the venue of the famous religious council in A.D. 1050, on which occasion Atīśa was received by the aged founder. Not far from the monastery of Tholing there is a hill with the ruins of the ancient castles of the Kings of Gugé the conveners of the great council. Even in its present state the hill looks very impressive with its remnants of palaces and temples, towers and battlements, standing against the monumental mass of a table mountain in the background.

When we expressed our intention to visit this place, the Abbot of Tholing assured us that there was nothing worth seeing, since all the palaces and temples had been thoroughly destroyed and that neither frescoes nor statues had survived. He was so emphatic about it that we could not help feeling that for some reason or other he wanted to prevent us from going there. Nevertheless we decided to make a day's excursion to the hill, if only for the purpose of sketching and taking photos of the picturesque surroundings.

The abbot was right in so far as we found no traces of ancient frescoes among the ruined buildings. But on the highest point of the hill we found a tall building perfectly intact and with a big Tibetan padlock hanging from the closed entrance. Naturally, we were intrigued to know what the building contained and why the abbot had hidden its existence from us. Its red colour and its shape suggested a temple, and the fact that it was locked proved that it was still in use, but not open to the public.

It was not difficult to climb on to the roof from one of the adjacent walls, and as the skylight was only closed from the outside with wooden shutters, without being locked, we could open them and look inside. We almost jumped backward, because we found ourselves face to face with a gigantic, many-headed monster, whose lowest head was that of a black bull. There were other ferocious faces protruding on both sides of the bull's head. Between its horns, at eye-level with us, a red demoniacal face stared at us; however, on the very top of this frightful pyramid of heads appeared the peaceful countenance of Mañjuśrī, the Dhyāni-Bodhisattva of transcendental knowledge.

The gigantic figure with which we were confronted was that of the most powerful and dreaded Yidam Yamāntaka, the Slayer of Death. The meaning of this fantastic figure is as profound as it is awe-inspiring. The God of Death *(Yama)* is represented in his terrible form as a bull-headed deity, while in reality he is none other than the merciful Avalokiteśvara who, in the stern form of the Lord and Judge of the Dead, holds the Mirror of Truth before deluded human beings, purifies them through the sufferings of purgatory, and finally leads them back to the path of liberation. Mañjuśrī, however, embodies the transcendental knowledge that death is ultimately illusion and that those who identify themselves with the ultimate reality, the plenum-void (*śūnyatā*) of their inner centre, overcome death and are liberated from the chains of *saṁsāra*, the rounds of rebirths in the six realms of delusion.

According to a popular legend, a saintly hermit, who had been meditating for a lifetime in a lonely cave, was about to attain complete liberation, when some robbers entered his cave with a stolen bull and killed it by severing its head, without being aware of the hermit's presence. When they discovered that the latter had been a witness of their deed, they killed him too by cutting off his head. But they had not counted on the supernatural power which he had acquired during his life-long penance. Hardly had they severed the head of the hermit when the latter rose, joined the bull's head to his body and thus transformed himself into the ferocious form of Yama. Deprived from reaching the highest aim of his penance and seized by an insatiable fury, he cut off the heads of the robbers, hung them round his neck as a garland and roamed through the world as a death-bringing demon, until he was vanquished by Mañjuśrī in the form of Yamāntaka, 'the Ender of Death'.

From a deeper point of view Yamāntaka represents the double nature of man, who shares his physical nature, his instincts, drives, and passions with the animals, and his spiritual nature with the divine forces of the universe. As a physical being he is mortal, as a spiritual being he is immortal. If his intellect is combined with his animal nature, demonic forces are born, while the intellect guided by his spiritual nature produces divine qualities. Yamāntaka combines in himself the animal, the demon, and the god, the primordial power of life in its aspects of creation and destruction, and the faculty of knowledge which ripens into the liberating wisdom.

We had never seen such a monumental figure of Yamāntaka, nor had there been an opportunity to photograph even a smaller statue of this kind, because generally it is too dark in the sanctuaries of the fearful deities and, moreover, women are not supposed to enter them. Li, therefore, took this rare opportunity to take a photograph of the Yidam's heads, that protruded beyond the lower roof of the temple on which we stood.

'What a pity that I cannot get the whole figure,' lamented Li, when we climbed down from the roof. 'Let us have a look at the lock!'

Well, she had a good look at it and decided that it could be opened with a little prodding. I tried to dissuade her, but before I could explain my reasons, she succeeded with her little penknife and resolutely entered the temple.

'There is nobody about,' she countered. 'We are miles away from any inhabited place, and there is no living soul in these ruins.'

We stood for a few moments in awed silence before the gigantic black figure of Yamāntaka, whose blackness is the colour of death and whose penis is erect, because procreation and death are inextricably bound up with each other. It is for this reason that Yama, the Lord of Death, holds the Wheel of Life in his claws. But while contemplating this tremendous conception of super-human reality—beyond the realm of beauty or ugliness—I could not suppress a feeling of danger at the back of my mind.

'Take your photo, and let us get out quickly,' I urged. 'One never knows whether somebody is not lurking round the corner. We might have been followed, and I do not like to think of what might happen to us if we were found here.'

Li saw the point, and after having taken a quick exposure we hurried out of the temple, snapped the lock, and walked down the lane by which we had come. Hardly had we turned the corner of the temple when we almost collided with the Abbot of Tholing, who apparently had been informed of our excursion and had followed us, accompanied by a servant. We greeted him with a somewhat exuberant joy—and our joy was not at all false, because we realised the danger we had escaped by a hair's breadth!

Had we been only one minute later I doubt whether we would have ever been allowed to proceed to Tsaparang.

After the encounter with the nun we continued our work undisturbed for about two weeks, happy that the danger had passed. Our happiness, however, came to a sudden end one evening, when returning from our work. We heard the sound of a drum coming from the valley, and the sound came nearer and nearer, as if a procession was slowly moving up the hill. Immediately we felt that new troubles were ahead and that our solitude would be broken. Indeed, soon we saw armed horsemen riding up from the foot of the hill, and Wangdu informed us that the Dzongpön of Tsaparang had arrived.

The following day, instead of working in the temples, we called upon the Dzongpön and explained the purpose of our stay in Tsaparang and the nature of our work. The Dzongpön listened politely, but did not seem to be convinced, and when we showed him our official papers, he told us that he could not take the responsibility of allowing us to work in the temples, unless he had received confirmation from Lhasa that the seals and signatures were genuine. When we asked how long it would take to send a messenger to Lhasa, he replied that it would take about two months to reach Lhasa and that an answer might take four to five months altogether. By that time our provisions would be exhausted and there was very little chance to replenish them locally—except for raw wheat, which we had to grind ourselves for our daily chapatis! Yet I kept up a stiff front and told the Dzongpön that we had no objection to a verification of our papers and that we would not mind waiting for an answer here in Tsaparang, while pursuing our studies.

Thereupon he tried to make out that we were only entitled to work in the temples and monasteries founded by Rinchen Zangpo and that the temples of Tsaparang were not founded by him, but only those of Tholing, where we might go and work.

I could now see that for some reason he wanted to prevent us from staying at Tsaparang, and I was at a loss how to prove that the Lhakhangs here were indeed founded by Rinchen Zangpo.

'But,' I said, 'I myself have read in ancient Tibetan books that these temples are mentioned among those built by Rinchen Zangpo.'

'Which book, for instance?' he demanded.

I realised the trap and knew that unless I could cite an authority big enough to be known and recognised by him I would not be able to impress him. I, therefore, did not mention the *History of the Kings of Gugé,* but rather had a blind shot: 'You will find the reference in your greatest historian's book *The Blue Records (Dep-ther sNgon-po)* by gZon-nud Pal-ldan.'

This obviously impressed him and convinced him that I was not unfamiliar with Tibetan literature. At any rate, he was not able to refute my contention; and feeling himself on uncertain ground, he preferred to drop the matter, saying that he would let us know his decision later.

Before taking our leave, I casually enquired whether it was possible to reach the summit of the Tsaparang rock on which the ruins of the royal palaces were situated, since we had not been able to discover any trace of a path or staircase leading there. The Dzongpön immediately assured us that the rock had become inaccessible on account of rock-falls which had completely obliterated the path that formerly led up to the summit. Besides this, he added, there was nothing but empty walls left of the palaces.

The memory of Tholing was only too fresh in my mind, and I was sure that he was keen to conceal the truth from us. I, therefore, did not show any further interest and merely remarked that it might have been pleasant to admire the view from there. Thus we dropped the matter and took our leave.

We returned to our hovel disheartened and depressed, because we felt that the Dzongpön was bent on preventing us from staying and working here. Now only a miracle could save us. Unable to do anything, we were so worried that we could hardly close our eyes during the night. Neither our money nor our provisions would enable us to wait all through the winter for an answer from Lhasa, especially as we had to consider the long and arduous journey back to India through unknown and probably difficult territory. We spent hours in silent meditation, feeling that only the intervention of higher powers could help us.

And indeed, they did help us! The next morning, instead of receiving orders to quit Tsaparang, as we had feared, the Dzongpön himself called on us, accompanied by servants with gifts of food, and explained that the nun, who had met us some time ago, had spoken to him and convinced him that we were genuine Nangpas ('Insiders', i.e. followers of the Buddha) and personal disciples of Tomo Géshé Rimpoché, whom he himself regarded as one of the greatest Lamas of Tibet and as his personal Guru. He felt sorry to have distrusted us, but now that he knew that we and he were 'Guru-bhais', he would permit us to continue our work, provided we could finish it within about a month, so that we could leave in time before the passes to India would be closed, because he would not like to take the responsibility of having us stranded here during a long and hard winter.

Though it seemed to us unlikely that we would be able to complete our work in so short a time, we promised to do our best, hoping that according to the usual vague Tibetan time-conceptions, the month could be slightly stretched. The main thing was to keep the Dzongpön in a good mood, though actually he had no right to set a time-limit to our work. Once he had left, he probably would forget about us, and if not, we might try to get another time-extension, even if it was only a week or a few days.

Fortunately the Dzongpön, after having provided us with another Lamyig for our return to India, left two days later. When taking leave, he expressed the hope of meeting us at Shipki, a village at the foot of the pass leading to India, where he would stay for some time at the end of the next month. We wished him a good journey and happily returned to our work, which had been interrupted for so many days.

8

THE LAMA OF PHIYANG

HARDLY HAD WE RETURNED to our Lhakhangs when the Dzongpön of Rudok arrived, accompanied by the Abbot of the Sakya Gompa of Phiyang. They reached Tsaparang in the evening, and the next morning the Phiyang Lama came up to the Red Temple just after we had finished our *pūjā* and were about to start our work. The Lama, an elderly man with a friendly face, fringed by a thin white beard, immediately impressed us as a person of sincere goodwill and religious devotion. His outward simplicity, his natural yet dignified bearing, and his quiet way of speaking made us instinctively feel that we had nothing to fear from him and that his questions were born of genuine religious interest and not from any motive of distrust. Sitting down in the warm sun outside the Red Temple, he immediately engaged me in a religious talk. After enquiring to which Chö-lug (sect or tradition) we belonged, he revealed that he himself—though being the head of a Sakya Gompa—was a follower of the Kargyüd and Nyingina traditions. I told him of our Kargyüd Guru as well as of Tomo Géshé Rimpoché, whereupon he said: 'What does it matter what school one follows, as there is only one thing that really matters: the practice of meditation.' Then he quoted a verse expressing these thoughts, which began with the words: 'Without meditation [*sgom*] there is no Dharma [*chos*], and wherever the Dharma is found, there is also meditation.'

I felt strangely elated in the presence of this old man, who was sitting humbly with us on the bare ground before the entrance of the temple, clad in his unassuming travelling robes, which did not distinguish him from the poorest Trapa. There was no curiosity in his talk; he was not interested in personal questions, from where we came and where we went from here or what we did, but only in matters of spiritual life and, most of all, in meditational practice. I could see that he was a man of great learning, but one who had left behind him the ambitions of mere scholarship, because he had realised the essence of the Buddha's message in his own life.

For the first time we did not feel sorry to interrupt our work, because since leaving our Gurus' monasteries in Southern Tibet, we had not met anybody of real spiritual attainment, which like the natural perfume of a flower makes itself known unobtrusively and quietly, pervading its surroundings, irrespective of whether people pay attention to it or not. We could not say why, but Phiyang Lama's presence radiated such peace that all our troubles and anxieties seemed to be blown away; our race against time, which had kept us in perpetual tension, had suddenly stopped and we felt happy and contented, as if time had ceased to exist. Nothing seemed to matter as long as we were in Phiyang Lama's presence, and we only wished that he could stay longer with us. But he told us that he was on his way to India on a pilgrimage to the holy places and that he had accepted the Dzongpön of Rudok's invitation to travel in his company only as long as they were following the same direction.

After we had returned from the temples in the company of Phiyang Lama, the Dzongpön joined us in our little hut, and since he was quite a pleasant young man, lively and full of eagerness to hear of our travels and especially of all the society people of Central Tibet whom we had met in various places, Li took out the photographs of our friends and acquaintances, many of whom were known to him. He was particularly interested in the photos of young ladies, and Li had some difficulty in dissuading him from keeping some of them, by explaining that she had no right to pass them on to others without having the permission of the persons concerned. Phiyang Lama was amused by the young man's enthusiasm, but he did not spoil his fun in any way, seeing how much the Dzongpön enjoyed talking about people and places of which he had pleasant remembrances and which he sorely missed in his far-off outpost at Rudok, not far from the Pangong Lake.

What a contrast between these two people: the gay young-man about town' and the quiet old sage! Yet they seemed to make good travelling companions: the young one by his good-natured jollity, the old one by his tolerant understanding of human nature and his unshakable equanimity.

They were leaving the following day, and when Phiyang Lama came to say goodbye to us, we felt genuinely sorry. In order to express our feelings in a more tangible way, we wanted to present him with a beautiful reproduction of the famous Sarnath Buddha (of the sixth century A.D.), which we had brought with us as a special gift for some high Lama, with whom we might come in touch on our journey. But to our surprise the Rimpoché declined our gift in all kindness, and we felt that his words were sincere and true, when he said: 'I thank you for your kindness, but I really do not need any outward picture of the Enlightened One, because the Buddha is ever present in my heart.' And then he blessed us and took his leave.

We suddenly felt a strange sense of loneliness, as if somebody whom we had known for long, somebody who was deeply connected with our own life, had left us. If it had not been for our work, we might have asked his permission to accompany him on his pilgrimage. Little did we know that our wish would be fulfilled in a manner we could not have dreamt of and which confirmed our first impression: that we had met a man with unusual spiritual attainments and the capacity as well as the will to transmit them to others.

9

A Race against Time and Obstacles

THE MOMENT PHIYANG Lama had left, time became again a reality and the race against it began anew. By now it had become clear to us that not only every day, but every minute of our working time, was precious. We would get up with the first ray of the sun that penetrated our cave-like dwelling through the chinks between the rough stone-blocks that formed its walls, and we would return only when it became too dark for our work in the temples and the sun sank behind the rocks. We dared not waste a moment on a midday meal and only cooked and ate after sunset. Sometimes we would even work on our tracings and notes in the light of a candle before going to sleep, as long as the warmth of our hot evening porridge kept our fingers from freezing. The temperature in our little room never rose above freezing-point, and often it happened that, when we neglected our cup of hot tea for a few minutes while talking, the tea would be frozen solid in the meantime.

To wash our hands and faces, we had to break the ice in our wash-basin, which froze over immediately after it had been filled from the wooden keg, which Wangdu brought every day from the stream in the valley and which had to be kept in his cave near the fireplace. Since fuel (consisting mainly of brushwood, rarely of yak dung) was scarce and had to be brought from a considerable distance down in the valley, it would only be used for cooking on the common fireplace between our cubicle and the cave entrance.

Our main food consisted of chapaties with a little rancid butter, which we had bought at Tholing Gompa at an exorbitant price, and in the evening we added to this a porridge of sweetened milk and wheat-flour. When finally even the Tholing butter came to an end, we had to send the Trapa of the Chamba Lhakhang first to Tholing and later, when the Gompa too was short of butter, to the Dogpas (nomadic herdsmen) of the Chang-Thang. The good man came back from there after a month with only two balls of somewhat 'mature' butter, sewn into raw hide (with the hair inside), weighing a little more than a pound each!

But the Buddhas of the Lhakhangs were feeding us with such inspiration that we gave little thought to physical food. Yet we could not help observing that our stores were diminishing at an alarming rate. We then discovered that there was a big hole in the wall, just behind the place where we kept our bags with foodstuffs. We quietly repaired the wall and moved our food to a safer place—out of reach of anybody who might thrust his arm through the hole.

For a few days everything went well, but then we noticed that pilferage was going on again. Could it be that the padlock, with which we locked the heavy wooden door of our cubicle every day before we left for our work, was opened in our absence? To make sure, we sealed it every morning. We never found the seal broken, nor anything wrong with the walls; but again foodstuffs were pilfered. We were sure that it could only be Wangdu or one of his friends or relatives, who came to visit him from time to time; but it was a riddle to us how anybody could get into the room without either opening the door or breaking through the wall. This latter possibility, however, had to be ruled out, because it would take too long (especially as the one or the other of us made a point of suddenly turning up at odd hours) and would leave traces, which we would be quick to detect, since we had been alerted by the previous experience.

Besides Wangdu, there was his brother-in-law, who served us alternately with him, because he claimed that he should also have an opportunity of earning some money. However, what first seemed to be a friendly arrangement between the two men developed into a kind of rivalry, and one day they quarrelled, and each of them tried to oust the other from our service. We were just inside the room, when a fight before our door started. Apparently each of them tried to push the other away and prevent him from entering. Suddenly, with a mighty crash they literally fell with the door into the room—and now we saw to our dismay that the door had come off from the hinges! So this was the solution of the riddle: every day, after we had locked the door and sealed the lock, the thief had simply lifted the door out of its hinges, taken whatever he wanted from our bags and put the door back. Thus, when we came back in the evening, we found our lock and its seal intact. From now on we sealed the hinges every day, and this was a complete success. No more foodstuffs were stolen.

Meanwhile a month and a half had passed and nothing was heard of the Dzongpön of Tsaparang who probably was now far away on the road to Shipki. Not finding us there, he would send for us, and by that time another month might have passed, which would allow us to finish our main work. On the other hand it might happen that the passes were already closed by heavy snowfalls in the outer Himalayas—in which case there would be little sense in trying to force us to return to India. We cared very little what might happen, as long as we could get on with our work.

It was in the middle of December when the feared blow fell. One evening a number of rough-looking fellows arrived and put up in Wangdu's cave, carousing noisily half the night. On the following morning a rather sinister-looking one-eyed man (the other had been blown out in a fight on the Chang-Thang, as we learned later) called on us and informed us that the Dzongpön had given orders that we had to leave Tsaparang and that he had been ordered to escort us to the frontier pass.

Since several of our panels were only half finished, I told the man that we would be ready to leave Tsaparang, if only the Dzongpön would give us a few days more to finish the work in hand. In order to play for time, I immediately wrote a letter to the Dzongpön and sent it off with one of his servants. I did not expect a favourable reply, but I knew that it would take at least a week for the man to return with the Dzongpön's answer. The latter, as we learned from his men, had come back from Shipki and was staying at Shangsha, his usual headquarters.

It worked out exactly as I had expected; the messenger came back after one week, and this was just sufficient for us to finish our work. Li had completed her set of frescoes of the Life of the Buddha and I had traced practically all the frescoes of the White Temple and most of the big ones above the Life of the Buddha in the Red Temple. Li had also succeeded in tracing a most interesting series of panels, representing scenes from the inauguration of the temple, which give a very good idea of contemporary life and show what the people, who built the temple, looked like.

One day after the messenger had returned, both the temples were sealed on the Dzongpön's order. It was a sad day, when we celebrated our last *pūjā* in each of these temples before the golden images that had smiled their blessings upon us daily for almost three months. Now that we took leave of them, it was like saying goodbye for ever to our dearest friends. To us they had been living embodiments of wisdom and compassion. They had given us courage and inspiration, and we had lived and worked under their protection. They had taught us the Dharma in wordless sermons of beauty, that would be enshrined in our hearts and live in us as the noblest vision of ultimate perfection. We left the temples with deep gratitude. Our task had been fulfilled and what we had gained, no worldly power could take away from us.

10

The Discovery of the Secret Path and the Temple of the Great Maṇḍala

After the temples had been sealed we had for the first time sufficient leisure to wander about among the ruins and in the surroundings and so we utilised this opportunity for sketching and taking photos. There was no dearth of beautiful motifs, and since our main work was accomplished, we felt free to devote ourselves to our own creative impulses with a good conscience. It was the only positive way to get over the sadness of leave-taking and to fill the emptiness that suddenly yawned before us.

While Li was busy sketching near the *chortens* at the back of the hill, I was exploring again the ruins which rose above the temples towards the foot of the isolated perpendicular rock, on which the castles of the kings were silhouetted against the sky, inaccessible and proud like the Castle of the Holy Grail. Again and again I could not help feeling that one last unsolved mystery was hidden among the ruins of the kings' palaces and that this was the reason why the Dzongpön tried to prevent us from staying longer at Tsaparang, fearing that one day we might find ways and means to get to the summit or to discover the secret path, if there was one.

These were the thoughts that went through my head while I was roaming about in a maze of ruined buildings, when finally I came to a halt at a steep rock and decided to give up the search. I was just about to turn back when I noticed three boulders, resting one upon the other at the foot of the rock, and suddenly it occurred to me that they could not have fallen like that by chance. Surely they could only have been placed in this way by human hands. But for what purpose? Was it merely to mark a certain spot or to indicate a certain direction to be followed, or did it serve a more immediate, tangible purpose, namely to reach something that otherwise would have been out of reach? I stepped on the boulders and stretched my hand upwards. And lo! My searching hand suddenly fitted into a small cavity, which I had not been able to detect from below. And now, while I drew myself up with one hand, my foot found a similar hold on the rock and my other hand reached a ledge, so that I could pull myself farther up, until I found myself at the lower end of a steeply rising gully, that seemed to have been eroded by rain-water. Scrambling up over the rubble that covered the ground, I soon came upon a flight of steps, which convinced me that I had found the beginning of the ancient stairway leading up to the palaces of the kings.

However, my joy was short-lived, since I soon lost myself again in a labyrinth of ruins, so that I finally had to return to my starting-point. There was only one alternative left, namely, to follow a steep ravine, half filled with fallen masonry. This proved to be a success, because now I found another flight of steps, better preserved than the previous one. It led to a spacious plateau and from it rose the perpendicular rock-wall of the summit of Tsaparang, towering several hundred feet above me. I searched in vain for a continuation of the staircase. So, probably, the Dzongpön had been right, when he told us that the way that once had led up to the castles had been completely destroyed.

But having come as far as this, I wanted at least to investigate the numerous caves which yawned at the base of the rock-wall, for I hoped to find remnants of frescoes or at least some ancient clay seals which were often deposited in such caves. But there was nothing of the kind. Instead of that I found what I had least expected: one of the caves proved to be the entrance to a tunnel that led upwards in a wide curve inside the rock, from time to time lit up by narrow openings in the outer rock-wall. With a beating heart I followed the tunnel, climbing higher and higher, filled with the greatest expectations and at the same time with a lurking fear to come again to a dead end or to be faced with some unsurmountable obstacle.

How great was, therefore, my joy, when I stepped into the light of the sun again and realised that I was standing on the very summit of Tsaparang, which for so long we had believed to be inaccessible. The view was in itself worth all the trouble of the climb. I could see now that the rocky spur, on which Tsaparang was built, had been carved out by two deep canyons, leading into the main canyon of the Langchen-Khambab, above which a wildly serrated range of rocky mountains rose into the clear blue sky like a non-ending procession of gothic cathedrals with innumerable towers and needle-sharp spires. Behind them appeared here and there snow-covered peaks, and in the bright sunlight the whole landscape scintillated in the most transparent colours.

I felt as if I was standing in the centre of an immense *maṇḍala* composed of unearthly colours and forms: a centre towards which all those forms and colours seemed to stand in a significant inner relationship, so that it became a focus of all those forces of heaven and earth that had shaped its surroundings. It is this geomantic principle according to which all great sanctuaries of Tibet have been built, in fact all seats of power, in which the spiritual element was always given predominance and was sought in perfect harmony with nature. Thus the castles of kings or other sovereign rulers were simultaneously strongholds of religion and sanctuaries of the Great Protectors and their secret cults. (They were 'secret' in the sense that they could only be performed within the circle of those who were trained through years of *sādhanā* and qualified by initiation, from which nobody was barred who was willing to fulfil the necessary preconditions and to abide by its rules.)

Conscious of all these facts, I wandered through the ruins of palaces and temples, silent witnesses of a great past, of great triumphs and tragedies, of human ambitions and passions, of worldly power and religious devotion. There was an eerie stillness in this place suspended, as it seemed, between heaven and earth—and perhaps, therefore, partaking of both: of the ecstasies of divine inspirations and the cruel sufferings of human greed and lust for power. Moving about as in a dream, in which past and present were interwoven into a fabric of four-dimensional reality, I suddenly stood before the half-open door of an almost completely preserved building, which by some miracle had escaped the general destruction.

With a strange feeling of expectancy I entered into the death-like stillness of a half-dark room, in which the secrets of centuries seemed to be present and to weigh upon me like the fate of an unfulfilled past. When finally my eyes had become accustomed to the darkness, my premonitions became certainty: I stood in the Holy of Holies of a mystery temple, the chamber of initiation, in which the great *maṇḍala,* 'the Sacred Circle of Highest Bliss', *(dPal hKhor-lo bDem-chog)* is revealed before the eyes of the initiate, in all its manifold forms of celestial splendour, divine figures and cosmic symbols.

It was Tomo Géshé Rimpoché who had brought me in touch for the first time with the mysterious world of this *maṇḍala,* and under his guidance it had become for me a living experience. For almost a year it formed the centre of my religious life—and even then I realised that I had only lifted a tiny corner of the veil that hides the supreme realisation of this profoundest of all profound Tantras, one of the earliest introduced in Tibet at the time of Padmasambhava and held in the highest esteem by Gelugpas as much as by the older sects of Tibetan Buddhism.

It contains the complete process of a world creation from the deepest centre of consciousness—the unfoldment of forms from the formless state of undifferentiated emptiness (*śūnyatā*) and unlimited potentiality—through the germ-syllables of the subtle elementary principles and the crystallisation of their essential forms and colours into a concentric image of the universe, spread out in ever widening rings of materialising worlds. Their essential and timeless centre is represented by the symbol of Mount Meru, the stable axis and the ideal cross-section of the universe, in which the hierarchy of divine beings and realms of existence—the increasingly intensified and purified manifestations, or *higher dimensions of consciousness*—are present. 'A miniature world is evolved, seething with elemental forces working in the universe as cosmic forces and in man as forces of body and spirit. Most of the quantities in this elaborate notation are taken from the body of indigenous religious teaching and mythology. Some are so universal and transparent that it reveals something, even to the outsider, of the force of this symbolical structure, and makes him intuitively feel that here we are assisting in the unfolding of a great spiritual drama, sweeping the mind up to heights of exaltation and nobility.'[1]

The realm of these higher dimensions is symbolised by a celestial temple, composed of the purest and most precious materials and containing the *maṇḍala* of highest bliss and supreme realisation, in which the spiritual hierarchies are arranged in concentric steps, rising towards the centre, in which the ultimate reality becomes conscious in the union of the divine figure of Demchog ('Highest Bliss') and his consort or *Prajñā* (transcendental knowledge) in the form of Dorjé Phagmo.

With the upper pair of his twelve arms, signifying the knowledge of the twelvefold formula of Interdependent Origination, Demchog tears apart the elephant-hide of ignorance, with his four faces, shining in the colours of the four basic elements (*mahābhūta*) of the universe, he permeates and encompasses the four directions of space with the four divine qualities of love, compassion, sympathetic joy, and equanimity. Each face has three eyes, because his vision penetrates the three worlds (the world of sense-desire, the world of Pure Form, and the world of Non-Form) and the three times (past, present, and future). The colour of his body is blue, because it represents the infinity, changelessness, and all-inclusiveness of space, as well as the ultimate principle of the metaphysical 'emptiness', the Plenum Void of *Śunyatā*.

1. From an article on the 'Srichakra-Sambhara-Tantra' by Johan van Manen, reprinted in *Shakti and Shakta* by Sir John Woodroffe (Luzac, London, 1929).

Dorjé Phagmo's body is red, to signify her passionate devotion to the good of all beings. She has only one face, which expresses the oneness of all things, and only two arms, which signify the two aspects of truth, the ultimate and the relative. She is naked because she is free from obscuring illusions. Her legs encircle the divine body of Demchog, who holds her in close embrace, indicating their complete and inseparable union in body and spirit, the oneness of supreme bliss and wisdom.

And all the divine figures, assembled around them in ascending steps, are likewise embraced by their wisdom-holding consorts, so that they appear like reflections of the central and highest truth on different levels of reality, and all of them are engaged in the same cosmic dance in the ecstatic experience of highest bliss, which flows from the union of *prajñā* and *upāya:* Wisdom and the means towards its realisation through active compassion and unselfish love. In fact, each of the figures embodies a certain quality or stage on the path of perfection, which is traced step by step in this profound and universal meditation.

'What must be done to make this meditation into a reality? Every concept in it must be vivified and drenched with life and power. Every god in it must be made into a living god, every power manipulated in it made into a potency. The whole structure must be made vibrant with forces capable of entering into sympathetic relation with the greater cosmic forces in the universe, created in imitation on a lower scale within the individual meditator himself. To the religious mind the universe is filled with the thoughts of the gods, with the powers of great intelligences and consciousnesses, radiating eternally through space and really constituting the world that is. "The world is only a thought in the mind of God." It must take years of strenuous practice even to build up the power to visualise and correctly produce this meditation as an internal drama.'[1] It is for this purpose that elaborate models of the *maṇḍala* are built up, in which the whole spiritual universe is minutely modelled with every detail and hundreds of divine and demonic figures, from the jewel-studded temple on the summit of Mount Meru down to the eight great

1. Johan van Manen, in his aforementioned essay.

cemeteries, the places of death and of initiation, in which Yogis and Siddhas underwent spiritual rebirth and transformation by experiencing the process of dying and overcoming the illusion of death. Because in order to be reborn the initiate has to go through the portals of death.

Remembering all this I stood upon the threshold of the temple, gazing with trepidation and expectancy into its dark interior. Slowly bit by bit the details of the *maṇḍala* stepped out of the darkness. But what had happened? The innumerable figures of divine beings, which had inhabited the *maṇḍala*, lay scattered in a wild heap all over the half-crumbled structure. The sanctuary had obviously been desecrated by pillaging hordes after the fall of Tsaparang at the collapse of the Gugé Dynasty. Yet the crude forces of violence had not been able to destroy the atmosphere of sanctity in this ancient place of initiation. The walls were still covered with frescoes of great beauty and depth of colour. They revealed a mystic dance of many-armed, many-headed deities, ecstatically embracing their consorts, terrible and awe-inspiring, beautiful and frightening at the same time: a revelation to the initiate, a horror to the ignorant intruder. Here life and death, creation and destruction, the forces of light and darkness, seemed to be inextricably interwoven in a cyclonic movement of transmutation and liberation.

I opened the door of the temple as wide as possible, but the light was not sufficient to take photographs of the frescoes, though I had my camera with me. But among the figures scattered over the *maṇḍala*, there was a Heruka (a heroic, four-armed form of Demchog), embraced by his knowledge-inspired Khadoma, and in these figures the moment, or, better, the timeless state of ecstasy in perfect union of Love and Wisdom, which results in Highest Bliss, was expressed with such consummate beauty, that I felt moved to lift the divine pair out of this chaos of destruction and carried it outside the temple, where I could take a photograph. I felt sorry to put the figures back into the temple, where surely they would perish with the rest of the doomed sanctuary, but I was glad to preserve at least a fraction of their beauty on my film for others to see and for myself as a lasting remembrance.

Before I closed the door of the temple behind me, I cast a last glance into the sanctuary and repeated the *mantras* with which the reality of the great *maṇḍala* of Demchog are invoked, *mantras* that a millennium ago were recited in this very place and brought to life the great visions that were enshrined in this temple. In the certainty that soon even the last traces of this *maṇḍala* would disappear, I was glad that I had been allowed this last glimpse and enabled to relive something of the spirit to which this place had been dedicated. The sanctity of such a place cannot be revived by outer renovation, but only through the inner action of devotion and the power of the mind, through which the creative faculty of *mantras* is realised.

I stepped again into the light of the sun, filled with grateful joy that even my last wish in Tsaparang had been fulfilled and that the mission I had set out to accomplish had been successfully completed. Before entering again the rock-tunnel on my way down, I surveyed for the last time the immense landscape and the ruins and canyons below me. And there, deep down, I saw a small human figure moving about and recognised Li sketching near the *chortens* at the foot of the hill. I called out to her—oblivious of the risk I took—and after looking about her in surprise, not knowing from where the sound of my voice came, she finally looked up and discovered me standing at the edge of the rock, on the very top of Tsaparang. She gave me a sign not to reveal my presence, since the Dzongpön's men might be lurking around, and I could only hope that my voice had not given me away. I dived at once into the rock-tunnel and hurried down as quickly as possible.

Since Li too wanted to see the Demchog Lhakhang, we both climbed up again the next morning, and though we had tried to avoid attention, by first starting in a different direction, the Dzongpön's men apparently had become suspicious, wondering where we had disappeared, and sent Wangdu in search of us. Hardly had we left the Demchog Lhakhang after a short *pūjā* and after Li had hurriedly taken some photos, when Wangdu emerged from the rock-tunnel, visibly agitated, because in all probability he had been instructed by the Dzongpön to prevent us from getting to the palaces of the kings and the hidden sanctuary. The fact that also he had denied more than once that there was any access to the summit of Tsaparang was sufficient proof for us.

However, we could not blame him for this, and we assured him that the Dzongpön would never come to know about it, if he would keep it from the Dzongpön's servants. This reassured him greatly, and in the afternoon he even consented to open for us the small Dorjé-Jigjé Lhakhang (the temple of Vajra-bhairava [Tib.: *rDorje hJigs-byed*], a synonym for *Yamāntaka),* which we had avoided so far, since we had assured the Dzongpön that we only wished to work in the main temples, dedicated to the peaceful deities. After our experience in Tholing, we knew only too well the Dzongpön's fear of arousing the wrath of the fierce deities if he would allow us to work in their sanctuary, which was just above the Red Temple. It was always locked, not only because it housed the powerful Protectors, but also because it served as a kind of store-room for all the most valuable metal images, which had been salvaged from various sanctuaries in the ruins of Tsaparang. The place really was a treasure-trove of the most exquisite metal statues we had ever seen. The execution of the many-armed fierce deities, many of them joined by their consorts *(yum),* was of the highest quality and showed a perfection in the treatment of metal that has never been surpassed anywhere in the world. But these priceless works of art were so crowded together in the small dark room that Li could take only very few photographs. Yet we were grateful even for this glimpse of these rare treasures.

Now nothing more remained for us but to start packing our things and to prepare for the long journey back to India. Though we felt sad, we knew that we had done all that was in our power and that our efforts had been richly rewarded.

11

Trek over the Frozen River

THE JOURNEY OVER the high mountain ranges that separate Western Tibet from Himachal Pradesh (the small Himalayan principalities) at the height of winter proved to be a dangerous undertaking and might have ended in disaster, if I had not resisted the plan of the Dzongpön's rascally one-eyed servant, who had been deputed to escort us to the frontier and who tried to get rid of his duty as soon as possible by pushing us somewhere over the frontier in a totally uninhabited region, where we would have perished from lack of food, shelter, and transport. His excuse was that the normal caravan route was already closed, but after having consulted my maps (which I had drawn before we left India, with the help of various maps of the Indo-Tibetan frontier region, which could not be bought at that time, but only consulted in government offices with special permission), I refused to fall in with his plan and insisted on joining the main caravan route and, if necessary, waiting there until the passes had opened again.

If we had thought that Tsaparang during December was a pretty cold place, we soon learned to think of it as warm and comfortable compared to the bitter cold and the icy winds we experienced on the highlands which we had to cross and where our simple canvas tent (which had seemed to us so sturdy and windproof) offered hardly any protection. We had no thermometer with us, but twenty degrees Celsius below zero would be a safe estimate. Our tent-sheets became so stiffly frozen that it required the greatest effort to fold and to roll them up in the morning, especially as our hands were numb and every movement had become torture. Even to take the camera out of its leather case and to adjust it for an exposure had become an almost insurmountable obstacle, so that we no longer had the energy to take photos. The effort to keep alive and moving absorbed all our forces.

Even at night we had to keep on our heavy Tibetan boots for fear that our feet would freeze and that in the morning we would not be able to get them again into the equally frozen boots. We slept with our hats on and with our blankets drawn over our heads, leaving only a small opening for breathing. But even our breath froze, and in the morning we found it laying on the blanket as a round wafer of ice. To use a handkerchief had become impossible; one might just as well have tried to wipe one's nose with a piece of crumpled cardboard. Moreover, my beard had become a mass of icicles, and from time to time I had to knock them off from under my nose, for which purpose a hammer would have been more adequate than a handkerchief.

Whenever there was an opportunity, i.e. whenever we got into an inhabited place in the valleys which lay across our path, the Dzongpön's man—whom we paid handsomely, as he had offered to be our servant and caravan leader—would spend his money in drink and gambling (as we had observed already in Tsaparang the night after his arrival), and sometimes he got so drunk that we did not see him for several days. Finally he disappeared altogether, so that we had to engage another servant—a man called Sherab—who during the coming months proved to be not only faithful, but a man whose human qualities soon made us feel towards him real friendship. He looked after our needs with touching solicitude, sparing no pains to make us comfortable and to protect us from exploitation. He never thought of his own advantage. After our experiences with Wangdu and the Dzongpön's servant, he was for us a real godsend, especially when avalanches suddenly blocked our way before we could reach the main Himalayan range, and we got stuck in a tiny Tibetan village just across the frontier in a valley surrounded by mighty snow-peaks and completely cut off from the outer world. This proved a blessing in disguise, because it was a real 'Shangrila', in which we spent almost a quarter of a year of unalloyed happiness in the company of simple but most lovable people and at the feet of the last of our Tibetan Gurus.

However, before we could reach this oasis of peace we still had half a month's journey before us. Just when we were nearing the safety of the main caravan road, we were informed that it was already closed. We had no means of ascertaining whether this was so or not, but the villagers, who informed us, declared themselves ready to guide us and to carry our luggage through the frozen gorges of the Langchen-Khambab. It was only during the coldest part of the winter that it was possible to travel through these gorges, which were so deep and narrow and threatened by rock-falls that no path could be made between the swirling waters of the river and the steep rocks which hemmed it in on both sides. Thus, it was only when the river was completely frozen that its surface could be used as a rough track, though it was impossible to employ yaks or horses. The reason for this soon became apparent: there was not even a path leading down into this tremendous canyon which cut through mountain-walls that rose not less than 8,000 feet on both sides of the roaring river. Moreover, no pack-animal could have walked on the ice, which due to the turbulence of the water did not form an even surface, but followed the shapes of the waves and cataracts underneath when it was not broken into a jumble of ice-blocks and -floes.

We therefore had to engage some twenty people for our luggage from the last village, where we had been staying for two days in order to visit a small but fantastically situated monastery on top of an isolated mountain, that looked as if it had been thrown up by a gigantic force and had become solid before it could fall back into the depth from which it had been hurled. The name of the monastery was Pekar Gompa, Pekar being one of the ancient, probably pre-buddhistic, telluric deities of Tibet, who had been retained as a protector of the country and the Buddhist faith.

The Dzongpön's man, who had turned up again, after some days' absence, apparently did not like to risk life and limb in the treacherous gorges of the Langchen-Khambab, especially as he might not be able to get back before the end of the winter if a sudden snowfall should block even this route.

So he took a tearful leave from us—probably thinking that we were going to our doom; or was it merely that he had had too much *chang*? At any rate we felt glad to leave him behind and to move on with a crowd of cheerful and friendly people, in whose company we felt safer in spite of the uncertainties of the days before us. The dangers of nature seemed to us always preferable to the unreliability of low characters, like this Dzongpön's servant.

When, after a few miles from the village, we came to the edge of the canyon, we all just slithered down a series of steep sand-falls till we reached the bottom of the gorge, several thousand feet below the level from which we had started. It then occurred to us that we had taken an irrevocable step, because it would have been impossible to climb up again on these moving sand-falls, especially with our heavy luggage! I don't know what we would have done, if the river had not yet been sufficiently frozen to bear our weight and the impact of falling luggage, when people slipped and crashed on the ice together with their loads. This happened every few moments, because the ice was as smooth as a mirror, but unfortunately not even, so that we, without loads, could hardly walk a few steps without falling.

Thus very little progress was made on that day, and when the evening came, we pitched camp on a narrow boulder-strewn strip of dry land. That night we felt for the first time comfortably warm—partly due to the lower altitude and the protection from wind, but also because the sky had become slightly overcast, as if a change of weather was imminent. There had been a lovely sunset, and our camp, surrounded by yellow reed-grass, was enveloped in a warm glow, which heightened our feeling of comfort and almost made us forget the ice of the river and the hazards of our trek. We were filled with a strange, unaccountable happiness, which made us oblivious of the past and the future and fully aware of the peace and the luminous beauty around us. Just as when we were stranded in the Valley of the Moon Castle, we experienced a kind of euphoria due to the utter strangeness of the situation, in which the world we had known ceased to exist, so that we felt a kind of release from all that had been or would be, and from all responsibility of decisions, accepting quietly and completely what was around us, a world in which we were entirely thrown back upon ourselves, as if we were the only people alive in the universe. The wonders of a journey consist far more of such intangible experiences and unexpected situations than of factual things and events of material reality.

Thus, to us this camp, though it happened in the middle of winter, remains in our remembrance the 'summer camp', as we called it that evening on the Langchen-Khambab, before we had retired into our tent. But how great was our surprise when we woke up the next morning and found ourselves snowed in and surrounded by a real winter landscape! We rubbed our eyes, awaking from our summer-dream and trying to cope with this new situation. Would we be able to continue our journey, and if not, what then? But we found our people quite unperturbed. They seemed to have slept in the snow as soundly as we in our tent. We could not help admiring them for their hardiness and their cheerful acceptance of all circumstances—and this reassured us greatly. In spite of the snow, the air appeared to us mild and pleasant. It demonstrated to us again the fact that in Tibet snowfalls seldom occur when it is very cold, and that snow therefore is welcome as a sign of milder weather.

After the intense cold of the highlands, where everything was frozen, but no snow was to be seen anywhere, except on the highest peaks, we now realised with astonishment how much less we felt the cold in this really wintry snow landscape—the mere sight of which would have made us shiver under normal circumstances, considering that Li was born and bred in Bombay on the shores of the Arabian Sea and that I myself spent the greater part of my life in tropical and subtropical countries. Our Tibetans definitely enjoyed the snow: in fact all along this river-trek they were exceedingly cheerful, and when we came to a place where there was a grove of small trees (a sight many of our highland Tibetans had never seen in their life) they got so excited over such an abundance of wood that they built big fires and sang and danced half the night. We too were caught up in the general spirit of merriment and enjoyed ourselves thoroughly, while preparing a mammoth amount of chapaties, listening to their songs and sharing their simple pleasures. We had all become one happy family! The whole scene was truly fantastic: the blazing fires in the snow, the colourful costumes of the people distributed in groups among the rocks and under the white tracery of twigs and branches, and all this in the wildest imaginable mountain scenery, which in its grimness formed the utmost contrast to the light-hearted playfulness of these brave people. They certainly were the merriest group we had ever travelled with, and the young women among them seemed to be as tireless as the men, in spite of carrying heavy loads all through the day over ice and boulder-strewn ground. They all slept on the snow, as if it was a featherbed, with no other protection than two sheepskins (the hair turned inside). Between those skins most of them slept naked, with their clothes rolled up as a pillow, a custom which we had also observed in other regions of Tibet. Even the women would strip down to the waist without concern. Probably they found it rather 'indecent' of us that we went to sleep with all our clothing on.

The snow—far from impeding our progress, as we had feared the morning after the heavy snowfall—was actually helping us, because now we were able to walk on the ice without slipping all the time, though, on the other hand, we had to be more careful of hidden crevices in the ice. Farther down the river—probably due to the stronger current—the ice was ripped open in many places, and if anybody had fallen into a crevice, nobody could have saved the unlucky person, because the current would have pulled the body under the ice before any help could be given. Fortunately we got through without an accident, and when after our six-day trek on the frozen river we finally emerged at the village of Tyak, near which the Lotsava Rinchen Zangpo was born, we felt quite sorry that our adventure had come to an end and even more so that we had to leave our friendly companions.

We now travelled on with Sherab, who arranged new teams of yaks, horses, and people from village to village, which was not difficult, as we were again on the regular caravan road. At Shipki we found no sign of the Dzongpön of Tsaparang, though we pitched our tent in the courtyard of the house which served him and other Tibetan officials as a temporary residence. We crossed the Shipki Pass without incident, in spite of high snow, and descended into the happy valley of Poo, our little 'Shangrila', which we reached towards the end of January.

12

The Happy Valley

Poo looked like any other Tibetan village and the people too were the same as on the other side of the Shipki-La, though the political frontier, dividing Tibet and India, was drawn across the pass. This, however, had no meaning to the people on both sides, who spoke the same language, practised the same religion and who moved freely to and fro, while having practically no contact with the population on the Indian side of the main Himalayan Range, which was still five days' journey away from here.

We had hoped to find a post office here, but we were informed that an Indian mail-runner came only once a month, and when we asked when we could expect the next one we were informed: 'In spring, when the passes over the Himalayas are open again.' 'When would this be?' we asked with some trepidation. 'Oh, in about three months' time!'

It was then that we realised that it would be four months before we could return to India, because the journey from here to the plains or the first bigger town, i.e. Simla, would take another month. We would not have minded this, if it had not been that both our money and our provisions had come to an end, and we wondered how we would pull through for so many months! However, this was no problem for the good old man who was in charge of the rest-house (which had been provided for the officials of the Public Works Department, in charge of the caravan road across the Shipki-La) and who very kindly gave us the permission to put up there on his own responsibility, since we could not communicate with the authorities. 'And if you are short of money,' he continued, 'I will give you as much as you need. You can return it to me when the mail comes or whenever it is convenient to you.'

'But we are complete strangers to you, and we have no means of establishing our bona fides,' we countered, whereupon he simply said: 'It is my duty to help you and, moreover, I trust you.'

His name was Namgyal and though he did not distinguish himself outwardly from the other villagers, wearing the rough, undyed homespuns and little round caps, characteristic of the inhabitants of these Himalayan valleys, he was highly respected in his community as a Nyingma Lama and a man of great religious devotion and knowledge. He treated us as if we were members of his own family, because, as he put it, we all belonged to the Ärya-kula, 'the noble family of the Buddha'. He missed no opportunity of discussing religious subjects with us and Sherab, and he even brought us some of his religious books, his most valued possessions, so that we could read and study them. Among them were the *Bardo Thödol,* the *Maṇi Kahbum,* and works dealing with the early history of Buddhism in Tibet and especially with Padmasambhava and the three great kings, Songtsen Gampo, Tisong Detsen, and Ralpachan. He would tell us, besides, many popular stories, of which he had a great repertoire, or he would read to us from one or the other of his books and discuss or explain points of particular interest.

The *Maṇi Kahbum* affected Sherab particularly, and one morning he came to us with tears in his eyes. He had read about the fate of those who had committed the sin of killing living beings, and he confessed that he had committed such a sin by setting traps for foxes. We consoled him by telling him that there is no sin that cannot be overcome and wiped out by a change of heart. He promised never to commit this sin again and was deeply moved when Namgyal spoke about the Buddhas' compassion and their self-sacrificing acts on their way to Buddhahood.

One day Namgyal invited us to his house and showed us his meditation and prayer-room (on the top floor), which contained the house altar with various images and thankas and a proper Lama's seat under a multicoloured canopy. His wife, an old and shrivelled lady, but with a face that showed strength and character, sang for us religious songs with a voice so beautiful, mellow, and tender, that one forgot her age. They both were ardent devotees of Padmasambhava, who seemed to be always present in their minds. To them Padmasambhava was none other than Śākyamuni Buddha in a new form and appearing to men in different disguises, compassionate as well as fierce, according to their needs. He was the ever-present protector and guide, who would stand by his devotees in danger and inspire them in their meditation. He was the special protector and friend of all animals and might even take their shape. Once, when the landscape was covered in deep snow, we heard the song of a bird. 'It is Him!' Namgyal said with great earnestness. On the tenth day of every Tibetan (lunar) month he was believed to descend among men and his devotees kept themselves ready on that day to receive him in mind and heart and in whatever form he might approach. Innumerable stories about him went from mouth to mouth, and they were all told in such a way as if they had happened quite recently. In fact, nobody thought of Padmasambhava as a figure of the remote past, but as somebody who had just passed through this valley and might return any moment. For the first time we realised the tremendous impact that Padmasambhava had on the Tibetan mind. He certainly was one of the most powerful personalities of Buddhist history. The miracle stories that grew up around him are nothing but the reflection of the unbounded admiration which his contemporaries and disciples felt for him, and if modern historians try to dismiss Padmasambhava as a 'sorcerer and a charlatan' or as a 'black magician', they only show their complete ignorance of human psychology in general and of religious symbolism in particular.

Would anybody, with any sense of fairness, dare to call Christ 'a sorcerer or a charlatan', because he turned water into wine, healed the incurable, roused the dead, exorcised evil spirits, defied Satan, resurrected from the grave after having been crucified and ascended to heaven in full view of his disciples? Why, therefore, should one ridicule the story of Padmasambhava's resurrection from the pyre, his victory over demons or whatever other miracles are ascribed to him? In fact, when missionaries came to Poo (many years ago) and told the people that Christ had sacrificed himself on the cross for the sake of humanity and had risen from the dead, they accepted this without hesitation and exclaimed: 'It was Him!', thoroughly convinced that Christ and Padmasambhava were actually the same person. Thus the missionaries finally had to give up, not because they were rejected, but because their teachings were readily accepted as a confirmation of those very truths which Śākyamuni and Padmasambhava and many other Buddhist saints had taught.

To us, certainly, Padmasambhava came to life, more than ever before, during our stay in Poo, where his memory was as fresh as if he had been here only a few days ago and might turn up any moment again.

Many great Lamas had passed through this valley on their pilgrimage either from Tibet to the holy places in India or from India to Mount Kailas. One of the most prominent among them was Tomo Géshé Rimpoché, whom Namgyal remembered with special veneration, because it was here that he had restored to life the girl that had been ailing for years and who on his command 'took her bed and walked away', to the open-mouthed surprise of those who had carried her on a stretcher and in the presence of the whole village. It was here that he exorcised the man who was possessed by a spirit and showed mercy even to that spirit by asking the villagers to build a small shrine for him as a dwelling-place, so that he would find rest and would no more trouble anyone. Modern people might look upon this as pure superstition; however, the effect proved the soundness of Tomo Géshé's advice: the man was cured and all his sufferings came to an end—whatever their actual cause might have been. A psychologist would probably be able to find a reasonable explanation in modern terminology for such phenomena and he would also admit that Tomo Géshé found the right remedy.

While listening to these and many other strange happenings, we came to hear a lot about the spirits that were supposed to inhabit certain localities. There was a group of old cedar trees not far from the village—the only trees in the otherwise bare landscape—and we were wondering how they could have survived not only the rigours of the climate (at an altitude of almost 9,000 feet), but even more the depredations of man in a place where wood was scarce and people had to roam far and wide to find fuel or wood for building. Namgyal explained that these trees were sacred and nobody would dare to touch them, because they were the abode of gods, and when we asked him how people knew this, he answered that they came and spoke to them and had even sometimes been seen. He said this in a matter-of-fact way, as if it was the most ordinary thing in the world, so that we felt almost guilty of ever having doubted such a possibility. To question such simple facts would have seemed to him the height of ignorance, and so we left it at that, little suspecting that one day we ourselves would witness the presence of these gods.

Tibetans are far more sensitive to psychic influences than most Westerners. They have not yet lost the capacity to communicate with the powers of their depth-consciousness or to understand their language, as revealed through dreams or other phenomena. One day Namgyal came and told us that he had seen in a dream a rainbow over our bungalow and that this could only mean a lucky event, like the arrival of some saintly person. And, indeed, the next day a Lama arrived and put up in a little outhouse belonging to our compound. We only saw him from a distance, while dismounting from his horse; and both the man as well as the horse seemed tired from a long journey. The Lama's robes were old and worn and the horse was limping and half blind. We were told that the Lama had returned from a long pilgrimage and would have to stay here until the passes were open.

Since the weather was cold and cloudy, we had remained in our room, but the following day the Lama himself called on us accompanied by Namgyal. How great was our joy and surprise when we recognised the Lama as our good old Abbot of Phiyang of whom we had taken tender farewells at Tsaparang, not expecting ever to meet him again. We had regretted this all the more, as we felt that here was a man from whom we could learn a great deal, especially in the field of meditational practice, and we felt almost cheated by fate that we should lose this rare opportunity the very moment it came our way.

Whether Phiyang Lama had foreseen that we were destined to meet again or not, one thing is sure: he had read our thoughts at that time, because now, before we could even mention our secret wish, he offered to instruct us in the most advanced methods of Tantric Sādhanā and Yoga practices.

As our room was not only bigger but warmer than Phiyang Lama's, since we kept a big fire going the whole day, thanks to Sherab's untiring concern for our well-being, Phiyang Lama came daily with Namgyal (who thus became our Guru-bhai) to instruct us and discuss our problems. It was a most fruitful time, because never was a teacher more eager to give from the wealth of his own experience than this new Guru of ours, who thus continued the good work of Tomo Géshé and Ajo Rimpoché, for which we shall ever remember him with deep gratitude. And in this gratitude we must include also our Guru-bhai Namgyal, who helped us in so many ways, and our faithful Sherab, who looked after us like a son, so that we could dedicate ourselves completely to our religious studies and practices.

When the news of Phiyang Lama's arrival and continued stay spread among the Poopas, many came to receive his blessings and finally the villagers requested him to perform a Tséwang for the whole community. The ceremony was to take place in the spacious courtyard between Phiyang Lama's quarters and our bungalow. A few days before the great ceremony he retired into his room—much to our regret, as we missed our daily meetings—though we understood that he required some time of solitude and intense concentration in order to prepare himself and to call up those forces which he wanted to communicate to others. But then it seemed to us that another Lama had joined him, probably to assist him during the forthcoming ritual, because we heard another voice much deeper than his own from time to time coming from his room. The long and sonorous recitations of the new voice were sometimes interrupted by Phiyang Lama's voice, but neither he nor the other Lama were ever seen outside. We were greatly intrigued as to who the new Lama could be, but nobody could give us any information. So, one or two days later, while passing Phiyang Lama's door, we heard again the voice of the other Lama, and since the door was wide open, we glanced inside. To our surprise we saw no other person in the room but only Phiyang Lama. He seemed to be oblivious of our presence, and the strange voice came out of him so deep and sonorous, as if another person was speaking through him. We quickly withdrew from the door.

When the great day came, a high throne was erected in the courtyard between our bungalow and the outhouse. The throne stood against a high revetment wall, covered with a decorative cloth curtain, while the courtyard was festively decorated with multicoloured bunting and streamers. Phiyang Lama in the full regalia of an abbot was seated on the throne, his head covered with the tall red cap worn by the Nyingma and Kargyütpa Orders, to which he originally belonged, though being now the head of a Sakya-Gompa. Nobody could have recognised in him the poor old pilgrim, who might have been taken as a mendicant friar on the day of his arrival. The man on the throne had the bearing of a king and the voice of a lion. His face was that of an inspired prophet, and every gesture expressed dignity and power. Whoever was present could feel that here was a man who not merely implored or invoked some unseen power, but one who had *become* that power, by having generated or focalised it within himself in a state of complete and sustained absorption and oneness with a particular aspect of transcendental reality. He had become the very embodiment of Tsépamé *(Tsé-dpag-med),* the Buddha of Infinite Life. His vision had become visible and communicable to all who attended the ritual, which held everybody spellbound and in a state of spiritual elation. The rhythm of mantric incantations and mystic gestures was like the weaving of a magic net, in which the audience was drawn together towards an invisible centre. The sense of participation was heightened when everybody received Tsépamé's blessings with a few drops of consecrated water and a small *tsé-ril,* a red consecrated pill of sweetened *tsampa,* representing the Wine and Bread of Life.

It was the most beautiful eucharistic rite we had ever witnessed, because it was performed by a man who had truly given his own blood and flesh, sacrificed his own personality, in order to make it a vessel of divine forces.

Never had I realised more thoroughly the importance of ritual in religion (and especially in community worship) and the folly of replacing it by preaching and sermonising. Ritual—if performed by those who are qualified by spiritual training and sincerity of purpose—appeals both to the heart and to the mind, and brings people in direct contact with a deeper and richer life than that of the intellect, in which individual opinions and dogmas get the upper hand.

13

Final Initiations

After the Tséwang Phiyang Lama continued his daily instructions and finally crowned them by giving us in short succession two esoteric initiations which completed the circle *(maṇḍala)* of our previous initiations and introduced us to many new aspects of meditative practice, belonging to the most ancient tradition of Tibetan Buddhism as preserved by the Nyingmapas (lit.: 'The Old Ones'). Thus we began to understand the various esoteric aspects of Padmasambhava, which have created such a sorry confusion among Western scholars, who neither understood the symbolic language of Padmasambhava's *Biography* nor that of his teachings, and who mixed up descriptions of mystic experience with historical facts and legendary accretions.

In these initiations all the psychic centres *(cakra)* were employed and activated, a process which I have tried to describe to some extent in my *Foundations of Tibetan Mysticism*. The different forms in which Padmasambhava appears depend on the psychic level from which he is viewed or on which he is experienced. His name, 'Lotus-born', indicates his spiritual birth from the 'lotus' or one of the psychic centres in the movement of his enlightenment or in the process of his spiritual realisation, which has to be re-enacted by each of his devotees, i.e. by all who have been initiated into his teachings and his way of ultimate liberation.

Thus Phiyang Lama not only became the last of our Tibetan Gurus, but he gave us the unique opportunity of experiencing for ourselves the completeness and harmony of Tibetan Buddhist tradition, marked by the great streams of Nyingmapa, Kargyütpa, and Gelugpa hierarchies, each of which had contributed valuable religious experience to the mainstream of Buddhist life. Though some of the powerful monasteries had been drawn into political rivalries (an inevitable concomitant of power) which were utilised by nations and warlike tribes beyond the borders of Tibet and disturbed the peace of the country, the validity of different religious traditions was always recognised. Reformers like Atīśa, Tsongkhapa, and others never rejected the traditions of earlier sects, but tried to synthesise their teachings and only criticised the faults of those among their followers, who had fallen from the high standard of their own professed ideals, and insisted on a re-establishment of those standards and the personal integrity of every member of the clergy.

Before Phiyang Lama left Poo he performed a very remarkable ceremony which culminated in a baptism or purification through fire, so to say a counterpart or natural complement to the Tséwang, the purification and spiritual renewal through the Water of Life. This ceremony (*me-dbang*) was remarkable for two things: for the unexpected interference of the local gods and for the way in which all the participants were actually enveloped by the flames of the fire, without anybody being hurt.

The procedure was as simple as it was ingenious and impressive. While Phiyang Lama intoned the *mantras* of consecration, he held an earthen bowl with fire in his left hand, and with the other he threw a fine incense powder (made of some local shrub or tree-bark) through the open flame, issuing from the bowl. The powder ignited instantly, and being thrown in the direction of the devotees, who were sitting in a group before the Lama, the fire enveloped them for a moment in a flash-like flame that vanished before it could burn anybody.

However, the first part of the ritual was more important, and it was here where the gods of the locality stepped into action. The ritual was concerned with the warding off and destruction of evil forces by the sacrificial fire, which was lit over the *maṇḍala* of the five Dhyāni buddhas, enclosed in a hexagram formed by two intersecting equilateral triangles, set in a square whose corners were protected by two vajra-hilted semi-circular chopping-knives. The firewood was carefully built up around the *maṇḍala,* and the whole structure rested on a raised platform in the centre of the open place in front of the Mani Temple. The Lama's throne stood with the back to the Mani Temple, facing the fire-altar, and the people sat around in a wide circle.

During the first part of the ceremony the Lama remained on his high seat, reciting *mantras* and invocations and wielding his magic dagger *(phurbu)* in various directions. He then descended from his throne and lit the sacrificial fire, into which ghee or oil was poured, so that it burned with a clear, smokeless flame. While chanting further invocations, he circled the sacred fire in a measured dance. In spite of his age and his heavy robes, he moved about with perfect ease, and every step and every *mudrā* was in harmony with the rhythm of his chant. His deep voice never wavered, his movements never faltered. His body seemed to be carried by a force generated and guided by the mind and maintained by a state of unshakable concentration.

It was in the middle of this liturgical dance that we observed a stir among the people sitting at the foot of a row of *chortens,* which formed one side of the square. A tall man got up, his body trembling and his eyes fixed as if in a trance. The people around him were visibly perturbed, and we felt that something strange and unforeseen was going to happen, something that had to do with the struggle between invisible opposing forces. Was it that the forces of darkness felt challenged and had risen to contend for supremacy?

The man's movements became more convulsive and somebody whispered: 'He has been seized by one of the gods!' No doubt the man was possessed, and nobody dared to interfere when, as in a trance, he moved towards the fire-altar, confronting the Lama and imitating his movements, as if challenging or mocking him. Everybody was horrified.

If the man succeeded in breaking up the ritual, disaster might follow. Two super-human powers seemed to face each other, measuring their strength. The tension became almost unbearable.

But the Lama, without missing a single step, without interrupting his incantations, moved on unperturbed, as if the possessed man were a mere phantom. The latter, however, persisted in his antics and handed to the Lama some scraps of paper or cloth, which he had snatched from one of the *chortens*. The Lama, without interrupting his movements, took them one by one and dropped them into the fire.

Now the spell was broken, and the possessed man rushed back towards the *chortens* and dashed his head against the stone foundation on which they stood, so that the blood spurted from his skull. It was a horrible sight, and we feared any moment to see the man's brains spilled on the ground. People now tried to hold him back and restrain him from

MAṆḌALA ON THE FIRE-ALTAR DURING THE MEWANG CEREMONY

killing himself; others were running about, shouting for wine and weapons to pacify the gods or whatever spirit had entered the man's body. His wife was weeping with fear. Apparently something was happening beyond anybody's control.

In the meantime the sacred dance had come to an end, and now the Lama enquired into the matter and was told that the local gods apparently objected to the performance of the ritual, as they had inhabited this place since time immemorial, even before the advent of Buddhism. The Lama immediately understood the situation and agreed that the gods should speak through the possessed man, who was their appointed medium.

By now a bowl of wine (or *chang*) and the emblems of the gods in the form of various weapons had been brought. The medium drank the wine and pierced his cheeks with iron spikes, and finally placed two swords upright on the ground, inserted their sharp points into his eyes and, leaning on them, he thus supported the weight of his body. A slip or the slightest loss of balance and his eyes would be gouged out, while the swords would penetrate his brain. It was too gruesome to contemplate! If I had not seen even more gruesome things of this kind among the Aissaouas in Northern Africa—I would not have believed my eyes.

After the medium had gone through all these tests of faith and devotion—or whatever the underlying meaning of these self-inflicted tortures or proofs of immunity might be—it seemed that the gods were satisfied and were ready to speak. The man sat down, trembling in every limb, but slowly quieting down. And now the gods spoke through him.

What they said was that, though this place was their rightful abode, they had neither been consulted nor invited to this ritual. If their permission and consent had been asked, they would have felt satisfied. They felt offended, because this common courtesy had not been shown to them.

The Phiyang Lama, towards whom these complaints were directed, answered, with great presence of mind and without losing his composure, that he had not intended to exclude anybody from the ritual, to which all beings of goodwill of all the realms of existence were welcome, but that, if he had known that this place was inhabited by them, he would have asked their permission and consent and would have invited them moreover to participate in this ritual for the benefit of all living beings. He, therefore, asked them to forgive this unintended offence and to give their consent to the completion of the ritual, as well as to participate in it for the benefit of all the people inhabiting their realm.

The gods accepted the apology and consented to the continuation of the ritual, which now proceeded without further disturbance.

This incident showed us again that invisible forces, whether we call them gods or spirits, divine or demoniacal powers, that influence the human mind, are not merely abstractions or the outcome of a sick mind, but realities with which every religion and psychology has to cope. I could very well understand now the type of forces against which Padmasambhava had to fight, and that such forces could only be conquered or subdued by calling up counterforces in the human mind, which is exactly the function of ritualistic magic, or magic ritual. We are dealing here with spiritual realities, not with theories, with actual forces, and not with religious doctrines. Modern psychology had to accept the facts of hypnotism, autosuggestion, extrasensory perception, telepathy, mediumism, psycho-kinesis, faith-healing, and the uncanny powers of our depth-consciousness—irrespective of whether it fitted into the prevailing scientific theories or not. And likewise Buddhism, whether it accepted or denied the value of these phenomena, had to cope with them on their own level.

Seen from this point of view, it becomes clear why Padmasambhava succeeded in establishing Buddhism in Tibet, while Śāntarakshita, an equally great scholar, but not a man of practical experience and insight into other people's minds, was not able to succeed. He confined himself to the teaching of ideas and doctrines, trying to convince people intellectually, appealing to their reasoning powers, but he had nothing with which to oppose or to convert the subtle forces of the mind below the threshold of the intellect.

14

THE MAGIC SMITH

AFTER THE FIRE baptism was over we enquired about the man through whom the gods had spoken and were told that he was a blacksmith, who after the death of the previous medium (who like him was a blacksmith) had been appointed by the gods. 'How did this happen?' we asked. 'Was the man of a particular religious character or did he possess particular psychic qualities or inclinations for spiritual things?' 'No, he was just an ordinary man, leading a normal life, but some time after the previous "Speaker of the Gods" had died, he was suddenly possessed one day, and since then the gods have spoken through him.'

Apparently there was always one man in the village who was thus called upon by the gods and had to accept this office. And he usually belonged to the blacksmith community. Is it that people who are mainly occupied with fire and metal are particularly vulnerable to the influences of psychic powers or are we here confronted with prehistoric traditions, going back to the times when metals for the first time were extracted from the stone and a new age of human history was dawning? At that time metal was regarded as having magic qualities and those who extracted and fashioned it were masters of a magic art. Heinrich Zimmer speaks in this connection of *'the magic smith'*, who released the world from the Stone Age. 'The hero who can draw the iron sword from the stone is not necessarily a great warrior, but always a powerful magician, lord over spiritual and material things.'

This prehistoric tradition seems to have been preserved in many parts of the world, in Africa as well as in the Hindu communities of the southern Himalayas, to give only two examples. This tradition has nothing to do with any particular religion, but seems to follow psychic practices—older than any known religion—in which the telluric forces of nature as well as the not yet conscious forces of the human psyche are aroused.

I found the most astonishing phenomena of this kind among the Aissaouas, a Mohammedan sect of mystics in North Africa, whose male members (consisting mainly of metal-workers, iron- and copper-smiths) used to meet every Friday in a special kind of mosque, reserved for their ecstatic religious practices. As a young man I was living among them for some time, wearing the usual Arab clothing, and thus I had several occasions to attend their religious meetings—though they were not averse to people of different faiths as long as they respected their religion and their customs.

Though their trances were self-induced with the help of ritual invocations, accompanied by the rhythm of drum-beats and slow swinging movements of their bodies, the effect was very similar to what we had seen at the fire ritual: once the trance had been achieved, another power seemed to take over and to make the body invulnerable to injury. Whatever name we may give to this power—whether we ascribe it to Allah or to certain faculties of that universal consciousness in which all living beings partake in the centre of their being and to which man may gain access, if he is ready to forget his little ego—what is important is to understand the power of the mind over matter, even in the crude forms in which this power may be applied on a primitive human level. To the Aissaouas the demonstration of the invulnerability of those who are filled with the thought of God, to the exclusion of all other thoughts, by repeating the sacred name (or *bīja-mantra*) of God (Allah), is a means to intensify their faith and an assurance of final redemption.

The ritual begins with rhythmic chanting of invocations to the sound of drums, during which the participants, standing in two rows, facing each other, are swaying to and fro. The men of each row have their arms interlocked, so that they sway like *one* body. From time to time a man would break out of the row, throw off his upper garments and strip down to the waist, whereupon the Imam, who presided over the function, would hand him one of the weapons, which were kept ready along one of the walls of the mosque. Most of the weapons consisted of iron spits of various length, with sharp points at one end, while the other was set into a hemispherical piece of wood, with the flat surface outside.

The purpose of these wooden ends (instead of a handle) became apparent when the Imam with a wooden sledgehammer began to drive the irons through various parts of the body of each of the men who approached him. It was a frightful sight to see the iron sink into the flesh inch by inch; but apparently the people experienced no pain, nor did I ever see a drop of blood. I observed very closely a man who had an iron spit driven through one cheek and saw it coming out through the other one without a trace of blood, and I was later on told that if blood came, it would be a sign that the person concerned had not attained the state of immunity, because his faith had not been strong enough or he had failed to concentrate on the name of God.

Some people were pierced by a number of such irons, but even then they continued swaying and dancing in unbroken ecstasy, until they collapsed with exhaustion. Wherever they fell, they remained lying on the floor, and the Imam immediately threw a white shroud over them. They had died the ritual death and were later on to be revived through a sacred formula, which was whispered into their ears by the Imam.

There were many different kinds of self-torture, or rather of exercises to prove the strength of faith and the completeness of surrender to God (because the idea was not to inflict pain, but to show that faith is stronger than pain). I remember, for instance, a man who threw himself with his full weight upon the sharp blade of a sword as if to disembowel himself. Yet the skin of his belly was not even scratched!

But more uncanny than all these feats was the transformation of men into animals, like pigs, dogs, and goats. I do not mean to say that the bodies of men changed into those animals, but their consciousness, their movements, their behaviour had so completely become that of animals that even though their human form was still there, one could clearly see them in their respective animal-forms. They moved on all fours and those who had become goats would, for instance, eat cactus leaves with long, sharp spikes, without hurting themselves. Others were eating broken glass and some would even swallow live scorpions—which almost made my stomach turn.

Finally the whole mosque was a pandemonium of dancing and swaying men, pierced with irons, raving animals and 'dead bodies' strewn all over. A mad ecstasy seemed to have gripped everybody in the mosque and was growing to such intensity that I felt it was dangerous to remain sane—as anybody who did not share the common frenzy might be run through with a spear or a sword, as being an alien element, an obstacle or denial of the state of consciousness that had seized everybody, except the Imam, who administered weapons and withdrew them when the time had come.

In the end everybody, including the 'animals', had succumbed to exhaustion and were covered with shrouds, as all the others who had fallen before them, and the mosque looked like a battlefield, strewn with the bodies of the 'dead'. The Imam now went from body to body, whispered the sacred words into their ears, and one after the other got up, as if nothing had happened. After the weapons had been pulled out, not even a scar remained!

When later I enquired why people—instead of entering a higher state of consciousness during their ecstasy—should degrade themselves to such an extent as to fall back into a state of animalhood, I was told that this was an act of humility, because the lower one makes oneself, the greater one can experience the glory of Allah by contrast.

I could see their point of view, though I could not share it. Like every virtue, so even humility and faith, when carried to the extreme, cease to be virtues. Self-abasement, which also in early and medieval Christianity was often carried to extremes, has never had a place in the Buddha's teaching, where self-reliance and responsibility for one's own actions replaced self-mortification and extreme asceticism, favoured by many of the Buddha's contemporaries. Nevertheless, even the followers of the Buddha have not always been able to avoid extremes, though the teaching of the Middle Way is a constant reminder and an efficient corrective.

Phiyang Lama's understanding and tolerant handling of the critical situation that arose during the fire ceremony showed that he was a worthy representative of that Middle Way, with a deep insight into the nature of the human mind.

15

FAREWELL TO TIBET

TOWARDS THE END of April news came that the passes were opening and that the caravan road had been dug out from the avalanches which had blocked it during the previous months. The hour of parting came near, and while we were assembling our caravan and preparing for our final return to India, Phiyang Lama set out for his Gompa in the district of Tsaparang. Before our beloved Guru left, he bade us to return to Tibet some day and to stay with him at his monastery. He gave us his 'Soldeb' *(gsol-hdebs),* a beautiful prayer composed by him, as a last gift and guidance. Whenever reciting it, we would be united with him in spirit.

On the morning of his departure we wanted to accompany him for a few miles, as a mark of respect and gratitude, but he firmly declined to accept this honour and insisted on walking alone. We bowed to his will, prostrated ourselves and received his last blessings. We all (Sherab included) had tears in our eyes when we saw him walking along the road, a solitary pilgrim—poorer even than on the day of his arrival, because his horse had died some weeks before. When grazing on the steep hillside, a short distance from our place, it had fallen into a deep ravine, probably due to its one blind eye. The Lama's few belongings had been carried ahead by some of the villagers, who had volunteered for this last labour of love for the Guru who had given so much to the village by his presence and his selfless service.

As soon as the solitary figure had disappeared from our eyes, I turned into the house and began to recite the Soldeb in order to get over the pangs of parting, and lo!—without knowing how it happened—the deep voice of the Guru sounded from my own chest! Li and Sherab came running in wonder and I heard them shouting: 'Has the Guru returned?' And then they saw me, and I could only say: 'Only his voice has returned!' Since then the voice has come back whenever I remembered the Guru, our beloved Lama of Phiyang.

Finally our caravan had been arranged after the usual delays and negotiations. We had asked Sherab to come with us, but he was afraid to venture into lower altitudes. Even in winter he often used to strip to the waist when working—especially when splitting big logs of fire-wood, which he had purchased from the villagers. He regarded Poo as a warm climate and an altitude of 9,000 feet was to him the lowest limit beyond which he would not dare to descend. He told us that he looked upon us as his father and his mother, and that he would like to serve us in every capacity. But he would die if he went into the lowlands of India, like so many of his countrymen who had never returned.

On the last day before our departure he carved a beautiful prayer-stone with the inscription '*Oṁ maṇi padme Hūṁ*'. We went with him to the Maṇiwall, where he deposited the tablet, while praying to be reborn with us in a future life, so that he might be able to serve us again. He then turned round to hide his tears and went away quickly, without looking back, because—as he had told us beforehand—if he did not go quickly and without looking back, it would break his heart.

The last to say goodbye to us was our dear friend and Guru-bhai, Namgyal. I embraced him and we both thanked him for all that he had done for us.

And so we left our 'Shangrila', the Valley of Happiness, and returned to the world, not knowing that Tibet's hour of fate had struck and that we would never see it again, except in our dreams. But we knew that the Gurus and the treasures of memory that this unforgettable country had bestowed on us would remain with us till the end of our days and that, if we succeeded in passing on to others even a part of those treasures and of our Gurus' teachings, we would feel that we had repaid a little of the debt of gratitude that we owe to Tibet and to our Teachers.

This is why this book had to be written and why we are determined to dedicate the rest of our lives to the completion of the work that fate entrusted to us at Tsaparang and to convey to the world in word, line, and colour the immortal heritage of Tibet.

EPILOGUE

GURU AND CHELA AND THE JOURNEY INTO THE LIGHT

SINCE IT WAS Tomo Géshé Rimpoché who opened to me the gates of Tibet, it is only fitting that I close this story of my Tibetan pilgrimage with a few words about his new incarnation, the present Tulku, Jigmé Nagawang Kalzang Rimpoché.

After our brief encounter at Gyantse at the end of 1947, we had not been able to catch up with him, and by the time we reached India he was again on his way to Sera, where conditions were regarded as safe enough for him to continue his studies. He remained there until 1959, when he passed his final examination as Géshé and was thus confirmed in his former title.

Hardly had he left Sera to take up his residence at Lhasa when the people rose against their Chinese oppressors and saved the Dalai Lama from becoming a prisoner or a tool of the Communists, who had tried to pose as the liberators of the poor—a lie that was once and for ever exploded, when it was exactly the 'poor' who, in spite of all inducements offered to them during the first years of Chinese occupation, revolted against their self-styled 'liberators'.

During these terrible events innumerable people came to Tomo Géshé Rimpoché who had been all the time in close collaboration with the Dalai Lama's supporters, seeking solace and encouragement. As in his former life, he lavishly distributed his life-giving '*ribus*' to all who asked for his help and his blessings. Many of the Khampas, who had heard of Tomo Géshé's fame and the miraculous powers ascribed to his '*ribus*', threw themselves fearlessly into the struggle for the liberation of the Dalai Lama and their beloved country.

The Chinese soon began to fear Tomo Géshé's '*ribus*' as much as the bullets of the Khampas. They arrested him and threw him into prison, where they tried to break his spirit by exposing him to the most inhuman conditions and humiliations, forced labour for sixteen hours a day on a starvation diet, demanding of him the lowest and dirtiest services and alternating this with the strictest solitary confinement without air and light.

Not long afterwards, people who had fled from Tibet reported that Tomo Géshé had been killed by the Chinese, who—as we were told—had poured boiling coal-tar over him, while he was sitting in meditation. According to their story, he had died without a word of complaint or a sign of fear.

We were deeply distressed, and the idea that our Guru should have chosen to return in a human body, only to die a martyr's death, before even having a chance to fulfil the mission for which he had come back, seemed to us a particularly cruel and senseless fate.

How great, therefore, was our joy when in 1961 we read a report that under diplomatic pressure from the Government of India and the personal interference of the Prime Minister, Pandit Nehru, the Chinese had released the Rimpoché and that he had arrived in Gangtok on the 24th of June 1961 after more than two years of imprisonment. The reason for his escape from imprisonment and death was that, being born in Gangtok (Sikkim), India could claim him as an Indian-protected person. Now we could see the deeper reason why Tomo Géshé, in spite of his wish to return to Dungkar Gompa, was not reborn in the Tomo Valley (as people might have expected), but just a short distance beyond the frontier of Tibet!

As I was not yet able to undertake the long journey from my present abode in the Western Himalayas to Yi-Gah Chö-Ling or Kalimpong, where Tomo Géshé lives alternately in his two main monasteries, I requested the Ven. Sangharakshita Thera, Head of the Triyāna Vardhana Vihāra, Kalimpong, to ask the Rimpoché whether he remembered me, his old disciple, and whether he had recognised me at Gyantse. His answer was plain and simple: 'I know him!'

We shall meet again, as soon as conditions will make it possible. By now I have reached the age of my old Guru, while he is now even younger than I was when I met him in his previous life. But old or young, the inner relationship between Guru and Chela remains, though the roles may be reversed outwardly. We shall meet again and again, till we both have fulfilled our tasks—till we both have become one with that ultimate light that is both our origin and our aim, and that unites us through many births and deaths and beyond.

It is this light that guided me through life, and now that I look back upon this life's long road, I can see it winding through a wide and variegated landscape, dominated by a mighty stream, the stream of spiritual tradition, that has been flowing from beginningless time and through the millenniums of human lives and endeavour. It embodies the experiences of untold generations of devotees, seers and singers, thinkers and poets, artists and scholars, sinners and saints. The sources of this stream are the Enlightened Ones, who ever and again manifest themselves among human beings, like Śākyamuni Buddha, whose message was of such universal significance that even after two and a half millenniums we have not yet exhausted the depth of its meaning and its manifold ways of expression and realisation.

The particular aspect under which this stream appeared in my life was that of Buddhism. Though I was fortunate enough to have had, even in early youth, the opportunity of informing myself of the main tenets of all great religions, without being influenced or compelled in any one or other direction, I chose Buddhism, because it was the very expression of my innermost nature and not something forced upon me by circumstances. I certainly was a Buddhist long before I was born!

However, it is always instructive to see how, at different times, different aspects of the same thing appeal to us. While in youth the rational side of Buddhism and the historical figure of the Buddha stood in the foreground of my religious conviction, the experiences of later years showed me the shallowness of intellectual reasoning and convinced me of the irrational (though not *anti*-rational) quality of Reality and of the spiritual character of the Buddha, by which the historical impulse of the past is transformed into a living force of the present, into a living reality within ourselves.

In applying the simile of the stream to the development and flow of Buddhist tradition through the last 2,500 years since the Parinirvāṇa of Buddha Śākyamuni, a vision flashed through my mind of the journey along this mighty river and of the infinite variety of vistas which it revealed to me. I will try to describe some of them, though I am conscious of the very personal nature of such a vision and of the inadequacy of words and symbols to depict it.

In the beginning the landscape was dominated by the mighty mountains of the Four Noble Truths: the Truth of Suffering, the Truth of its Causes, the Truth of Liberation, and the Truth of the Path of Liberation. The first of these mountains looked dark and sinister and was covered with ashes and black volcanic rock, bare of all vegetation, while an ominous indigo-coloured cloud hovered over it like a pall of doom.

The second mountain belched forth fire and smoke, and streams of incandescent lava licked the sides of the summit with red glowing tongues, while a rain of stone and fire crushed and extinguished all life around the raging mountain. And a thunderous voice filled the air: 'Verily, I tell you, the world is on fire. It burns with the fire of greed, with the fire of hate, with the fire of delusion!'

The third mountain was bathed in brilliant sunshine and its peak gleamed with eternal snow in the deep blue sky-unearthly, pure, far beyond the reach of mortals.

But a fourth mountain loomed beside it, rising in eight lofty steps; and from the last and highest of them a multi-coloured radiance issued and threw a rainbow bridge towards the white, gleaming peak of the third mountain that towered above all the others.

And again the Buddha's voice filled the air: 'The path of deliverance is found, the Eightfold Path that leads through Right Understanding, Right Aspirations, Right Speech, Right Action, Right Livelihood, Right Effort, Right Awareness and Right Meditation to the final liberation of Nirvana.'

There were lovely groves at the foot of the Mountain of Liberation, and many who wanted to prepare themselves for the steep ascent retired into their peace and protection from the heat of the fierce sun, and devoted themselves to a life of renunciation and contemplation. And they built walls around themselves to keep out the world and its disturbing influences. But the more they shut out the world, the less they were aware of those mighty mountains, and the sound of the great river became fainter and fainter.

Finally, the walls became so high that even the Mountain of Liberation was lost to sight. But the recluses preserved the memory of the four mountains and of the Eightfold Path, leading to the summit of the Mountain of Liberation; and they wrote many a learned tome on the dangers and wonders of those mountains. And though the world, which they had shut out, still fed them and clothed them, they felt that they had become independent of it; and thus there was no more necessity to leave their sheltered grove and to set out for a strenuous climb, which only few had attempted and even fewer accomplished. And those few had never returned.

But the river flowed on as ever.

Thus many a year passed by in this cool and pleasant grove, until one day the call of the river reached some of the recluses, whose yearning for liberation had not yet been lulled to sleep. And at the same time they also heard the call of the world, the voices of innumerable suffering beings inhabiting the river valley, and like them yearning to be free. In order to save them all, they built a big ship and set out on the great adventure of the river. But the farther they travelled, the more they realised that the river in some mysterious way carried them towards the very aim they had been striving for from the outset and that however many pilgrims joined the vessel, there was room enough for all. The vessel seemed to grow with the number of the pilgrims. Thus all the world was welcome to it.

And now they also began to realise that the Eightfold Path leads right through the world and that its first step is the recognition that there is nothing that separates us from our fellow-pilgrims, unless it be the illusion of our own uniqueness or superiority. A wave of warm love broke from their hearts and enveloped their fellow-pilgrims and all that lives, until they felt wide and open and free as the sky.

Their spiritual path and the river had become one and flowed towards the setting sun, into which it seemed to merge. And the radiance of the Waters of Life mingled with the radiance of the Sun of Enlightenment; and it seemed as if the lonely mountain of individual liberation received its glory only from the reflected light that emanated from the river and the setting sun into which it flowed.

And the radiance of the setting sun was filled with innumerable Buddhas and Bodhisattvas: all those who had gone before and all those who were still to come—because it is the realm where time is extinguished and past and future are one with the eternal present. Therefore the setting sun, towards which the river flows, will never set, and its radiance will never be extinguished for those who travel along the river.

And so I will close this book with an invocation

TO THE BUDDHA OF INFINITE LIGHT

Who is meditated upon while facing the setting sun, when the day's work is accomplished and the mind is at peace:

AMITĀBHA!

Thou who liveth within my heart,
Awaken me to the immensity of thy spirit,
To the experience of thy living presence!
Deliver me from the bonds of desire,
From the slavery of small aims,
From the delusion of narrow egohood!

Enlighten me with the light of thy wisdom,
Suffuse me with the incandescence of thy love,
Which includes and embraces the darkness,

Like the light that surrounds the dark core of the flame,
Like the love of a mother that surrounds
The growing life in the darkness of her womb,
Like the earth protecting the tender germ of the seed.

Let me be the seed of thy living light!
Give me the strength to burst the sheath of selfhood,
And like the seed that dies in order to be reborn,
Let me fearlessly go through the portals of death,
So that I may awaken to the greater life:
The all-embracing life of thy love,
The all-embracing love of thy wisdom.

Kasar Devi Ashram, Kumaon Himalaya, India, *November 1964*

Appendices

I. The Kings of Lhasa

TIBET ITSELF, WHEN at the height of its military power in the seventh and eighth centuries A.D. (when even China had to pay tribute to Tibet), succumbed to the spiritual superiority of a creed which contradicted the very concept of worldly power. And what the mighty armies of the Chinese Empire had not been able to accomplish was achieved by the subtle influence of two high-minded women, who became the consorts of the great Tibetan king Songtsen Gampo (*Srong-btsan Gam-po*: 629–50 A.D.) and who not only converted him to Buddhism, but actively propagated the Dharma in the country of their adoption. The one was a princess of the royal house of Nepal, the other the daughter of the Emperor of China, who had been defeated by Songtsen Gampo. The Emperor's daughter, however, agreed to become Songtsen Gampo's wife only on condition that she should be allowed to take with her into 'the country of the barbarians' the precious image of Lord Buddha, which was believed to have been made during the lifetime of the Enlightened One, and which was regarded as the greatest treasure of the Imperial Family.

Since the Emperor could not refuse his daughter's hand to so powerful a monarch as Songtsen Gampo, he had to yield. And thus the image came to

Lhasa, where it was housed in a wonderful temple—the famous Jokhang—which up to the present day is the greatest sanctuary in Lhasa and, indeed, in the whole of Tibet. Miraculous properties are ascribed to the image of the Precious Lord (Jovo Rimpoché as it is called), and in fact it became a focus of spiritual power, which soon transformed Lhasa into a Buddhist centre—much to the dismay of the priests of the ancient Bön faith, the original religion of Tibet, in which the terrifying powers of local spirits and deities were mainly invoked.

However, so long as Buddhism remained restricted to Lhasa and to a few temples, the Bön resistance did not show itself much in the open. It grew in the same proportion in which Buddhism spread, until under King Tisong Detsen[1] it found a skilful leader in the person of his minister Mazhang.

Though the King was an ardent Buddhist, as his father and his grandfather had been, he was not able to oppose Mazhang, who had not only the support of the Bön clergy but also a strong following among the aristocracy, many of whom still clung to the traditions of the old shamanistic cult. But before Mazhang succeeded in his scheme of driving out Buddhism he was killed by his adversaries, and now Tisong Detsen redoubled his efforts to place Buddhism on a firm basis. For this purpose he invited Indian scholars to teach and to reorganise the new faith.

Thus the famous Buddhist scholar Śāntarakshita from the monastic university of Nālanda—which in those days played as important a role in the East as Oxford today in the West—accepted the King's invitation. But the opposition of the Böns was too strong for him, and he was obliged to return to India after a short time.

But the King did not give up, and when Śāntarakshita told him of the powerful Tantric Sage Padmasambhava, he immediately sent messengers to invite him to Tibet. Padmasambhava, one of the most colourful and vigorous personalities of Buddhist history, who had studied Tantric Buddhism in the monastic universities of Eastern India, was versed in magic as well as in philosophy and was thus able to fight the Böns (who were said to be masters of magic power) with their own weapons.

Instead of merely repudiating the local deities of the Böns, he had the wisdom and understanding of human nature to incorporate them as protectors of the Dharma in the Buddhist system. In this way, by respecting the national feelings and loyalties of the people and without destroying the ancient traditions of the country, he gave a new impetus to Buddhism and succeeded in building the

1. Khri-srong-lde-btsan.

first big monastery in Tibet (Samyé; spelled *bSam-yas)* after the model of the university of Otantapuri. The work was started in the year 787 A.D. and completed in 799.

The last of the great religious kings was Ralpachan (also known as Ti-tsuk-de-tsen [*khrī-btsugs-lde-btsan*], 817–36 A.D.) who, encouraged by the success of his predecessor, introduced many reforms in favour of Buddhism. But being too impatient in the furtherance of his aims, the Bön opposition flared up again and Ralpachan was murdered, while his younger brother Langdarma,[1] who had allied himself with the Bön party, was proclaimed king.

The latter immediately began to persecute the Buddhists, destroying their temples and libraries and killing and driving out their monks and influential supporters. It seemed to be the end of Buddhism in Tibet.

But a hermit who lived in the vicinity of Lhasa and who was said to be the incarnation of one of the fierce protecting deities, who had been incorporated into the Buddhist faith by Padmasambhava, made an end of this cruel persecution. He entered Lhasa in the garb of a 'black magician' of the Bön Order, dressed in a black cloak, wearing the black, skull-surmounted hat of that order, and riding on a black horse.

Arriving in the open square before the King's palace, he dismounted and began to perform a ritual dance in which bow and arrows were used as symbolical weapons for subduing evil spirits. The King stepped on to the balcony of the palace to watch the dance, when suddenly the black magician let fly one of his arrows and killed the King on the spot.

Before the people could realise what had happened, the black magician jumped upon his horse and disappeared in the direction of the Kyi River (on the banks of which Lhasa is situated). By the time the people reached the bank, he had crossed the river. But even on the other side nobody could find or had seen the black rider on the black horse. What had happened? The rider had turned his white-lined cloak inside out, while the black colour with which the horse had been dyed had come off in the river, so that a white rider on a white horse emerged on the other side.

Thus the three years of Langdarma's reign of terror came to a sudden end. But there was not a single Buddhist institution left in Central Tibet from which the revival of the religion could be started. There were not even books from which to teach the Dharma, and the few scattered monks, who had survived or dared to return after Langdarma's death, were helpless in the face of the damage done and without the backing of a stable monarchy or the leadership of an outstanding personality.

1. *gLang-dar-ma.*

The assassination of Ralpachan had been the beginning of the dissolution of the Tibetan empire, and after Langdarma's death there was nobody with sufficient authority to stop the process of decay. Thus Lhasa ceased to be the capital of Tibet, which was divided into a number of independent kingdoms and principalities of feudal lords.

Palkhortsan, the grandson of Langdarma, established a kingdom in Western Tibet, which he subsequently divided between his three sons. The eldest received the province of Mang-yul, the middle son the province of Purang, and the youngest, Detsun-gon by name, received Shang-Shung and the three provinces of Gugé, of which Tsaparang and Tholing became alternately the capitals.

II. THE RISE AND FALL OF THE KINGS OF GUGÉ

THE SONS AND grandsons of King Detsun-gon were inspired by the same religious fervour as their illustrious forefathers, the three Dharmarajas of Tibet: Songtsen Gampo, Tisong Detsen, and Ralpachan. So we read in the Tibetan chronicle *Pag-sam-jon-zang* that King Khoré—whose religious name was Lha-Lama Yeshé-ö—gave his kingdom to his younger brother, Song-ngé, while he himself and his two sons entered the Buddhist Order and became monks.

Yeshé-ö realised that whatever had been preserved of the Buddhist religion after the fall of the Lhasa dynasty was in danger of degenerating if a new set of religious teachers and adequate translations of the original scriptures were not obtained. So he followed the example of Songtsen Gampo, selected a group of intelligent young men and sent them to Kashmir to study Sanskrit under competent teachers for a period of ten years, so that they would be able to translate and teach the Buddha-dharma on their return to Tibet.

But few Tibetans can endure lower altitudes and a warm climate for long. Out of the thirteen who had been sent to India by Songtsen Gampo for the study of Buddhism, only one had survived the rigours of the climate. The same fate befell the group of young men sent out by Yeshé-ö. Nineteen died before their mission was fulfilled, and only two returned to their country. One of these was the Lotsava (translator) Rinchen Zangpo, and with him started the revival of Buddhism in Western Tibet.

Like Padmasambhava, Rinchen Zangpo was not only a great scholar but a great personality, who inspired all those who came in touch with him. Wherever he went, he spread the knowledge of the Dharma, built temples and monasteries, *stūpa* and libraries (to which he himself contributed a great number of books), encouraged arts and crafts, and introduced sculpture and fresco-painting of the highest order.

No less than 108 temples and monasteries are claimed to have originated under the guidance of this many-sided genius, who himself is said to have been a gifted artist. Among the temples ascribed to him are those of Tholing and Tsaparang. Their frescoes and statues belong to the finest achievements of Tibetan art.

Yeshé-ö was succeeded by King Lhade (his younger brother's son) who invited the scholar Subhūtri Śrī Sānti from Kashmir, while two of his sons, Shiva-ö and Changchub-ö, invited the famous Bengali Pandit Dīpankara Srī Jñāna, one of the leading lights of the university of Vikramaśīla, to their residence at Tholing. A delegation with rich presents was sent to Vikramaśīla, but Atīśa, as Dīpankara is called in Tibet, declined the invitation, for his services were equally needed in his own country.

The King, who then resided at Tholing and who, according to one tradition, is identified with Yeshé-ö, thought that his presents had been too small and therefore organised an expedition to the northern border of his country, where gold could be found. But unfortunately he fell into the hands of his enemy, the King of Garlog, whose country lay across the borders and who demanded a huge sum as ransom.

Changchub-ö thereupon collected funds for the release of his father; but when he reached Garlog it was found that the amount was not sufficient. Before returning, in order to procure the missing sum, he met his father. The King, however, exhorted him not to spend all his gold on an old man like him, who at the best had only a few years more to live, but to send it instead to Atīśa and to tell him that he prized his visit more than his life, which he would gladly sacrifice for the cause of the Dharma. Changchub-ö took leave from his father with a heavy heart. He was never to see him again.

Another delegation was sent to India. When they arrived at Vikramaśīla and told Atīśa all that had happened, the great teacher was deeply moved and exclaimed: 'Verily, this King was a Bodhisattva! What else can I do but obey the will of so great a saint!'

It was not easy, however, for Atīśa to relinquish his many responsibilities, and it took him eighteen months before he could free himself from his various duties and start for Tibet. Of the gold with which he had been presented, he kept nothing for himself, but distributed it among the professors and pupils of Vikramaśīla and other religious institutions.

In the year 1042 Atīśa reached Tholing and was received by the King, his ministers, and the members of the clergy. Among them was also the eighty-five-year-old Lotsava Rinchen Zangpo. Being the Elder in the Sangha, Rinchen Zangpo remained seated when Atīśa entered the congregation; but after Atīśa had delivered his first religious discourse, Rinchen Zangpo was so deeply impressed that he got up and paid his respects to him.

Atīśa spent two years in Western Tibet and then proceeded to Central Tibet, where he succeeded in reorganising the scattered Buddhist groups and in re-establishing the purity and supremacy of the Dharma. He founded the Kadampa Order, which later on developed into the most powerful sect of Lamaism, the Gelugpas. These established the reign of the Dalai Lamas and made Lhasa again the spiritual and temporal capital of Tibet.

However, Tholing and Tsaparang retained for many a century their importance as cultural and political centres of Western Tibet, though Tholing reached the peak of its fame in the year 1075, when the great religious council took place in the Golden Temple of Tholing under King Tseldé. The greatest scholars and the highest spiritual dignitaries from all parts of Tibet took part in this council, which marked the final triumph and consolidation of the Buddhist revival of Tibet and the beginning of a new era.

Slowly the scene of political and cultural activity shifted back to Central Tibet, and the last glance of the vanishing splendour of the kingdom of Gugd is the report of Padre Andrade, a Portuguese priest, who was the first European to penetrate into the Land of the Snows, attracted by the fame of the royal court of Tsaparang.

Padre Andrade reached Tsaparang in the year 1625 and was received with great hospitality by the King, who paid him high honour and, in the true spirit of Buddhist tolerance, allowed him to preach his religion. To him a man who had travelled round half the world for the sake of his Dharma was certainly worth hearing and deserved the greatest respect.

Truth cannot harm truth. Therefore, whatever was true in the religion of the stranger could only enhance and bear out the teachings of the Buddhas and Bodhisattvas. Was it not possible that in the countries of the West many a Bodhisattva (a saint on the way to Buddhahood, or the emanation of an enlightened being) had arisen, of whom the people of the East had not yet heard? So, out of the goodness of his heart, the King of Gugé wrote the following letter to Father Antonio de Andrade in the year 1625:

'We the King of the Kingdoms of Pontenté, rejoicing at the arrival in our lands of Padre Antonio Franguim [as the Portuguese were called in India teach us a holy law, take him for our Chief Lama and give him full authorit teach the holy law to our people. We shall not allow that anyone molest hi this and we shall issue orders that he be given a site and all the help neede build a house of prayer.'

And the King gave even his own garden to the stranger, a gift which u the conditions of Tibet, where gardens are scarce and a rare luxury, was than a mere polite gesture.

But, alas, the King in his unsuspecting goodness did not know tha stranger had come not merely to exchange true and beautiful thoughts those who were striving after similar ideals, but to destroy what others taught, in order to replace it by what he regarded as the sole truth. The co was inevitable and took forms which none of the protagonists of the en drama-who both believed sincerely in the righteousness of their intenti had foreseen.

The King's favours aroused the suspicions of the Lamas, which wer firmed by the uncompromising attitude of the stranger, and soon the disc spread and the political opponents of the King saw their opportunity.

While Padre Andrade, encouraged by his success in Tsaparang, proc to Lhasa in order to extend his activities over the whole of Tibet, a revolt out, the King was overthrown, and with him the Gugé dynasty and the g Tsaparang came to an end. Around 1650 the kingdom of Gugé disap from the map of Tibet and came under the domination of Lhasa.

When, one hundred years later, Padre Desideri, attracted by the ent tic account of Padre Andrade, travelled to Tsaparang in the hope of con or reviving the former's mission, he found the city abandoned and in ruin so it is to the present day. The roofs of palaces and monasteries have fa but the main temples are still well preserved and their frescoes have r their glowing colours and their minutely executed line-work. The golden stand, as if protected by the magic of their beauty, wrapped in the sil centuries, dreaming of the times when Buddhas and great saints inhabi earth, or as if waiting for the advent of the Great Loving One, the Maitreya, who will bring again the message of peace and goodwill into th torn human world.

Like Padmasambhava, Rinchen Zangpo was not only a great scholar but a great personality, who inspired all those who came in touch with him. Wherever he went, he spread the knowledge of the Dharma, built temples and monasteries, *stūpa* and libraries (to which he himself contributed a great number of books), encouraged arts and crafts, and introduced sculpture and fresco-painting of the highest order.

No less than 108 temples and monasteries are claimed to have originated under the guidance of this many-sided genius, who himself is said to have been a gifted artist. Among the temples ascribed to him are those of Tholing and Tsaparang. Their frescoes and statues belong to the finest achievements of Tibetan art.

Yeshé-ö was succeeded by King Lhade (his younger brother's son) who invited the scholar Subhūtri Śrī Sānti from Kashmir, while two of his sons, Shiva-ö and Changchub-ö, invited the famous Bengali Pandit Dīpankara Srī Jñāna, one of the leading lights of the university of Vikramaśīla, to their residence at Tholing. A delegation with rich presents was sent to Vikramaśīla, but Atīśa, as Dīpankara is called in Tibet, declined the invitation, for his services were equally needed in his own country.

The King, who then resided at Tholing and who, according to one tradition, is identified with Yeshé-ö, thought that his presents had been too small and therefore organised an expedition to the northern border of his country, where gold could be found. But unfortunately he fell into the hands of his enemy, the King of Garlog, whose country lay across the borders and who demanded a huge sum as ransom.

Changchub-ö thereupon collected funds for the release of his father; but when he reached Garlog it was found that the amount was not sufficient. Before returning, in order to procure the missing sum, he met his father. The King, however, exhorted him not to spend all his gold on an old man like him, who at the best had only a few years more to live, but to send it instead to Atīśa and to tell him that he prized his visit more than his life, which he would gladly sacrifice for the cause of the Dharma. Changchub-ö took leave from his father with a heavy heart. He was never to see him again.

Another delegation was sent to India. When they arrived at Vikramaśīla and told Atīśa all that had happened, the great teacher was deeply moved and exclaimed: 'Verily, this King was a Bodhisattva! What else can I do but obey the will of so great a saint!'

It was not easy, however, for Atīśa to relinquish his many responsibilities, and it took him eighteen months before he could free himself from his various duties and start for Tibet. Of the gold with which he had been presented, he kept nothing for himself, but distributed it among the professors and pupils of Vikramaśīla and other religious institutions.

In the year 1042 Atīśa reached Tholing and was received by the King, his ministers, and the members of the clergy. Among them was also the eighty-five-year-old Lotsava Rinchen Zangpo. Being the Elder in the Sangha, Rinchen Zangpo remained seated when Atīśa entered the congregation; but after Atīśa had delivered his first religious discourse, Rinchen Zangpo was so deeply impressed that he got up and paid his respects to him.

Atīśa spent two years in Western Tibet and then proceeded to Central Tibet, where he succeeded in reorganising the scattered Buddhist groups and in re-establishing the purity and supremacy of the Dharma. He founded the Kadampa Order, which later on developed into the most powerful sect of Lamaism, the Gelugpas. These established the reign of the Dalai Lamas and made Lhasa again the spiritual and temporal capital of Tibet.

However, Tholing and Tsaparang retained for many a century their importance as cultural and political centres of Western Tibet, though Tholing reached the peak of its fame in the year 1075, when the great religious council took place in the Golden Temple of Tholing under King Tseldé. The greatest scholars and the highest spiritual dignitaries from all parts of Tibet took part in this council, which marked the final triumph and consolidation of the Buddhist revival of Tibet and the beginning of a new era.

Slowly the scene of political and cultural activity shifted back to Central Tibet, and the last glance of the vanishing splendour of the kingdom of Gugd is the report of Padre Andrade, a Portuguese priest, who was the first European to penetrate into the Land of the Snows, attracted by the fame of the royal court of Tsaparang.

Padre Andrade reached Tsaparang in the year 1625 and was received with great hospitality by the King, who paid him high honour and, in the true spirit of Buddhist tolerance, allowed him to preach his religion. To him a man who had travelled round half the world for the sake of his Dharma was certainly worth hearing and deserved the greatest respect.

Truth cannot harm truth. Therefore, whatever was true in the religion of the stranger could only enhance and bear out the teachings of the Buddhas and Bodhisattvas. Was it not possible that in the countries of the West many a Bodhisattva (a saint on the way to Buddhahood, or the emanation of an enlightened being) had arisen, of whom the people of the East had not yet heard? So, out of the goodness of his heart, the King of Gugé wrote the following letter to Father Antonio de Andrade in the year 1625:

'We the King of the Kingdoms of Pontenté, rejoicing at the arrival in our lands of Padre Antonio Franguim [as the Portuguese were called in India] to teach us a holy law, take him for our Chief Lama and give him full authority to teach the holy law to our people. We shall not allow that anyone molest him in this and we shall issue orders that he be given a site and all the help needed to build a house of prayer.'

And the King gave even his own garden to the stranger, a gift which under the conditions of Tibet, where gardens are scarce and a rare luxury, was more than a mere polite gesture.

But, alas, the King in his unsuspecting goodness did not know that the stranger had come not merely to exchange true and beautiful thoughts with those who were striving after similar ideals, but to destroy what others had taught, in order to replace it by what he regarded as the sole truth. The conflict was inevitable and took forms which none of the protagonists of the ensuing drama-who both believed sincerely in the righteousness of their intentions—had foreseen.

The King's favours aroused the suspicions of the Lamas, which were confirmed by the uncompromising attitude of the stranger, and soon the discontent spread and the political opponents of the King saw their opportunity.

While Padre Andrade, encouraged by his success in Tsaparang, proceeded to Lhasa in order to extend his activities over the whole of Tibet, a revolt broke out, the King was overthrown, and with him the Gugé dynasty and the glory of Tsaparang came to an end. Around 1650 the kingdom of Gugé disappeared from the map of Tibet and came under the domination of Lhasa.

When, one hundred years later, Padre Desideri, attracted by the enthusiastic account of Padre Andrade, travelled to Tsaparang in the hope of continuing or reviving the former's mission, he found the city abandoned and in ruins—and so it is to the present day. The roofs of palaces and monasteries have fallen in, but the main temples are still well preserved and their frescoes have retained their glowing colours and their minutely executed line-work. The golden statues stand, as if protected by the magic of their beauty, wrapped in the silence of centuries, dreaming of the times when Buddhas and great saints inhabited the earth, or as if waiting for the advent of the Great Loving One, the Buddha Maitreya, who will bring again the message of peace and goodwill into the strife-torn human world.

INDEX